AF541322

Generations of Economists

Generations of Economists

Dharmendra Kumar

RANDOM PUBLICATIONS
NEW DELHI (INDIA)

Generations of Economists

ISBN 978-93-5111-636-3

Published in 2015 in India by

RANDOM PUBLICATIONS

4376-A/4B, Gali Murari Lal, Ansari Road
New Delhi-110 002
Phone : +9111-43580356, 011-23289044, 011-43142548
e-mail: sales@randompublications.com,
info@randompublications.com, randomexports@gmail.com

Reprinted 2019

Type Setting by : Friends Media, Delhi-110089
Digitally Printed at : Replika Press Pvt. Ltd.

Preface

Economics is the social science studying the production, distribution and consumption of goods and services. It is a complex social science that spans from mathematics to psychology. At its most basic, however, economics considers how a society provides for its needs. Its most basic need is survival; which requires food, clothing and shelter. Once those are covered, it can then look at more sophisticated commodities such as services, personal transport, entertainment, the list goes on. Today, this social science known as "Economics" tends to refer only to the type of economic thought which political economists refer to as Neoclassical Economics. It developed in the 18th century based on the idea that Economics can be analysed mathematically and scientifically.

The professionalization of economics, reflected in academia, has been described as "the main change in economics since around 1900."[1] Economists debate the path they believe their profession should take. It is, primarily, a debate between a scholastic orientation, focused on mathematical techniques, and a public discourse orientation, which is more focused on communicating to lay people pertinent economic principles as they relate to public policy. Surveys among economists indicate a preference for a shift toward the latter. However, these preferences expressed in private often differ with what is actually acted out in the public eye.

Economists work in many fields including academia, government and in the private sector, where they may also "...study data and statistics in order to spot trends in economic activity, economic confidence levels, and consumer attitudes. They assess this information using advanced methods in statistical analysis, mathematics, computer programming [and] they make recommendations about ways to improve the efficiency of a system or take advantage of trends as they begin."

Most economists are concerned with practical applications of economic policy in a particular area, such as finance, labour, agriculture, transportation, real estate, environment, natural resources, energy, or health. They use their understanding of economic relationships to advise business firms, insurance companies, banks, securities firms, industry and trade associations, labour unions, government agencies, and others. On the other hand, economists who are primarily theoreticians may use mathematical models to develop theories on the causes of business cycles and inflation, or the effects of unemployment and tax legislation.

Philosophy has to be deductive, poetry romantic, plays and fiction humorous, and politics intriguing if they are to catch my attention, writes Kaushik Basu. All these interests are on display in An Economists Miscellany, which brings together an eclectic collection of writings on the world of academe, politics, and policy.

This book is useful for students, teachers and researchers engaged in library and information science research.

I would like to thank my team for standing beside me throughout my career and writing this book. My special thanks go to "Random Publications" who have published the book.

– Dharmendra Kumar

Contents

1

Economist

AN INTRODUCTION TO ECONOMIST

An economist is a professional in the social science discipline of economics. The individual may also study, develop, and apply theories and concepts from economics and write about economic policy. Within this field there are many sub-fields, ranging from the broad philosophical theories to the focused study of minutiae within specific markets, macroeconomic analysis, microeconomic analysis or financial statement analysis, involving analytical methods and tools such as econometrics, statistics, economics computational models, financial economics, mathematical finance and mathematical economics. A generally accepted interpretation in academia is that an economist is one who has attained a Ph.D. in economics, teaches economic science, and has published literature in a field of economics.

IN ACADEMIA

The professionalization of economics, reflected in academia, has been described as "the main change in economics since around 1900." Economists debate the path they believe their profession should take. It is, primarily, a debate between a scholastic orientation, focused on mathematical techniques, and a public discourse orientation, which is more focused on communicating to lay people pertinent economic principles as they relate to public policy. Surveys among economists indicate a preference for a shift towards the latter. However, these preferences expressed in private often differ with what is actually acted out in the public eye.

Most major universities have an economics faculty, school or department, where academic degrees are awarded in economics. However, many prominent economists come from a background in mathematics, business, political science, law, sociology, or history. Getting a PhD in economics takes six years, on average, with a median of 5.3 years.

The Nobel Memorial Prize in Economics, established by Sveriges Riksbank in 1968, is a prize awarded to economists each year for outstanding intellectual contributions in the field of economics. The prize winners are announced in October every year. They receive their awards (a prize amount, a gold medal and a diploma) on December 10, the anniversary of Alfred Nobel's death.

PROFESSIONS

Economists work in many fields including academia, government and in the private sector, where they may also "...study data and statistics in order to spot trends in economic activity, economic confidence levels, and consumer attitudes. They assess this information using advanced methods in statistical analysis, mathematics, computer programmeming [and] they make recommendations about ways to improve the efficiency of a system or take advantage of trends as they begin."

In contrast to regulated professions such as engineering, law or medicine, there is not a legally-required educational requirement or license for economists. In academia, to be called an economist requires a Ph.D. degree in Economics. In the US government, on the other hand, a person can be hired as an economist provided that they have a degree that included or was supplemented by 21 semester hours in economics and three hours in statistics, accounting, or calculus.

A professional working inside of one of many fields of economics or having an academic degree in this subject is often considered to be an economist. In addition to government and academia, economists are also employed in banking, finance, accountancy, commerce, marketing, business administration, lobbying and non- or not-for profit organizations.

Politicians often consult economists before enacting economic policy, and many statesmen have academic degrees in economics.

ECONOMISTS BY COUNTRY

Economics graduates are employable in varying degrees, depending on the regional economic scenario and labour market conditions at the time for a given country. Apart from the specific understanding of the subject, employers value the skills of numeracy and analysis, the ability to communicate and the capacity to grasp broad issues which the graduates acquire at the university or college. Whilst only a few economics graduates may be expected to become professional economists, many find it a base for entry into a career in finance – including accounting, insurance, tax and banking, or management. A number of economics graduates from around the world have been successful in obtaining employment in a variety of major national and international firms in the financial and commercial sectors, and in manufacturing, retailing and IT, as well as in the public sector – for example, in the health and education sectors, or in government and politics. Small numbers go on to undertake postgraduate studies, either in economics, research, teacher training or further qualifications in specialist areas.

UNITED STATES

According to the United States Department of Labour, there were around 15,000 non-academic economists in the United States in 2008, with a median salary of roughly $83,000, and with the top ten percent earning more than $147,040 annually. About 135 colleges and universities grant about 900 new Ph.D.s every year. Incomes are highest for those in the private sector, followed by the federal government, with academia paying the lowest incomes. As of January 2013 PayScale.com showed Ph.D. economists' salary ranges as follows: All Ph.D. economists, $61,000 to $160,000; Ph.D. corporate economists, $71,000 to $207,000; economics full professors, $89,000 to $137,000; economics associate professors, $59,000 to $156,000, and economics assistant professors, $72,000 to $100,000.

UNITED KINGDOM

The largest single professional grouping of economists in the UK are the more than 1000 members of the Government Economic Service, who work in 30 government departments and agencies.

Analysis of destination surveys for economics graduates from a number of selected top schools of economics in the United Kingdom (ranging from Newcastle University to theLondon School of Economics), shows nearly 80 percent in employment six months after graduation – with a wide range of roles and employers, including regional, national and international organisations, across many sectors. This figure compares very favourably with the national picture, with 64 percent of economics graduates in employment.

NOTABLE ECONOMISTS

Current well-known economists include 2008 Nobel Memorial Prize in Economic Sciences winner Paul Krugman, a public intellectual and advocate of modern liberal policies;Alan Greenspan, a former chairman of the Federal Reserve; Ben Bernanke, another former Chairman of the Federal Reserve; Joseph Stiglitz, an American economist, Nobel Memorial Prize in Economics winner, critic of inequality and the governance of globalization, and Chief Economist of the World Bank.

NATURE OF THE WORK

Economists study the ways a society uses scarce resources such as land, labour, raw materials, and machinery to produce goods and services. They analyze the costs and benefits of distributing and consuming these goods and services. Economists conduct research, collect and analyze data, monitor economic trends, and develop forecasts. Their research might focus on topics such as energy costs, inflation, interest rates, farm prices, rents, imports, or employment.

Most economists are concerned with practical applications of economic policy in a particular area, such as finance, labour, agriculture, transportation, real estate, environment, natural resources, energy, or health. They use their understanding of economic relationships to advise business firms, insurance companies, banks, securities firms, industry and trade associations, labour unions, government agencies, and others. On the other hand, economists who are primarily theoreticians may use mathematical models to develop theories on the causes of business cycles and inflation, or the effects of unemployment and tax legislation.

Depending on the topic under study, economists devise methods and procedures for obtaining the data they need. For example, sampling techniques may be used to conduct a survey, and econometric modeling techniques may be used to develop forecasts. Preparing reports usually is an important part of the economist's job. He or she may be called upon to review and analyze all the relevant data, prepare tables and charts, and write up the results in clear, concise language. Being able to present economic and statistical concepts in a meaningful way is particularly important for economists whose research is policy directed.

Economists who work for government agencies assess economic conditions in the United States and abroad and estimate the economic effects of specific changes in legislation or public policy. For example, they may study how the dollar's fluctuation against foreign currencies affects import and export markets. Most government economists are in the fields of agriculture, business, finance, labour, transportation, utilities, urban economics, or international trade. Economists in the U.S. Department of Commerce study domestic production, distribution, and consumption of commodities or services; those in the Federal Trade Commission prepare industry analyses to assist in enforcing Federal statutes designed to eliminate unfair, deceptive, or monopolistic practices in interstate commerce; and those in the Bureau of Labour Statistics analyze data on prices, wages, employment, productivity, and safety and health. An economist working for a state or local government might analyze regional or local data on trade and commerce, industrial and commercial growth, and employment and unemployment, and project labour force trends.

WORKING CONDITIONS

Economists working for government agencies and private firms have structured work schedules. They may work alone writing reports, preparing statistical charts, and using computers and calculators. Or they may be an integral part of a research team. Most work under pressure of deadlines and tight schedules, and sometimes must work overtime. Their routine may be interrupted by special requests for data, letters, meetings, or conferences. Travel may be necessary to collect data or attend conferences.

Economics faculty have flexible work schedules, and may divide their time among teaching, research, consulting, and administration.

EMPLOYMENT

Economists and marketing research analysts held about 51,000 jobs in 1992. Private industry particularly economic and marketing research firms, management consulting firms, banks, securities and commodities brokers, and computer and data processing companies employed 7 out of 10 salaried workers. The remainder, primarily economists, were employed by a wide range of government agencies, primarily in the Federal Government. The Departments of State, Labour, Agriculture, and Commerce are the largest Federal employers of economists. A number of economists combine a full-time job in government or business with part-time or consulting work in academia or another setting.

Employment of economists analysts is concentrated in large cities for example, New York City, Washington, D.C., and Chicago. Some economists work abroad for companies with major international operations; for the Department of State and other U.S. Government agencies; and for international organizations, including the World Bank and the United Nations.

Besides the jobs described above, many economists held economics faculty positions in colleges and universities.

TRAINING, OTHER QUALIFICATIONS, AND ADVANCEMENT

A bachelor's degree with a major in economics is sufficient for many entry-level research, administrative, management trainee, and sales jobs. Economics majors can choose from a variety of courses, ranging from those which are intensely mathematical like microeconomics, macroeconomics, and econometrics, to more philosophical courses like the history of economic thought. Because of the importance of quantitative skills to economists, courses in mathematics, statistics, econometrics, sampling theory and survey design, and computer science are highly recommended.

Aspiring economists can gain experience gathering and analyzing data, conducting interviews or surveys, and writing reports on their findings while in college. This experience can prove invaluable later in obtaining a full-time position in the field, since much of their work in the beginning centers around these duties.

Beginning workers also may do considerable clerical work, such as copying data, editing and coding questions, and tabulating survey results. With further experience, economists eventually are assigned their own research projects. Graduate training increasingly is required for many economist jobs, and for advancement to more responsible positions. Economics includes many specialties at the graduate level, such as advanced economic theory, mathematical economics, econometrics, history of economic thought, international economics, and labour economics. Students should select graduate schools strong in specialties in which they are interested. Some schools help graduate students find internships or part-time employment in government agencies, economic consulting firms, financial institutions, or marketing research firms. Like undergraduate students, work experience and contacts can be useful in testing career preferences and learning about the job market for economists.

In the Federal Government, candidates for beginning economist positions generally need a college degree with a minimum of 21 semester hours of economics and 3 hours of statistics, accounting, or calculus. Competition is keen, however, and additional education or experience may be required for some jobs.

For a job as a college instructor in many junior colleges and some 4-year schools, a master's degree is the minimum requirement. In most colleges and universities, however, a Ph.D. is necessary for appointment as an instructor. Similar to other disciplines, a Ph.D. and extensive publication are required for a professorship and for tenure.

In government, industry, research organizations, and consulting firms, economists who have a graduate degree usually can qualify for more responsible research and administrative positions. A Ph.D. is necessary for top positions in many organizations. Many corporation and government executives have a strong background in economics or marketing.

Persons considering careers as economists should be able to work accurately with detail since much time is spent on data analysis. Patience and persistence are necessary qualities since economists may spend long hours on independent study and problem solving. At the same time, they must be able to work well with others. Economists must be objective and systematic in their work and be able to present their findings, both orally and in writing, in a clear, meaningful way. Creativity and intellectual curiosity are essential for success in these fields, just as they are in other areas of scientific endeavor.

JOB OUTLOOK

Employment of economists is expected to grow about as fast as the average for all occupations through the year 2005. Most job openings, however, are likely to result from the need to replace experienced workers who transfer to other occupations, or retire or leave the labour force for other reasons.

Opportunities for economists should be best in private industry and in research and consulting firms, as some companies contract out for economic research services rather than support a staff of full-time economists. The growing complexity of the global economy and increased reliance on quantitative methods of analyzing business trends, forecasting sales, and planning purchasing and production should spur demand for economists. The continued need for economic analyses by lawyers, accountants, engineers, health services administrators, education administrators, urban and regional planners, environmental scientists, and others also should result in additional jobs for economists. Other organizations, including trade associations, unions, and non-profit organizations, may offer job opportunities for economists. Employment of economists in the Federal Government should decline in line with the rate of growth projected for the Federal workforce as a whole. Slower than average employment growth is expected among economists in State and local government.

A strong background in economic theory, mathematics, statistics, and econometrics provides the tools for acquiring any specialty within the field. Those skilled in quantitative techniques and their application to economic modeling and forecasting and marketing research, including the use of computers, should have the best job opportunities.

Persons who graduate with a bachelor's degree in economics through the year 2005 should face keen competition for the limited number of economist positions for which they qualify. Related work experience conducting research, developing surveys, or analyzing data, for example while in school is a major asset in this competitive job market. Many graduates will find employment in government, industry, and business as management or sales trainees, or as research or administrative assistants.

Economists with good quantitative skills are qualified for research analyst positions in a broad range of fields. Those with strong backgrounds in mathematics, statistics, survey design, and computer science may be hired by private firms for marketing research work. Those who meet State certification requirements may become high school economics teachers. The demand for secondary school economics teachers is expected to grow as economics becomes an increasingly important and popular course.

Candidates who hold a master's degree in economics have better employment prospects than bachelor's degree holders. Some businesses and research and consulting firms seek master's degree holders who have strong computer and quantitative skills and can perform complex research, but do not command the high salary of a Ph.D. Master's degree holders are likely to face competition for teaching positions in colleges and universities; however, some may gain positions in junior and community colleges.

Opportunities will be best for Ph.D.'s. Ph.D. graduates should have opportunities to work as economists in private industry, research and consulting firms, and government. In addition, employment prospects for economists in colleges and universities should improve due to an expected wave of retirements among college faculty.

ECONOMISTS - WHAT THEY DO

Economists study how society distributes resources, such as land, labour, raw materials, and machinery, to produce goods and services. They conduct research, collect and analyze data, monitor economic trends, and develop forecasts on a wide variety of issues, including energy costs, inflation, interest rates, exchange rates, business cycles, taxes, and employment levels, among others.

Economists develop methods for obtaining the data they need. For example, sampling techniques may be used to conduct a survey, and various mathematical modeling techniques may be used to develop forecasts. Preparing reports, including tables and charts, on research results also is an important part of an economist's job, as is presenting economic and statistical concepts in a clear and meaningful way for those who do not have a background in economics. Some economists also perform economic analysis for the media.

Many economists specialize in a particular area of economics, although general knowledge of basic economic principles is essential. Microeconomists study the supply and demand decisions of individuals and firms, such as how profits can be maximized and the quantity of a good or service that consumers will demand at a certain price. Industrial economists and organizational economists study the market structure of particular industries in terms of the number of competitors within those industries and examine the market decisions of competitive firms and monopolies.

These economists also may be concerned with antitrust policy and its impact on market structure. Macroeconomists study historical trends in the whole economy and forecast future trends in areas such as unemployment, inflation, economic growth, productivity, and investment. Monetary economists and financial economists do work that is similar to that done by macroeconomists. These workers study the money and banking system and the effects of changing interest rates. International economists study global financial markets, currencies and exchange rates, and the effects of various trade policies such as tariffs. Labour economists and demographic economists study the supply and demand for labour and the determination of wages.

These economists also try to explain the reasons for unemployment and the effects of changing demographic trends, such as an aging population and increasing immigration, on labour markets. Public finance economists are involved primarily in studying the role of the government in the economy and the effects of tax cuts, budget deficits, and welfare policies.

Econometricians investigate all areas of economics and apply mathematical techniques such as calculus, game theory, and regression analysis to their research. With these techniques, they formulate economic models that help explain economic relationships that can be used to develop forecasts about business cycles, the effects of a specific rate of inflation on the economy, the effects of tax legislation on unemployment levels, and other economic phenomena. Many economists apply these areas of economics to health, education, agriculture, urban and regional economics, law, history, energy, the environment, and other issues.

Economists working for corporations are involved primarily in microeconomic issues, such as forecasting consumer demand and sales of the firm's products. Some analyze their competitors' market share and advise their company on how to handle the competition. Others monitor legislation passed by Congress, such as environmental and worker safety regulations, and assess how new laws will affect the corporation. Corporations with many international branches or subsidiaries might employ economists to monitor the economic situations in countries where they do business or to provide a risk assessment of a country into which the company is considering expanding.

Economists working in economic consulting or research firms sometimes perform the same tasks as economists working for corporations. However, economists in consulting firms also perform much of the macroeconomic analysis and forecasting conducted in the United States. Their analyses and forecasts are frequently published in newspapers and journal articles.

Another large employer of economists is government. Economists in the Federal Government administer most of the surveys and collect the majority of the economic data about the United States. For example, economists in the U.S. Department of Commerce collect and analyze data on the production, distribution, and consumption of commodities produced in the United States, and economists employed by the U.S. Department of Labour collect and analyze data on the domestic economy, including data on prices, wages, employment, productivity, and safety and health.

Economists who work for government agencies also assess economic conditions in the United States and abroad to estimate the effects of specific changes in legislation and public policy. Government economists advise policy makers in areas such as the deregulation of industries, the effects of changes to Social Security, the effects of tax cuts on the budget deficit, and the effectiveness of imposing tariffs on imported goods. An economist working in State or local government might analyze data on the growth of school-age or prison populations and on employment and unemployment rates to project future spending needs.

2

World's Famous Economists

ADAM SMITH

Adam Smith (16 June 1723 NS (5 June 1723 OS) – 17 July 1790) was a Scottish moral philosopher and a pioneer of political economy. One of the key figures of the Scottish Enlightenment, Smith is best known for two classic works: *The Theory of Moral Sentiments*(1759), and *An Enquiry into the Nature and Causes of the Wealth of Nations* (1776).

The latter, usually abbreviated as *The Wealth of Nations*, is considered his *magnum opus* and the first modern work of economics. Smith is cited as the "father of modern economics" and is still among the most influential thinkers in the field of economics today.

Smith studied social philosophy at the University of Glasgow and at Balliol College, Oxford, where he was one of the first students to benefit from scholarships set up by fellow Scot, John Snell. After graduating, he delivered a successful series of public lectures at the University of Edinburgh, leading him to collaborate with David Hume during the Scottish Enlightenment.

Smith obtained a professorship at Glasgow teaching moral philosophy, and during this time he wrote and published *The Theory of Moral Sentiments*. In his later life, he took a tutoring position that allowed him to travel throughout Europe, where he met other intellectual leaders of his day. Smith laid the foundations of classical free market economic theory.

The Wealth of Nations was a precursor to the modern academic discipline of economics. In this and other works, he expounded upon how rational self-interest and competition can lead to economic prosperity.

Smith was controversial in his own day and his general approach and writing style were often satirised byTory writers in the moralising tradition of William Hogarth and Jonathan Swift.

In 2005, *The Wealth of Nations* was named among the 100 Best Scottish Books of all time. Former UK Prime Minister Margaret Thatcher, it is said, used to carry a copy of the book in her handbag.

BIOGRAPHY

Early Life

Smith was born in Kirkcaldy, in the County of Fife, in Scotland. His father, also of the same name, was a Scottish *Writer to the Signet* (senior solicitor, advocate, and prosecutor (Judge Advocate) and also served as comptroller of the Customs in Kirkcaldy. In 1720 he married Margaret Douglas, daughter of the landed Robert Douglas of Strathendry, also in Fife. His father died two months after he was born, leaving his mother a widow. The date of Smith's baptism into the Church of Scotland at Kirkcaldy was 5 June 1723, and this has often been treated as if it were also his date of birth, which is unknown. Although few events in Smith's early childhood are known, the Scottish journalist John Rae, Smith's biographer, recorded that Smith was abducted by gypsies at the age of three and released when others went to rescue him. Smith was close to his mother, who probably encouraged him to pursue his scholarly ambitions. He attended the Burgh School of Kirkcaldy—characterised by Rae as "one of the best secondary schools of Scotland at that period"—from 1729 to 1737, he learned Latin, mathematics, history, and writing.

Formal Education

Smith entered the University of Glasgow when he was fourteen and studied moral philosophy under Francis Hutcheson. Here, Smith developed his passion for liberty, reason, and free speech. In 1740 Smith was the graduate scholar presented to undertake postgraduate studies at Balliol College, Oxford, under the Snell Exhibition.

Adam Smith considered the teaching at Glasgow to be far superior to that at Oxford, which he found intellectually stifling. In Book V, Chapter II of *The Wealth of Nations*, Smith wrote: "In the University of Oxford, the greater part of the public professors have, for these many years, given up altogether even the pretence of teaching." Smith is also reported to have complained to friends that Oxford officials once discovered him reading a copy of David Hume's *Treatise on Human Nature*, and they subsequently confiscated his book and punished him severely for reading it.According to William Robert Scott, "The Oxford of [Smith's] time gave little if any help towards what was to be his lifework." Nevertheless, Smith took the opportunity while at Oxford to teach himself several subjects by reading many books from the shelves of the large Bodleian Library.

When Smith was not studying on his own, his time at Oxford was not a happy one, according to his letters. Near the end of his time there, Smith began suffering from shaking fits, probably the symptoms of a nervous breakdown. He left Oxford University in 1746, before his scholarship ended. In Book V of *The Wealth of Nations*, Smith comments on the low quality of instruction and the meagre intellectual activity at English universities, when compared to their Scottish counterparts. He attributes this both to the rich endowments of the colleges at Oxford and Cambridge, which made the income of professors independent of their ability to attract students, and to the fact that distinguished men of letters could make an even more comfortable living as ministers of the Church of England.

Adam Smith's discontent at Oxford might be in part due to the absence of his beloved teacher in Glasgow, Francis Hutcheson. Hutcheson was well regarded as one of the most prominent lecturers at the University of Glasgow in his day and earned the approbation of students, colleagues, and even ordinary residents with the fervour and earnestness of his orations (which he sometimes opened to the public). His lectures endeavoured not merely to teach philosophy but to make his students embody that philosophy in their lives, appropriately acquiring the epithet, the preacher of philosophy. Unlike Smith, Hutcheson was not a system builder; rather it was his magnetic personality and method of lecturing that so influenced his students and caused the greatest of those to reverentially refer to him as "the never to be forgotten Hutcheson" – a title that Smith in all his correspondence used to describe only two people, his good friend David Hume and influential mentor Francis Hutcheson.

Teaching Career

Smith began delivering public lectures in 1748 in University of Edinburgh, sponsored by the Philosophical Society of Edinburgh under the patronage of Lord Kames. His lecture topics included rhetoric and *belles-lettres*, and later the subject of "the progress of opulence". On this latter topic he first expounded his economic philosophy of "the obvious and simple system of natural liberty". While Smith was not adept at public speaking, his lectures met with success.

In 1750, he met the philosopher David Hume, who was his senior by more than a decade. In their writings covering history, politics, philosophy, economics, and religion, Smith and Hume shared closer intellectual and personal bonds than with other important figures of the Scottish Enlightenment.

In 1751, Smith earned a professorship at Glasgow University teaching logic courses, and in 1752 he was elected a member of the Philosophical Society of Edinburgh, having been introduced to the society by Lord Kames. When the head of Moral Philosophy died the next year, Smith took over the position. He worked as an academic for the next thirteen years, which he characterised as "by far the most useful and therefore by far the happiest and most honourable period [of his life]".

Smith published *The Theory of Moral Sentiments* in 1759, embodying some of his Glasgow lectures. This work was concerned with how human morality depends on sympathy between agent and spectator, or the individual and other members of society. Smith defined "mutual sympathy" as the basis of moral sentiments. He based his explanation, not on a special "moral sense" as the Third Lord Shaftesbury and Hutcheson had done, nor on utility as Hume did, but on mutual sympathy, a term best captured in modern parlance by the twentieth-century concept of empathy, the capacity to recognise feelings that are being experienced by another being.

Following the publication of *The Theory of Moral Sentiments*, Smith became so popular that many wealthy students left their schools in other countries to enroll at Glasgow to learn under Smith. After the publication of *The Theory of Moral Sentiments*, Smith began to give more attention to jurisprudence and economics in his lectures and less to his theories of morals. For example, Smith lectured that the cause of increase in national wealth is labour, rather than the nation's quantity of gold or silver, which is the basis formercantilism, the economic theory that dominated Western European economic policies at the time.

In 1762, the University of Glasgow conferred on Smith the title of Doctor of Laws (LL.D.). At the end of 1763, he obtained an offer from Charles Townshend – who had been introduced to Smith by David Hume – to tutor his stepson, Henry Scott, the young Duke of Buccleuch. Smith then resigned from his professorship to take the tutoring position. He subsequently attempted to return the fees he had collected from his students because he resigned in the middle of the term, but his students refused.

Tutoring and Travels

Smith's tutoring job entailed touring Europe with Scott, during which time he educated Scott on a variety of subjects – such as proper Polish.He was paid £300 per year (plus expenses) along with a £300 per year pension; roughly twice his former income as a teacher. Smith first travelled as a tutor to Toulouse, France, where he stayed for one and a half years. According to his own account, he found Toulouse to be somewhat boring, having written to Hume that he "had begun to write a book to pass away the time". After touring the south of France, the group moved to Geneva, where Smith met with the philosopher Voltaire.

From Geneva, the party moved to Paris. Here Smith came to know several great intellectual leaders of the time; invariably having an effect on his future works. This list included: Benjamin Franklin, Turgot, Jean D'Alembert, André Morellet, Helvétius, and, notably, François Quesnay, the head of the Physiocratic school. So impressed with his ideas Smith considered dedicating *The Wealth of Nations* to him – had Quesnay not died beforehand. Physiocrats were opposed to mercantilism, the dominating economic theory of the time. Illustrated in their motto Laissez faire et laissez passer, le monde va de lui même! (Let do and let pass, the world goes on by itself!). They were also known to have declared that only agricultural activity produced real wealth; merchants and industrialists (manufacturers) did not. This however, did not represent their true school of thought, but was a mere "smoke screen" manufactured to hide their actual criticisms of the nobility and church; arguing that they made up the only real clients of merchants. The wealth of France was virtually destroyed by Louis XIV and Louis XV in ruinous wars, by aiding the American insurgents against the British, and perhaps most destructive (in terms of public perceptions) was what was seen as the excessive consumption of goods and services deemed to have no economic contribution – unproductive labour. Assuming that nobility and church are essentially detractors from economic growth, the feudal system of agriculture in France was the only sector important to maintain the wealth of the nation. Given that the English economy of the day yielded an income distribution that stood in contrast to that which existed in France, Smith concluded that the teachings and beliefs of Physiocrats were, "with all [their] imperfections [perhaps], the nearest approximation to the truth that has yet been published upon the subject of political economy". The distinction between productive versus unproductive labour – the physiocratic *classe steril* – was a predominant issue in the development and understanding of what would become classical economic theory.

Later Years

In 1766, Henry Scott's younger brother died in Paris, and Smith's tour as a tutor ended shortly thereafter. Smith returned home that year to Kirkcaldy, and he devoted much of the next ten years to his magnum opus. There he befriended Henry Moyes, a young blind man who showed precocious aptitude. As well as teaching Moyes, Smith secured the patronage of David Hume and Thomas Reid in the young man's education. In May 1773, Smith was elected fellow of the Royal Society of London, and was elected a member of the Literary Club in 1775. *The Wealth of Nations* was published in 1776 and was an instant success, selling out its first edition in only six months.

In 1778, Smith was appointed to a post as commissioner of customs in Scotland and went to live with his mother in Panmure House in Edinburgh's Canongate. Five years later, as a member of the Philosophical Society of Edinburgh when it received its royal charter, he automatically became one of the founding members of the Royal Society of Edinburgh, and from 1787 to 1789 he occupied the honourary position of Lord Rector of the University of Glasgow. He died in the northern wing of Panmure House in Edinburgh on 17 July 1790 after a painful illness and was buried in the Canongate Kirkyard. On his death bed, Smith expressed disappointment that he had not achieved more.

Smith's literary executors were two friends from the Scottish academic world: the physicist and chemist Joseph Black, and the pioneering geologist James Hutton. Smith left behind many notes and some unpublished material, but gave instructions to destroy anything that was not fit for publication. He mentioned an early unpublished *History of Astronomy* as probably suitable, and it duly appeared in 1795, along with other material such as *Essays on Philosophical Subjects*.

Smith's library went by his will to David Douglas, Lord Reston (son of his cousin Colonel Robert Douglas of Strathendry, Fife), who lived with Smith. It was eventually divided between his two surviving children, Cecilia Margaret (Mrs. Cunningham) and David Anne (Mrs. Bannerman). On the death of her husband, the Rev. W. B. Cunningham of Prestonpans in 1878, Mrs. Cunningham sold some of the books. The remainder passed to her son, Professor Robert Oliver Cunningham of Queen's College, Belfast, who presented a part to the library of Queen's College. After his death the remaining books were sold. On the death of Mrs. Bannerman in 1879 her portion of the library went intact to the New College (of the Free Church), Edinburgh.

PERSONALITY AND BELIEFS

Character

Not much is known about Smith's personal views beyond what can be deduced from his published articles. His personal papers were destroyed after his death at his request. He never married, and seems to have maintained a close relationship with his mother, with whom he lived after his return from France and who died six years before his own death.

Smith was described by several of his contemporaries and biographers as comically absent-minded, with peculiar habits of speech and gait, and a smile of "inexpressible benignity". He was known to talk to himself, a habit that began during his childhood when he would smile in rapt conversation with invisible companions.

He also had occasional spells of imaginary illness, and he is reported to have had books and papers placed in tall stacks in his study. According to one story, Smith took Charles Townshend on a tour of a tanning factory, and while discussing free trade, Smith walked into a huge tanning pit from which he needed help to escape.

He is also said to have put bread and butter into a teapot, drunk the concoction, and declared it to be the worst cup of tea he ever had. According to another account, Smith distractedly went out walking in his nightgown and ended up 15 miles (24 km) outside of town, before nearby church bells brought him back to reality.

James Boswell who was a student of Smith's at Glasgow University, and later knew him at the Literary Club, says that Smith thought that speaking about his ideas in conversation might reduce the sale of his books, and so his conversation was unimpressive. According to Boswell, he once told Sir Joshua Reynolds that 'he made it a rule when in company never to talk of what he understood'.

Smith, who is reported to have been an odd-looking fellow, has been described as someone who "had a large nose, bulging eyes, a protruding lower lip, a nervous twitch, and a speech impediment".

Smith is said to have acknowledged his looks at one point, saying, "I am a beau in nothing but my books." Smith rarely sat for portraits, so almost all depictions of him created during his lifetime were drawn from memory. The best-known portraits of Smith are the profile by James Tassie and two etchings byJohn Kay. The line engravings produced for the covers of 19th century reprints of *The Wealth of Nations* were based largely on Tassie's medallion.

Religious Views

There has been considerable scholarly debate about the nature of Smith's religious views. Smith's father had shown a strong interest in Christianity and belonged to the moderate wing of the Church of Scotland. The fact that Adam Smith received the Snell Exhibition suggests that he may have gone to Oxford with the intention of pursuing a career in the Church of England.

Anglo-American economist Ronald Coase has challenged the view that Smith was a deist, based on the fact that Smith's writings never explicitly invoke God as an explanation of the harmonies of the natural or the human worlds. According to Coase, though Smith does sometimes refer to the "Great Architect of the Universe", later scholars such as Jacob Viner have "very much exaggerated the extent to which Adam Smith was committed to a belief in a personal God", a belief for which Coase finds little evidence in passages such as the one in the *Wealth of Nations* in which Smith writes that the curiosity of mankind about the "great phenomena of nature", such as "the generation, the life, growth and dissolution of plants and animals", has led men to "enquire into their causes", and that "superstition first attempted to satisfy this curiosity, by referring all those wonderful appearances to the immediate agency of the gods.

Philosophy afterwards endeavoured to account for them, from more familiar causes, or from such as mankind were better acquainted with than the agency of the gods".

Some other authors argue that Smith's social and economic philosophy is inherently theological and that his entire model of social order is logically dependent on the notion of God's action in nature.

Smith was also a close friend and later the executor of David Hume, who was commonly characterised in his own time as an atheist. The publication in 1777 of Smith's letter to William Strahan, in which he described Hume's courage in the face of death in spite his irreligiosity, attracted considerable controversy.

PUBLISHED WORKS

The Theory of Moral Sentiments

In 1759, Smith published his first work, *The Theory of Moral Sentiments*. He continued making extensive revisions to the book, up until his death. Although *The Wealth of Nations* is widely regarded as Smith's most influential work, it is believed that Smith himself considered *The Theory of Moral Sentiments* to be a superior work.

In the work, Smith critically examines the moral thinking of his time, and suggests that conscience arises from social relationships. His goal in writing the work was to explain the source of mankind's ability to form moral judgements, in spite of man's natural inclinations towards self-interest. Smith proposes a theory of sympathy, in which the act of observing others makes people aware of themselves and the morality of their own behaviour.

Scholars have traditionally perceived a conflict between *The Theory of Moral Sentiments* and *The Wealth of Nations*; the former emphasises sympathy for others, while the latter focuses on the role of self-interest. In recent years, however, some scholars of Smith's work have argued that no contradiction exists. They claim that in *The Theory of Moral Sentiments*, Smith develops a theory of psychology in which individuals seek the approval of the "impartial spectator" as a result of a natural desire to have outside observers sympathise with them. Rather than viewing *The Theory of Moral Sentiments* and *The Wealth of Nations* as presenting incompatible views of human nature, some Smith scholars regard the works as emphasising different aspects of human nature that vary depending on the situation. Furthermore, Ekelund and Hebert argue that self-interest is present in both works and that "in the former, sympathy is the moral faculty that holds self-interest in check, whereas in the latter, competition is the economic faculty that restrains self-interest."

The Wealth of Nations

There is a fundamental disagreement between classical and neo-classical economists about the central message of Smith's most influential work: *An Enquiry into the Nature and Causes of the Wealth of Nations*. Neo-classical economists emphasise Smith's invisible hand, a concept mentioned in the middle of his work – Book IV, Chapter II – and classical economists believe that Smith stated his programme for promoting the "wealth of nations" in the first sentences.

Smith used the term "the invisible hand" in "History of Astronomy" referring to "the invisible hand of Jupiter" and twice – each time with a different meaning – the term "an invisible hand": in *The Theory of Moral Sentiments* (1759) and in *The Wealth of Nations* (1776). This last statement about "an invisible hand" has been interpreted as "the invisible hand" in numerous ways.

It is therefore important to read the original: As every individual, therefore, endeavours as much as he can both to employ his capital in the support of domestic industry, and so to direct that industry that its produce may be of the greatest value; every individual necessarily labours to render the annual revenue of the society as great as he can.

He generally, indeed, neither intends to promote the public interest, nor knows how much he is promoting it. By preferring the support of domestic to that of foreign industry, he intends only his own security; and by directing that industry in such a manner as its produce may be of the greatest value, he intends only his own gain, and he is in this, as in many other cases, led by an invisible hand to promote an end which was no part of his intention. Nor is it always the worse for the society that it was no part of it.

By pursuing his own interest he frequently promotes that of the society more effectually than when he really intends to promote it. I have never known much good done by those who affected to trade for the public good. It is an affectation, indeed, not very common among merchants, and very few words need be employed in dissuading them from it.

Those who regard that statement as Smith's central message also quote frequently Smith's dictum:

It is not from the benevolence of the butcher, the brewer, or the baker, that we expect our dinner, but from their regard to their own interest. We address ourselves, not to their humanity but to their self-love, and never talk to them of our own necessities but of their advantages.

Smith's statement about the benefits of "an invisible hand" is certainly meant to answer Mandeville's contention that "Private Vices... may be turned into Public Benefits".

It shows Smith's belief that when an individual pursues his self-interest, he indirectly promotes the good of society. Self-interested competition in the free market, he argued, would tend to benefit society as a whole by keeping prices low, while still building in an incentive for a wide variety of goods and services. Nevertheless, he was wary of businessmen and warned of their "conspiracy against the public or in some other contrivance to raise prices". Again and again, Smith warned of the collusive nature of business interests, which may form cabals or monopolies, fixing the highest price "which can be squeezed out of the buyers".

Smith also warned that a business-dominated political system would allow a conspiracy of businesses and industry against consumers, with the former scheming to influence politics and legislation. Smith states that the interest of manufacturers and merchants "...in any particular branch of trade or manufactures, is always in some respects different from, and even opposite to, that of the public...The proposal of any new law or regulation of commerce which comes from this order, ought always to be listened to with great precaution, and ought never be adopted till after having been long and carefully examined, not only with the most scrupulous, but with the most suspicious attention."

The neo-classical interest in Smith's statement about "an invisible hand" originates in the possibility to see it as a precursor of neo-classical economics and its General Equilibrium concept. Samuelson's "Economics" refers 6 times to Smith's "invisible hand". To emphasise this relation, Samuelson quotes Smith's "invisible hand" statement putting "general interest" where Smith wrote "public interest". Samuelson concluded: "Smith was unable to prove the essence of his invisible-hand doctrine. Indeed, until the 1940s no one knew how to prove, even to state properly, the kernel of truth in this proposition about perfectly competitive market."

Very differently, classical economists see in Smith's first sentences his programme to promote "The Wealth of Nations". Taking up the physiocratical concept of the economy as a circular process means that to have growth the inputs of period2 must excel the inputs of period1.

Therefore the outputs of period1 not used or usable as input of period2 are regarded as unproductive labour as they do not contribute to growth. This is what Smith had learned in France with Quesnay. To this French insight that unproductive labour should be pushed back to use more labour productively, Smith added his own proposal, that productive labour should be made even more productive by deepening the division of labour. Deepening the division of labour means under competition lower prices and thereby extended markets. Extended markets and increased production lead to a new step of reorganising production and inventing new ways of producing which again lower prices, etc., etc.. Smith's central message is therefore that under dynamic competition a growth machine secures "The Wealth of Nations". It predicted England's evolution as the workshop of the World, underselling all its competitors. The opening sentences of the "Wealth of Nations" summarise this policy:

The annual labour of every nation is the fund which originally supplies it with all the necessaries and conveniences of life which it annually consumes.... [T]his produce... bears a greater or smaller proportion to the number of those who are to consume it....[B]ut this proportion must in every nation be regulated by two different circumstances;

- First, by the skill, dexterity, and judgement with which its labour is generally applied; and,
- Secondly, by the proportion between the number of those who are employed in useful labour, and that of those who are not so employed.

Criticism and Dissent

Alfred Marshall criticised Smith's definition of economy on several points. He argued that man should be equally important as money, services are as important as goods, and that there must be an emphasis on human welfare, instead of just wealth. Nobel Prize-winning economist Joseph E. Stiglitz says, on the topic of one of Smith's better known ideas: "the reason that the invisible hand often seems invisible is that it is often not there."

Other Works

Shortly before his death, Smith had nearly all his manuscripts destroyed. In his last years, he seemed to have been planning two major treatises, one on the theory and history of law and one on the sciences and arts.

The posthumously published *Essays on Philosophical Subjects*, a history of astronomy down to Smith's own era, plus some thoughts on ancient physics and metaphysics, probably contain parts of what would have been the latter treatise.

Lectures on Jurisprudence were notes taken from Smith's early lectures, plus an early draft of *The Wealth of Nations*, published as part of the 1976 Glasgow Edition of the works and correspondence of Smith. Other works, including some published posthumously, include *Lectures on Justice, Police, Revenue, and Arms* (1763) (first published in 1896); and *Essays on Philosophical Subjects* (1795).

LEGACY

In Economics and Moral Philosophy

The Wealth of Nations was a precursor to the modern academic discipline of economics. In this and other works, Smith expounded how rational self-interest and competition can lead to economic prosperity. Smith was controversial in his own day and his general approach and writing style were often satirised by Tory writers in the moralising tradition of Hogarth and Swift, as a discussion at the University of Winchester suggests.In 2005, *The Wealth of Nations* was named among the 100 Best Scottish Books of all time. Former UK Prime Minister Margaret Thatcher, it is said, used to carry a copy of the book in her handbag.

In light of the arguments put forward by Smith and other economic theorists in Britain, academic belief in mercantalism began to decline in England in the late 18th century. During the Industrial Revolution, Britain embraced free trade and Smith's laissez-faire economics, and via the British Empire, used its power to spread a broadly liberal economic model around the world, characterised by open markets, and relatively barrier free domestic and international trade.

George Stigler attributes to Smith "the most important substantive proposition in all of economics". It is that, under competition, owners of resources (for example labour, land, and capital) will use them most profitably, resulting in an equal rate of return in equilibrium for all uses, adjusted for apparent differences arising from such factors as training, trust, hardship, and unemployment. Paul Samuelson finds in Smith's pluralist use of supply and demand as applied to wages, rents, profit a valid and valuable anticipation of the general equilibrium modelling ofWalras a century later. Smith's allowance for wage increases in the short and intermediate term from capital accumulation and invention contrasted with Malthus, Ricardo, andKarl Marx in their propounding a rigid subsistence–wage theory of labour supply.

On the other hand, Joseph Schumpeter dismissed Smith's contributions as unoriginal, saying "His very limitation made for success. Had he been more brilliant, he would not have been taken so seriously. Had he dug more deeply, had he unearthed more recondite truth, had he used more difficult and ingenious methods, he would not have been understood. But he had no such ambitions; in fact he disliked whatever went beyond plain common sense. He never moved above the heads of even the dullest readers. He led them on gently, encouraging them by trivialities and homely observations, making them feel comfortable all along."

Classical economists presented competing theories of those of Smith, termed the "labour theory of value". Later Marxian economics descending from classical economics also use Smith's labour theories, in part. The first volume of Karl Marx's major work, *Capital*, was published in German in 1867. In it, Marx focused on the labour theory of value and what he considered to be the exploitation of labour by capital. The labour theory of value held that the value of a thing was determined by the labour that went into its production. This contrasts with the modern contention of neo-classical economics, that the value of a thing is determined by what one is willing to give up to obtain the thing.

The body of theory later termed "neo-classical economics" or "marginalism" formed from about 1870 to 1910. The term "economics" was popularised by such neo-classical economists as Alfred Marshall as a concise synonym for "economic science" and a substitute for the earlier, broader term "political economy" used by Smith. This corresponded to the influence on the subject of mathematical methods used in the natural sciences. Neo-classical economics systematised supply and demand as joint determinants of price and quantity in market equilibrium, affecting both the allocation of output and the distribution of income. It dispensed with the labour theory of value of which Smith was most famously identified with in classical economics, in favour of a marginal utility theory of value on the demand side and a more general theory of costs on the supply side.

The bicentennial anniversary of the publication of *The Wealth of Nations* was celebrated in 1976, resulting in increased interest for *The Theory of Moral Sentiments* and his other works throughout academia. After 1976, Smith was more likely to be represented as the author of both *The Wealth of Nations* and *The Theory of Moral Sentiments*, and thereby as the founder of a moral philosophy and the science of economics. His *homo economicus* or "economic man" was also more often represented as a moral person. Additionally, economists David Levy and Sandra Peart in "The Secret History of the Dismal Science" point to his opposition to hierarchy and beliefs in inequality, including racial inequality, and provide additional support for those who point to Smith's opposition to slavery, colonialism, and empire.

They show the caricatures of Smith drawn by the opponents of views on hierarchy and inequality in this online article. Emphasized also are Smith's statements of the need for high wages for the poor, and the efforts to keep wages low.

In The "Vanity of the Philosopher": From Equality to Hierarchy in Postclassical Economics Peart and Levy also cite Smith's view that a common street porter was not intellectually inferior to a philosopher, and point to the need for greater appreciation of the public views in discussions of science and other subjects now considered to be technical. They also cite Smith's opposition to the often expressed view that science is superior to common sense.

Smith also explained the relationship between growth of private property and civil government:

"Men may live together in society with some tolerable degree of security, though there is no civil magistrate to protect them from the injustice of those passions. But avarice and ambition in the rich, in the poor the hatred of labour and the love of present ease and enjoyment, are the passions which prompt to invade property, passions much more steady in their operation, and much more universal in their influence.

Wherever there is great property there is great inequality. For one very rich man there must be at least five hundred poor, and the affluence of the few supposes the indigence of the many.

The affluence of the rich excites the indignation of the poor, who are often both driven by want, and prompted by envy, to invade his possessions. It is only under the shelter of the civil magistrate that the owner of that valuable property, which is acquired by the labour of many years, or perhaps of many successive generations, can sleep a single night in security.

He is at all times surrounded by unknown enemies, whom, though he never provoked, he can never appease, and from whose injustice he can be protected only by the powerful arm of the civil magistrate continually held up to chastise it. The acquisition of valuable and extensive property, therefore, necessarily requires the establishment of civil government. Where there is no property, or at least none that exceeds the value of two or three days' labour, civil government is not so necessary.

Civil government supposes a certain subordination. But as the necessity of civil government gradually grows up with the acquisition of valuable property, so the principal causes which naturally introduce subordination gradually grow up with the growth of that valuable property. (...) Men of inferior wealth combine to defend those of superior wealth in the possession of their property, in order that men of superior wealth may combine to defend them in the possession of theirs. All the inferior shepherds and herdsmen feel that the security of their own herds and flocks depends upon the security of those of the great shepherd or herdsman; that the maintenance of their lesser authority depends upon that of his greater authority, and that upon their subordination to him depends his power of keeping their inferiors in subordination to them.

They constitute a sort of little nobility, who feel themselves interested to defend the property and to support the authority of their own little sovereign in order that he may be able to defend their property and to support their authority. Civil government, so far as it is instituted for the security of property, is in reality instituted for the defence of the rich against the poor, or of those who have some property against those who have none at all."

Portraits, Monuments, and Banknotes

Smith has been commemorated in the UK on banknotes printed by two different banks; his portrait has appeared since 1981 on the £50 notes issued by the Clydesdale Bank in Scotland, and in March 2007 Smith's image also appeared on the new series of £20 notes issued by the Bank of England, making him the first Scotsman to feature on an English banknote.

A large-scale memorial of Smith by Alexander Stoddart was unveiled on 4 July 2008 in Edinburgh. It is a 10 feet (3.0 m)-tall bronze sculpture and it stands above the Royal Mile outside St Giles' Cathedral in Parliament Square, near the Mercat cross. 20th-century sculptor Jim Sanborn (best known for the*Kryptos* sculpture at the United States Central Intelligence Agency) has created multiple pieces which feature Smith's work.

At Central Connecticut State University is *Circulating Capital*, a tall cylinder which features an extract from *The Wealth of Nations* on the lower half, and on the upper half, some of the same text but represented in binary code.

At the University of North Carolina at Charlotte, outside the Belk College of Business Administration, is *Adam Smith's Spinning Top*. Another Smith sculpture is atCleveland State University. He also appears as the narrator in the 2013 play *The Low Road*, centred on a proponent on laissez-faire economics in the late eighteenth century but dealing obliquely with thefinancial crisis of 2007–2008 and the recession which followed – in the premiere production, he was portrayed by Bill Paterson.

Residence

Adam Smith resided at Panmure house from 1778–90. This residence has now been purchased by the Edinburgh Business School at Heriot Watt University and fundraising has begun to restore it. Part of the Northern end of the original building appears to have been demolished in the 19th century to make way for an iron foundry.

As a Symbol of Free Market Economics

Smith has been celebrated by advocates of free market policies as the founder of free market economics, a view reflected in the naming of bodies such as the Adam Smith Institute in London, the Adam Smith Society and the Australian Adam Smith Club, and in terms such as the Adam Smith necktie.

Alan Greenspan argues that, while Smith did not coin the term *laissez-faire*, "it was left to Adam Smith to identify the more-general set of principles that brought conceptual clarity to the seeming chaos of market transactions". Greenspan continues that *The Wealth of Nations* was "one of the great achievements in human intellectual history". P. J. O'Rourke describes Smith as the "founder of free market economics".

However, other writers have argued that Smith's support for *laissez-faire* (which in French means leave alone) has been overstated. Herbert Stein wrote that the people who "wear an Adam Smith necktie" do it to "make a statement of their devotion to the idea of free markets and limited government", and that this misrepresents Smith's ideas. Stein writes that Smith "was not pure or doctrinaire about this idea.

He viewed government intervention in the market with great skepticism...yet he was prepared to accept or propose qualifications to that policy in the specific cases where he judged that their net effect would be beneficial and would not undermine the basically free character of the system. He did not wear the Adam Smith necktie." In Stein's reading, *The Wealth of Nations* could justify the Food and Drug Administration, the Consumer Product Safety Commission, mandatory employer health benefits, environmentalism, and "discriminatory taxation to deter improper or luxurious behaviour".

Similarly, Vivienne Brown stated in *The Economic Journal* that in the 20th century United States, Reaganomics supporters, the *Wall Street Journal*, and other similar sources have spread among the general public a partial and misleading vision of Smith, portraying him as an "extreme dogmatic defender of *laissez-faire* capitalism and supply-side economics". In fact, *The Wealth of Nations* includes the following statement on the payment of taxes:

"The subjects of every state ought to contribute towards the support of the government, as nearly as possible, in proportion to their respective abilities; that is, in proportion to the revenue which they respectively enjoy under the protection of the state."

Some commentators have argued that Smith's works show support for a progressive, not flat, income tax and that he specifically named taxes that he thought should be required by the state, among them luxury goods taxes and tax on rent.

Additionally, Smith outlined the proper expenses of the government in *The Wealth of Nations, Book V, Ch. I*. Included in his requirements of a government is to enforce contracts and provide justice system, grant patents and copy rights, provide public goods such as infrastructure, provide national defence and regulate banking. It was the role of the government to provide goods "of such a nature that the profit could never repay the expense to any individual" such as roads, bridges, canals, and harbours.

He also encouraged invention and new ideas through his patent enforcement and support of infant industry monopolies. he supported public education and religious institutions as providing general benefit to the society. Finally he outlined how the government should support the dignity of the monarch or chief magistrate, such that they are equal or above the public in fashion.

He even states that monarchs should be provided for in a greater fashion than magistrates of a republic because "we naturally expect more splendor in the court of a king than in the mansion-house of a doge". In addition, he was in favour of retaliatory tariffs and believed that they would eventually bring down the price of goods. He even stated in Wealth of Nations:

"The recovery of a great foreign market will generally more than compensate the transitory inconvenience of paying dearer during a short time for some sorts of goods."

Economic historians such as Jacob Viner regard Smith as a strong advocate of free markets and limited government (what Smith called "natural liberty") but not as a dogmatic supporter of *laissez-faire*.

Economist Daniel Klein believes using the term "free market economics" or "free market economist" to identify the ideas of Smith is too general and slightly misleading. Klein offers six characteristics central to the identity of Smith's economic thought and argues that a new name is needed to give a more accurate depiction of the "Smithian" identity. Economist David Ricardo set straight some of the misunderstandings about Smith's thoughts on free market. Most people still fall victim to the thinking that Smith was a free market economist without exception, though he was not. Ricardo pointed out that Smith was in support of helping infant industries. Smith believed that the government should subsidise newly formed industry, but he did fear that when the infant industry grew into adulthood it would be unwilling to surrender the government help.Smith also supported tariffs on imported goods to counteract an internal tax on the same good. Smith also fell to pressure in supporting some tariffs in support for national defence. Some have also claimed, Emma Rothschild among them, that Smith supported a minimum wage.

Though, Smith had written in his book *The Wealth of Nations*:

"The price of labour, it must be observed, cannot be ascertained very accurately anywhere, different prices being often paid at the same place and for the same sort of labour, not only according to the different abilities of the workmen, but according to the easiness or hardness of the masters. Where wages are not regulated by law, all that we can pretend to determine is what are the most usual; and experience seems to show that law can never regulate them properly, though it has often pretended to do so."

Smith also noted the inequality of bargaining power:

A landlord, a farmer, a master manufacturer, a merchant, though they did not employ a single workman, could generally live a year or two upon the stocks which they have already acquired. Many workmen could not subsist a week, few could subsist a month, and scarce any a year without employment. In the long run the workman may be as necessary to his master as his master is to him; but the necessity is not so immediate.

ALAN GREENSPAN

Alan Greenspan (born March 6, 1926) is an American economist who served as Chairman of the Federal Reserve of the United States from 1987 to 2006. He currently works as a private adviser and provides consulting for firms through his company, Greenspan Associates LLC. First appointed Federal Reserve chairman by President Ronald Reagan in August 1987, he was reappointed at successive four-year intervals until retiring on January 31, 2006 after the second-longest tenure in the position.

Greenspan came to the Federal Reserve Board from a successful consulting career. Although he was subdued in his public appearances, favourable media coverage raised his profile to a point that several observers likened him to a "rock star".Democratic leaders of Congress criticized him for politicizing his office because of his support for Social Security privatization and tax cuts, which they felt would increase the deficit. The easy-money policies of the Fed during Greenspan's tenure have been suggested to be a leading cause of the subprime mortgage crisis, which occurred within months of his departure from the Fed, and have, said *The Wall Street Journal*, "tarnished his reputation".

EARLY LIFE AND EDUCATION

Greenspan was born in the Washington Heights area of New York City. His father Herbert Greenspan was of Romanian-Jewish descent and his mother Rose Goldsmith of Hungarian-Jewish descent. His father worked as a stockbroker and market analyst in New York City.

Greenspan attended George Washington High School from 1940 until he graduated in June 1943, where one of his classmates wasJohn Kemeny. He played clarinet and saxophone along with classmate Stan Getz. He further studied clarinet at the Juilliard School from 1943 to 1944. Among his bandmates in the Woody Herman band was Leonard Garment, Richard Nixon's Special Counsel. In 1945 Greenspan attended New York

University where he earned a B.S. degree in economics *summa cum laude* in 1948 and an M.A. degree in economics in 1950. At Columbia University, under the tutelage of Arthur Burns, he pursued advanced economic studies but dropped out.

In 1977, Greenspan obtained a PhD degree in economics from New York University. His dissertation is not available from the university since it was removed at Greenspan's request in 1987, when he became Chairman of the Federal Reserve Board. In April 2008, however, *Barron's* obtained a copy, and notes that it includes "a discussion of soaring housing prices and their effect on consumer spending; it even anticipates a bursting housing bubble".

CAREER

Before the Federal Reserve

During his economic studies at New York University, Greenspan worked under Eugene Banks, a managing director at the Wall Street investment bank Brown Brothers Harriman, working in the firm's equity research department. From 1948 to 1953, Greenspan worked as an economic analyst at The National Industrial Conference Board, a business and industry oriented think-tank in New York City.

From 1955 to 1987, when he was appointed as chairman of the Federal Reserve, Greenspan was chairman and president of Townsend-Greenspan & Co., Inc., an economic consulting firm in New York City, a 32-year stint interrupted only from 1974 to 1977 by his service as Chairman of the Council of Economic Advisers under President Gerald Ford.

In mid-1968, Greenspan agreed to serve Richard Nixon as his coordinator on domestic policy in the nomination campaign. Greenspan has also served as a corporate director for Aluminum Company of America (Alcoa); Automatic Data Processing; Capital Cities/ABC, Inc.; General Foods; J.P. Morgan & Co.; Morgan Guaranty Trust Company; Mobil Corporation; and the Pittston Company. He was a director of the Council on Foreign Relations foreign policy organization between 1982 and 1988. He also served as a member of the influential Washington-based financial advisory body, the Group of Thirty in 1984.

Chairman of the Federal Reserve

What I've learned at the Federal Reserve is a new language which is called "Fed-speak". You soon learn to mumble with great incoherence.

— Alan Greenspan

On June 2, 1987, President Ronald Reagan nominated Greenspan as a successor to Paul Volcker as chairman of the Board of Governors of the Federal Reserve, and the Senate confirmed him on August 11, 1987. Investor, author and commentator Jim Rogershas said that Greenspan lobbied to get this chairmanship.

Two months after his confirmation Greenspan said immediately following the 1987 stock market crash that the Fed "affirmed today its readiness to serve as a source of liquidity to support the economic and financial system" George H. W. Bush blamed Fed policy for not winning a second term. Democratic president Bill Clinton reappointed Greenspan, and consulted him on economic matters. Greenspan lent support to Clinton's 1993 deficit reduction programme. Greenspan, while still fundamentally monetarist in orientation, had eclectic views on the economy, and his monetary policy decisions largely followed standard Taylor rule prescriptions.

In 2000, Greenspan raised interest rates several times; these actions were believed by many to have caused the bursting of the dot-com bubble. According to Nobel laureatePaul Krugman, however, "he didn't raise interest rates to curb the market's enthusiasm; he didn't even seek to impose margin requirements on stock market investors. Instead, he waited until the bubble burst, as it did in 2000, then tried to clean up the mess afterwards."

In January 2001, Greenspan, in support of President Bush's proposed tax decrease, stated that the federal surplus could accommodate a significant tax cut while paying down the national debt.

In autumn 2001, as a decisive reaction to the September 11 attacks and various corporate scandals which undermined the economy, the Greenspan-led Federal Reserve initiated a series of interest cuts that brought down the Federal Funds rate to 1perc ent in 2004. While presenting the Federal Reserve's Monetary Policy Report in July 2002, he said that "It is not that humans have become any more greedy than in generations past. It is that the avenues to express greed had grown so enormously." and suggested that financial markets need to be regulated. His critics, led by Steve Forbes, attributed the rapid rise in commodity prices and gold to Greenspan's loose monetary policy, which Forbes believed had caused excessive asset inflation and a weak dollar. By late 2004, the price of gold was higher than its 12-year moving average.

On May 18, 2004, Greenspan was nominated by President George W. Bush to serve for an unprecedented fifth term as chairman of the Federal Reserve. He was previously appointed to the post by Presidents Reagan, George H. W. Bush, and Clinton.

In a May 2005 speech, Greenspan stated: "Two years ago at this conference I argued that the growing array of derivatives and the related application of more-sophisticated methods for measuring and managing risks had been key factors underlying the remarkable resilience of the banking system, which had recently shrugged off severe shocks to the economy and the financial system. At the same time, I indicated some concerns about the risks associated with derivatives, including the risks posed by concentration in certain derivatives markets, notably the over-the-counter (OTC) markets for U.S. dollar interest rate options."

Greenspan opposed tariffs against People's Republic of China for its refusal to let the yuan rise, suggesting instead that any American workers displaced by Chinese tradecould be compensated through unemployment insurance and retraining programmes.

Greenspan's term as a member of the Board ended on January 31, 2006, and Ben Bernanke was confirmed as his successor.

As chairman of the board, Greenspan did not give any broadcast interviews from 1987 through 2005.

After the Federal Reserve

Immediately upon leaving the Fed, Greenspan formed an economic consulting firm, Greenspan Associates LLC. He also accepted an honourary (unpaid) position at HM Treasury in the United Kingdom.

On February 26, 2007, Greenspan forecast a possible recession in the U.S. before or in early 2008. Stabilizing corporate profits are said to have influenced his comments. The following day, the Dow Jones Industrial Average decreased by 416 points, losing 3.3perc ent of its value. In May 2007, Greenspan was hired as a special consultant by Pacific Investment Management Company (PIMCO) to participate in their quarterly economic forums and speak privately with the bond managers about Fed interest rate policy.

In August 2007, Deutsche Bank announced that it would be retaining Greenspan as a senior advisor to its investment banking team and clients.

In mid-January 2008, hedge fund Paulson & Co. hired Greenspan as an adviser. According to the terms of their agreement he was not to advise any other hedge fund while working for Paulson. (During 2007 Paulson had foreseen the collapse of the sub-prime housing market and hired Goldman Sachs to package their sub-prime holdings into derivatives and sell them. Some economic commentators blamed this collapse on Greenspan's policies while at the Fed.)

On April 30, 2009, Greenspan offered a defence of the H-1B visa programme, telling a U.S. Senate subcommittee that the visa quota is "far too small to meet the need" and saying that it protects U.S. workers from global competition, creating a "privileged elite". Testifying on immigration reform before the Subcommittee on Immigration, Border Security and Citizenship, he said more skilled immigration was needed "as the economy copes with the forthcoming retirement wave of skilled baby boomers".

Memoir

Greenspan wrote a memoir titled *The Age of Turbulence: Adventures in a New World*, published September 17, 2007. Greenspan says that he wrote this book in longhand mostly while soaking in the bathtub, a habit he regularly employs ever since an accident in 1971, when he injured his back. Greenspan wrote:

To this day, the bathtub is where I get many of my best ideas. My assistants have gotten used to typing from drafts scrawled on damp yellow pads—a chore that got much easier once we found a kind of pen whose ink doesn't run. Immersed in my bath, I'm as happy as Archimedes as I contemplate the world.

Greenspan discusses in his book, among other things, his history in government and economics, capitalism and other economic systems, current issues in the global economy, and future issues that face the global economy. In the book Greenspan criticizes President George W. Bush, Vice President Dick Cheney, and the Republican-controlled Congress for abandoning the Republican Party's principles on spending and deficits. Greenspan's criticisms of President Bush include his refusal to veto spending bills, sending the country into increasingly deep deficits, and for "putting political imperatives ahead of sound economic policies".

Greenspan writes, "They swapped principle for power. They ended up with neither. They deserved to lose [the 2006 election]." Of all the presidents with whom he worked, he praises Bill Clinton above all others, saying that Clinton maintained "a consistent, disciplined focus on long-term economic growth." Although he respected what he saw as Richard Nixon's immense intelligence, Greenspan found him to be "sadly paranoid, misanthropic and cynical". He said of Gerald Ford that he "was as close to normal as you get in a president, but he was never elected".

As for advice regarding future U.S. economic policy, one change Greenspan recommends is for the U.S. to improve its primary and secondary education systems. He asserts this would narrow the unusually large gap between the minority of high income earners and the majority of workers, whose wages have not grown proportionately with globalization and the nation's GDP growth.

OBJECTIVISM

In the early 1950s, Greenspan began an association with novelist and philosopher Ayn Rand. Greenspan was introduced to Rand by his first wife, Joan Mitchell. Rand nicknamed Greenspan "the undertaker" because of his penchant for dark clothing and reserved demeanor. Although Greenspan was initially a logical positivist, he was converted to Rand's philosophy of Objectivism by her associate Nathaniel Branden. He became one of the members of Rand's inner circle, the Ayn Rand Collective, who read *Atlas Shrugged* while it was being written. During the 1950s and 1960s Greenspan was a proponent of Objectivism, writing articles for Objectivist newsletters and contributing several essays for Rand's 1966 book *Capitalism: The Unknown Ideal* including an essay supporting the gold standard. Rand stood beside him at his 1974 swearing-in as Chair of the Council of Economic Advisers. Greenspan and Rand remained friends until her death in 1982.

He has come under criticism from Harry Binswanger, who believes his actions while at work for the Federal Reserve and his publicly expressed opinions on other issues show abandonment of Objectivist and free market principles.

When questioned in relation to this, however, he has said that in a democratic society individuals have to make compromises with each other over conflicting ideas of how money should be handled. He said he himself had to make such compromises, because he believes that "we did extremely well" without a central bank and with a gold standard.

In a Congressional hearing on October 23, 2008, Greenspan admitted that his free-market ideology shunning certain regulations was flawed. When asked about free markets and Rand's ideas in an interview on April 4, 2010, however, Greenspan clarified his stance on *laissez faire* capitalism and asserted that in a democratic society there could be no better alternative. He stated that the errors that were made stemmed not from the principle, but from the application of competitive markets in "assuming what the nature of risks would be."

RECEPTION

Housing Bubble

In the wake of the subprime mortgage and credit crisis in 2007, Greenspan stated that there was a bubble in the US housing market, warning in 2007 of "large double digit declines" in home values "larger than most people expect". Greenspan also noted, however, "I really didn't get it until very late in 2005 and 2006."

Greenspan stated that the housing bubble was "fundamentally engendered by the decline in real long-term interest rates", though he also claims that long-term interest rates are beyond the control of central banks because "the market value of global long-term securities is approaching $100 trillion" and thus these and other asset markets are large enough that they "now swamp the resources of central banks".

Following the September 11, 2001 attacks, the Federal Open Market Committee voted to reduce the federal funds rate from 3.5perc ent to 3.0perc ent. Then, after the accounting scandals of 2002, the Fed dropped the federal funds rate from then current 1.25perc ent to 1.00perc ent. Greenspan stated that this drop in rates would have the effect of leading to a surge in home sales and refinancing, adding that "Besides sustaining the demand for new construction, mortgage markets have also been a powerful stabilizing force over the past two years of economic distress by facilitating the extraction of some of the equity that homeowners have built up over the years."

According to some, however, Greenspan's policies of adjusting interest rates to historic lows contributed to a housing bubble in the US. The Federal Reserve acknowledged the connection between lower interest rates, higher home values, and the increased liquidity the higher home values bring to the overall economy: "Like other asset prices, house prices are influenced by interest rates, and in some countries, the housing market is a key channel of monetary policy transmission."

In a speech in February 2004, Greenspan suggested that more homeowners should consider taking out adjustable-rate mortgages (ARMs) where the interest rate adjusts itself to the current interest in the market. The fed own funds rate was at a then all-time-low of 1perc ent. A few months after his recommendation, Greenspan began raising interest rates, in a series of rate hikes that would bring the funds rate to 5.25perc ent about two years later. A triggering factor in the 2007 subprime mortgage financial crisis is believed to be the many subprime ARMs that reset at much higher interest rates than what the borrower paid during the first few years of the mortgage.

In 2008, Greenspan expressed great frustration that the speech he made on February 23, 2004 was used to criticize him on ARMs and the subprime mortgage crisis, and stated that he had made countervailing comments eight days after it that praised traditional fixed-rate mortgages. In that speech, Greenspan had suggested that lenders should offer to home purchasers a greater variety of "mortgage product alternatives" other than traditional fixed-rate mortgages. Greenspan also praised the rise of the subprime mortgage industry and the tools which it uses to assess credit-worthiness in an April 2005 speech:

Innovation has brought about a multitude of new products, such as subprime loans and niche credit programmes for immigrants. Such developments are representative of the market responses that have driven the financial services industry throughout the history of our country... With these advances in technology, lenders have taken advantage of credit-scoring models and other techniques for efficiently extending credit to a broader spectrum of consumers.... Where once more-marginal applicants would simply have been denied credit, lenders are now able to quite efficiently judge the risk posed by individual applicants and to price that risk appropriately.

These improvements have led to rapid growth in subprime mortgage lending; indeed, today subprime mortgages account for roughly 10 percent of the number of all mortgages outstanding, up from just 1 or 2 percent in the early 1990s.

The subprime mortgage industry collapsed in March 2007, with many of the largest lenders filing for bankruptcy protection in the face of spiraling foreclosure rates. For these reasons, Greenspan has been criticized for his role in the rise of the housing bubble and the subsequent problems in the mortgage industry, as well as "engineering" the housing bubble itself.

In 2004 Businessweek magazine analysts argued: "It was the Federal Reserve-engineered decline in rates that inflated the housing bubble... the most troublesome aspect of the price runup is that many recent buyers are squeezing into houses that they can barely afford by taking advantage of the lower rates available from adjustable-rate mortgages. That leaves them fully exposed to rising rates.

In September 2008 Joseph Stiglitz stated that Greenspan "didn't really believe in regulation; when the excesses of the financial system were noted, (he and others) called for self-regulation – an oxymoron." Greenspan, according to *The New York Times,* says he himself is blameless. On April 6, 2005, Greenspan called for a substantial increase in the regulation of Fannie Mae and Freddie Mac: "Appearing before the Senate Banking Committee, the Fed chairman, Alan Greenspan, said the enormous portfolios of the companies — nearly a quarter of the home-mortgage market — posed significant risks to the nation's financial system should either company face significant problems.

"Despite this, Greenspan still claims to be a firm believer in free markets, although in the 2007 publication of his biography, he writes, "History has not dealt kindly with the aftermath of protracted periods of low risk premiums" as seen before the credit crisis of 2008.

In 2009 Robert Reich wrote that "Greenspan's worst move was to contribute to the giant housing bubble and the worst worldwide crash since the Great Depression. In 2004 he lowered interest rates to 1perc ent, enabling banks to borrow money for free, adjusted for inflation. Naturally, the banks wanted to borrow as much as they possibly could, then lend it out, earning nice profits. The situation screamed for government oversight of lending institutions, lest the banks lend to unfit borrowers. He refused, trusting the market to weed out bad credit risks. It did not."

In Congressional testimony on October 23, 2008, Greenspan finally conceded error on regulation. *The New York Times* wrote, "a humbled Mr. Greenspan admitted that he had put too much faith in the self-correcting power of free markets and had failed to anticipate the self-destructive power of wanton mortgage lending.... Mr. Greenspan refused to accept blame for the crisis but acknowledged that his belief in deregulation had been shaken." Although many Republican lawmakers tried to blame the housing bubble on Fannie Mae and Freddie Mac, Greenspan placed far more blame on Wall Street for bundling subprime mortgages into securities.

Late 2000s Recession

In March 2008, Greenspan wrote an article for the *Financial Times'* Economists' Forum in which he said that the 2008-financial crisis in the United States is likely to be judged as the most wrenching since the end of World War II. In it he argued: "We will never be able to anticipate all discontinuities in financial markets." He concluded: "It is important, indeed crucial, that any reforms in, and adjustments to, the structure of markets and regulation not inhibit our most reliable and effective safeguards against cumulative economic failure: market flexibility and open competition.

" The article attracted a number of critical responses from forum contributors, who, finding causation between Greenspan's policies and the discontinuities in financial markets that followed, criticized Greenspan mainly for what many believed to be his unbalanced and immovable ideological suppositions about global capitalism and free competitive markets. Notable critics included J. Bradford DeLong, Paul Krugman, Alice Rivlin, Michael Hudson, andWillem Buiter.

Greenspan responded to his critics in a follow-up article in which he defended his ideology as applied to his conceptual and policy framework, which, among other things, prohibited him from exerting real pressure against the burgeoning housing bubble or, in his words, "leaning against the wind". Greenspan argued, "My view of the range of dispersion of outcomes has been shaken, but not my judgement that free competitive markets are by far the unrivaled way to organize economies.

" He concluded: "We have tried regulation ranging from heavy to central planning. None meaningfully worked. Do we wish to retest the evidence?" The *Financial Times* associate editor and chief economics commentator, Martin Wolf, responded to the discussion with an article defending Greenspan primarily as a scapegoat for the market turmoil. Several notable contributors in defence of Greenspan included Stephen Roach, Allan Meltzer, and Robert Brusca.

An October 15, 2008, article in the *Washington Post* analyzing the origins of the economic crisis claims that Greenspan vehemently opposed any regulation of derivatives, and actively sought to undermine the office of the Commodity Futures Trading Commission when the Commission sought to initiate regulation of derivatives.

Meanwhile, Greenspan recommended improving mark-to-market regulations to avoid having derivatives or other complex assets marked to a distressed or illiquid market during times of material adverse conditions as seen during the late 2000s credit crisis.

Greenspan was not alone in his opposition to derivatives regulation. In a 1999 government report that was a key driver in the passage of the Commodity Futures Modernization Act of 2000—legislation that clarified that most over-the-counter derivatives were outside the regulatory authority of any government agency—Greenspan was joined by Treasury Secretary Lawrence Summers, Securities and Exchange Commission Chairman Arthur Levitt, and Commodity Futures Trading Commission Chairman William Ranier in concluding that "under many circumstances, the trading of financial derivatives by eligible swap participants should be excluded from the CEA" (Commodity Exchange Act). Other government agencies also supported that view.

In Congressional testimony on October 23, 2008, Greenspan acknowledged that he was "partially" wrong in opposing regulation and stated "Those of us who have looked to the self-interest of lending institutions to protect shareholder's equity – myself especially – are in a state of shocked disbelief." Referring to his free-market ideology, Greenspan said: "I have found a flaw. I don't know how significant or permanent it is. But I have been very distressed by that fact." Representative Henry Waxman (D-CA) then pressed him to clarify his words. "In other words, you found that your view of the world, your ideology, was not right, it was not working," Waxman said. "Absolutely, precisely," Greenspan replied. "You know, that's precisely the reason I was shocked, because I have been going for 40 years or more with very considerable evidence that it was working exceptionally well." Greenspan admitted fault in opposing regulation of derivatives and acknowledged that financial institutions didn't protect shareholders and investments as well as he expected.

Matt Taibbi described the Greenspan put and its bad consequences saying: "every time the banks blew up a speculative bubble, they could go back to the Fed and borrow money at zero or one or two percent, and then start the game all over", thereby making it "almost impossible" for the banks to lose money. He also called Greenspan a "classic con man" who, through political savvy, "flattered and bullshitted his way up the Matterhorn of American power and... jacked himself off to the attention of Wall Street for 20 consecutive years."

In the documentary film *Inside Job* Greenspan is cited as one of the persons responsible for the Economic Meltdown of 2008. He is also named in Time Magazine as one of the "25 People to Blame for the Financial Crisis".

Political Views and Alleged Politicization of Office

Greenspan describes himself as a "lifelong libertarian Republican".

In March 2005, in reaction to Greenspan's support of President Bush's plan to partially privatize Social Security, Democratic Senate Minority Leader Harry Reid attacked Greenspan as "one of the biggest political hacks we have in Washington" and criticized him for supporting Bush's 2001 tax cut plan.

Then-Democratic House Minority LeaderNancy Pelosi added that there were serious questions about the Fed's independence as a result of Greenspan's public statements. Greenspan also received criticism from Democratic Congressman Barney Frank and others for supporting Bush's Social Security plans favouring private accounts. Greenspan had said Bush's model has "the seeds of developing full funding by its very nature. As I've said before, I've always supported moves to full funding in the context of a private account." Others, like Republican Senator Mitch McConnell, disagreed that Greenspan was too deferential to Bush, stating that Greenspan "has been an independent player at the Fed for a long time under both parties and made an enormous positive contribution".

Economist Paul Krugman wrote that Greenspan was a "three-card maestro" with a "lack of sincerity" who, "by repeatedly shilling for whatever the Bush administration wants, has betrayed the trust placed in the Fed chairman". Republican Senator Jim Bunning, who opposed Greenspan's fifth reconfirmation, charged that Greenspan should comment only on monetary policy, not fiscal policy.Greenspan had used his position as Fed Chairman to comment upon fiscal policy as early as 1993, however, when he supported President Clinton's deficit reduction plan, which included tax increases and budget cuts.

In an October 2011 lecture addressing the Occupy movement, Noam Chomsky characterized portions of Greenspan's February 1997 testimony to the U.S. Senate as an example of the self-serving attitudes of the so-called 1perc ent. In that testimony, Greenspan had stated that growing worker insecurity is a significant factor keeping inflation and inflation expectation low, thereby promoting long term investment.

PERSONAL LIFE

Greenspan has married twice. His first marriage was to an artist named Joan Mitchell in 1952; the marriage ended in annulment less than a year later. He dated newswomanBarbara Walters in the late 1970s. In 1984, Greenspan began dating journalist Andrea Mitchell. Greenspan at the time was 58; Mitchell is 20 years younger. In 1997, they were married by Supreme Court Justice Ruth Bader Ginsburg.

HONOURS

In 2004, Greenspan received the Dwight D. Eisenhower Medal for Leadership and Service, from Eisenhower Fellowships. In 2005, he became the first recipient of the Harry S. Truman Medal for Economic Policy, presented by the Harry S. Truman Library Institute. In 2007, Greenspan was the recipient of the inaugural Thomas Jefferson Foundation Medal in Citizen Leadership, presented by the University of Virginia.

On December 14, 2005, he was awarded an honourary Doctor of Commercial Science degree by New York University, his fourth degree from that institution. On April 19, 2012, Greenspan received the Eugene J. Keogh Award for Distinguished Public Service from NYU.

AMARTYA SEN

Amartya Kumar Sen (born 3 November 1933) is an Indian economist and philosopher who since 1972 has taught and worked in the United Kingdom and the United States. He has made contributions to welfare economics, social choice theory, economic and social justice, economic theories of famines, and indexes of the measure of well-being of citizens of developing countries. He was awarded the Nobel Memorial Prize in Economic Sciences in 1998 for his work in welfare economics.

He is currently the Thomas W. Lamont University Professor and Professor of Economics and Philosophy at Harvard University. He serves as the chancellor of Nalanda University. He is also a senior fellow at the Harvard Society of Fellows, a distinguished fellow ofAll Souls College, Oxford, an honourary fellow of Darwin College, Cambridge and a Fellow of Trinity College, Cambridge, where he served as Master from 1998 to 2004. He is also known for being one of the strongest champions of rationalism, secularism, andegalitarianism in India, and he has condemned the ghettoization of Ambedkar as a Dalit leader.

EARLY LIFE AND EDUCATION

Sen was born in Santiniketan, West Bengal, India, to Ashutosh Sen and Amita Sen. Rabindranath Tagore gave Amartya Sen his name. Sen's family was from Wari and Manikganj, Dhaka, both in present-day Bangladesh. His father Ashutosh Sen was a professor of chemistry at Dhaka University who moved with his family to West Bengal in 1945 and worked at various government institutions, including the West Bengal Public Service Commission (of which he was the chairman), and the Union Public Service Commission. Sen's mother Amita Sen was the daughter of Kshiti Mohan Sen, a well-known scholar of ancient and medieval India and close associate of Rabindranath Tagore. He served as the Vice Chancellor of Visva-Bharati University for some years.

Sen began his high-school education at St Gregory's School in Dhaka in 1940. From fall 1941, Sen studied at Visva-Bharati University school. He later went to Presidency College, Kolkata, where earned a B.A. in Economics, with a minor in Mathematics. In 1953, he moved to Trinity College, Cambridge, where he earned a second B.A. in Economics in 1955. He was elected President of the Cambridge Majlis. While Sen was officially a Ph.D. student at Cambridge (though he had finished his research in 1955-6), he was offered the position of Professor and Head of the Economics Department of the newly created Jadavpur University in Calcutta. He served in that position, starting the new Economics Department, during 1956 to 1958.

Meanwhile, Sen was elected to a Prize Fellowship at Trinity College, which gave him four years of freedom to do anything he liked; he made the radical decision to studyphilosophy. That proved to be of immense help to his later research. Sen explained: "The broadening of my studies into philosophy was important for me not just because some of my main areas of interest in economics relate quite closely to philosophical disciplines (for example, social choice theory makes intense use of mathematical logic and also draws on moral philosophy, and so does the study of inequality and deprivation), but also because I found philosophical studies very rewarding on their own". His interest in philosophy, however, dates back to his college days at Presidency, where he read books on philosophy and debated philosophical themes.

To Sen, Cambridge was like a battlefield. There were major debates between supporters of Keynesian economics on the one hand, and the "neo-classical" economists skeptical of Keynes, on the other.Sen was lucky to have close relations with economists on both sides of the divide.

Meanwhile, thanks to its good "practice" of democratic and tolerant social choice, Sen's own college, Trinity College, was somewhat removed from the discord. However, because of a lack of enthusiasm for social choice theory in both Trinity and Cambridge, Sen had to choose a different subject for his Ph.D. thesis, which was on "The Choice of Techniques" in 1959, though the work had been completed much earlier (except for some valuable advice from his adjunct supervisor in India, Professor A. K. Dasgupta, given to Sen while teaching and revising his work at Jadavpur) under the supervision of the "brilliant but vigorously intolerant" post-Keynesian, Joan Robinson.

Quentin Skinner notes that Sen was a member of the secret society Cambridge Apostlesduring his time at Cambridge.

PROFESSORSHIPS

Between 1960 and 1961, Sen was a visiting Professor at Massachusetts Institute of Technology in the United States. He was also a visiting Professor at UC-Berkeley andCornell. He taught as Professor of Economics between 1963 and 1971 at the Delhi School of Economics (where he completed his *magnum opus* Collective Choice and Social Welfare by 1969),.This is a period considered to be a Golden Period in the history of DSE. In 1972, he joined the London School of Economics as a Professor of Economics where he taught until 1977.

From 1977 to 1986 he taught at the University of Oxford, where he was first a Professor of Economics and Fellow of Nuffield College, and then the Drummond Professor of Political Economy and a Fellow of All Souls College from 1980. In 1987, he joined Harvard as the Thomas W. Lamont University Professor of Economics.

In 1998 he was appointed as Master of Trinity College, Cambridge. In January 2004, Sen returned to Harvard. He also established the Eva Colorni Trust at the former London Guildhall University in the name of his deceased wife.

MEMBERSHIP AND ASSOCIATIONS

He has served as president of the Econometric Society (1984), the International Economic Association (1986–1989), the Indian Economic

Association (1989) and the American Economic Association (1994). He has also served as President of the Development Studies Association and the Human Development and Capabilities Association.

He serves as the Chair of the International Advisory Board of the Centre for Human and Economic Development Studies at Peking University in China.

RESEARCH

Sen's papers in the late 1960s and early 1970s helped develop the theory of social choice, which first came to prominence in the work by the American economist Kenneth Arrow, who, while working at the RAND Corporation, had most famously shown that all voting rules, be they majority rule or two thirds-majority or status quo, must inevitably conflict with some basic democratic norm.

Sen's contribution to the literature was to show under what conditions Arrow's impossibility theorem would indeed come to pass as well as to extend and enrich the theory of social choice, informed by his interests in history of economic thought and philosophy.

In 1981, Sen published *Poverty and Famines: An Essay on Entitlement and Deprivation* (1981), a book in which he argued that famine occurs not only from a lack of food, but from inequalities built into mechanisms for distributing food.

Sen also argued that the Bengal famine was caused by an urban economic boom that raised food prices, thereby causing millions of rural workers to starve to death when their wages did not keep up.

Sen's interest in famine stemmed from personal experience. As a nine-year-old boy, he witnessed the Bengal famine of 1943, in which three million people perished.

This staggering loss of life was unnecessary, Sen later concluded.He presents data that there was an adequate food supply in Bengal at the time, but particular groups of people including rural landless labourers and urban service providers like haircutters did not have the means to buy food as its price rose rapidly due to factors that include British military acquisition, panic buying, hoarding, and price gouging, all connected to the war in the region.

In *Poverty and Famines*, Sen revealed that in many cases of famine, food supplies were not significantly reduced.

In Bengal, for example, food production, while down on the previous year, was higher than in previous non-famine years.

Thus, Sen points to a number of social and economic factors, such as declining wages, unemployment, rising food prices, and poor food-distribution, which led to starvation.

His capabilities approach focuses on positive freedom, a person's actual ability to be or do something, rather than on negative freedom approaches, which are common in economics and simply focuses on non-interference. In the Bengal famine, rural laborers' negative freedom to buy food was not affected. However, they still starved because they were not positively free to do anything, they did not have the functioning of nourishment, nor the capability to escape morbidity. In addition to his important work on the causes of famines, Sen's work in the field of development economics has had considerable influence in the formulation of the "Human Development Report", published by the United Nations Development Programme.

This annual publication that ranks countries on a variety of economic and social indicators owes much to the contributions by Sen among other social choice theorists in the area of economic measurement of poverty and inequality.

Sen's revolutionary contribution to development economics and social indicators is the concept of "capability" developed in his article "Equality of What". He argues that governments should be measured against the concrete capabilities of their citizens.

This is because top-down development will always trump human rights as long as the definition of terms remains in doubt (is a "right" something that must be provided or something that simply cannot be taken away?). For instance, in the United States citizens have a hypothetical "right" to vote. To Sen, this concept is fairly empty. In order for citizens to have a capacity to vote, they first must have "functionings".

These "functionings" can range from the very broad, such as the availability of education, to the very specific, such as transportation to the polls. Only when such barriers are removed can the citizen truly be said to act out of personal choice. It is up to the individual society to make the list of minimum capabilities guaranteed by that society. For an example of the "capabilities approach" in practice, see Martha Nussbaum's *Women and Human Development*.

He wrote a controversial article in *The New York Review of Books* entitled "More Than 100 Million Women Are Missing", analyzing the mortality impact of unequal rights between the genders in the developing world, particularly Asia. Other studies, including one by Emily Oster, had argued that this is an overestimation, though Oster has since then recanted her conclusions.

Welfare economics seeks to evaluate economic policies in terms of their effects on the well-being of the community. Sen, who devoted his career to such issues, was called the "conscience of his profession".

His influential monograph *Collective Choice and Social Welfare* (1970), which addressed problems related to individual rights (including formulation of the liberal paradox), justice and equity, majority rule, and the availability of information about individual conditions, inspired researchers to turn their attention to issues of basic welfare. Sen devised methods of measuring poverty that yielded useful information for improving economic conditions for the poor. For instance, his theoretical work on inequality provided an explanation for why there are fewer women than men in India and China despite the fact that in the

West and in poor but medically unbiased countries, women have lower mortality rates at all ages, live longer, and make a slight majority of the population. Sen claimed that this skewed ratio results from the better health treatment and childhood opportunities afforded boys in those countries, as well as sex-selective abortions.

Governments and international organizations handling food crises were influenced by Sen's work. His views encouraged policy makers to pay attention not only to alleviating immediate suffering but also to finding ways to replace the lost income of the poor—for example through public works—and to maintain stable prices for food.

A vigorous defender of political freedom, Sen believed that famines do not occur in functioning democracies because their leaders must be more responsive to the demands of the citizens. In order for economic growth to be achieved, he argued, social reforms—such as improvements in education and public health—must precede economic reform.

In 2009, Sen published a new book called *The Idea of Justice*. Based on his previous work in welfare economics and social choice theory, but also on his philosophical thoughts, he presented his own theory of justice that he meant to be an alternative to the influential modern theories of justice of John Rawls or John Harsanyi.

In opposition to Rawls but also earlier justice theoreticians Immanuel Kant, Jean-Jacques Rousseau or David Hume, and inspired by the philosophical works of Adam Smith and Mary Wollstonecraft, Sen developed a theory that is both comparative and realizations-oriented (instead of being transcendental and institutional).

However, he still regards institutions and processes as being important. As an alternative to Rawls's veil of ignorance, Sen chose the thought experiment of an impartial spectator as the basis of his theory of justice.

He also stressed the importance of public discussion (understanding democracy in the sense of John Stuart Mill) and a focus on people's capabilities (an approach that he had co-developed), including the notion of universal human rights, in evaluating various states with regard to justice.

PERCEPTIONS: IN COMPARISONS

Sen has been called "the Conscience of the profession" and "the Mother Teresa of Economics" for his work on famine, human development theory, welfare economics, the underlying mechanisms of poverty, gender inequality, and political liberalism.

However, he denies the comparison to Mother Teresa, saying that he has never tried to follow a lifestyle of dedicated self-sacrifice. Amartya Sen also added his voice to the campaign against the anti-gay Section 377 of the Indian Penal Code.

INDIA: UNIVERSITY MENTOR FOR GROWTH AND REVIVAL

Nalanda International University Project

In May 2007, he was appointed as chairman of Nalanda Mentor Group to examine the framework of international cooperation, and proposed structure of partnership, which would govern the establishment of Nalanda International University Project as an international centre of education seeking to revive the ancient centre of higher learning which was present in India from the 5th century to 1197.

On 19 July 2012, Sen was named the first chancellor of the proposed Nalanda University (NU). Teaching began in August 2014.

MEDIA AND CULTURE

A 57-minute documentary named *Amartya Sen: A Life Re-examined* directed by Suman Ghosh details his life and work.

A 2001 portrait of Sen by Annabel Cullen is in Trinity College's collection. A 2003 portrait of Sen hangs in the National Portrait Gallery in London.

PERSONAL LIFE AND BELIEFS

Sen has been married three times. His first wife was Nabaneeta Dev Sen, an Indian writer and scholar, by whom he had two daughters: Antara, a journalist and publisher, andNandana, a Bollywood actress. Their marriage broke up shortly after they moved to London in 1971.

Later on, Sen married his second wife, Eva Colorni, who died fromstomach cancer in 1985. He has two children by Eva, a daughter Indrani, who is a journalist in New York, and a son Kabir, a hip hop artist, MC, and music teacher at Shady Hill School. In 1991, Sen married Emma Georgina Rothschild, who serves as the Jeremy and Jane Knowles Professor of History at Harvard University.

The Sens have a house in Cambridge, Massachusetts, which is the base from which they teach during the academic year. They also have a home in Cambridge, England, where Sen is a Fellow of Trinity College, Cambridge, and Rothschild is a Fellow of Magdalene College.

He usually spends his winter holidays at his home in Santiniketan in West Bengal, India, where he used to go on long bike rides until recently. Asked how he relaxes, he replies: "I read a lot and like arguing with people."

Sen is an atheist and holds that this can be associated with Hinduism of the atheist schools, like Lokayata.

In an interview for the magazine *California*, which is published by the University of California, Berkeley, he noted:

" In some ways people had got used to the idea that India was spiritual and religion-oriented. That gave a leg up to the religious interpretation of India, despite the fact that Sanskrit had a larger atheistic literature than what exists in any other classical language. Madhava Acharya, the remarkable 14th century philosopher, wrote this rather great book called *Sarvadarshansamgraha*, which discussed all the religious schools of thought within the Hindu structure. The first chapter is on the philosophy of Lokayata – a very strong presentation of the argument in favour of theism and materialism. "

ACADEMIC ACHIEVEMENTS, AWARDS AND HONOURS

Sen has received over 90 honourary degrees from universities around the world.

- 1954 He received the Adam Smith Prize.
- 1981: He was elected a Foreign Honourary Member of the American Academy of Arts and Sciences.
- 1982: He was awarded honourary fellowship by the Institute of Social Studies.
- 1998: He received the Nobel Memorial Prize in Economic Sciences for his work in welfare economics.
- 1999: He received the Bharat Ratna "the highest civilian award in India" by the President of India.
- 1999: He was offered the honourary citizenship of Bangladesh by Sheikh Hasina in recognition of his achievements in winning the Nobel Prize, and given that his ancestral origins were in what has become the modern state of Bangladesh
- 2000: He was awarded the order of Companion of Honour, UK.
- 2000: He received Leontief Prize for his outstanding contribution to economic theory from the Global Development and Environment Institute.
- 2000: He was awarded the Eisenhower Medal for Leadership and Service USA;
- 2000: He was the 351st Commencement Speaker of Harvard University.
- 2002: He received the International Humanist Award from the International Humanist and Ethical Union.
- 2003: He was conferred the Lifetime Achievement Award by the Indian Chamber of Commerce.
- He is awarded the Life Time Achievement award by Bangkok-based United Nations Economic and Social Commission for Asia and the Pacific (UNESCAP)
- 2005: Honourary degree, University of Pavia

- 2010: He was chosen to deliver the Demos Annual Lecture 2010
- 2011: The National Humanities Medal
- 2012: Sash in a special category Order of the Aztec Eagle
- 2013: He was made a Commander of the French Legion of Honour
- 2013: The 25 Greatest Global Living Legends In India by NDTV

BENJAMIN GRAHAM

Benjamin Graham (real name Grossbaum) (May 8, 1894 – September 21, 1976) was a British-born American professionalinvestor. Graham is considered the father of value investing, an investment approach he began teaching at Columbia Business School in 1928 and subsequently refined with David Dodd through various editions of their famous book *Security Analysis*.

Graham had many disciples in his lifetime, a number of whom went on to become successful investors themselves. Graham's most well-known disciples include Warren Buffett, William J. Ruane, Irving Kahn and Walter J. Schloss, among others.

Buffett, who credits Graham as grounding him with a sound intellectual investment framework, described him as the second most influential person in his life after his own father. In fact, Graham had such an overwhelming influence on his students that two of them, Buffett and Kahn, named their sons Howard Graham Buffett and Thomas Graham Kahn after him. Graham also taught at the UCLA Anderson School of Management.

LIFE AND CAREER

Early Life

Benjamin Graham was born Benjamin Grossbaum in London, England, to Jewish parents. He moved to New York City with his family when he was one year old. After the death of his father and experiencing poverty, he became a good student, graduating from Columbia University, as salutatorian of his class, at the age of 20. He received an invitation for employment as an instructor in English, mathematics, and philosophy, but took a job on Wall Street eventually starting the Graham-Newman Partnership. Early in his professional life, Graham made a name for himself with "The Northern Pipeline Affair", involving John D. Rockefeller.

Career

His book, *Security Analysis,* with David Dodd, was published in 1934 and has been considered a bible for serious investors since it was written. It and *The Intelligent Investor* published in 1949 (4th revision, with Jason Zweig, 2003), are his two most widely acclaimed books. Warren Buffettdescribes *The Intelligent Investor* as "the best book about investing ever written." Graham exhorted the stock market participant to first draw a fundamental distinction between investment and speculation. In *Security Analysis*, he proposed a clear definition of investment that was distinguished from what he deemed speculation. It read, "An investment operation is one which, upon thorough analysis, promises safety of principal and an adequate return. Operations not meeting these requirements are speculative."

Graham wrote that the owner of equity stocks should regard them first and foremost as conferring part ownership of a business. With that perspective in mind, the stock owner should not be too concerned with erratic fluctuations in stock prices, since in the short term, the stock market behaves like a voting machine, but in the long term it acts like a weighing machine (*i.e.* its true value will in the long run be reflected in its stock price). Graham distinguished between the passive and the active investor.

The passive investor, often referred to as a defensive investor, invests cautiously, looks for value stocks, and buys for the long term. The active investor, on the other hand, is one who has more time, interest, and possibly more specialized knowledge to seek out exceptional buys in the market. Graham recommended that investors spend time and effort to analyze the financial state of companies.

When a company is available on the market at a price which is at a discount to its intrinsic value, a "margin of safety" exists, which makes it suitable for investment.

Graham wrote that investment is most intelligent when it is most businesslike, a statement which Warren Buffett regarded as the most important words about investment ever written.

Graham said that the stock investor is neither right nor wrong because others agreed or disagreed with him; he is right because his facts and analysis are right. Graham's favourite allegory is that of Mr. Market, a fellow who turns up every day at the stock holder's door offering to buy or sell his shares at a different price. Usually, the price quoted by Mr. Market seems plausible, but occasionally it is ridiculous.

The investor is free to either agree with his quoted price and trade with him, or to ignore him completely. Mr. Market doesn't mind this, and will be back the following day to quote another price. The point is that the investor should not regard the whims of Mr. Market as determining the value of the shares that the investor owns.

He should profit from market folly rather than participate in it. The investor is best off concentrating on the real life performance of his companies and receiving dividends, rather than being too concerned with Mr. Market's often irrational behaviour.

Graham was critical of the corporations of his day for obfuscated and irregular financial reporting that made it difficult for investors to discern the true state of the business's finances. He was an advocate of dividend payments to shareholders rather than businesses keeping all of their profits as retained earnings. He also criticized those who advised that some types of stocks were a good buy at any price, because of the prospect of sustained stock price growth, without a good analysis of the business's actual financial condition. These observations remain relevant today.

Legacy

Graham's most famous student is Warren Buffett. According to Buffett, Graham said that he wished every day to do something foolish, something creative, and something generous. Buffett said that Graham excelled most at the last.

Some of Graham's most famous disciples, who have drawn on the works of several Columbia Business School alumni, many of whom were direct disciples of Benjamin Graham himself, include famous Value Investors such as Warren Buffett, Charlie Munger, Philip Fisher, Walter Schloss, Peter Lynch, John Templeton, Mohnish Pabrai, Amit Ayare,Whitney Tilson, Prem Watsa, Lauren Templeton, Jerome Chazen and many more.

Alongside his revolutionary work in investment finance, Graham also made significant contributions to economic theory. Most notably, he devised a new basis for both U.S. and global currency.

PERSONAL LIFE

According to *The Snowball*, after his son's death, Graham had an affair with his deceased son's girlfriend Malou (Marie Louise Amingues) who was several years older to his son, and used to travel to France frequently to visit her. He later separated from his wife Estey in New York, after she refused his offer of living in New York for six months and France for six months. Marie Louise was content to live with Graham without marriage.

BERTIL GOTTHARD OHLIN

Bertil Gotthard Ohlin (23 April 1899 – 3 August 1979) was a Swedish economist and politician. He was a professor of economics at the Stockholm School of Economics from 1929 to 1965. He was also leader of the People's Party, asocial-liberal party which at the time was the largest party in opposition to the governing Social Democratic Party, from 1944 to 1967. He served briefly as Minister for Trade from 1944 to 1945 in the Swedish coalition government during World War II.

Ohlin's name lives on in one of the standard mathematical model of international free trade, the Heckscher–Ohlin model, which he developed together with Eli Heckscher. He was jointly awarded the Nobel Memorial Prize in Economic Sciences in 1977 together with the British economist James

Meade "for their pathbreaking contribution to the theory of international trade and internationalcapital movements".

BIOGRAPHY

Having received his B.A. from Lund University 1917 and his MSc. from Stockholm School of Economics in 1919. He obtained an M.A. from Harvard University in 1923 and his doctorate from Stockholm University in 1924. In 1925 he became a professor at theUniversity of Copenhagen. In 1929 he debated with John Maynard Keynes, contradicting the latter's view on the consequences of the heavy war reparations payments imposed on Germany. (Keynes predicted a war caused by the burden of debt, Ohlin thought that Germany could afford the reparations.) The debate was important in the modern theory of unilateral international payments.

In 1930 Ohlin succeeded Eli Heckscher, his teacher, as a professor of economics, at the Stockholm School of Economics. In 1933 Ohlin published a work that made him world renowned, *Interregional and International Trade*. In this Ohlin built an economic theory of international trade from earlier work by Heckscher and his own doctoral thesis. It is now known as the Heckscher–Ohlin model, one of the standard model economists use to debate trade theory.

The model was a break-through because it showed how comparative advantage might relate to general features of a country'scapital and labour, and how these features might change through time. The model provided a basis for later work on the effects of protection on real wages, and has been fruitful in producing predictions and analysis; Ohlin himself used the model to derive theHeckscher–Ohlin theorem, that nations would specialize in industries most able to utilize their mix of national resources efficiently. Today, the theory has been largely disproved, yet it is still a useful framework by which to understand international trade.

Later, Ohlin and other members of the "Stockholm school" extended Knut Wicksell's economic analysis to produce a theory of the macroeconomy anticipating Keynesianism.

Ohlin was party leader of the liberal Liberal People's Party from 1944 to 1967, the main opposition party to the Social DemocratGovernments of the era, and from '44 to '45 was *minister of commerce* in the wartime government. His daughter Anne Wibble, representing the same party, served as Minister of Finance from 1991 to 1994.

In 2009, a street adjacent to the Stockholm School of Economics was named after Ohlin: "Bertil Ohlins Gata".

HECKSCHER–OHLIN THEOREM

The Heckscher–Ohlin Theorem, which is concluded from the Heckscher–Ohlin model of international trade, states: trade between countries is in proportion to their relative amounts of capital and labour. In countries with an abundance of capital, wage rates tend to be high; therefore, labour-intensive products, *e.g.* textiles, simple electronics, etc., are more costly to produce internally. In contrast, capital-intensive products, *e.g.* automobiles, chemicals, etc., are less costly to produce internally.

Countries with large amounts of capital will export capital-intensive products and import labour-intensive products with the proceeds. Countries with high amounts of labour will do the reverse. The following conditions must be true:

- The major factors of production, namely labour and capital, are not available in the same proportion in both countries.
- The two goods produced either require more capital or more labour.
- Labour and capital do not move between the two countries.
- There are no costs associated with transporting the goods between countries.
- The citizens of the two trading countries have the same needs.

The theory does not depend on total amounts of capital or labour, but on the amounts per worker. This allows small countries to trade with large countries by specializing in production of products that use the factors which are more available than its trading partner.

The key assumption is that capital and labour are not available in the same proportions in the two countries. That leads to specialization, which in turn benefits the country's economic welfare. The greater the difference between the two countries, the greater the gain from specialization.

Wassily Leontief made a study of the theory that seemed to invalidate it. He noted that the United States had a lot of capital; therefore, it should export capital-intensive products and import labour-intensive products. Instead, he found that it exported products that used more labour than the products it imported. This finding is known as the Leontief paradox.

DANIEL KAHNEMAN

Daniel Kahneman (born March 5, 1934) is an Israeli-American psychologist. He shared the 2002 Nobel Memorial Prize in Economic Sciences with Vernon L. Smith. Kahneman is notable for his work on the psychology of judgement anddecision-making, behavioural economics and hedonic psychology.

With Amos Tversky and others, Kahneman established a cognitive basis for common human errors that arise from heuristics and biases, and developed prospect theory. He was awarded the 2002 Nobel Memorial Prize in Economics for his work in prospect theory.

In 2011, he was named by *Foreign Policy* magazine to its list of top global thinkers. In the same year, his book *Thinking, Fast and Slow*, which summarizes much of his research, was published and became a best seller.

Currently, he is professor emeritus of psychology and public affairs at Princeton University's Woodrow Wilson School. Kahneman is a founding partner of TGG Group, a business and philanthropy consulting company. He is married to Royal Society Fellow Anne Treisman.

BIOGRAPHY

Daniel Kahneman was born in Tel Aviv in 1934, where his mother was visiting relatives. He spent his childhood years in Paris,France, where his parents had emigrated from Lithuania in the early 1920s. Kahneman and his family were in Paris when it was occupied by Nazi Germany in 1940. His father was picked up in the first major round-up of French Jews, but he was released after six weeks due to the intervention of his employer.

The family was on the run for the remainder of the war, and it survived intact except for the death of Kahneman's father due to diabetes in 1944. Daniel Kahnemann and his family then moved to British Mandatory Palestine in 1948, just before the creation of the state of Israel .

Kahneman has written of his experience in Nazi-occupied France, explaining in part why he entered the field of psychology:

It must have been late 1941 or early 1942. Jews were required to wear the Star of David and to obey a 6 p.m. curfew. I had gone to play with a Christian friend and had stayed too late. I turned my brown sweater inside out to walk the few blocks home. As I was walking down an empty street, I saw a German soldier approaching.

He was wearing the black uniform that I had been told to fear more than others – the one worn by specially recruited SS soldiers. As I came closer to him, trying to walk fast, I noticed that he was looking at me intently. Then he beckoned me over, picked me up, and hugged me. I was terrified that he would notice the star inside my sweater.

He was speaking to me with great emotion, in German. When he put me down, he opened his wallet, showed me a picture of a boy, and gave me some money. I went home more certain than ever that my mother was right: people were endlessly complicated and interesting.

Kahneman received his bachelor of science degree with a major in psychology and a minor in mathematics from the Hebrew University of Jerusalem in 1954. After earning his undergraduate degree, he served in the psychology department of the Israeli Defence Forces.

One of his responsibilities was to evaluate candidates for officer's training school, and to develop tests and measures for this purpose. In 1958, he went to the United States to study for his PhD in Psychology from the University of California at Berkeley.

Daniel Kahneman is married to Anne Treisman, a fellow professor of psychology at Princeton University.

Academic Career

Cognitive Psychology

Kahneman began his academic career as a lecturer in psychology at the Hebrew University of Jerusalem in 1961. He was promoted to senior lecturer in 1966. His early work focused on visual perception and attention. For example, his first publication in the prestigious journal *Science* was entitled "Pupil Diameter and Load on Memory".

During this period, Kahneman was a visiting scientist at the University of Michigan (1965–66) and the Applied Psychology Research Unit in Cambridge (1968/1969, summers). He was a fellow at the Centre for Cognitive Studies and a lecturer in psychology at Harvard University in 1966/1967.

Judgement and Decision-Making

This period marks the beginning of Kahneman's lengthy collaboration with Amos Tversky. Together, Kahneman and Tversky published a series of seminal articles in the general field of judgement and decision-making, culminating in the publication of their prospect theory in 1979. Kahneman was awarded the Nobel Memorial Prize in Economics in 2002 for his work on prospect theory.

In his Nobel biography, Kahneman states that his collaboration with Tversky began after Kahneman had invited Tversky to give a guest lecture to one of Kahneman's seminars at Hebrew University in 1968 or 1969. Their first jointly written paper, "Belief in the Law of Small Numbers," was published in 1971.

They published seven articles in peer-reviewed journals in the years 1971–1979. Aside from "Prospect Theory," the most important of these articles was "Judgement Under Uncertainty: Heuristics and Biases", which was published in the prestigious journal *Science* and introduced the notion of anchoring.

Kahneman left Hebrew University in 1978 to take a position at the University of British Columbia. This move had little or no immediate effect on his collaborations with Tversky, for Tversky moved on to Stanford University that same year.

Behavioural Economics

Kahneman and Tversky were both fellows at the Centre for Advanced Study in the Behavioural Sciences at Stanford University in the academic year 1977–1978. A young economist named Richard Thaler was a visiting professor at the Stanford branch of the National Bureau of Economic Research during that same year. According to Kahneman, "[Thaler and I] soon became friends, and have ever since had a considerable influence on each other's thinking". Building on prospect theory and Kahneman and Tversky's body of work, Thaler published "Towards a Positive Theory of Consumer Choice" in 1980, a paper which Kahneman has called "the founding text in behavioural economics".

Kahneman and Tversky both became heavily involved in the development of this new approach to economic theory, and their involvement in this movement had the effect of reducing the intensity and exclusivity of their earlier period of joint collaboration. They would continue to publish together until the end of Tversky's life, but the period when Kahneman published almost exclusively with Tversky ended in 1983, when he published two papers with Anne Treisman, his wife since 1978.

Hedonic Psychology

In the 1990s, Kahneman's research focus began to gradually shift in emphasis towards the field of "hedonic psychology". This subfield is closely related to the positive psychology movement, which was steadily gaining in popularity at the time. According to Kahneman and colleagues,

Hedonic psychology...is the study of what makes experiences and life pleasant or unpleasant. It is concerned with feelings of pleasure and pain, of interest and boredom, of joy and sorrow, and of satisfaction and dissatisfaction. It is also concerned with the whole range of circumstances, from the biological to the societal, that occasion suffering and enjoyment.

It is difficult to determine precisely when Kahneman's research began to focus on hedonics, although it likely stemmed from his work on the economic notion of utility. After publishing multiple articles and chapters in all but one of the years spanning the period 1979–1986 (for a total of 23 published works in 8 years), Kahneman published exactly one chapter during the years 1987–1989. After this hiatus, articles on utility and the psychology of utility began to appear.

In 1992, Varey and Kahneman introduced the method of evaluating moments and episodes as a way to capture "experiences extended across time". While Kahneman continued to study decision-making, hedonic psychology was the focus of an increasing number of publications, culminating in a volume co-edited with Ed Diener and Norbert Schwarz, scholars of affect and well-being.

Together with David Schkade, Kahneman developed the notion of the focusing illusion to explain in part the mistakes people make when estimating the effects of different scenarios on their future happiness (also known as affective forecasting, which has been studied extensively by Daniel Gilbert).

The "illusion" occurs when people consider the impact of one specific factor on their overall happiness, they tend to greatly exaggerate the importance of that factor, while overlooking the numerous other factors that would in most cases have a greater impact. A good example is provided by Kahneman and Schkade's 1998 paper "Does living in California make people happy? A focusing illusion in judgements of life satisfaction". In that paper, students in the Midwest and in California reported similar levels of life satisfaction, but the Midwesterners thought their Californian peers would be happier.

The only distinguishing information the Midwestern students had when making these judgements was the fact that their hypothetical peers lived in California. Thus, they "focused" on this distinction, thereby overestimating the effect of the weather in California on its residents' satisfaction with life.

Teaching

Kahneman is currently a senior scholar and faculty member emeritus at Princeton University's Department of Psychology and Woodrow Wilson School of Public and International Affairs. He is also a fellow at Hebrew University and a Gallup Senior Scientist.

Personal

Kahneman is married to the award-winning cognitive psychologist Anne Treisman. They live in Berkeley, California, during the summer.

AWARDS AND RECOGNITION

- In 2002, Kahneman received the Nobel Memorial Prize in Economics, despite being a research psychologist, for his work in prospect theory. Kahneman states he has never taken a single economics course – that everything that he knows of the subject he and Tversky learned from their collaborators Richard Thaler and Jack Knetsch.
- Kahneman, co-recipient with Tversky, earned the 2003 University of Louisville Grawemeyer Award for Psychology.
- In 2007, he was presented with the American Psychological Association's Award for Outstanding Lifetime Contributions to Psychology.
- On November 6, 2009, he was awarded an honourary doctorate from the department of Economics at Erasmus University in Rotterdam, Netherlands. In his acceptance speech Kahneman said, "when you live long enough, you see the impossible become reality." He was referring to the fact that he would never have expected to be honoured as an economist when he started his studies into what would become Behavioural Economics.
- In both 2011 and 2012, he made the Bloomberg 50 most influential people in global finance.
- On November 9, 2011, he was awarded the Talcott Parsons Prize by the American Academy of Arts and Sciences.
- His book, *Thinking, Fast and Slow* was the winner of the 2011 *Los Angeles Times* Book Award for Current Interest.

- In 2012 his book, *Thinking, Fast and Slow*, was awarded the National Academy of Sciences Communication Award for the best book published in 2011.
- In 2012 he was accepted as corresponding academician at the Real Academia Española (Economic and Financial Sciences).
- On August 8, 2013, President Barack Obama announced that Daniel Kahneman would be a recipient of the Presidential Medal of Freedom.

FRANCO MODIGLIANI

Franco Modigliani (June 18, 1918 – September 25, 2003) was an Italian economist naturalized American, a professor at the MIT Sloan School of Management and MIT Department of Economics who won the Nobel Memorial Prize in Economics in 1985.

LIFE AND CAREER

Born in railway colony, Modigliani left Italy because of his Jewish origin and antifascist views. He first went to Paris with the family of his then-girlfriend, Serena, whom he married in 1939, and then to the United States. From 1942 to 1944, he taught at Columbia University and Bard College as an instructor in economics and statistics. In 1944, he obtained his D. Soc. Sci. from the New School for Social Research working under Jacob Marschak. In 1946, he became a naturalized citizen of the United States, and in 1948, he joined the University of Illinois at Urbana-Champaign faculty.

When he was a professor at the Graduate School of Industrial Administration of Carnegie Mellon University in the 1950s and early 1960s, Modigliani made two path-breaking contributions to economic science:

- Along with Merton Miller, he formulated the important Modigliani–Miller theorem in corporate finance (1958). This theorem demonstrated that under certain assumptions, the value of a firm is not affected by whether it is financed by equity (selling shares) or debt (borrowing money).
- He was also the originator of the life-cycle hypothesis, which attempts to explain the level of saving in the economy. Modigliani proposed that consumers would aim for a stable level of consumption throughout their lifetime, for example by saving during their working years and spending during their retirement.

In 1962, he joined the faculty at MIT, achieving distinction as an Institute Professor, where he stayed until his death. In 1985 he received MIT's James R. Killian Faculty Achievement Award.

Modigliani also co-authored the textbooks, "Foundations of Financial Markets and Institutions" and "Capital Markets: Institutions and Instruments" with Frank J. Fabozzi of Yale School of Management.

In the 1990s he teamed up with Francis Vitagliano to work on a new credit card, and he also helped to oppose changes to a patent law that would be harmful to inventors.

He is the co-author of Rethinking Pension Reform (2009), Cambridge University Press, and along with Arun Muralidhar, critiqued the privatization model of Social Security reform proposed by the World Bank (in the 1990s) and President Bush in the early 2000s, and offered a better alternative to reform Social Security systems globally.

FRIEDRICH VON HAYEK

Friedrich Hayek CH (8 May 1899 – 23 March 1992), born in Austria-Hungary as Friedrich August von Hayek and frequently referred to as F. A. Hayek, was an Austrian, later British, economist and philosopher best known for his defence of classical liberalism. Hayek shared the Nobel Memorial Prize in Economic Sciences (with Gunnar Myrdal) for his "pioneering work in the theory of money and economic fluctuations and... penetrating analysis of the interdependence of economic, social and institutional phenomena".

Hayek was a major political thinker of the twentieth century, and his account of how changing prices communicate informationwhich enables individuals to co-ordinate their plans is widely regarded as an important achievement in economics.

Hayek served in World War I and said that his experience in the war and his desire to help avoid the mistakes that had led to the war led him to his career. Hayek lived in Austria, Great Britain, the United States and Germany, and became a British subject in 1938. He spent most of his academic life at the London School of Economics (LSE), the University of Chicago, and the University of Freiburg.

In 1984, he was appointed a member of the Order of the Companions of Honour by Queen Elizabeth II on the advice of Prime Minister Margaret Thatcher for his "services to the study of economics". He was the first recipient of the Hanns Martin Schleyer Prize in 1984. He also received the US Presidential Medal of Freedom in 1991 from President George H. W. Bush. In 2011, his article "The Use of Knowledge in Society" was selected as one of the top 20 articles published in *The American Economic Review*during its first 100 years.

EARLY LIFE

Hayek was born in Vienna. The son of August von Hayek, a Prussian doctor in the municipal health service. Hayek's grandfathers were prominent academics working in the fields of statistics and biology. His paternal line had been raised to the ranks of the Bohemian nobility for its services to the state. Similarly, a generation before his maternal forebears had also been raised to the lower noble rank. However, after 1919 titles of nobility were banned by law in Austria, and the "von Hayek" family became simply the Hayek family. Hence, after 1919, Hayek's legal name became "Friedrich Hayek", not "Friedrich von Hayek". Hayek's father turned his work on regional botany into a highly esteemed botanical treatise, continuing the family's scholarly traditions.

On his mother's side, Hayek was second cousin to the philosopher Ludwig Wittgenstein. His mother often played with Wittgenstein's sisters, and had known Ludwig well. As a result of their family relationship, Hayek became one of the first to read Wittgenstein's *Tractatus Logico-Philosophicus* when the book was published in its original German edition in 1921.

Although Hayek met Wittgenstein on only a few occasions, Hayek said that Wittgenstein's philosophy and methods of analysis had a profound influence on his own life and thought. In his later years, Hayek recalled a discussion of philosophy with Wittgenstein, when both were officers during World War I.

After Wittgenstein's death, Hayek had intended to write a biography of Wittgenstein and worked on collecting family materials; and he later assisted biographers of Wittgenstein.

At his father's suggestion, Hayek, as a teenager, read the genetic and evolutionary works of Hugo de Vries and the philosophical works of Ludwig Feuerbach. In school Hayek was much taken by one instructor's lectures on Aristotle's ethics.

In 1917, Hayek joined an artillery regiment in the Austro-Hungarian Army and fought on the Italian front. Much of Hayek's combat experience was spent as a spotter in an aeroplane. Hayek suffered damage to his hearing in his left ear during the war, and was decorated for bravery. During this time Hayek also survived the 1918 flu pandemic.

Hayek then decided to pursue an academic career, determined to help avoid the mistakes that had led to the war. Hayek said of his experience, "The decisive influence was really World War I. It's bound to draw your attention to the problems of political organization." He vowed to work for a better world.

EDUCATION AND CAREER

At the University of Vienna, Hayek earned doctorates in law and political science in 1921 and 1923 respectively; and he also studied philosophy, psychology, and economics.

For a short time, when the University of Vienna closed, Hayek studied in Constantin von Monakow's Institute of Brain Anatomy, where Hayek spent much of his time staining brain cells.

Hayek's time in Monakow's lab, and his deep interest in the work of Ernst Mach, inspired Hayek's first intellectual project, eventually published as *The Sensory Order*(1952). It located connective learning at the physical and neurological levels, rejecting the "sense data" associationism of the empiricists and logical positivists. Hayek presented his work to the private seminar he had created with Herbert Furth called the Geistkreis.

During Hayek's years at the University of Vienna, Carl Menger's work on the explanatory strategy of social science and Friedrich von Wieser's commanding presence in the classroom left a lasting influence on him.

Upon the completion of his examinations, Hayek was hired by Ludwig von Mises on the recommendation of Wieser as a specialist for the Austrian government working on the legal and economic details of the Treaty of Saint Germain. Between 1923 and 1924 Hayek worked as a research assistant to Prof.Jeremiah Jenks of New York University, compiling macroeconomic data on the American economy and the operations of the US Federal Reserve.

Initially sympathetic to Wieser's democratic socialism, Hayek's economic thinking shifted away from socialism and towards the classical liberalism of Carl Menger after reading von Mises' book *Socialism*.

It was sometime after reading *Socialism* that Hayek began attending von Mises' private seminars, joining several of his university friends, including Fritz Machlup, Alfred Schutz, Felix Kaufmann, and Gottfried Haberler, who were also participating in Hayek's own, more general, private seminar. It was during this time that he also encountered and befriended noted political philosopher Eric Voegelin, with whom he retained a long-standing relationship.

With the help of Mises, in the late 1920s Hayek founded and served as director of the Austrian Institute for Business Cycle Research, before joining the faculty of the London School of Economics (LSE) in 1931 at the behest of Lionel Robbins.

Upon his arrival in London, Hayek was quickly recognised as one of the leading economic theorists in the world, and his development of the economics of processes in time and the co-ordination function of prices inspired the ground-breaking work of John Hicks, Abba Lerner, and many others in the development of modern microeconomics.

In 1932, Hayek suggested that private investment in the public markets was a better road to wealth and economic co-ordination in Britain than government spending programmes, as argued in a letter he co-signed with Lionel Robbins and others in an exchange of letters with John Maynard Keynes in *The Times*.

The nearly decade long deflationary depression in Britain dating from Churchill's decision in 1925 to return Britain to the gold standard at the old pre-war, pre-inflationary par was the public policy backdrop for Hayek's single public engagement with Keynes over British monetary and fiscal policy, otherwise Hayek and Keynes agreed on many theoretical matters, and their economic disagreements were fundamentally theoretical, having to do almost exclusively with the relation of the economics of extending the length of production to the economics of labour inputs.

Economists who studied with Hayek at the LSE in the 1930s and the 1940s include Arthur Lewis, Ronald Coase, John Kenneth Galbraith, Abba Lerner, Nicholas Kaldor, George Shackle, Thomas Balogh, Vera Smith, L. K. Jha, Arthur Seldon, Paul Rosenstein-Rodan, and Oskar Lange. Hayek also taught or tutored many other LSE students, including David Rockefeller.

Unwilling to return to Austria after the Anschluss brought it under the control of Nazi Germany in 1938, Hayek remained in Britain and became a British subject in 1938. He held this status for the remainder of his life, but he did not live in Great Britain after 1950. He lived in the United States from 1950 to 1962 and then mostly in Germany but also briefly in Austria.

The Road to Serfdom

Hayek was concerned about the general view in Britain's academia that fascism was a capitalist reaction to socialism and *The Road to Serfdom* arose from those concerns. It was written between 1940 and 1943. The title was inspired by the French classical liberal thinker Alexis de Tocqueville's writings on the "road to servitude".

It was first published in Britain by Routledge in March 1944 and was quite popular, leading Hayek to call it "that unobtainable book", also due in part to wartime paper rationing. When it was published in the United States by the University of Chicago in September of that year, it achieved greater popularity than in Britain.

At the arrangement of editor Max Eastman, the American magazine *Reader's Digest* also published an abridged version in April 1945, enabling *The Road to Serfdom* to reach a far wider audience than academics. The book is widely popular among those advocating individualism and classical liberalism.

Chicago

In 1950, Hayek left the London School of Economics for the University of Chicago, where he became a professor in the Committee on Social Thought. Senior university officials at Chicago wanted the Economics Department to hire him but they declined to do so. Hayek's friend Milton Friedman was highly critical of Hayek's economics writings, *Prices and Production* and his book on capital theory.

Hayek at the time was working in political theory, not economics, and was hostile to the positivist approach the Department embraced. Hayek had frequent contacts with some members of the Department of Economics, and his political views resembled those of many of the Chicago School activists. In terms of ideology, said Friedman, the majority of the Chicago economics department "was on Hayek's side." Hayek actively promoted Aaron Director, who was active in the Chicago School in helping to fund and establish what became the

"Law and Society" programme in the University of Chicago Law School. Hayek,Frank Knight, Friedman and George Stigler worked together in forming the Mont Pèlerin Society, an international forum for libertarian economists. Hayek and Friedman cooperated in support of the Intercollegiate Society of Individualists, later renamed theIntercollegiate Studies Institute, an American student organisation devoted to libertarian ideas.

Hayek's first class at Chicago was a faculty seminar on the philosophy of science attended by many of the University's most notable scientists of the time, including Enrico Fermi, Sewall Wright and Leó Szilárd. During his time at Chicago, Hayek worked on the philosophy of science, economics, political philosophy, and the history of ideas. Hayek's economics notes from this period have yet to be published. Hayek received a Guggenheim Fellowship in 1954.

After editing a book on John Stuart Mill's letters he planned to publish two books on the liberal order, *The Constitution of Liberty* and "The Creative Powers of a Free Civilization" (eventually the title for the second chapter of *The Constitution of Liberty*). He completed *The Constitution of Liberty* in May 1959, with publication in February 1960. Hayek was concerned "with that condition of men in which coercion of some by others is reduced as much as is possible in society". Hayek was disappointed that the book did not receive the same enthusiastic general reception as *The Road to Serfdom* had sixteen years before.

Freiburg, Los Angeles, and Salzburg

From 1962 until his retirement in 1968, he was a professor at the University of Freiburg, West Germany, where he began work on his next book, *Law, Legislation and Liberty*. Hayek regarded his years at Freiburg as "very fruitful". Following his retirement, Hayek spent a year as a visiting professor of philosophy at the University of California, Los Angeles, where he continued work on*Law, Legislation and Liberty*, teaching a graduate seminar by the same name and another on the philosophy of social science. Primary drafts of the book were completed by 1970, but Hayek chose to rework his drafts and finally brought the book to publication in three volumes in 1973, 1976 and 1979.

He became a professor at the University of Salzburg from 1969 to 1977; he then returned to Freiburg, where he spent the rest of his days. When Hayek left Salzburg in 1977, he wrote, "I made a mistake in moving to Salzburg." The economics department was small, and the library facilities were inadequate.

Nobel Laureate

On 9 October 1974, it was announced that Hayek would be awarded the Nobel Memorial Prize in Economics, along with Swedish socialist economist Gunnar Myrdal. The reasons for the two of them winning the prize are described in the Nobel committee's press release. He was surprised at being given the award and believed that he was given it with Myrdal to balance the award with someone from the opposite side of the political spectrum.

During the Nobel ceremony in December 1974, Hayek met the Russian dissident Aleksandr Solzhenitsyn. Hayek later sent him a Russian translation of *The Road to Serfdom*.Although he spoke with apprehension at his award speech about the danger which the authority of the prize would lend to an economist, the prize brought much greater public awareness of Hayek and has been described by his biographer as "the great rejuvenating event in his life".

LATER YEARS

United Kingdom Politics

In February 1975, Margaret Thatcher was elected leader of the British Conservative Party. The Institute of Economic Affairs arranged a meeting between Hayek and Thatcher in London soon after.

During Thatcher's only visit to the Conservative Research Department in the summer of 1975, a speaker had prepared a paper on why the "middle way" was the pragmatic path the Conservative Party should take, avoiding the extremes of left and right. Before he had finished, Thatcher "reached into her briefcase and took out a book.

It was Hayek's *The Constitution of Liberty*. Interrupting our pragmatist, she held the book up for all of us to see. 'This', she said sternly, 'is what we believe', and banged Hayek down on the table".

In 1977, Hayek was critical of the Lib-Lab pact, in which the British Liberal Party agreed to keep the British Labour government in office. Writing to *The Times*, Hayek said, "May one who has devoted a large part of his life to the study of the history and the principles of liberalism point out that a party that keeps a socialist government in power has lost all title to the name 'Liberal'. Certainly no liberal can in future vote 'Liberal'".

Hayek was criticised by Liberal politicians Gladwyn Jebb and Andrew Phillips, who both claimed that the purpose of the pact was to discourage socialist legislation.

Lord Gladwyn pointed out that the German Free Democrats were in coalition with the German Social Democrats. Hayek was defended by Professor Antony Flew who stated that the German Social Democrats, unlike the British Labour Party, had, since the late 1950s, abandoned public ownership of the means of production, distribution and exchange and had instead embraced the social market economy.

In 1978, Hayek came into conflict with the Liberal Party leader, David Steel, who claimed that liberty was possible only with "social justice and an equitable distribution of wealth and power, which in turn require a degree of active government intervention" and that the Conservative Party were more concerned with the connection between liberty and private enterprise than between liberty and democracy. Hayek claimed that a limited democracy might be better than other forms of limited government at protecting liberty but that an unlimited democracy was worse than other forms of unlimited government because "its government loses the power even to do what it thinks right if any group on which its majority depends thinks otherwise".

Hayek stated that if the Conservative leader had said "that free choice is to be exercised more in the market place than in the ballot box, she has merely uttered the truism that the first is indispensable for individual freedom while the second is not: free choice can at least exist under a dictatorship that can limit itself but not under the government of an unlimited democracy which cannot".

Influence on Central European Politics

US President Ronald Reagan listed Hayek as among the two or three people who most influenced his philosophy and welcomed Hayek to the White House as a special guest.In the 1970s and 1980s, the writings of Hayek were also a major influence on many of the leaders of the "velvet" revolution in Central Europe during the collapse of the oldSoviet Empire. Here are some supporting examples:

There is no figure who had more of an influence, no person had more of an influence on the intellectuals behind the Iron Curtain than Friedrich Hayek. His books were translated and published by the underground and black market editions, read widely, and undoubtedly influenced the climate of opinion that ultimately brought about the collapse of the Soviet Union.

—Milton Friedman (Hoover Institution)

The most interesting among the courageous dissenters of the 1980s were the classical liberals, disciples of F. A. Hayek, from whom they had learned about the crucial importance of economic freedom and about the often-ignored conceptual difference between liberalism and democracy.

—Andrzej Walicki (History, Notre Dame)

Estonian Prime Minister Mart Laar came to my office the other day to recount his country's remarkable transformation. He described a nation of people who are harder-working, more virtuous – yes, more virtuous, because the market punishes immorality – and more hopeful about the future than they've ever been in their history. I asked Mr. Laar where his government got the idea for these reforms. Do you know what he replied? He said, "We read Milton Friedman and F. A. Hayek."

—US Representative Dick Armey

I was 25 years old and pursuing my doctorate in economics when I was allowed to spend six months of post-graduate studies in Naples, Italy. I read the Western economic textbooks and also the more general work of people like Hayek. By the time I returned to Czechoslovakia, I had an understanding of the principles of the market. In 1968, I was glad at the political liberalism of the Dubcek Prague Spring, but was very critical of the Third Way they pursued in economics.

—Václav Klaus (former President of the Czech Republic)

Recognition

In 1980, Hayek, a non-practicing Roman Catholic, was one of twelve Nobel laureates to meet with Pope John Paul II, "to dialogue, discuss views in their fields, communicate regarding the relationship between Catholicism and science, and 'bring to the Pontiff's attention the problems which the Nobel Prize Winners, in their respective fields of study, consider to be the most urgent for contemporary man'".

In 1984, he was appointed as a member of the Order of the Companions of Honour (CH) by Queen Elizabeth II of the United Kingdom on the advice of the British Prime Minister Margaret Thatcher for his "services to the study of economics". Hayek had hoped to receive a baronetcy, and after he was awarded the CH he sent a letter to his friends requesting that he be called the English version of Friedrich (Frederick) from now on.

After his 20 min audience with the Queen, he was "absolutely besotted" with her according to his daughter-in-law, Esca Hayek. Hayek said a year later that he was "amazed by her. That ease and skill, as if she'd known me all my life." The audience with the Queen was followed by a dinner with family and friends at the Institute of Economic Affairs. When, later that evening, Hayek was dropped off at the Reform Club, he commented: "I've just had the happiest day of my life."

In 1991, US President George H. W. Bush awarded Hayek the Presidential Medal of Freedom, one of the two highest civilian awards in the United States, for a "lifetime of looking beyond the horizon".

Hayek died in 1992 in Freiburg, Germany, and was buried in the Neustift am Wald cemetery in the northern outskirts of Vienna. In 2011, his article The Use of Knowledge in Society was selected as one of the top 20 articles published in the American Economic Review during its first 100 years.

The New York University *Journal of Law and Liberty* holds an annual lecture in his honour.

WORK

The Business Cycle

Hayek's principal investigations in economics concerned capital, money, and the business cycle. Mises had earlier applied the concept of marginal utility to the value of money in his *Theory of Money and Credit* (1912), in which he also proposed an explanation for "industrial fluctuations" based on the ideas of the old British Currency School and of Swedish economist Knut Wicksell. Hayek used this body of work as a starting point for his own interpretation of the business cycle, elaborating what later became known as the "Austrian Theory of the Business Cycle". Hayek spelled out the Austrian approach in more detail in his book, published in 1929, an English translation of which appeared in 1933 as *Monetary Theory and the Trade Cycle*.

There he argued for a monetary approach to the origins of the cycle. In his *Prices and Production* (1931), Hayek argued that the business cycle resulted from the central bank's inflationary credit expansion and its transmission over time, leading to a capital misallocation caused by the artificially low interest rates.

Hayek claimed that "the past instability of the market economy is the consequence of the exclusion of the most important regulator of the market mechanism, money, from itself being regulated by the market process".

Hayek's analysis was based on Böhm-Bawerk's concept of the "average period of production" and on the effects that monetary policy could have upon it. In accordance with the reasoning later outlined in his essay *The Use of Knowledge in Society* (1945), Hayek argued that a monopolistic governmental agency like a central bank can neither possess the relevant information which should govern supply of money, nor have the ability to use it correctly.

In 1929, Lionel Robbins assumed the helm of the London School of Economics (LSE). Eager to promote alternatives to what he regarded as the narrow approach of the school of economic thought that then dominated the English-speaking academic world (centred at the University of Cambridge and deriving largely from the work of Alfred Marshall), Robbins invited Hayek to join the faculty at LSE, which he did in 1931. According to Nicholas Kaldor, Hayek's theory of the time-structure of capital and of the business cycle initially "fascinated the academic world" and appeared to offer a less "facile and superficial" understanding of macroeconomics than the Cambridge school's.

Also in 1931, Hayek critiqued Keynes's *Treatise on Money* (1930) in his "Reflections on the pure theory of Mr. J. M. Keynes" and published his lectures at the LSE in book form as *Prices and Production*. Unemployment and idle resources are, for Keynes, caused by a lack of effective demand; for Hayek, they stem from a previous, unsustainable episode of easy money and artificially low interest rates.

The Economic Calculation Problem

Building on the earlier work of Ludwig von Mises and others, Hayek also argued that while in centrally planned economies an individual or a select group of individuals must determine the distribution of resources, these planners will never have enough information to carry out this allocation reliably. This argument, first proposed by Max Weber, says that the efficient exchange and use of resources can be maintained only through the price mechanism in free markets.

In 1935, Hayek published *Collectivist Economic Planning*, a collection of essays from an earlier debate that had been initiated by Ludwig von Mises. Hayek included Mises's essay, in which Mises argued that rational planning was impossible under socialism.

Some socialists such as H. D. Dickinson and Oskar Lange, responded by invoking general equilibrium theory, which they argued disproved Mises's thesis. They noted that the difference between a planned and a free market system lay in who was responsible for solving the equations.

They argued, if some of the prices chosen by socialist managers were wrong, gluts or shortages would appear, signalling them to adjust the prices up or down, just as in a free market. Through such a trial and error, a socialist economy could mimic the efficiency of a free market system, while avoiding its many problems.

Hayek challenged this vision in a series of contributions. In "Economics and Knowledge" (1937), he pointed out that the standard equilibrium theory assumed that all agents have full and correct information. In the real world, however, different individuals have different bits of knowledge, and furthermore, some of what they believe is wrong.

In *The Use of Knowledge in Society* (1945), Hayek argued that the price mechanism serves to share and synchronise local and personal knowledge, allowing society's members to achieve diverse, complicated ends through a principle of spontaneous self-organization.

He contrasted the use of the price mechanism with central planning, arguing that the former allows for more rapid adaptation to changes in particular circumstances of time and place. Thus, he set the stage for Oliver Williamson's later contrast between markets and hierarchies as alternative co-ordination mechanisms for economic transactions.

He used the term catallaxy to describe a "self-organizing system of voluntary co-operation". Hayek's research into this argument was specifically cited by the Nobel Committee in its press release awarding Hayek the Nobel prize.

Against Collectivism

Hayek was one of the leading academic critics of collectivism in the 20th century. Hayek argued that all forms of collectivism (even those theoretically based on voluntary co-operation) could only be maintained by a central authority of some kind. In Hayek's view, the central role of the state should be to maintain the rule of law, with as little arbitrary intervention as possible. In his popular book, *The Road to Serfdom* (1944) and in subsequent academic works, Hayek argued that socialism required central economic planning and that such planning in turn leads towards totalitarianism.

From *The Road to Serfdom:*

Although our modern socialists' promise of greater freedom is genuine and sincere, in recent years observer after observer has been impressed by the unforeseen consequences of socialism, the extraordinary similarity in many respects of the conditions under "communism" and "fascism".

Hayek posited that a central planning authority would have to be endowed with powers that would impact and ultimately control social life, because the knowledge required for centrally planning an economy is inherently decentralised, and would need to be brought under control.

Hayek also wrote that the state can play a role in the economy, and specifically, in creating a "safety net". He wrote, "There is no reason why, in a society which has reached the general level of wealth ours has, the first kind of security should not be guaranteed to all without endangering general freedom; that is: some minimum of food, shelter and clothing, sufficient to preserve health.

Nor is there any reason why the state should not help to organize a comprehensive system of social insurance in providing for those common hazards of life against which few can make adequate provision."

Investment and Choice

Perhaps more fully than any other economist, Hayek investigated the choice theory of investment. He examined the inter-relations between *non-permanent* production goods and "latent" or potentially economic *permanent* resources – building on the choice theoretical insight that, "processes that take more time will evidently not be adopted unless they yield a greater return than those that take less time".

Hayek's work on the microeconomics of the choice theoretics of investment, non-permanent goods, *potential* permanent resources, and *economically-adapted* permanent resources mark a central dividing point between his work in areas of macroeconomics and that of most all other economists.

Hayek's work on the macroeconomic subjects ofcentral planning, trade cycle theory, the division of knowledge, and entrepreneurial adaptation especially, differ greatly from the opinions of macroeconomic "Marshallian" economists in the tradition of John Maynard Keynes and the microeconomic "Walrasian" economists in the tradition of Abba Lerner.

Philosophy of Science

During the World War II, Hayek started doing the 'Abuse of Reason' project. His goal was to show how a number of then-popular doctrines and beliefs, doctrines with which he disagreed, had a common origin in some fundamental misconceptions about the social science. In his philosophy of science, which has much in common with that of his good friend Karl Popper, Hayek was highly critical of what he termed *scientism*: a false understanding of the methods of science that has been mistakenly forced upon the social sciences, but that is contrary to the practices of genuine science.

Usually, scientism involves combining the philosophers' ancient demand for demonstrative justification with the associationists' false view that all scientific explanations are simple two-variable linear relationships.

Hayek points out that much of science involves the explanation of complex multivariable and non-linear phenomena, and the social science of economics and undesigned order compares favourably with such complex sciences as Darwinian biology.

These ideas were developed in *The Counter-Revolution of Science: Studies in the Abuse of Reason*, 1952 and in some of Hayek's later essays in the philosophy of science such as "Degrees of Explanation" and "The Theory of Complex Phenomena".

Psychology

In *The Sensory Order: An Enquiry into the Foundations of Theoretical Psychology* (1952), Hayek independently developed a "Hebbian learning" model of learning and memory – an idea which he first conceived in 1920, prior to his study of economics.

Hayek's expansion of the "Hebbian synapse" construction into a global brain theory has received continued attention in neuroscience, cognitive science, computer science, behavioural science, and evolutionary psychology, by scientists such as Gerald Edelman, and Joaquin Fuster.

Hayek posited two orders, the sensory order that we experience, and the natural order that natural science has revealed. Hayek thought that the sensory order is in fact a product of the brain. He characterized the brain as a highly complex but self-ordering, hierarchical classification system, a huge network of connections.

Spontaneous Order

Hayek viewed the free price system not as a conscious invention (that which is intentionally designed by man), but as spontaneous order or what he referred to as "that which is the result of human action but not of human design". Thus, Hayek put the *price mechanism* on the same level as, for example, language.

Hayek attributed the birth of civilization to private property in his book *The Fatal Conceit* (1988).

He explained that price signals are the only means of enabling each economic decision maker to communicate tacit knowledge or dispersed knowledge to each other, to solve the economic calculation problem.

Social and Political Philosophy

In the latter half of his career Hayek made a number of contributions to social and political philosophy, which he based on his views on the limits of human knowledge, and the idea of *spontaneous order* in social institutions. He argues in favour of a society organised around a market order, in which the apparatus of state is employed almost (though not entirely) exclusively to enforce the legal order (consisting of abstract rules, and not particular commands) necessary for a market of free individuals to function.

These ideas were informed by a moral philosophy derived from epistemological concerns regarding the inherent limits of human knowledge. Hayek argued that his ideal individualistic, free-market polity would be self-regulating to such a degree that it would be 'a society which does not depend for its functioning on our finding good men for running it'.

Hayek disapproved of the notion of 'social justice'. He compared the market to a game in which 'there is no point in calling the outcome just or unjust' and argued that 'social justice is an empty phrase with no determinable content'; likewise "the results of the individual's efforts are necessarily unpredictable, and the question as to whether the resulting distribution of incomes is just has no meaning".

He generally regarded government redistribution of income or capital as an unacceptable intrusion upon individual freedom: "the principle of distributive justice, once introduced, would not be fulfilled until the whole of society was organized in accordance with it. This would produce a kind of society which in all essential respects would be the opposite of a free society."

With regard to a safety net, Hayek advocated "some provision for those threatened by the extremes of indigence or starvation, be it only in the interest of those who require protection against acts of desperation on the part of the needy".

As referenced in the section on "The economic calculation problem", Hayek wrote that "there is no reason why... the state should not help to organize a comprehensive system of social insurance". Summarizing on this topic, Wapshott writes "[Hayek] advocated mandatory universal health care and unemployment insurance, enforced, if not directly provided, by the state." In the 1973 *Law, Legislation, and Liberty,* Hayek wrote:

There is no reason why in a free society government should not assure to all, protection against severe deprivation in the form of an assured minimum income, or a floor below which nobody need descend.

To enter into such an insurance against extreme misfortune may well be in the interest of all; or it may be felt to be a clear moral duty of all to assist, within the organised community, those who cannot help themselves. So long as such a uniform minimum income is provided outside the market to all those who, for any reason, are unable to earn in the market an adequate maintenance, this need not lead to a restriction of freedom, or conflict with the Rule of Law. And in *The Road to Serfdom:*

Nor is there any reason why the state should not assist the individuals in providing for those common hazards of life against which, because of their uncertainty, few individuals can make adequate provision.

Where, as in the case of sickness and accident, neither the desire to avoid such calamities nor the efforts to overcome their consequences are as a rule weakened by the provision of assistance – where, in short, we deal with genuinely insurable risks – the case for the state's helping to organize a comprehensive system of social insurance is very strong.

Wherever communal action can mitigate disasters against which the individual can neither attempt to guard himself nor make the provision for the consequences, such communal action should undoubtedly be taken.

CRITIQUES

Business Cycle Critiques

Keynes asked his friend Piero Sraffa to respond publicly to Hayek's challenge; instead of formulating an alternative theory, Sraffa elaborated on the logical inconsistencies of Hayek's argument, especially concerning the effect of inflation-induced "forced savings" on the capital sector and about the definition of a "natural" interest rate in a growing economy.

Others who responded negatively to Hayek's work on the business cycle included John Hicks, Frank Knight, and Gunnar Myrdal. Kaldor later wrote that Hayek's *Prices and Production* had produced "a remarkable crop of critics" and that the total number of pages in British and American journals dedicated to the resulting debate "could rarely have been equalled in the economic controversies of the past."

Hayek continued his research on monetary and capital theory, revising his theories of the relations between credit cycles and capital structure in *Profits, Interest and Investment*(1939) and *The Pure Theory of Capital* (1941), but his reputation as an economic theorist had by then fallen so much that those works were largely ignored, except for scathing critiques by Nicholas Kaldor.

Lionel Robbins himself, who had embraced the Austrian theory of the business cycle in *The Great Depression* (1934), later regretted having written that book and accepted many of the Keynesian counter-arguments.

Hayek never produced the book-length treatment of "the dynamics of capital" that he had promised in the *Pure Theory of Capital.* After 1941, he continued to publish works on the economics of information, political philosophy, the theory of law, and psychology, but seldom on macroeconomics. At the University of Chicago, Hayek was not part of the economics department and did not influence the rebirth of neo-classical theory which took place there. When, in 1974, he shared the Nobel Memorial Prize in Economics with Gunnar

Myrdal, the latter complained about being paired with an "ideologue". Milton Friedman declared himself "an enormous admirer of Hayek, but not for his economics. I think *Prices and Production* is a very flawed book. I think his [*Pure Theory of Capital*] is unreadable. On the other hand, *The Road to Serfdom* is one of the great books of our time."

Critiques of his Concept of Collectivist Rationalism

Arthur M. Diamond argues Hayek's problems arise when he goes beyond claims that can be evaluated within economic science. Diamond argued that: "The human mind, Hayek says, is not just limited in its ability to synthesize a vast array of concrete facts, it is also limited in its ability to give a deductively sound ground to ethics. Here is where the tension develops, for he also wants to give a reasoned moral defence of the free market.

He is an intellectual skeptic who wants to give political philosophy a secure intellectual foundation. It is thus not too surprising that what results is confused and contradictory."

Chandran Kukathas argued: "The central dilemma of Hayek's political philosophy is, given his view of the limited role reason can play in social life, how is it possible to mount a systematic defence of liberalism without falling victim to the very kinds of rationalism he criticises? This difficulty stays unresolved in Hayek's political thought because it is informed by two incompatible assumptions about what reason can achieve."

Norman Barry similarly notes that the "critical rationalism" in Hayek's writings appears incompatible with "a certain kind of fatalism, that we must wait for evolution to pronounce its verdict."

New Right Critiques

Alain de Benoist of the *Nouvelle Droite* (New Right) produced a highly critical essay on Hayek's work in an issue of *Telos*, citing the flawed assumptions behind Hayek's idea of "spontaneous order" and the authoritarian, totalising implications of his free-market ideology.

Hayek's Views on Pinochet's Chile

Hayek visited Chile in the 1970s and 1980s during the Government Junta of general Augusto Pinochet and accepted being named Honourary Chairman of the *Centro de Estudios Públicos*, the think tank formed by the economists who transformed Chile into a free market economy.

Asked about the liberal, non-democratic rule by a Chilean interviewer, Hayek is translated from German to Spanish to English as having said, "As long term institutions, I am totally against dictatorships.

But a dictatorship may be a necessary system for a transitional period. [...] Personally I prefer a liberal dictatorship to democratic government devoid of liberalism.

My personal impression – and this is valid for South America – is that in Chile, for example, we will witness a transition from a dictatorial government to a liberal government." In a letter to the *London Times*, he defended the Pinochet regime and said that he had "not been able to find a single person even in much maligned Chile who did not agree that personal freedom was much greater under Pinochet than it had been under Allende."

Hayek admitted that "it is not very likely that this will succeed, even if, at a particular point in time, it may be the only hope there is.", he explained, however, "It is not certain hope, because it will always depend on the goodwill of an individual, and there are very few individuals one can trust.

But if it is the sole opportunity which exists at a particular moment it may be the best solution despite this. And only if and when the dictatorial government is visibly directing its steps towards limited democracy".

For Hayek, the supposedly stark difference between authoritarianism and totalitarianism has much importance and Hayek places heavy weight on this distinction in his defence of transitional dictatorship. For example, when Hayek visited Venezuela in May 1981, he was asked to comment on the prevalence of "totalitarian" regimes in Latin America.

In reply, Hayek warned against confusing "totalitarianism with authoritarianism," and said that he was unaware of "any totalitarian governments in Latin America. The only one was Chile under Allende". For Hayek, however, the word 'totalitarian' signifies something very specific: the wants to "organize the whole of society" to attain a "definite social goal" and—in stark contrast to "liberalism and individualism".

Hayek urged British Prime Minister Margaret Thatcher to adopt economic reforms similar to Chile's.

INFLUENCE AND RECOGNITION

Hayek's influence on the development of economics is widely acknowledged. Hayek is the second-most frequently cited economist (after Kenneth Arrow) in the Nobel lectures of the prize winners in economics, particularly since his lecture was critical of the field of orthodox economics and neo-classical modelisation. A number of Nobel Laureates in economics, such as Vernon Smith and Herbert A. Simon, recognise Hayek as the greatest modern economist.

Another Nobel winner, Paul Samuelson, believed that Hayek was worthy of his award but nevertheless claimed that "there were good historical reasons for fading memories of Hayek within the mainstream last half of the twentieth century economist fraternity. In 1931, Hayek's *Prices and Production* had enjoyed an ultra-short Byronic success.

In retrospect hindsight tells us that its mumbo-jumbo about the period of production grossly misdiagnosed the macroeconomics of the 1927–1931 (and the 1931–2007) historical scene". Despite this comment, Samuelson spent the last 50 years of his life obsessed with the problems of capital theory identified by Hayek and Böhm-Bawerk, and Samuelson flatly judged Hayek to have been right and his own teacher, Joseph Schumpeter, to have been wrong on the central economic question of the 20th century, the feasibility of socialist economic planning in a production goods dominated economy.

Hayek is widely recognised for having introduced the time dimension to the equilibrium construction and for his key role in helping inspire the fields of growth theory, information economics, and the theory of spontaneous order.

The "informal" economics presented in Milton Friedman's massively influential popular work *Free to Choose* (1980), is explicitly Hayekian in its account of the price system as a system for transmitting and co-ordinating knowledge. This can be explained by the fact that Friedman taught Hayek's famous paper "The Use of Knowledge in Society" (1945) in his graduate seminars.

In 1944 he was elected as a Fellow of the British Academy, after he was nominated for membership by Keynes.

Harvard economist and former Harvard University President Lawrence Summers explains Hayek's place in modern economics: "What's the single most important thing to learn from an economics course today? What I tried to leave my students with is the view that the invisible hand is more powerful than the [un]hidden hand.

Things will happen in well-organized efforts without direction, controls, plans. That's the consensus among economists. That's the Hayek legacy."

By 1947, Hayek was an organiser of the Mont Pelerin Society, a group of classical liberals who sought to oppose what they saw as socialism in various areas. He was also instrumental in the founding of the Institute of Economic Affairs, the free-market think tank that inspired Thatcherism. He was in addition a member of the Philadelphia Society.

Hayek had a long-standing and close friendship with philosopher of science Karl Popper, also from Vienna. In a letter to Hayek in 1944, Popper stated, "I think I have learnt more from you than from any other living thinker, except perhaps Alfred Tarski."

Popper dedicated his *Conjectures and Refutations* to Hayek. For his part, Hayek dedicated a collection of papers, *Studies in Philosophy, Politics, and Economics*, to Popper and, in 1982, said that "ever since his *Logik der Forschung* first came out in 1934, I have been a complete adherent to his general theory of methodology".

Popper also participated in the inaugural meeting of the Mont Pelerin Society. Their friendship and mutual admiration, however, do not change the fact that there are important differences between their ideas. Hayek also played a central role in Milton Friedman's intellectual development. Friedman wrote:

"My interest in public policy and political philosophy was rather casual before I joined the faculty of the University of Chicago. Informal discussions with colleagues and friends stimulated a greater interest, which was reinforced by Friedrich Hayek's powerful book The Road to Serfdom, by my attendance at the first meeting of the Mont Pelerin Society in 1947, and by discussions with Hayek after he joined the university faculty in 1950. In addition, Hayek attracted an exceptionally able group of students who were dedicated to a libertarian ideology.

They started a student publication, The New Individualist Review, which was the outstanding libertarian journal of opinion for some years. I served as an adviser to the journal and published a number of articles in it...."

Hayek's greatest intellectual debt was to Carl Menger, who pioneered an approach to social explanation similar to that developed in Britain by Bernard Mandeville and the Scottish moral philosophers in the Scottish Enlightenment. He had a wide-reaching influence on contemporary economics, politics, philosophy, sociology, psychology and anthropology.

For example, Hayek's discussion in *The Road to Serfdom* (1944) about truth, falsehood and the use of language influenced some later opponents ofpostmodernism.

Hayek and Conservatism

Hayek received new attention in the 1980s and 1990s with the rise of conservative governments in the United States, United Kingdom, and Canada. After winning the United Kingdom general election, 1979, Margaret Thatcher appointed Keith Joseph, the director of the Hayekian Centre for Policy Studies, as her secretary of state for industry in an effort to redirect parliament's economic strategies.

Likewise, David Stockman, Ronald Reagan's most influential financial official in 1981 was an acknowledged follower of Hayek.

Hayek wrote an essay, "Why I Am Not a Conservative", in which he disparaged conservatism for its inability to adapt to changing human realities or to offer a positive political programme, remarking, "Conservatism is only as good as what it conserves".

Although he noted that modern day conservatism shares many opinions on economics with classical liberals, particularly a belief in the free market, he believed it's because conservatism wants to "stand still", whereas liberalism embraces the free market because it "wants to go somewhere".

Hayek identified himself as a classical liberal but noted that in the United States it had become almost impossible to use "liberal" in its original definition, and the term "libertarian" has been used instead. However, for his part, Hayek found this term "singularly unattractive" and offered the term "Old Whig" (a phrase borrowed from Edmund Burke) instead. In his later life, he said, "I am becoming a Burkean Whig." However, Whiggery as a political doctrine had little affinity for classical political economy, the tabernacle of the Manchester School and William Gladstone.

His essay has served as an inspiration to other liberal-minded economists wishing to distinguish themselves from conservative thinkers, for example James M. Buchanan's essay "Why I, Too, Am Not a Conservative: The Normative Vision of Classical Liberalism".

A common term in much of the world for what Hayek espoused is "neo-liberalism". A British scholar, Samuel Brittan, concluded in 2010, "Hayek's book [*The Constitution of Liberty*] is still probably the most comprehensive statement of the underlying ideas of the moderate free market philosophy espoused by neo-liberals." Brittan adds that although Raymond Plant (2009) comes out in the end against Hayek's doctrines, Plant gives *The Constitution of Liberty* a "more thorough and fair-minded analysis than it has received even from its professed adherents".

In *Why F A Hayek is a Conservative*, British policy analyst Madsen Pirie believes Hayek mistakes the nature of the conservative outlook. Conservatives, he says, are not averse to change – but like Hayek, they are highly averse to change being imposed on the social order by people in authority who think they know how to run things better. They wish to allow the market to function smoothly and give it the freedom to change and develop. It is an outlook, says Pirie, that Hayek and conservatives both share.

PERSONAL LIFE

In August 1926, Hayek married Helen Berta Maria von Fritsch (1901–1960), a secretary at the civil service office where Hayek worked. They had two children together.Friedrich and Helen divorced in July 1950 and he married Helene Bitterlich (1900–1996) just a few weeks later, moving to Arkansas to take advantage of permissive divorce laws. On Hayek's religious views, he was an agnostic.

GEORGE JOSEPH STIGLER

George Joseph Stigler (January 17, 1911 – December 1, 1991) was a U.S. economist. He won the Nobel Memorial Prize in Economic Sciences in 1982, and was a key leader of the Chicago School of Economics, along with Milton Friedman.

Stigler was born in Seattle, Washington, of German descent. He graduated from the University of Washington in 1931 with a B.A and then spent a year at Northwestern University from which he obtained his M.B.A in 1932. It was during his studies at Northwestern that Stigler developed an interest in economics and decided on an academic career. Due to a tuition scholarship that he received from the University of Chicago, Stigler enrolled at the university in 1933 to study economics and went on to earn his Ph.D. in economics from the University of Chicago in 1938.

His teaching experience began in 1936 at Iowa State College where he taught until 1938. He spent much of World War II at Columbia University, performing mathematical and statistical research for the Manhattan Project. He then spent one year at Brown University. He served on the Columbia faculty from 1947 to 1958.

While at Chicago, he was greatly influenced by Frank Knight, his dissertation supervisor. Friedman, a friend for over sixty years, comments upon it as remarkable since only three or four students ever managed to complete their PhD dissertation under Knight in his 28 years at Chicago. Jacob Viner and Henry Simons also influenced him and, among his students, W. Allen Wallis and Milton Friedman.

Stigler is best known for developing the *Economic Theory of Regulation*, also known as capture, which says that interest groups and other political participants will use the regulatory and coercive powers of government to shape laws and regulations in a way that is beneficial to them. This theory is a component of the public choice field of economics. He also carried out extensive research in thehistory of economic thought.

Stigler's most important contribution to economics was disseminated in his landmark article titled "The Economics of Information".According to Friedman, Stigler "essentially created a new area of study for economists." In this article, Stigler stressed the importance of information by writing, "One should hardly have to tell academicians that information is a valuable resource: knowledge is power. And yet it occupies a slum dwelling in the town of economics."

His 1962 article "Information in the Labour Market" developed the theory of search unemployment.

He was known for his sharp sense of humor, and wrote a number of spoof essays. In his book *The Intellectual and the Marketplace*, for instance, he proposed *Stigler's Law of Demand and Supply Elasticities,* that "all demand curves are inelastic and all supply curves are inelastic too."

The essay referenced studies that found many goods and services to be inelastic over the long run, as well as offering a supposed theoretical proof; he ended by announcing that his next essay would demonstrate that the price system does not exist.

Another essay, on "Truth in Teaching," described the consequences of a (fictional) set of court decisions that held universities legally responsible for the consequences of teaching errors. The Stigler diet was named after him.

Stigler wrote numerous articles on the history of economics, published in the leading journals and republished 14 of them in 1965. The review in the *American Economic Review* said "many of these essays have become such well-known landmarks that no scholar in this field should be unfamiliar with them" and praised, "The lucid prose, penetrating logic, and wry humor which have become the author's trademarks." However, economist Deirdre McCloskey later referred to Stigler as "among the worst historians of economic thought in the history of the discipline" who "read a lot but was defective in paying attention."

Stigler was a founding member of the Mont Pelerin Society, and was president from 1976 to 1978. He received National Medal of Science in 1987.

GERARD DEBREU

Gérard Debreu (July 4, 1921 – December 31, 2004) was a French economist and mathematician, who also came to have United States citizenship. Best known as a professor of economics at the University of California, Berkeley, where he began work in 1962, he won the 1983 Nobel Memorial Prize in Economics.

BIOGRAPHY

His father was the business partner of his maternal grandfather in lace manufacturing, a traditional industry in Calais. Debreu was orphaned at an early age, as his father committed suicide and his mother died of natural causes.

Prior to the start of World War II, he received his baccalauréat and went to Ambert to begin preparing for the entrance examination of a grande école. Later on, he moved from Ambert to Grenoble to complete his preparation, both places being in Vichy France during World War II.

In 1941, he was admitted to the École Normale Supérieure in Paris, along with Marcel Boiteux (fr). He was influenced by Henri Cartan and theBourbaki writers. When he was about to take the final examinations in 1944, the Normandy landings occurred and he, instead, enlisted in the French army. He was transferred for training to Algeria and then served in the occupying French forces in Germany until July 1945.

Debreu passed the Agrégation de Mathématiques exams at the end of 1945 and the beginning of 1946. By this time, he had become interested in economics, particularly in the general equilibrium theory of Léon Walras. From 1946 to 1948, he was an assistant in the Centre National de la Recherche Scientifique. During these two and a half years, he made the transition from mathematics to economics.

In 1948, Debreu went to the United States on a Rockefeller Fellowship which allowed him to visit several American universities, as well as those in Uppsala and Oslo in 1949–50.

Debreu married Françoise Bled in 1946 and they had two daughters, Chantal and Florence, born in 1946 and 1950 respectively.

Debreu died in Paris at the age of 83 of natural causes on New Year's Eve, 2004, and was interred in Père Lachaise Cemetery.

ACADEMIC CAREER

Debreu began working as a Research Associate and joined the Cowles Commission at the University of Chicago in the summer of 1950. He remained there for five years, returning to Paris periodically.

In 1954, he published a breakthrough paper, entitled *Existence of an Equilibrium for a Competitive Economy*, together with Kenneth Arrow, in which they provided a definitive mathematical proof of the existence of a general equilibrium, using topological rather thancalculus-based methods. In 1955, he moved to Yale University.

In 1959, he published his classical monograph, *Theory of Value: An Axiomatic Analysis of Economic Equilibrium* (Cowles Foundation Monographs Series), which is one of the most important works in mathematical economics. He also studied several problems in the theory of cardinal utility, in particular the additive decomposition of a utility function defined on a Cartesian productof sets.

In this monograph, Debreu set up an axiomatic foundation for competitive markets. He also established the existence of an equilibrium using a novel approach. The main idea of his argument is to show that there exists a price system for which the aggregate excess demand correspondence vanishes. He did so by proving a type of fixed-point theorem that is based on the Kakutani fixed-point theorem.

Debreu introduced the concept of uncertainty and showed how it could be incorporated into the deterministicmodel. Here, he introduced the notion of a contingent commodity, which is a promise to deliver a good should a certain state of nature be realized. This concept is very frequently used in financial economics, where it is known as the "Arrow–Debreu security".

In 1960–61, he worked at the Centre for Advanced Study in the Behavioural Sciences at Stanford and devoted most of his time to the complex proof that appeared in 1962 of a general theorem on the existence of an economic equilibrium.

In January 1962, he started working at the University of California, Berkeley, where he held the titles of University Professor and Class of 1958 Professor of Economics and Mathematics Emeritus.

During his leaves in the late 1960s and 1970s, he visited universities in Leiden, Cambridge, Bonn and Paris.

His later studies centered mainly on the theory of differentiable economies, where he showed that, in general, aggregate excess demand functions vanish at a finite number of points – basically, he showed that economies have a finite number of price equilibria.

In 1976, he received the French Legion of Honour. He was awarded the 1983 Bank of Sweden Prize in Economic Sciences in Memory of Alfred Nobel, for having incorporated new analytical methods into economic theory and for his rigourous reformulation of general equilibrium theory. He was a member of the International Academy of Science.

In 1990, he served as President of the American Economic Association.

GUNNAR MYRDAL

Karl Gunnar Myrdal (6 December 1898 – 17 May 1987) was a Swedish Nobel laureate economist, sociologist, and politician. In 1974, he received the Nobel Memorial Prize in Economic Sciences with Friedrich Hayek for "their pioneering work in the theory of money and economic fluctuations and for their penetrating analysis of the interdependence of economic, social and institutional phenomena." He is best known in the United States for his study of race relations, which culminated in his book *An American Dilemma: The Negro Problem and Modern Democracy*. The study was influential in the 1954 landmark U.S. Supreme Court Decision *Brown v. Board of Education*.

CHILDHOOD

Myrdal was born on 6 December 1898 in Gustafs, Sweden, to Karl Adolf Pettersson (1876–1934), a railroad employee, and his wife Anna Sofia Karlsson (1878–1965). He took the name *Myrdal* in 1914 after his ancestors farm Myr in Dalarna.

EDUCATION AND EARLY CAREER

There is a possibly apocryphal story about an interaction between him and Gustav Cassel, where Cassel was reported to say, "Gunnar, you should be more respectful to your elders, because it is we who will determine your promotion," and he replied, "Yes, but it is we who will write your obituaries."

Gunnar Myrdal graduated with a law degree from Stockholm University in 1923 and a doctorate in economics in 1927. In 1919, he met Alva Reimer, whom he married in 1924.

In Gunnar Myrdal's doctoral dissertation, published in 1927, he examined the role of expectations in price formation. His analysis strongly influenced the Stockholm school. He built on Knut Wicksell´s theories of Cumulative process of endogenous money, stressing the importance of Knightian uncertainty and Ex ante and Ex post expectations role in the economic process.

Between 1925 and 1929 he studied in Britain and Germany. He was a Rockefeller Fellow and visited the United States in 1929–1930. During this period he published his first books, including *The Political Element in the Development of Economic Theory*. Returning to Europe, he served for one year as associate professor in the Graduate Institute of International Studies,

Geneva, Switzerland. Gunnar Myrdal was at first fascinated by the abstract mathematical models coming into fashion in the 1920, and helped found the Econometric Society in London. Later, however, he accused the movement of ignoring the problem of distribution of wealth in its obsession with economic growth, of using faulty statistics and substituting Greek letters for missing data in its formulas and of flouting logic.

He wrote, "Correlations are not explanations and besides, they can be as spurious as the high correlation in Finland between foxes killed and divorces." Professor Myrdal was an early supporter of the theses of John Maynard Keynes, although he maintained that the basic idea of adjusting national budgets to slow or speed an economy was first developed by him and articulated in his book *Monetary Economics*, published in 1932, four years prior to Keynes' *General Theory of Employment, Interest and Money*.

William Barber's comment upon Myrdal's work on monetary theory goes like this:

"If his contribution had been available to readers of English before 1936, it is interesting to speculate whether the 'revolution' in macroeconomic theory of the depression decade would be referred to as 'Myrdalian' as much as 'Keynesian'"

Economist G. L. S. Shackle claimed the importance of Gunnar Myrdal´s analysis by which saving and investment are allowed to adjust ex ante to each other. However, the reference to ex ante and ex post analysis has become so usual in modern macroeconomics that the position of Keynes to not include it in his work was currently considered as an oddity, if not a mistake. As Shackle put it:

Myrdalian ex ante language would have saved the General Theory from describing the flow of investment and the flow of saving as identically, tautologically equal, and within the same discourse, treating their equality as a condition which may, or not, be fulfilled.

Gunnar Myrdal also developed the key concept Circular Cumulative Causation, a multi-causal approach where the core variables and their linkages are delineated.

CAREER

Gunnar Myrdal became professor at the Stockholm School of Economics 1933. At the Stockholm School of Economics he became good friends with Bertil Ohlin, professor in economics at the same university 1929-1965. The two became the leading proponents of the Stockholm school. Myrdal was professor of economics at Stockholm School of Economics for 15 years, until 1947.

He became a Social Democratic Member of Parliament from 1933 and from 1945 to 1947 he served as Trade Minister in Tage Erlander's government.

During this period he was heavily criticised for his financial agreement with the Soviet Union. At the same time he was accused of being responsible for the Swedish monetary crisis in 1947.

He coauthored with his wife, Alva Myrdal, the *Crisis in the Population Question*. The work of Gunnar and Alva inspired policies adopted by the Minister of Social Affairs, Gustav Möller, to provide social support to families.

Gunnar Myrdal headed a comprehensive study of sociological, economic, anthropological and legal data on race relations in the United States funded by the Carnegie Corporation, starting in 1938.

The result of the effort was Gunnar Myrdal's best-known work, *An American Dilemma: The Negro Problem and Modern Democracy*, published in 1944, written with the collaboration of R. M. E. Sterner and Arnold Rose. He characterized the problem of race relations as a dilemma because of a perceived conflict between high ideals, embodied in what he called the "American Creed," on the one hand and poor performance on the other.

In the generations since the Civil War, the U.S. had been unable to put its human rights ideals into practice for the African-American tenth of its population. This book was cited by the U.S. Supreme Court in its 1954 decision in*Brown v. Board of Education*, which outlawed racial segregation in public schools. Myrdal planned on doing a similar study on gender inequality, but he could not find funding for this project and never completed it.

During World War II, Gunnar Myrdal was staunchly, publicly anti-Nazi. Together with his wife, Alva, he wrote *Contact with America* in 1941, which praised the United States' democratic institutions.

Gunnar Myrdal became the Executive Secretary of the United Nations Economic Commission for Europe in 1947. During his tenure, he founded one of the leading centers economic research and policy development. After ten years in the position, Dr. Myrdal resigned as Executive Secretary in 1957.

In 1956 and 1957, he was able to publish *An International Economy, Problems and Prospects*, *Rich Lands and Poor* and *Economic Theory and Underdeveloped Regions.*

Myrdal was also a signatory of the 1950 UNESCOstatement *The Race Question*, which rebuts the theories of racial supremacy and purity, and also influenced the *Brown v. Board of Education* decision.

Between 1960 and 1967, he was a professor of international economics at Stockholm University. In 1961, he founded the Institute for International Economic Studies at the University. Throughout the 1960s, he worked on a comprehensive study of trends and policies in South Asia for the Twentieth Century Fund.

The study culminated in his three-volume *Asian Drama: An Enquiry into the Poverty of Nations*, published in 1968. In 1970, he published a companion book called *The Challenge of World Poverty*, where he laid out what he believed to be the chief policy solutions to the problems he outlined in *Asian Drama.* Gunnar Myrdal strongly opposed the Vietnam War. In *Asian Drama*, Myrdal predicted that land reform and pacification would fail in Vietnam and urged the United States to begin negotiations with North Vietnam. After returning to Sweden, he headed the Swedish Vietnam Committee and became co-chair of International Commission of Enquiry Into U.S. War Crimes in Indochina.

He also presided over the Stockholm International Peace Research Institute, an international watch-dog for the arms trade. He was one of the signers of the Humanist Manifesto.

In 1971 both he and his wife received honourary doctorates from Gustavus Adolphus College in Saint Peter, Minnesota.

He shared the Bank of Sweden Prize in Economic Sciences (otherwise known as the Nobel Memorial Prize in Economics) with Friedrich Hayek in 1974 but argued for its abolition because it had been given to such "reactionaries" as Friedrich Hayek and Milton Friedman.

PERSONAL LIFE

Myrdal was married to politician and diplomat Alva Myrdal in 1924, and together had two daughters, Kaj Fölster (mother of Swedish economist Stefan Fölster) and Sissela Bok, and a son, Jan Myrdal.

Myrdal was hospitalized for two months before he died in a hospital in Danderyd, near Stockholm, on May 17, 1987. His daughter Kaj Fölster and his grandson, Janken Myrdal, were present.

CONTRIBUTIONS TO THE PHILOSOPHY OF KNOWLEDGE

Gunnar Myrdal's scientific influence was not limited to economics. Through the introduction to "Asian Drama" with the title "The Beam in our Eyes" (a biblical reference; cf. Matthew 7:1–2) he introduced the approach mentioned as scientific relativism of values.

This behavioural approach is narrowly connected to behaviouralism and is built on the idea that the logical gulf between "is" and "ought" is more sophisticated than just dividing premises into categories.

The articles edited in "Value in Social Theory" underlines Myrdal's importance to political science. As political science normally is considered more descriptive as economics one might get the idea that Myrdal should not have dealt systematically with the values applied to economics. On the contrary, Myrdal connected social science, political science and economics as a practitioner.

Myrdal published many notable works, both before and after *American Dilemma* and, among many other contributions to social and public policy, founded and chaired theStockholm International Peace Research Institute.

Internationally revered as a father-figure of social policy, he contributed to social democratic thinking throughout the world, in collaboration with friends and colleagues in the political and academic arenas. Sweden and Britain were among the pioneers of a welfare state and books by Myrdal (*Beyond the Welfare State* – New Haven, 1958) and Richard Titmuss (*Essays on "The Welfare State"* – London, 1958) unsurprisingly explore similar themes. Myrdal's theoretical key concept "circular cumulative causation" contributed to the development of modern Non-equilibrium economics.

QUOTES BY GUNNAR MYRDAL

- "Education means an assimilation of white American culture. It decreases the dissimilarity of the Negroes from other Americans."
- "The study of women's intelligence and personality has had broadly the same history as the one we record for Negroes. As in the case of the Negro, women themselves have often been brought to believe in their inferiority of endowment."
- "White prejudice and discrimination keep the Negro low in standards of living, health, education, manners and morals. This, in its turn, gives support to white prejudice. White prejudice and Negro standards thus mutually 'cause' each other."
- "Correlations are not explanations and besides, they can be as spurious as the high correlation in Finland between foxes killed and divorces."
- "The only possible way of decreasing Negro population is by means of controlling fertility." (An American Dilemma, The Growth of the Negro Population)

HENRY GEORGE

Henry George (September 2, 1839 – October 29, 1897) was an American writer, politician and political economist, who was the most influential proponent of the land value tax and the value capture of land/natural resource rents, an idea known at the time as*Single-Tax*.

His immensely popular writing is credited with sparking several reform movements of the Progressive Era and ultimately inspiring the broad economic philosophy often referred to today as Georgism, the main tenet of which is that people legitimately own value they fairly create, but that resources and common opportunities, most importantly the value of land, belongs equally to all humanity.

His most famous work, *Progress and Poverty* (1879), sold millions of copies worldwide, probably more than any other American book before that time. It is a treatise on inequality, the cyclic nature of industrialized economies, and the use of the land value tax as a remedy.

BIOGRAPHY

Life and Career

George was born in Philadelphia, Pennsylvania, to a lower-middle-class family, the second of ten children of Richard S. H. George and Catharine Pratt (Vallance) George. His father was a publisher of religious texts and a devout Episcopalian, and sent George to the Episcopal Academy in Philadelphia.

George chafed at his religious upbringing and left the academy without graduating.Instead he convinced his father to hire a tutor and supplemented this with avid reading and attending lectures at the Franklin institute. His formal education ended at age 14 and he went to sea as a foremast boy at age 15 in April 1855 on the *Hindoo*, bound for Melbourne and Calcutta.

He ended up in the West in 1858 and briefly considered prospecting for gold but instead started work the same year in San Francisco as a type setter. In California George fell in love with Annie Corsina Fox, an eighteen-year-old girl from Sydney who had been orphaned and was living with an uncle.

The uncle, a prosperous, strong-minded man, was opposed to his niece's impoverished suitor. But the couple, defying him, eloped and married in late 1861, with Henry dressed in a borrowed suit and Annie bringing only a packet of books.

The marriage was a happy one and four children were born to them. Fox's mother was Irish Catholic, and while George remained an Evangelical Protestant, the children were raised Catholic. On November 3, 1862 Annie gave birth to future United States Representative from New York, Henry George, Jr. (1862–1916). Early on, even with the birth of future sculptor, Richard F. George (1865 – September 28, 1912), the family was near starvation.

After deciding against gold mining in British Columbia George was hired as a printer for the newly created San Francisco *Times*, and was able to immediately submit editorials for publication, including the popular *What the Railroads Will Bring Us.*, which remained required reading in California schools for decades. George climbed the ranks of the *Times*, eventually becoming managing editor in the summer of 1867.

George worked for several papers, including four years (1871–1875) as editor of his own newspaper *San Francisco Daily Evening Post* and time running the *Reporter*, a Democratic anti-monopoly publication. The George family struggled but George's increasing reputation and involvement in the newspaper industry lifted them from poverty.

George's other two children were both daughters. The first was Jennie George, (c. 1867–1897), later to become Jennie George Atkinson.George's other daughter was Anna Angela George (b. 1879), who would become mother of both future dancer and choreographer, Agnes de Mille and future actress Peggy George (who was born Margaret George de Mille).

Economic and Political Philosophy

George began as a Lincoln Republican, but then became a Democrat. He was a strong critic of railroad and mining interests, corrupt politicians, land speculators, and labour contractors. He first articulated his views in an 1868 article entitled "What the Railroad Will Bring Us."

George argued that the boom in railroad construction would benefit only the lucky few who owned interests in the railroads and other related enterprises, while throwing the greater part of the population into abject poverty.

This had led to him earning the enmity of the Central Pacific Railroad's executives, who helped defeat his bid for election to the California State Assembly.

One day in 1871 George went for a horseback ride and stopped to rest while overlooking San Francisco Bay. He later wrote of the revelation that he had:

I asked a passing teamster, for want of something better to say, what land was worth there. He pointed to some cows grazing so far off that they looked like mice, and said, 'I don't know exactly, but there is a man over there who will sell some land for a thousand dollars an acre.'

Like a flash it came over me that there was the reason of advancing poverty with advancing wealth. With the growth of population, land grows in value, and the men who work it must pay more for the privilege.

Furthermore, on a visit to New York City, he was struck by the apparent paradox that the poor in that long-established city were much worse off than the poor in less developed California.

These observations supplied the theme and title for his 1879 book *Progress and Poverty*, which was a great success, selling over 3 million copies. In it George made the argument that a sizeable portion of the wealth created by social and technological advances in a free market economy is possessed by land owners and monopolists viaeconomic rents, and that this concentration of unearned wealth is the main cause of poverty.

George considered it a great injustice that private profit was being earned from restricting access to natural resources while productive activity was burdened with heavy taxes, and indicated that such a system was equivalent to slavery – a concept somewhat similar to wage slavery.

This is also the work in which he made the case for a land value tax in which governments would tax the value of the land itself, thus preventing private interests from profiting upon its mere possession, but allowing the value of all improvements made to that land to remain with investors.

George was in a position to discover this pattern, having experienced poverty himself, knowing many different societies from his travels, and living in California at a time of rapid growth. In particular he had noticed that the construction of railroads in California was increasing land values and rents as fast as or faster than wages were rising. In 1880, now a popular writer and speaker, George moved to New York City, becoming closely allied with the Irish nationalist community despite being of English ancestry.

From there he made several speaking journeys abroad to places such as Ireland and Scotland where access to land was (and still is) a major political issue. In 1886 George campaigned for mayor of New York City as the candidate of the United Labour Party, the short-lived political society of the Central Labour Union.

He polled second, more than the Republican candidate Theodore Roosevelt. The election was won by Tammany Hall candidate Abram Stevens Hewitt by what many of George's supporters believed was fraud. In the 1887 New York state elections George came in a distant third in the election for Secretary of State of New York.

The United Labour Party was soon weakened by internal divisions: the management was essentially Georgist, but as a party of organized labour it also included some Marxistmembers who did not want to distinguish between land and capital, many Catholic members who were discouraged by the excommunication of Father Edward McGlynn, and many who disagreed with George's free trade policy.

George had particular trouble with Terrence V. Powderly, president of the Knights of Labour, a key member of the United Labour coalition. While initially friendly with Powderly, George vigorously opposed the tariff policies which Powderly and many other labour leaders thought vital to the protection of American workers.

George's strident criticism of the tariff set him against Powderly and others in the labour movement.

Death

George's first stroke occurred in 1890, after a global speaking tour concerning land rights and the relationship between rent and poverty. This stroke greatly weakened him, and he never truly recovered. Despite this, George tried to remain active in politics.

Against the advice of his doctors, George campaigned for New York City mayor again in 1897, this time as an Independent Democrat. The strain of the campaign precipitated a second stroke, leading to his death four days before the election.

An estimated 100,000 people attended his funeral at Grand Central Palace, with countless more crowding outside and lining the streets of the funeral procession. On Sunday, October 30, 1897, the Reverend Lyman Abbott delivered an address, "Henry George: A Remembrance".

Commentators disagreed on whether it was the largest funeral in New York history or the largest since the death of Abraham Lincoln.

POLICY PROPOSALS

Single Tax on Land

Henry George is best known for his argument that the economic rent of land should be shared by society rather than being owned privately. The clearest statement of this view is found in *Progress and Poverty*: "We must make land common property."

By taxing land values, society could recapture the value of its common inheritance, and eliminate the need for taxes on productive activity. George believed that this would provide disincentives towards land speculation, but would continue to incentivize development, as landlords would not suffer tax penalties for any industry or edifice constructed on their land.

Many environmentalists, such as Bolton Hall and Ralph Borsodi, have agreed with the idea of the earth as the common property of humanity.

The US Green Party platform has endorsed the idea of ecological tax reform, including land value taxation and substantial taxes or fees on pollution as a replacement for "command and control" regulation.

Free Trade

George was opposed to tariffs, which were at the time both the major method of protectionist trade policy and an important source of federal revenue (the federal income taxhaving not yet been introduced).

He believed that tariffs kept prices high for consumers, while failing to produce any increase in wages. He also thought that tariffs protected monopolistic companies from competition, thus augmenting their power. Later in his life, free trade became a major issue in federal politics and his book *Protection or Free Trade* was read into the Congressional Record by five Democratic congressmen.

Secret Ballot

George was one of the earliest, strongest and most prominent advocates for adoption of the secret ballot in the United States. George's first article in support of the secret ballot was entitled "Bribery in Elections" and published in the *Overland Review* of December 1871.

His second article was "Money in Elections," published in the *North American Review* of March 1883. The first state to adopt the secret ballot, also called The Australian Ballot, was Massachusetts in 1888 under the leadership of Richard Henry Dana III.

By 1891, more than half the states had adopted it also. For a more complete discussion of the adoption of the Australian Ballot, see Saltman, Roy G., (2006), *The History and Politics of Voting Technology,* Palgrave Macmillan, NY, pp. 96–103.

Currency and National Debt

George supported the use of government issued paper currency such as the greenback. He opposed the use of metallic currency (such as gold or silver), and money issued by private commercial banks.

Other Proposals

Henry George also proposed the following reforms:

- To have government own and manage all right-of-way "natural" monopolies,
- To dramatically reduce the size of the military,
- To replace contract patronage with the direct employment of government workers, with civil-service protections,
- To make urban public transportation free to the people,
- To extend suffrage to women, and even to have one house of Congress entirely male and the other entirely female.

LEGACY

Henry George's idea known as Georgism had enormous influence in his time but slowly waned throughout the 1900s. Non-etheless, it would be difficult to overstate George's impact on turn of the century reform movements and intellectual culture. George's self-published Progress and Poverty was the first popular economics text and one of the most widely printed books ever written.

The book's explosive world-wide popularity is often marked as the beginning of the Progressive Era and various political parties, clubs, and charitable organizations around the world were founded on George's ideas.

George's message appeals broadly across thepolitical spectrum and has attracted strong support from labour movements, socialists, anarchists, abolitionists, suffragists, middle-class reformers, wealthy industrialists and investors.

As a result, Henry George is still claimed as a primary intellectual influence by both the classical libertarian and socialist movements. Edwin Markham expressed a common sentiment when he said, "Henry George has always been to me one of the supreme heroes of humanity."

A large number of famous individuals, particularly Progressive Era figures, claim inspiration from George's idea, now known asGeorgism. Franklin D. Roosevelt praised George as "one of the really great thinkers produced by our country" and bemoaned the fact that George's writings were not better known and understood.

John Dewey wrote, "It would require less than the fingers of the two hands to enumerate those who from Plato down rank with him," and that "No man, no graduate of a higher educational institution, has a right to regard himself as an educated man in social thought unless he has some first-hand acquaintance with the theoretical contribution of this great American thinker." In 1892, Alfred Russel Wallace stated that George's *Progress and Poverty*was "undoubtedly the most remarkable and important book of the present century." Albert Jay Nock wrote that anyone who rediscovers Henry George will find that "George was one of the first half-dozen [greatest] minds of the nineteenth century, in all the world."

The social scientist and economist John A. Hobson observed in 1897 that "Henry George may be considered to have exercised a more directly powerful formative and educative influence over English radicalism of the last fifteen years than any other man." Many others agree with Hobson.

George Bernard Shaw asserts with first hand knowledge that George was responsible for inspiring 5 out of 6 progressives of the 1880s who would also form socialist organizations such as the Fabian Society. The controversial People's Budget and the *Land Values (Scotland) Bill* were inspired by Henry George and resulted in the Parliament Act 1911 to reform of the House of Lords, which had blocked Georgist land reform. In Denmark, the Danmarks Retsforbund (known in English as the Justice Party or Single-Tax Party) was founded in 1919. The party's platform is based upon the land tax principles of Henry George.

The party was elected to parliament for the first time in 1926, and they were moderately successful in the post-war period and managed to join a governing coalition with the Social Democrats and the Social Liberal Party from the years 1957–60, with diminishing success afterwards.

Non-political means have also been attempted to further the cause. A number of "Single Tax Colonies" were started, such as Arden, Delaware and Fairhope, Alabama. A follower of George, Lizzie Magie, created a board game called The Landlord's Game in 1904 to demonstrate his theories, which later turned into the popular board gameMonopoly.

Henry George's popularity waned gradually during the 20th century. However, there are still Georgist organizations. Many influential people who remain famous, such as George Bernard Shaw, were influenced inspired by George or identify as Georgists. In his last book, *Where do we go from here: Chaos or Community?*, Martin Luther King, Jrreferenced Henry George in support of a guaranteed minimum income.

Bill Moyers has quoted Henry George and identified George as a "great personal hero". Albert Einstein wrote that "Men like Henry George are are rare unfortunately.

One cannot imagine a more beautiful combination of intellectual keenness, artistic form and fervent love of justice. Every line is written as if for our generation. The spreading of these works is a really deserving cause, for our generation especially has many and important things to learn from Henry George."

Before reading *Progress and Poverty*, Helen Keller was a socialist who believed that Georgism was a good step in the right direction. She later wrote of finding "in Henry George's philosophy a rare beauty and power of inspiration, and a splendid faith in the essential nobility of human nature."

The Robert Schalkenbach Foundation publishes copies of George's works and related texts on economic reform and sponsors academic research into his policy proposals. The Lincoln Institute of Land Policy was founded to promote the ideas of Henry George but now focuses more generally on land economics and policy. The Henry George School of Social Science of New York and its satellite schools teach classes and conduct outreach.

Mason Gaffney, an American economist and a major Georgist critic of neo-classical economics, argued that neo-classical economics was designed and promoted by landowners and their hired economists to divert attention from George's extremely popular philosophy that since land and resources are provided by nature, and their value is given by society, land value – rather than labour or capital – should provide the tax base to fund government and its expenditures.

Although both advocated worker's rights, Henry George and Karl Marx were antagonists. Marx saw the Single Tax platform as a step backwards from the transition to communism. On his part, Henry George predicted that if Marx's ideas were tried, the likely result would be a dictatorship.

Henry George Theorem

In 1977, Joseph Stiglitz showed that under certain conditions, spending by the government on public goods will increase aggregate land rents by an equal amount. This result has been dubbed by economists the Henry George Theorem, as it characterizes a situation where Henry George's "single tax" is not only efficient, it is also the only tax necessary to finance public expenditures.

ECONOMIC CONTRIBUTIONS

George developed what he saw as a crucial feature of his own theory of economics in a critique of an illustration used by Frédéric Bastiat in order to explain the nature ofinterest and profit. Bastiat had asked his readers to consider James and William, both carpenters. James has built himself a plane, and has lent it to William for a year.

Would James be satisfied with the return of an equally good plane a year later? Surely not! He'd expect a board along with it, as interest. The basic idea of a theory of interest is to understand why.

Bastiat said that James had given William over that year "the power, inherent in the instrument, to increase the productivity of his labour," and wants compensation for that increased productivity. George did not accept this explanation. He wrote, "I am inclined to think that if all wealth consisted of such things as planes, and all production was such as that of carpenters – that is to say, if wealth consisted but of the inert matter of the universe, and production of working up this inert matter into different shapes – that interest would be but the robbery of industry, and could not long exist."

But some wealth is inherently fruitful, like a pair of breeding cattle, or a vat of grape juice soon to ferment into wine. Planes and other sorts of inert matter (and the most lent item of all – money itself) earn interest indirectly, by being part of the same "circle of exchange" with fruitful forms of wealth such as those, so that tying up these forms of wealth over time incurs an opportunity cost.

George's theory had its share of critiques. Austrian school economist Eugen von Böhm-Bawerk, for example, expressed a negative judgement of George's discussion of the carpenter's plane. In his treatise, *Capital and Interest*, he wrote:

The separation of production into two groups, in one of which the vital forces of nature form a distinct element in addition to labour, while in the other they do not, is entirely untenable[...] The natural sciences have long ago told us that the cooperation of nature is universal. [...] The muscular movement of the man who planes would be of very little use, if the natural powers and properties of the steel edge of the plane did not come to his assistance.

Later, George argued that the role of time in production is pervasive. In *The Science of Political Economy*, he writes:

[I]f I go to a builder and say to him, "In what time and at what price will you build me such and such a house?" he would, after thinking, name a time, and a price based on it.

This specification of time would be essential.... This I would soon find if, not quarreling with the price, I ask him largely to lessen the time.... I might get the builder somewhat to lessen the time... ; but only by greatly increasing the price, until finally a point would be reached where he would not consent to build the house in less time no matter at what price. He would say [that the house just could not be built any faster].

The importance... of this principle – that all production of wealth requires time as well as labour – we shall see later on; but the principle that time is a necessary element in all production we must take into account from the very first.

According to Oscar B. Johannsen, "Since the very basis of the Austrian concept of value is subjective, it is apparent that George's understanding of value paralleled theirs. However, he either did not understand or did not appreciate the importance of marginal utility."

Another spirited response came from British biologist T.H. Huxley in his article "Capital – the Mother of Labour," published in 1890 in the journal *The Nineteenth Century*. Huxley used the principles of energy science to undermine George's theory, arguing that, energetically speaking, labour is unproductive.

HERBERT SIMON

Herbert Alexander Simon (June 15, 1916 – February 9, 2001) was an American political scientist, economist, sociologist,psychologist, and professor—most notably at Carnegie Mellon University—whose research ranged across the fields of cognitive psychology, cognitive science, computer science, public administration, economics, management, philosophy of science, sociology, and political science.

With almost a thousand highly cited publications, he was one of the most influential social scientists of the twentieth century.

Simon was among the founding fathers of several of today's important scientific domains, including artificial intelligence, information processing, decision-making, problem-solving, attention economics, organization theory, complex systems, and computer simulation of scientific discovery.

He coined the terms *bounded rationality* and *satisficing*, and was the first to analyze the architecture of complexity and to propose apreferential attachment mechanism to explain power law distributions.

He also received many top-level honours later in life. These include: becoming a fellow of the American Academy of Arts and Sciences in 1959; election to the National Academy of Sciences in 1967; the ACM's Turing Award for making "basic contributions to artificial intelligence, the psychology of human cognition, and list processing" (1975); the Nobel Memorial Prize in Economics "for his pioneering research into the decision-making process within economic organizations" (1978); the National Medal of Science (1986); and the APA's Award for Outstanding Lifetime Contributions to Psychology (1993).

As a testament to his interdisciplinary approach, Simon was affiliated with such varied Carnegie Mellon departments as the School of Computer Science, Tepper School of Business, departments of Philosophy, Social and Decision Sciences, and Psychology. Simon received an honourary Doctor of Political science degree from University of Pavia in 1988 and an honourary Doctor of Laws(LL.D.) degree from Harvard University in 1990.

EARLY LIFE AND EDUCATION

Herbert Alexander Simon was born in Milwaukee, Wisconsin on June 15, 1916. His father, Arthur Simon (1881–1948), was an electrical engineer who had come to the United States from Germany in 1903 after earning his engineering degree from theTechnische Hochschule of Darmstadt. An inventor who was granted "several dozen patents", his father also was an independent patent attorney.

Herbert's mother, Edna Marguerite Merkel, was an accomplished pianist whose ancestors had come fromPrague and Cologne. Herbert's European ancestors had been piano makers, goldsmiths, and vintners. Simon's father was

Jewish and his mother came from a family with Jewish, Lutheran, and Catholic backgrounds. Simon called himself an atheist.

Herbert Simon was educated as a child in the public school system in Milwaukee where he developed an interest in science. He found schoolwork to be interesting, but rather easy.

Unlike many children, Simon was exposed to the idea that human behaviour could be studied scientifically at a relatively young age due to the influence of his mother's younger brother, Harold Merkel, who had studied economics at the University of Wisconsin–Madison under John R. Commons.

Through his uncle's books on economics and psychology, Simon discovered the social sciences.

Among his earliest influences, Simon has cited Richard Ely's economics textbook, Norman Angell's *The Great Illusion*, and Henry George's *Progress and Poverty*. In 1933, Simon entered the University of Chicago, and following those early influences, he studied the social sciences and mathematics. He was interested in biology, but chose not to study it because of his "colour-blindness and awkwardness in the laboratory".

He chose instead to focus on political science and economics. His most important mentor at the University was Henry Schultz who was an econometrician and mathematical economist.

Simon received both his B.A. (1936) and his Ph.D. (1943) in political science, from the University of Chicago, where he studied under Harold Lasswell and Charles Edward Merriam.

After enrolling in a course on "Measuring Municipal Governments," Simon was invited to be a research assistant for Clarence Ridley, with whom he coauthored the book,*Measuring Municipal Activities*, in 1938, the same year that he and Dorothea married. Eventually his studies led him to the field of organizational decision-making, which would become the subject of his doctoral dissertation.

ACADEMIC CAREER

From 1939 to 1942, Simon acted as director of a research group at the University of California, Berkeley. When the grant to the group was exhausted, he joined the faculty ofIllinois Institute of Technology, where he was a professor of political science from 1942 to 1949 and also served as department chairman.

Back in Chicago, he began participating in the seminars held by the staff of the Cowles Commission who at that time included Trygve Haavelmo, Jacob Marschak, and Tjalling Koopmans.

He thus began a more in-depth study of economics in the area of institutionalism. Marschak brought Simon in to assist in the study he was currently undertaking with Sam Schurr of the "prospective economic effects of atomic energy". In 1949, Simon became a professor of administration and chairman of the Department of Industrial Management at Carnegie Tech (later to become Carnegie Mellon University).

Until his death in 2001, he continued to teach in various departments at Carnegie Mellon, including psychology and computer science, and occasionally was a visiting fellow at one or more other universities.

From 1950 to 1955, Simon studied mathematical economics and during this time, together with David Hawkins, discovered and proved the Hawkins–Simon theorem on the "conditions for the existence of positive solution vectors for input-output matrices."

He also developed theorems on near-decomposability and aggregation. Having begun to apply these theorems to organizations, by 1954 Simon determined that the best way to study problem-solving was to simulate it with computer programmes, which led to his interest in computer simulation of human cognition. Founded during the 1950s, he was among the first members of the Society for General Systems Research.

Simon had a keen interest in the arts. He was a friend of Robert Lepper and Richard Rappaport. Rappaport also painted Simon's commissioned portrait at Carnegie Mellon University.

In January 2001, Simon underwent surgery at UPMC Presbyterian to remove a cancerous tumor in his abdomen. Although the surgery was successful, Simon later succumbed to the complications that followed.

STUDY OF DECISION-MAKING

Administrative Behaviour, from 1947, was based on Simon's doctoral dissertation. It served as the foundation for his life's work. The centerpiece of this book is the behavioural and cognitive processes of making rational human choices, that is, decisions.

By his definition, an operational administrative decision should be correct and efficient, and it must be practical to implement with a set of coordinated means.

Any such decision involves a choice selected from a number of alternatives, directed towards an organizational goal or subgoal. Realistic options were defined as having real consequences consisting of personnel actions or non-actions modified by environmental facts and values.

In practice, some of the alternatives may be conscious or unconscious; some of the consequences may be unintended as well as intended; and some of the means and ends may be imperfectly differentiated, incompletely related, or poorly detailed.

The task of rational decision making is to select the alternative that results in the more preferred set of all the possible consequences. This task may be divided into three required steps:

- The identification and listing of all the alternatives;
- The determination of all the consequences resulting from each of the alternatives; and
- the comparison of the accuracy and efficiency of each of these sets of consequences.

Any given individual or organization attempting to implement this model in a real situation would be unable to comply with the three requirements. It is highly improbable that one could know all the alternatives, or all the consequences that follow each alternative.

The resulting question would be: given the inevitable limits on rational decision making, what other techniques or behavioural processes can a person or organization bring to bear to achieve approximately the best result? Simon writes:

The human being striving for rationality and restricted within the limits of his knowledge has developed some working procedures that partially overcome these difficulties. These procedures consist in assuming that he can isolate from the rest of the world a closed system containing a limited number of variables and a limited range of consequences.

Administrative Behaviour, as a text, addresses a wide range of human behaviours, cognitive abilities, management techniques, personnel policies, training goals and procedures, specialized roles, criteria for evaluation of accuracy and efficiency, and all of the ramifications of communication processes. Simon is particularly interested in how these factors directly and indirectly influence the making of decisions.

Weaving in and out of the practical functioning of all of these organizational factors are two universal elements of human social behaviour that Simon addresses in Chapter VII—The Role of Authority, and in Chapter X—Loyalties, and Organizational Identification.

Authority is a well studied, primary mark of organizational behaviour, and is straightforwardly defined in the organizational context as the ability and right of an individual of higher rank to determine the decision of an individual of lower rank.

The actions, attitudes, and relationships of the dominant and subordinate individuals constitute components of role behaviour that may vary widely in form, style, and content, but do not vary in the expectation of obedience by the one of superior status, and willingness to obey from the subordinate.

Authority is highly influential on the formal structure of the organization, including patterns of communication, sanctions, and rewards, as well as on the establishment of goals, objectives, and values of the organization.

Decisions can be complex admixtures of facts and values. Information about facts, especially empirically-proven facts or facts derived from specialized experience, are more easily transmitted in the exercise of authority than are the expressions of values. Simon is primarily interested in seeking identification of the individual employee with the organizational goals and values. Following Lasswell, he states that "a person identifies himself with a group when, in making a decision, he evaluates the several alternatives of choice in terms of their consequences for the specified group".

A person may identify himself with any number of social, geographic, economic, racial, religious, familial, educational, gender, political, and sports groups. Indeed, the number and variety are unlimited.

The fundamental problem for organizations is to recognize t personal and group identifications may either facilitate or obstruct correct decision making for the organization. A specific organization has to determine deliberately, and specify in appropriate detail and clear language, its own goals, objectives, means, ends, and values.

Chester Barnard pointed out that "the decisions that an individual makes as a member of an organization are quite distinct from his personal decisions". Personal choices may be determined whether an individual joins a particular organization, and continue to be made in his or her extra–organizational private life.

As a member of an organization, however, that individual makes decisions not in relationship to personal needs and results, but in an impersonal sense as part of the organizational intent, purpose, and effect. Organizational inducements, rewards, and sanctions are all designed to form, strengthen, and maintain this identification. The correctness of administrative decisions is measured by two major criteria:

- Adequacy of achieving the desired objective; and
- The efficiency with which the result was obtained. Many members of the organization may focus on adequacy, but the overall administrative management must pay particular attention to the efficiency with which the desired result was obtained.

Simon's contributions to research in the area of administrative decision-making have become increasingly mainstream in the business community thanks to the growth of management consulting.

ARTIFICIAL INTELLIGENCE AND PSYCHOLOGY

Simon was a pioneer in the field of artificial intelligence, creating with Allen Newell the Logic Theory Machine (1956) and the General Problem Solver (GPS) (1957) programmes.

GPS may possibly be the first method developed for separating problem solving strategy from information about particular problems. Both programmes were developed using theInformation Processing Language (IPL) (1956) developed by Newell, Cliff Shaw, and Simon.

Donald Knuth mentions the development of list processing in IPL, with the linked listoriginally called "NSS memory" for its inventors. In 1957, Simon predicted that computer chess would surpass human chess abilities within "ten years" when, in reality, that transition took about forty years.

In the early 1960s psychologist Ulric Neisser asserted that while machines are capable of replicating 'cold cognition' behaviours such as reasoning, planning, perceiving, and deciding, they would never be able to replicate 'hot cognition' behaviours such as pain, pleasure, desire, and other emotions.

Simon responded to Neisser's views in 1963 by writing a paper on emotional cognition, which he updated in 1967 and published in *Psychological Review*.

Simon's work on emotional cognition was largely ignored by the artificial intelligence research community for several years, but subsequent work on emotions by Sloman and Picard helped refocus attention on Simon's paper and eventually, made it highly influential on the topic. Simon also collaborated with James G. March on several works in organization theory.

With Allen Newell, Simon developed a theory for the simulation of human problem solving behaviour using production rules. The study of human problem solving required new kinds of human measurements and, with Anders Ericsson, Simon developed the experimental technique of verbal protocol analysis.

Simon was interested in the role of knowledge in expertise. He said that to become an expert on a topic required about ten years of experience and he and colleagues estimated that expertise was the result of learning roughly 50,000 chunks of information. A chess expert was said to have learned about 50,000 chunks or chess position patterns.

Simon also was interested in how humans learn and, with Edward Feigenbaum, he developed the EPAM (Elementary Perceiver and Memorizer) theory, one of the first theories of learning to be implemented as a computer programme. EPAM was able to explain a large number of phenomena in the field of verbal learning.

Later versions of the model were applied to concept formation and the acquisition of expertise. With Fernand Gobet, he has expanded the EPAM theory into the CHREST computational model. The theory explains how simple chunks of information form the building blocks of schemata, which are more complex structures. CHREST has been used predominantly, to simulate aspects of chess expertise.

He was awarded the ACM A.M. Turing Award along with Allen Newell in 1975. "In joint scientific efforts extending over twenty years, initially in collaboration with J. C. (Cliff) Shawat the RAND Corporation, and subsequentially [*sic*] with numerous faculty and student colleagues at Carnegie Mellon University, they have made basic contributions to artificial intelligence, the psychology of human cognition, and list processing."

SOCIOLOGY AND ECONOMICS

Herbert Simon has been credited for revolutionary changes in microeconomics. He is responsible for the concept of organizational decision-making as it is known today.

He also was the first to discuss this concept in terms of uncertainty; *i.e.* it is impossible to have perfect and complete information at any given time to make a decision. While this notion was not entirely new, Simon is best known for its origination. It was in this area that he was awarded the Nobel Prize in 1978.

At the Cowles Commission, Simon's main goal was to link economic theory to mathematics and statistics. His main contributions were to the fields of general equilibrium andeconometrics. He was greatly influenced by the marginalist debate that began in the 1930s.

The popular work of the time argued that it was not apparent empirically that entrepreneurs needed to follow the marginalist principles of profit-maximization/cost-minimization in running organizations.

The argument went on to note that profit-maximization was not accomplished, in part, because of the lack of complete information. In decision-making, Simon believed that agents face uncertainty about the future and costs in acquiring information in the present.

These factors limit the extent to which agents may make a fully rational decision, thus they possess only "bounded rationality" and must make decisions by "satisficing," or choosing that which might not be optimal, but which will make them happy enough.

Simon was known for his research on industrial organization. He determined that the internal organization of firms and the external business decisions thereof, did not conform to the Neo-classical theories of "rational" decision-making. Simon wrote many articles on the topic over the course of his life mainly focusing on the issue of decision-making within the behaviour of what he termed "bounded rationality".

"Rational behaviour, in economics, means that individuals maximize their utility function under the constraints they face (*e.g.*, their budget constraint, limited choices,...) in pursuit of their self-interest. This is reflected in the theory of subjective expected utility.

The term, bounded rationality, is used to designate rational choice that takes into account the cognitive limitations of both knowledge and cognitive capacity.

Bounded rationality is a central theme in behavioural economics. It is concerned with the ways in which the actual decision-making process influences decisions. Theories of bounded rationality relax one or more assumptions of standard expected utility theory". Simon determined that the best way to study these areas was through computer simulation modeling. As such, he developed an interest in computer science. Herbert Simon's main interests in computer science were in artificial intelligence, human-computer interaction, principles of the organization of humans and machines as information processing systems, the use of computers to study (by modeling) philosophical problems of the nature of intelligence and of epistemology, and the social implications of computer technology.

Some of Simon's economic research was directed towards understanding technological change in general and the information processing revolution in particular.

PEDAGOGY

Simon's work has strongly influenced John Mighton, developer of a programme that has achieved significant success in improving mathematics performance among elementary and high school students.

Mighton cites a 2000 paper by Simon and two co-authors that counters arguments by French mathematics educator, Guy Brousseau, and others suggesting that excessive practice hampers children's understanding:

The criticism of practice (called 'drill and kill,' as if this phrase constituted empirical evaluation) is prominent in constructivist writings. Nothing flies more in the face of the last 20 years of research than the assertion that practice is bad.

All evidence, from the laboratory and from extensive case studies of professionals, indicates that real competence only comes with extensive practice. In denying the critical role of practice one is denying children the very thing they need to achieve real competence.

The instructional task is not to 'kill' motivation by demanding drill, but to find tasks that provide practice while at the same time sustaining interest.

— John R. Anderson, Lynne M. Reder, and Herbert A. Simon, 'Applications and misapplications of cognitive psychology to mathematics education', *Texas Educational Review* 6 (2000)

CRITICISM

In the 1972 book "What Computers Can't Do", the American philosopher Hubert Dreyfus criticized Simon for claiming that the computer programmes of the day already exhibited intelligent behaviour.

Dreyfus also criticized Simon's optimism about the eventual success of AI as a result of a psychological theory of heuristics.

This critique was partly based on the phenomenological claim that certain forms of intelligent human behaviour can not be reduced to rule following. For a more detailed summary of the criticism, see Hubert Dreyfus's views on artificial intelligence.

PERSONAL INFORMATION

For 63 years Simon was married to Dorothea and they had three children, Katherine, Peter, and Barbara. His wife died in 2002, during the year following his death in 2001.

JAMES TOBIN

James Tobin (March 5, 1918 – March 11, 2002) was an American economist who, in his lifetime, served on the Council of Economic Advisors and the Board of Governors of the Federal Reserve System, and taught at Harvard and Yale Universities. He developed the ideas of Keynesian economics, and advocated government intervention to stabilize output and avoid recessions.

His academic work included pioneering contributions to the study of investment, monetary and fiscal policy and financial markets. He also proposed an econometric model for censored endogenous variables, the well-known "Tobit model". Tobin received the Nobel Memorial Prize in Economic Sciences in 1981.

Outside of academia, Tobin was widely known for his suggestion of a tax on foreign exchange transactions, now known as the "Tobin tax". This was designed to reduce speculation in the international currency markets, which he saw as dangerous and unproductive.

LIFE AND CAREER

Early Life

Tobin was born on March 5, 1918 in Champaign, Illinois. His father was Louis Michael Tobin, (b. 1879) a journalist working at theUniversity of Illinois at Urbana-Champaign.

His father had fought in World War I, was a member of the first Greek Organization at Illinois (Delta Tau Delta fraternity Beta Upsilon chapter), and was credited as the inventor of 'Homecoming'. His mother, Margaret Edgerton Tobin (b. 1893), was a social worker.

Tobin followed primary school at the University Laboratory High School of Urbana, Illinois, a laboratory school in the university's campus.

In 1935, on his father's advice, Tobin took the entrance exams for Harvard University. Despite no special preparation for the exams, he passed and was admitted with a national scholarship from the university.

Here among the faculty he would meet Joseph Schumpeter, Alvin Hansen, Gottfried Haberler,Sumner Slichter, Seymour Harris, Edward Mason, Edward Chamberlin, John Kenneth Galbraith and Wassily Leontief. During his studies he first read Keynes' *The General Theory of Employment, Interest and Money*, published in 1936. Tobin graduated summa cum laude in

1939 with a thesis centered on a critical analysis of Keynes' mechanism for introducing equilibrium "involuntary" unemployment. His first published article, in 1941, was based on this senior's thesis.

Tobin immediately started graduate studies, also at Harvard, earning his M.A. degree in 1940. His fellow graduate students included Paul Samuelson, Lloyd Metzler, Abram Bergson, Richard Musgrave and Richard M. Goodwin.

In 1941, he interrupted graduate studies to work for the Office of Price Administration and Civilian Supply and the War Production Board in Washington, D.C..

The next year, after the United States entered World War II, he enrolled in the US Navy, spending the war as an officer on a destroyer. At the end of the war he returned to Harvard and resumed studies, receiving his Ph.D. in 1947 with a thesis on the consumption function written under the supervision of Joseph Schumpeter.

In 1947 Tobin was elected a Junior Fellow of Harvard's Society of Fellows, which allowed him the freedom and funding to spend the next three years studying and doing research.

Academic Activity and Consultancy

In 1950 Tobin moved to Yale University, where he remained for the rest of his career. He joined the Cowles Foundation, which moved to Yale in 1955, also serving as its president between 1955–1961 and 1964-1965. His main research interest was to provide microfoundations to Keynesian economics, with a special focus on monetary economics. In 1957 he was appointed Sterling Professor at Yale.

Besides teaching and research, Tobin was also strongly involved in the public life, writing on current economic issues and serving as an economic expert and policy consultant. During 1961–62, he served as a member of John F. Kennedy's Council of Economic Advisors, under the chairman Walter Heller, then acted as a consultant between 1962–68.

Here, in close collaboration with Arthur Okun, Robert Solow and Kenneth Arrow, he helped design the Keynesian economic policy implemented by the Kennedy administration. Tobin also served for several terms as a member of the Board of Governors of Federal Reserve System Academic Consultants and as a consultant of the US Treasury Department.

Tobin was awarded the John Bates Clark Medal in 1955 and, in 1981, the Nobel Memorial Prize in Economics. He was a fellow of several professional associations, holding the position of president of the American Economic Association in 1971. In 1972 Tobin, along with fellow Yale economics professor William Nordhaus, published *Is Growth Obsolete?*, an article that introduced the Measure of Economic Welfare as the first model for economic sustainability assessment, and economic sustainability measurement.

In 1988 Tobin formally retired from Yale, but continued to deliver some lectures as Professor Emeritus and continued to write. He died on March 11, 2002, in New Haven, Connecticut. Tobin was a trustee of Economists for Peace and Security.

Personal life

James Tobin married Elizabeth Fay Ringo, a former M.I.T. student of Paul Samuelson, on September 14, 1946. They had four children: Margaret Ringo (born in 1948), Louis Michael (born in 1951), Hugh Ringo (born in 1953) and Roger Gill (born in 1956). In late June, 2009, the family announced via a private e-mail that Tobin's wife had died at the age of 90.

Legacy

In August 2009 in a roundtable interview in Prospect magazine, Adair Turner supported the idea of new global taxes on financial transactions, warning that the "swollen" financial sector paying excessive salaries had grown too big for society. Lord Turner's suggestion that a "Tobin tax" – named after James Tobin – should be considered for financial transactions made headlines around the world.

Tobin's Tobit model of regression with censored endogenous variables (Tobin 1958a) is a standard econometric technique. His "q" theory of investment, theBaumol-Tobin model of the transactions demand for money (Tobin 1956), and his model of liquidity preference as behaviour towards risk (the asset demand for money) (Tobin 1958b) are all staples of economics textbooks.

In his 1958 article Tobin also led the way in showing how to deal with utility maximization under uncertainty with an infinite number of possible states. As Palda explains "One way to get out of the mess of figuring out asset prices using a model of maximizing the expected utility of investing in stocks is to make assumptions about either preferences or the probabilities of the different possible states of the world.

Nobellist James Tobin (1958) took this line and discovered that in some cases you do not need to worry about the utility of income in thousands of states, and the attached probabilities, to solve the consumer's choice on how to spread income among states.

When preferences contain only a linear and a squared term (a case of diminishing returns) or the probabilities of different stock returns follow a normal distribution (an equation that contains a linear and squared terms as parameters), a simple formulation of a person's investment choices becomes possible. Under Tobin's assumptions we can reformulate the person's decision problem as being one of trading off risk and expected return. Risk, or more precisely the variance of your investment portfolio creates spread in the returns you expect. People are willing to assume more risk only if compensated by a higher level of expected return.

One can thus think of a tradeoff people are willing to make between risk and expected return. They invest in risky assets to the point at which their willingness to trade off risk and return is equal to the rate at which they able to trade them off. It is difficult to exaggerate how brilliant is the simplification of the investment problem that flows from these assumptions. Instead of worrying about the investor's optimization problem in potentially millions of possible states of the world, one need only worry about how the investor can trade off risk and return in the stock market."

JAN TINBERGEN

Jan Tinbergen (April 12, 1903 – June 9, 1994) was a Dutch economist. He was awarded the first Bank of Sweden Prize in Economic Sciences in Memory of Alfred Nobel in 1969, which he shared with Ragnar Frisch for having developed and applied dynamic models for the analysis of economic processes. Tinbergen was a founding trustee of Economists for Peace and Security.

BIOGRAPHY

Jan Tinbergen was the eldest of five children of Dirk Cornelis Tinbergen and Jeannette van Eek. His brother Nikolaas "Niko" Tinbergen would also win a Nobel Prize (for physiology, during 1973) for his work in ethology, while his youngest brother Luukwould become a famous ornithologist. Between 1921 and 1925, Tinbergen studied mathematics and physics at the University of Leiden under Paul Ehrenfest. During those years at Leiden he had numerous discussions with Ehrenfest, Kamerlingh Onnes,Hendrik Lorentz, Pieter Zeeman, and Albert Einstein.

After graduating, Tinbergen fulfilled his community service in the administration of a prison in Rotterdam and at the Central Bureau of Statistics (CBS) in The Hague. He then returned to the University of Leiden and in 1929 defended his PhD thesis titled "Minimumproblemen in de natuurkunde en de economie" (Minimisation problems in Physics and Economics).

This topic was suggested by Ehrenfest and allowed Tinbergen to combine his interests in mathematics, physics, economics and politics. At that time, CBS established a new department of business surveys and mathematical statistics, and Tinbergen became its first chairman, working at CBS until 1945.

Access to the vast CBS data helped Tinbergen in testing his theoretical models. In parallel, starting from 1931 he was professor of statistics at the University of Amsterdam, and in 1933 he was appointed associate professor of mathematics and statistics at The Netherlands School of Economics, Rotterdam, where he stayed until 1973.

From 1929 to 1945 he worked for the Dutch statistical office and briefly served as consultant to the League of Nations (1936–1938). In 1945 he became the first director of the Netherlands Bureau for Economic Policy Analysis and left this position in 1955 to focus on education.

He spent one year as a visiting professor at the Harvard University and then returned to the Dutch Economic Institute (the successor of the Netherlands School of Economics).

In parallel, he provided consulting services to international organizations and governments of various developing countries, such as United Arab Republic, Turkey, Venezuela, Surinam, Indonesia and Pakistan.

Tinbergen was a member of the Royal Netherlands Academy of Arts and Science and of the International Academy of Science. In 1956 he founded the Econometric Institute at the Erasmus Universiteit Rotterdam together with Henri Theil, who also was his successor in Rotterdam. The Tinbergen Institute was named in his honour. The International Institute of Social Studies (ISS) awarded its Honourary Fellowship to Jan Tinbergen in 1962.

WORK

Tinbergen became known for his 'Tinbergen Norm', which is the principle that, if the ratio between the greatest and least income in a company exceeds 5, it will not help the company and may be counterproductive.

Tinbergen developed the first national comprehensive macroeconomic model, which he first developed in 1936 for the Netherlands, and later applied to the United States and the United Kingdom.

In his work on macroeconomic modelling and economic policy making, Tinbergen classified some economic quantities as *targets* and others as *instruments*. Targets are those macroeconomic variables the policy maker wishes to influence, whereas instruments are the variables that the policy maker can control directly. Tinbergen emphasized that achieving the desired values of a certain number of targets requires the policy maker to control an equal number of instruments.

Tinbergen's classification remains influential today, underlying the theory of monetary policy used by central banks. Many central banks today regard the inflation rate as their target; the policy instrument they use to control inflation is the short-term interest rate.

Tinbergen's work on macroeconomic models was later continued by Lawrence Klein, contributing to another Nobel Memorial Prize in Economic Sciences. For his cultural contributions, he was given the Gouden Ganzenveer in 1985. Tinbergen's econometric modelling lead to a lively debate with well several known participants including J.M. Keynes, Ragnar

Frisch and Milton Friedman. The debate is sometime referred to as the Tinbergen debate.

JEREMY BENTHAM

Jeremy Bentham (15 February [O.S. 4 February] 1748 – 6 June 1832) was a British philosopher, jurist, and social reformer. He is regarded as the founder of modern utilitarianism.

Bentham became a leading theorist in Anglo-American philosophy of law, and a political radical whose ideas influenced the development of welfarism. He advocated individual and economic freedom, the separation of church and state, freedom of expression, equal rights for women, the right to divorce, and the decriminalising of homosexual acts.

He called for the abolition of slavery, the abolition of the death penalty, and the abolition of physical punishment, including that of children. He has also become known in recent years as an early advocate of animal rights.

Though strongly in favour of the extension of individual legal rights, he opposed the idea of natural law and natural rights, calling them "non-sense upon stilts".

Bentham's students included his secretary and collaborator James Mill, the latter's son, John Stuart Mill, the legal philosopher John Austin, as well as Robert Owen, one of the founders of utopian socialism. Bentham has been described as the "spiritual founder" ofUniversity College London, though he played little direct part in its foundation.

LIFE

Bentham was born in Houndsditch, London, into a wealthy family that supported the Tory party. He was reportedly a child prodigy: he was found as a toddler sitting at his father's desk reading a multi-volume history of England, and he began to study Latin at the age of three. He had one surviving sibling, Samuel Bentham, with whom he shared a close bond.

He attended Westminster School and, in 1760, at age 12, was sent by his father to The Queen's College, Oxford, where he completed his Bachelor's degree in 1763 and his Master's degree in 1766. He trained as a lawyer and, though he never practised, was called to the bar in 1769. He became deeply frustrated with the complexity of the English legal code, which he termed the "Demon of Chicane".

When the American colonies published their Declaration of Independence in July 1776, the British government did not issue any official response but instead secretly commissioned London lawyer and pamphleteer John Lind to publish a rebuttal. His 130-page tract was distributed in the colonies and contained an essay titled "Short Review of the Declaration" written by Bentham, a friend of Lind's, which attacked and mocked the

Americans' political philosophy. Among his many proposals for legal and social reform was a design for a prison building he called the Panopticon. He spent some sixteen years of his life developing and refining his ideas for the building, and hoped that the government would adopt the plan for a National Penitentiary, and appoint him as contractor-governor.

Although the prison was never built, the concept had an important influence on later generations of thinkers. Twentieth-century French philosopher Michel Foucault argued that the Panopticon was paradigmatic of several 19th-century "disciplinary" institutions.

Bentham became convinced that his plans for the Panopticon had been thwarted by the King and an aristocratic elite acting in their own interests. It was largely because of his brooding sense of injustice that he developed his ideas of "sinister interest" – that is, of the vested interests of the powerful conspiring against a wider public interest – which underpinned many of his broader arguments for reform.

More successful was his cooperation with Patrick Colquhoun in tackling the corruption in the Pool of London. This resulted in the Thames Police Bill of 1798, which was passed in 1800. The bill created the Thames River Police, which was the first preventive police force in the country and was a precedent for Robert Peel's reforms 30 years later.

Bentham was in correspondence with many influential people. Adam Smith, for example, opposed free interest rates before he was made aware of Bentham's arguments on the subject. As a result of his correspondence with Mirabeau and other leaders of the French Revolution, Bentham was declared an honourary citizen of France. He was an outspoken critic of the revolutionary discourse of natural rights and of the violence that arose after the Jacobins took power (1792). Between 1808 and 1810, he held a personal friendship with Latin American Independence Precursor Francisco de Miranda and paid visits to Miranda's Grafton Way house in London.

In 1823, he co-founded the *Westminster Review* with James Mill as a journal for the "Philosophical Radicals" – a group of younger disciples through whom Bentham exerted considerable influence in British public life. One such young writer was Edwin Chadwick, who wrote on hygiene, sanitation and policing and was a major contributor to thePoor Law Amendment Act. Bentham employed him as a secretary and bequeathed him a large legacy.

An insight into his character is given in Michael St. John Packe's *The Life of John Stuart Mill*:

During his youthful visits to Bowood House, the country seat of his patron Lord Lansdowne, he had passed his time at falling unsuccessfully in love with all the ladies of the house, whom he courted with a clumsy jocularity, while playing chess with them or giving them lessons on the harpsichord. Hopeful to the last, at the age of eighty he wrote again to one of them, recalling to her memory the far-off days when she had "presented him, in ceremony, with the flower in the green lane" [citing Bentham's memoirs]. To the end of his life he could not hear of Bowood without tears swimming in his eyes, and he was forced to exclaim, "Take me forward, I entreat you, to the future – do not let me go back to the past."

A psychobiographical study by Philip Lucas and Anne Sheeran argues that he may have had Asperger's syndrome.

DEATH AND THE AUTO-ICON

Bentham died on 6 June 1832 aged 84 at his residence in Queen Square Place in Westminster, London. He had continued to write up to a month before his death, and had made careful preparations for the dissection of his body after death and its preservation as an auto-icon.

As early as 1769, when Bentham was just twenty-one years old, he made a will leaving his body for dissection to a family friend, the physician and chemist George Fordyce, whose daughter, Maria Sophia (1765–1858), married Jeremy's brother Samuel Bentham. A paper written in 1830, instructing Thomas Southwood Smith to create the auto-icon, was attached to his last will, dated 30 May 1832.

On 8 June 1832, two days after his death, invitations were distributed to a select group of friends, and on the following day at 3 p.m., Southwood Smith delivered a lengthy oration over Bentham's remains in the Webb Street School of Anatomy & Medicine in Southwark, London. The printed oration contains a frontispiece with an engraving of Bentham's body partly covered by a sheet.

Afterwards, the skeleton and head were preserved and stored in a wooden cabinet called the "Auto-icon", with the skeleton padded out with hay and dressed in Bentham's clothes.

Originally kept by his disciple Thomas Southwood Smith, it was acquired by University College London in 1850. It is normally kept on public display at the end of the South Cloisters in the main building of the college; however, for the 100th and 150th anniversaries of the college, and in 2013, it was brought to the meeting of the College Council, where it was listed as "present but not voting".

Bentham had intended the Auto-icon to incorporate his actual head, mummified to resemble its appearance in life. However, Southwood Smith's experimental efforts at mummification, based on practices of the indigenous people of New Zealand and involving placing the head under an air pump over sulphuric acid and simply drawing off the fluids, although technically successful, left the head looking distastefully macabre, with dried and darkened skin stretched tautly over the skull.

The Auto-icon was therefore given a wax head, fitted with some of Bentham's own hair. The real head was displayed in the same case as the Auto-icon for many years, but became the target of repeatedstudent pranks. It is now locked away securely. A 360-degree rotatable, high-resolution 'Virtual Auto-Icon' is available at the UCL Bentham Project's web site.

WORK

Utilitarianism

Bentham's ambition in life was to create a "Pannomion", a complete utilitarian code of law. He not only proposed many legal and social reforms, but also expounded an underlying moral principle on which they should be based.

This philosophy of utilitarianism took for its "fundamental axiom", *it is the greatest happiness of the greatest number that is the measure of right and wrong*". Bentham claimed to have borrowed this concept from the writings of Joseph Priestley, although the closest that Priestley in fact came to expressing it was in the form "the good and happiness of the members, that is the majority of the members of any state, is the great standard by which every thing relating to that state must finally be determined".

The "greatest happiness principle", or the principle of utility, forms the cornerstone of all Bentham's thought. By "happiness", he understood a predominance of "pleasure" over "pain". He wrote in *The Principles of Morals and Legislation*:

Nature has placed mankind under the governance of two sovereign masters, pain and pleasure. It is for them alone to point out what we ought to do, as well as to determine what we shall do.

On the one hand the standard of right and wrong, on the other the chain of causes and effects, are fastened to their throne. They govern us in all we do, in all we say, in all we think...

He also suggested a procedure for estimating the moral status of any action, which he called the Hedonistic or felicific calculus. Utilitarianism was revised and expanded by Bentham's student John Stuart Mill. In Mill's hands, "Benthamism" became a major element in the liberal conception of state policy objectives.

In his exposition of the felicific calculus, Bentham proposed a classification of 12 pains and 14 pleasures, by which we might test the "happiness factor" of any action.Non-etheless, it should not be overlooked that Bentham's "hedonistic" theory (a term from J.J.C. Smart), unlike Mill's, is often criticized for lacking a principle of fairness embodied in a conception of justice.

In *Bentham and the Common Law Tradition*, Gerald J. Postema states: "No moral concept suffers more at Bentham's hand than the concept of justice. There is no sustained, mature analysis of the notion..." Thus, some critics object, it would be acceptable to torture one person if this would produce an amount of happiness in other people outweighing the unhappiness of the tortured individual. However, as P.J. Kelly argued in *Utilitarianism and Distributive Justice: Jeremy Bentham and the Civil Law*, Bentham had a theory of justice that prevented such consequences. According to Kelly, for Bentham the law "provides the basic framework of social interaction by delimiting spheres of personal inviolability within which individuals can form and pursue their own conceptions of well-being".

It provides security, a precondition for the formation of expectations. As the hedonic calculus shows "expectation utilities" to be much higher than natural ones, it follows that Bentham does not favour the sacrifice of a few to the benefit of the many.

Bentham's *An Introduction to the Principles of Morals and Legislation* focuses on the principle of utility and how this view of morality ties into legislative practices.

His principle of utility regards "good" as that which produces the greatest amount of pleasure and the minimum amount of pain and "evil" as that which produces the most pain without the pleasure. This concept of pleasure and pain is defined by Bentham as physical as well as spiritual. Bentham writes about this principle as it manifests itself within the legislation of a society.

He lays down a set of criteria for measuring the extent of pain or pleasure that a certain decision will create.

The criteria are divided into the categories of intensity, duration, certainty, proximity, productiveness, purity, and extent. Using these measurements, he reviews the concept of punishment and when it should be used as far as whether a punishment will create more pleasure or more pain for a society.

He calls for legislators to determine whether punishment creates an even more evil offence.

Instead of suppressing the evil acts, Bentham argues that certain unnecessary laws and punishments could ultimately lead to new and more dangerous vices than those being punished to begin with, and calls upon legislators to measure the pleasures and pains associated with any legislation and to form laws in order to create the greatest good for the greatest number.

He argues that the concept of the individual pursuing his or her own happiness cannot be necessarily declared "right", because often these individual pursuits can lead to greater pain and less pleasure for a society as a whole. Therefore, the legislation of a society is vital to maintain the maximum pleasure and the minimum degree of pain for the greatest number of people.

Economics

Bentham's opinions about monetary economics were completely different from those of David Ricardo; however, they had some similarities to those of Henry Thornton. He focused on monetary expansion as a means of helping to create full employment. He was also aware of the relevance of forced saving, propensity to consume, the saving-investment relationship, and other matters that form the content of modern income and employment analysis. His monetary view was close to the fundamental concepts employed in his model of utilitarian decision making. His work is considered to be an early precursor of modern welfare economics.

Bentham stated that pleasures and pains can be ranked according to their value or "dimension" such as intensity, duration, certainty of a pleasure or a pain. He was concerned with maxima and minima of pleasures and pains; and they set a precedent for the future employment of the maximisation principle in the economics of the consumer, the firm and the search for an optimum in welfare economics.

Law reform

Bentham was the first person to aggressively advocate for the codification of *all* of the common law into a coherent set of statutes; he was actually the person who coined the verb "to codify" to refer to the process of drafting a legal code.

He lobbied hard for the formation of codification commissions in both England and the United States, and went so far as to write to President James Madison in 1811 to volunteer to write a complete legal code for the young country. After he learned more about American law and realized that most of it was state-based, he promptly wrote to the governors of every single state with the same offer.

During his lifetime, Bentham's codification efforts were completely unsuccessful. Even today, they have been completely rejected by almost every common law jurisdiction, including England. However, his writings on the subject laid the foundation for the moderately successful codification work of David Dudley Field II in the United States a generation later.

Animal Rights

Bentham is widely regarded as one of the earliest proponents of animal rights, and has even been hailed as "the first patron saint of animal rights". He argued that the ability to suffer, not the ability to reason, should be the benchmark, or what he called the "insuperable line".

If reason alone were the criterion by which we judge who ought to have rights, human infants and adults with certain forms of disability might fall short, too. In 1789, alluding to the limited degree of legal protection afforded to slaves in the French West Indies by the Code Noir, he wrote:

The day has been, I am sad to say in many places it is not yet past, in which the greater part of the species, under the denomination of slaves, have been treated by the law exactly upon the same footing, as, in England for example, the inferior races of animals are still. The day *may* come when the rest of the animal creation may acquire those rights which never could have been witholden from them but by the hand of tyranny.

The French have already discovered that the blackness of the skin is no reason a human being should be abandoned without redress to the caprice of a tormentor.

It may one day come to be recognised that the number of the legs, the villosity of the skin, or the termination of the *os sacrum* are reasons equally insufficient for abandoning a sensitive being to the same fate.

What else is it that should trace the insuperable line? Is it the faculty of reason or perhaps the faculty of discourse? But a full-grown horse or dog, is beyond comparison a more rational, as well as a more conversable animal, than an infant of a day or a week or even a month, old. But suppose the case were otherwise, what would it avail? The question is not, Can they *reason*? nor, Can they *talk*? but, Can they *suffer*?

Earlier in that paragraph, Bentham makes clear that he accepted that animals could be killed for food, or in defence of human life, provided that the animal was not made to suffer unnecessarily.

Bentham did not object to medical experiments on animals, providing that the experiments had in mind a particular goal of benefit to humanity, and had a reasonable chance of achieving that goal.

He wrote that otherwise he had a "decided and insuperable objection" to causing pain to animals, in part because of the harmful effects such practices might have on human beings. In a letter to the editor of the *Morning Chronicle* in March 1825, he wrote:

I never have seen, nor ever can see, any objection to the putting of dogs and other inferior animals to pain, in the way of medical experiment, when that experiment has a determinate object, beneficial to mankind, accompanied with a fair prospect of the accomplishment of it.

But I have a decided and insuperable objection to the putting of them to pain without any such view. To my apprehension, every act by which, without prospect of preponderant good, pain is knowingly and willingly produced in any being whatsoever, is an act of cruelty; and, like other bad habits, the more the correspondent habit is indulged in, the stronger it grows, and the more frequently productive of its bad fruit.

I am unable to comprehend how it should be, that to him to whom it is a matter of amusement to see a dog or a horse suffer, it should not be matter of like amusement to see a man suffer; seeing, as I do, how much more morality as well as intelligence, an adult quadruped of those and many other species has in him, than any biped has for some months after he has been brought into existence; nor does it appear to me how it should be, that a person to whom the production of pain, either in the one or in the other instance, is a source of amusement, would scruple to give himself that amusement when he could do so under an assurance of impunity.

Gender and Sexuality

Bentham said that it was the placing of women in a legally inferior position that made him choose, at the age of eleven, the career of a reformist. Bentham spoke for a complete equality between sexes.

The essay *Offences Against One's Self,* argued for the liberalisation of laws prohibiting homosexual sex. The essay remained unpublished during his lifetime for fear of offending public morality.

It was published for the first time in 1931. Bentham does not believe homosexual acts to be unnatural, describing them merely as "irregularities of the venereal appetite".

The essay chastises the society of the time for making a disproportionate response to what Bentham appears to consider a largely private offence – public displays or forced acts being dealt with rightly by other laws.

Privacy

For Bentham, transparency had moral value. For example, journalism puts power-holders under moral scrutiny. However, Bentham wanted such transparency to apply to everyone.

This he describes by picturing the world as a gymnasium in which each "gesture, every turn of limb or feature, in those whose motions have a visible impact on the general happiness, will be noticed and marked down".

Both "transparency and surveillance are a positive way of making all things present in order to generate understanding and make life better for all".

Bentham and University College London

Bentham is widely associated with the foundation in 1826 of the London University (the institution that, in 1836, became University College London), though he was 78 years old when the University opened and played only an indirect role in its establishment.

His direct involvement was limited to his buying a single £100 share in the new University, making him just one of over a thousand shareholders.

Bentham and his ideas can non-etheless be seen as having inspired several of the actual founders of the University. He strongly believed that education should be more widely available, particularly to those who were not wealthy or who did not belong to the established church; in Bentham's time, membership of the Church of England and the capacity to bear considerable expenses were required of students entering the Universities of Oxford and Cambridge.

As the University of London was the first in England to admit all, regardless of race, creed or political belief, it was largely consistent with Bentham's vision.

There is some evidence that, from the sidelines, he played a "more than passive part" in the planning discussions for the new institution, although it is also apparent that "his interest was greater than his influence".

He failed in his efforts to see his disciple John Bowring appointed professor of English or History, but he did oversee the appointment of another pupil, John Austin, as the first professor of Jurisprudence in 1829.

The more direct associations between Bentham and UCL – the College's custody of his Auto-icon and of the majority of his surviving papers – postdate his death by some years: the papers were donated in 1849, and the Auto-icon in 1850.

A large painting by Henry Tonkshanging in UCL's Flaxman Gallery depicts Bentham approving the plans of the new university, but it was executed in 1922 and the scene is entirely imaginary. Since 1959 (when the Bentham Committee was first established) UCL has hosted the Bentham Project, which is progressively publishing a definitive edition of Bentham's writings.

UCL now endeavours to acknowledge Bentham's influence on its foundation, while avoiding any suggestion of direct involvement, by describing him as its "spiritual founder".

Bentham and Literature

The national poet and man of letters of the recently liberated, and divided by the Treaty of Berlin, Bulgaria Ivan Vazov refers to Bentham in his 1881 poem.

Legacy

The Faculty of Laws at University College London occupies Bentham House, next to the main UCL campus.

Bentham's name was adopted by the Australian litigation funder IMF Limited to become Bentham IMF Limited on 28 November 2013, in recognition of Bentham being "among the first to support the utility of litigation funding".

JOHN C HARSANYI

John Charles Harsanyi (May 29, 1920 – August 9, 2000) was a Hungarian-American economist and Nobel Memorial Prize in Economic Sciences winner.

He is best known for his contributions to the study of game theory and its application to economics, specifically for his developing the highly innovative analysis of games of incomplete information, so-called Bayesian games.

He also made important contributions to the use of game theory and economic reasoning in political and moral philosophy (specifically utilitarian ethics) as well as contributing to the study of equilibrium selection. For his work, he was a co-recipient along with John Nash and Reinhard Selten of the 1994 Nobel Memorial Prize in Economics.

BIOGRAPHY

John C. Harsanyi was born in Budapest, Hungary on May 29, 1920, the son of a pharmacy owner. His parents converted from Judaism to Catholicism a year before he was born.

He attended high school at the Lutheran Gymnasium in Budapest. During high school, he became one of the best problem solvers of the KöMaL, the Mathematical and Physical Monthly for Secondary Schools. Founded in 1893, this periodical is generally credited with a large share of Hungarian students' success in mathematics. He also won the first prize in the Eötvös mathematics competition Eötvös for high school students.

Although he wanted to study mathematics and philosophy, his father sent him to France in 1939 to enroll in chemical engineering at the University of Lyon. However, because of the start of World War II, Harsanyi returned to Hungary to study pharmacology at theUniversity of Budapest (today: Eötvös Loránd University), earning a diploma in 1944.

As a pharmacology student, Harsanyi escaped conscription into the Hungarian Army which, as a person of Jewish descent, would have meant forced labour.

However, in 1944 (after the fall of the Horthy regime and the seizure of power by the Arrow Cross Party) his military deferment was cancelled and he was compelled to join a forced labour unit on the Eastern Front. After seven months of forced labour, when the German authorities decided to deport his unit to a concentration camp in Austria, John Harsanyi managed to escape and found sanctuary for the rest of the war in a Jesuit house.

Postwar

After the end of the war, Harsanyi returned to the University of Budapest for graduate studies in philosophy and sociology, earning his Ph.D. in both subjects in 1947. Then a devout Catholic, he simultaneously studied theology, also joining lay ranks of the Dominican Order. He later abandoned Catholicism, becoming an atheist for the rest of his life.

Harsanyi spent the academic year 1947–1948 on the faculty of the Institute of Sociology of the University of Budapest, where he met Anne Klauber, his future wife. He was forced to resign the faculty because of openly expressing his anti-Marxist opinions, while Anne faced increasing peer pressure to leave him for the same reason.

Harsanyi remained in Hungary for the following two years attempting to sell his family's pharmacy without losing it to the authorities.

After it became apparent that the communist party would confiscate the pharmacy in 1950, he fled with Anne and her parents by illegally crossing the border with Austria and then going to Australia where Klauber's parents had some friends.

Australia

The two did not marry until they arrived in Australia because Klauber's immigration papers would need to be changed to reflect her married name. The two arrived with her parents on December 30, 1950 and they looked to marry immediately. Harsanyi and Klauber were married on January 2, 1951.

Neither spoke much English and understood little of what they were told to say to each other. Harsanyi later explained to his new wife that she had promised to cook better food than she usually did.

Harsanyi's Hungarian degrees were not recognized in Australia, but they earned him credit at the University of Sydney for a master's degree. Harsanyi worked in a factory during the day and studied economics in the evening at the University of Sydney, finishing with a M.A. in 1953.

While studying in Sydney, he started publishing research papers in economic journals, including the *Journal of Political Economy* and the *Review of Economic Studies*. The degree allowed him to take a teaching position in 1954 at the University of Queensland in Brisbane. While in Brisbane, Harsanyi's wife became a fashion designer for a small factory.

Later Years

In 1956, Harsanyi received a Rockefeller scholarship that enabled him and Anne to spend the next two years in the United States, at Stanford University and, for a semester, at the Cowles Foundation.

At Stanford Harsanyi wrote a dissertation in game theory under the supervision of Kenneth Arrow, earning a second PhD in economics in 1959, while Anne earned an MA in psychology. Harsanyi's student visa expired in 1958 and the two returned to Australia.

After working for a short time as a researcher at the Australian National University in Canberra, Harsanyi became frustrated with the lack of interest in game theory in Australia.

With the help of Kenneth Arrow and James Tobin, he was able to move to the United States, taking a position as professor of economics at the Wayne State University in Detroitbetween 1961–1963. In 1964, he moved to Berkeley, California, he remained at the University of California, Berkeley until retiring in 1990. Shortly after arriving in Berkeley, he and Anne had a child, Tom.

While teaching at Berkeley, John Harsanyi did extensive research in game theory. From 1966 to 1968, Harsanyi was part of a team of game theorists tasked with advising the United States Arms Control and Disarmament Agency in collaboration with Mathematica, a consulting group from Princeton University led byHarold Kuhn and Oskar Morgenstern.

John Harsanyi died in 2000 from a heart attack in Berkeley, California, after suffering for a time from Alzheimer's disease.

JOHN MAYNARD KEYNES

John Maynard Keynes, 1st Baron Keynes, CB, FBA (5 June 1883 – 21 April 1946) was a British economistwhose ideas have fundamentally affected the theory and practice of modern macroeconomics and informed the economic policies of governments.

He built on and greatly refined earlier work on the causes of business cycles, and he is widely considered to be one of the founders of modern macroeconomics and the most influential economist of the 20th century. His ideas are the basis for the school of thought known as Keynesian economics and its various offshoots.

In the 1930s, Keynes spearheaded a revolution in economic thinking, overturning the older ideas of neo-classical economics that held that free markets would, in the short to medium term, automatically provide full employment, as long as workers were flexible in their wage demands.

Keynes instead argued that aggregate demand determined the overall level of economic activity and that inadequate aggregate demand could lead to prolonged periods of high unemployment. According to Keynesian economics, state intervention was necessary to moderate "boom and bust" cycles of economic activity.

He advocated the use of fiscal andmonetary measures to mitigate the adverse effects of economic recessions and depressions. Following the outbreak of World War II, Keynes's ideas concerning economic policy were adopted by leading Western economies.

In 1942, Keynes was awarded ahereditary peerage as Baron Keynes of Tilton in the County of Sussex. Keynes died in 1946; but, during the 1950s and 1960s, the success of Keynesian economics resulted in almost all capitalist governments adopting its policy recommendations.

Keynes's influence waned in the 1970s, partly as a result of problems that began to afflict the Anglo-American economies from the start of the decade and partly because of critiques from Milton Friedman and other economists who were pessimistic about the ability of governments to regulate the business cycle with fiscal policy.

However, the advent of the global financial crisis of 2007–08 caused a resurgence in Keynesian thought. Keynesian economics provided the theoretical underpinning for economic policies undertaken in response to the crisis by President George W.

Bush of the United States, Prime Minister Gordon Brown of the United Kingdom, and other heads of governments.

In 1999, *Time* magazine included Keynes in their list of the 100 most important and influential people of the 20th century, commenting that: "His radical idea that governments should spend money they don't have may have saved capitalism." He has been described by *The Economist* as "Britain's most famous 20th-century economist." In addition to being an economist, Keynes was also a civil servant, a director of the Bank of England, a part of the Bloomsbury Group of intellectuals, a patron of the arts and an art collector, a director of the British Eugenics Society, an advisor to several charitable trusts, a successful private investor, a writer, a philosopher, and a farmer.

EARLY LIFE AND EDUCATION

John Maynard Keynes was born in Cambridge, Cambridgeshire, England, to an upper-middle-class family. His father, John Neville Keynes, was an economist and a lecturer in moral sciences at the University of Cambridge and his mother Florence Ada Keynes a local social reformer.

Keynes was the first born, and was followed by two more children – Margaret Neville Keynes in 1885 and Geoffrey Keynes in 1887. Geoffrey became a surgeon and Margaret married the Nobel Prize-winning physiologist Archibald Hill.

According to the economist and biographer Robert Skidelsky, Keynes's parents were loving and attentive. They remained in the same house throughout their lives, where the children were always welcome to return.

Keynes would receive considerable support from his father, including expert coaching to help him pass his scholarship exams and financial help both as a young man and when his assets were nearly wiped out at the onset of Great Depression in 1929.

Keynes's mother made her children's interests her own, and according to Skidelsky, "because she could grow up with her children, they never outgrew home".

At the age of five and a half, in January 1889, Keynes started at the Kindergarten of the Perse School for Girls for five mornings a week. He quickly showed a talent for arithmetic, but his health was poor leading to several long absences.

He was tutored at home by a governess, Beatrice Mackintosh, and his mother. At eight and a half, in January 1892, he started as a day pupil at St Faith's preparatory school. By 1894 Keynes was top of his class and excelling at mathematics.

In 1896 St Faith's headmaster, Ralph Goodchild, wrote that Keynes was "head and shoulders above all the other boys in the school" and was confident that Keynes could get a scholarship to Eton.

Keynes won a scholarship to Eton College in 1897, where he displayed talent in a wide range of subjects, particularly mathematics, classics and history.

At Eton, Keynes experienced the first "love of his life" in Dan Macmillan, older brother of the future Prime Minister Harold Macmillan. Despite his middle-class background, Keynes mixed easily with upper-class pupils. In 1902

Keynes left Eton for King's College, Cambridge after receiving a scholarship for this also to study mathematics. Alfred Marshall begged Keynes to become an economist, although Keynes's own inclinations drew him towards philosophy – especially the ethical system of G. E. Moore.

Keynes joined the Pitt Club and was an active member of the semi-secretive Cambridge Apostles society, a debating club largely reserved for the brightest students. Like many members, Keynes retained a bond to the club after graduating and continued to attend occasional meetings throughout his life. Before leaving Cambridge, Keynes became the President of the Cambridge Union Society and Cambridge University Liberal Club.

In May 1904 he received a first class B.A. in mathematics. Aside from a few months spent on holidays with family and friends, Keynes continued to involve himself with the university over the next two years. He took part in debates, further studied philosophy and attended economics lectures informally as a graduate student. He also studied for his 1905 Tripos and 1906 civil service exams.

The economist Harry Johnson wrote that the optimism imparted by Keynes's early life is a key to understanding his later thinking. Keynes was always confident he could find a solution to whatever problem he turned his attention to, and retained a lasting faith in the ability of government officials to do good.

Keynes's optimism was also cultural, in two senses – he was of the last generation raised by an empire still at the height of its power, in its own eyes and by much of the world (at least outwardly) seen as pre-eminent in both power and benevolence. Keynes was also of the last generation who felt entitled to govern by culture, rather than by expertise.

According to Skidelsky, the sense of cultural unity current in Britain from the 19th century to the end of World War I provided a framework with which the well-educated could set various spheres of knowledge in relation to each other and to life, enabling them to confidently draw from different fields when addressing practical problems.

CAREER

Keynes's Civil Service career began in October 1906, as a clerk in the India Office. He enjoyed his work at first, but by 1908 had become bored and resigned his position to return to Cambridge and work on probability theory, at first privately funded only by two dons at the university – his father and the economist Arthur Pigou.

In 1909 Keynes published his first professional economics article in the *Economics Journal*, about the effect of a recent global economic downturn on India. Also in 1909, Keynes accepted a lectureship in economics funded personally by Alfred Marshall. Keynes's earnings rose further as he began to take on pupils for private tuition, and on being elected a fellow. In 1911 Keynes was made editor of *The Economic Journal*. By 1913 he had published his first book, *Indian Currency and Finance*. He was then appointed to the Royal Commission on Indian Currency and Finance – the same topic as his book – where Keynes showed considerable talent at applying economic theory to practical problems.

His written work was published under the name "J M Keynes", though to his family and friends he was known as Maynard. (His father, John Neville Keynes, was also always known by his middle name).

World War I

The British Government called on Keynes's expertise during the First World War. While he did not formally re-join the civil service in 1914, Keynes traveled to London at the government's request a few days before hostilities started. Bankers had been pushing for the suspension of specie payments – the convertibility of banknotes into gold – but with Keynes's help the Chancellor of the Exchequer (then Lloyd George) was persuaded that this would be a bad idea, as it would hurt the future reputation of the city if payments were suspended before absolutely necessary.

In January 1915 Keynes took up an official government position at the Treasury. Among his responsibilities were the design of terms of credit between Britain and its continental allies during the war, and the acquisition of scarce currencies.

According to economist Robert Lekachman, Keynes's "nerve and mastery became legendary" because of his performance of these duties, as in the case where he managed to assemble – with difficulty – a small supply of Spanish pesetas. The secretary of the Treasury was delighted to hear Keynes had amassed enough to provide a temporary solution for the British Government.

But Keynes did not hand the pesetas over, choosing instead to sell them all to break the market: his boldness paid off, as pesetas then became much less scarce and expensive.

In the 1917 King's Birthday Honours, Keynes was appointed Companion of the Order of the Bath for his wartime work, and his success led to the appointment that would have a huge effect on Keynes's life and career; Keynes was appointed financial representative for the Treasury to the 1919 Versailles peace conference. He was also appointed Officer of the Belgian Order of Leopold.

Versailles Peace Conference

Keynes's experience at Versailles was influential in shaping his future outlook, yet it was not a successful one for him. Keynes's main interest had been in trying to prevent Germany's compensation payments (World War I reparations) being set so high it would traumatise innocent German people, damage the nation's ability to pay and sharply limit her ability to buy exports from other countries – thus hurting not just Germany's own economy but that of the wider world.

Unfortunately for Keynes, conservative powers in the coalition that emerged from the 1918 coupon election were able to ensure that both Keynes himself and the Treasury were largely excluded from formal high-level talks concerning reparations.

Their place was taken by the Heavenly Twins – the judge Lord Sumner and the banker Lord Cunliffewhose nickname derived from the "astronomically" high war compensation they wanted to demand from Germany. Keynes was forced to try to exert influence mostly from behind the scenes.

The three principal players at Versailles were Britain's Lloyd George, France's Clemenceau and America's President Wilson. It was only Lloyd George to whom Keynes had much direct access; until the 1918 election he had some sympathy with Keynes's view but while campaigning had found his speeches were only well received by the public if he promised to harshly punish Germany, and had therefore committed to extracting high payments.

Lloyd George did however win some loyalty from Keynes with his actions at the Paris conference by intervening against the French to ensure the dispatch of much-needed food supplies to German civilians.

Clemenceau also pushed for high reparations; generally France argued for an even more severe settlement than Britain. Wilson initially favoured relatively lenient treatment of Germany – he feared too harsh conditions could foment the rise of extremism, and wanted Germany to be left sufficient capital to pay for imports. To Keynes's dismay, Lloyd George and Clemenceau were able to pressure Wilson to agree to very high repayments being imposed.

Towards the end of the conference, Keynes came up with a plan that he argued would not only help Germany and other impoverished central European powers but also be good for the world economy as a whole. It involved the writing down of war debts which would have the effect of increasing international trade all round.

Lloyd George agreed it might be acceptable to the British electorate. However, America was against it; the US was then the largest creditor and by this time Wilson had started to believe in the merits of a harsh peace as a warning to future aggressors. Hence despite his best efforts, the end result of the conference was a treaty which disgusted Keynes both on moral and economic grounds, and led to his resignation from the Treasury.

In June 1919 he turned down an offer to become chairman of the British Bank of Northern Commerce, a job that promised a salary of £2000 in return for a morning per week of work.

Keynes's analysis on the predicted damaging effects of the treaty appeared in the highly influential book, *The Economic Consequences of the Peace*, published in 1919. This work has been described as Keynes's best book, where he was able to bring all his gifts to bear – his passion as well as his skill as an economist. In addition to economic analysis, the book contained pleas to the reader's sense of compassion:

I cannot leave this subject as though its just treatment wholly depended either on our own pledges or on economic facts. The policy of reducing Germany to servitude for a generation, of degrading the lives of millions of human beings, and of depriving a whole nation of happiness should be abhorrent and detestable, –abhorrent and detestable, even if it were possible, even if it enriched ourselves, even if it did not sow the decay of the whole civilised life of Europe.

Also present was striking imagery such as "year by year Germany must be kept impoverished and her children starved and crippled" along with bold predictions which were later justified by events:

If we aim deliberately at the impoverishment of Central Europe, vengeance, I dare predict, will not limp. Nothing can then delay for very long that final war between the forces of Reaction and the despairing convulsions of Revolution, before which the horrors of the late German war will fade into nothing.

Keynes's predictions of disaster were borne out when the German economy suffered the hyperinflation of 1923, and again by the collapse of the Weimar Republic and the outbreak of World War II.

Only a fraction of reparations were ever paid. *The Economic Consequences of the Peace* gained Keynes international fame, but also caused him to be regarded as anti-establishment – it was not until after the outbreak of World War II that Keynes was offered a directorship of a major British Bank, or an acceptable offer to return to government with a formal job.

However, Keynes was still able to influence government policy making through his network of contacts, his published works and by serving on government committees; this included attending high-level policy meetings as a consultant.

In the 1920s

Keynes had completed his *A Treatise on Probability* before the war, but published it in 1921. The work was a notable contribution to the philosophical and mathematical underpinnings of probability theory, championing the important view that *probabilities* were no more or less than truth values intermediate between simple truth and falsity.

Keynes developed the first upper-lower probabilistic intervalapproach to probability in chapters 15 and 17 of this book, as well as having developed the first decision weight approach with his conventional coefficient of risk and weight, *c*, in chapter 26. In addition to his academic work, the 1920s saw Keynes active as a journalist selling his work internationally and working in London as a financial consultant. In 1924 Keynes wrote an obituary for his former tutor Alfred Marshall which Schumpeter called "the most brilliant life of a man of science I have ever read." Marshall's widow was "entranced" by the memorial, while Lytton Strachey rated it as one of Keynes's "best works".

In 1922 Keynes continued to advocate reduction of German reparations with *A Revision of the Treaty*. He attacked the post World War I deflation policies with *A Tract on Monetary Reform* in 1923 – a trenchant argument that countries should target stability of domestic prices, avoiding deflation even at the cost of allowing their currency to depreciate.

Britain suffered from high unemployment through most of the 1920s, leading Keynes to recommend the depreciation of sterling to boost jobs by making British exports more affordable. From 1924 he was also advocating a fiscal response, where the government could create jobs by spending on public works.

During the 1920s Keynes's pro stimulus views had only limited effect on policy makers and mainstream academic opinion – according to Hyman Minsky one reason was that at this time his theoretical justification was "muddled".

The *Tract* had also called for an end to the gold standard. Keynes advised it was no longer a net benefit for countries such as Britain to participate in the gold standard, as it ran counter to the need for domestic policy autonomy. It could force countries to pursue deflationary policies at exactly the time when expansionary measures were called for to address rising unemployment.

The Treasury and Bank of England were still in favour of the gold standard and in 1925 they were able to convince the then Chancellor Winston Churchill to re-establish it, which had a depressing effect on British industry. Keynes responded by writing *The Economic Consequences of Mr. Churchill* and continued to argue against the gold standard until Britain finally abandoned it in 1931.

During the Great Depression

Keynes had begun a theoretical work to examine the relationship between unemployment, money and prices back in the 1920s. The work, *Treatise on Money*, was published in 1930 in two volumes.

A central idea of the work was that if the amount of money being saved exceeds the amount being invested – which can happen if interest rates are too high – then unemployment will rise. This is in part a result of people not wanting to spend too high a proportion of what employers pay out, making it difficult, in aggregate, for employers to make a profit.

Keynes was deeply critical of the British government's austerity measures during the Great Depression. He believed that budget deficits were a good thing, a product of recessions. He wrote, "For Government borrowing of one kind or another is nature's remedy, so to speak, for preventing business losses from being, in so severe a slump as to present one, so great as to bring production altogether to a standstill."

At the height of the Great Depression, in 1933, Keynes published *The Means to Prosperity*, which contained specific policy recommendations for tackling unemployment in a global recession, chiefly counter cyclical public spending.

*The Means to Prosperity*contains one of the first mentions of the multiplier effect. While it was addressed chiefly to the British Government, it also contained advice for other nations affected by the global recession.

A copy was sent to the newly elected President Roosevelt and other world leaders. The work was taken seriously by both the American and British governments, and according to Skidelsky, helped pave the way for the later acceptance of Keynesian ideas, though it had little immediate practical influence. In the 1933 London Economic Conferenceopinions remained too diverse for a unified course of action to be agreed upon.

Keynesian-like policies were adopted by Sweden and Germany, but Sweden was seen as too small to command much attention, and Keynes was deliberately silent about the successful efforts of Germany as he was dismayed by their imperialist ambitions and their treatment of Jews.

Apart from Great Britain, Keynes's attention was primarily focused on the United States. In 1931, he received considerable support for his views on counter-cyclical public spending in Chicago, then America's foremost centre for economic views alternative to the mainstream. However, orthodox economic opinion remained generally hostile regarding fiscal intervention to mitigate the depression, until just before the outbreak of war.

In late 1933 Keynes was persuaded by Felix Frankfurter to address President Roosevelt directly, which he did by letters and face to face in 1934, after which the two men spoke highly of each other.However according to Skidelsky, the consensus is that Keynes's efforts only began to have a more than marginal influence on US economic policy after 1939.

Keynes's *magnum opus*, *The General Theory of Employment, Interest and Money* was published in 1936. It was researched and indexed by one of Keynes's favourite students, later the economist David Bensusan-Butt. The work served as a theoretical justification for the interventionist policies Keynes favoured for tackling a recession.

The *General Theory* challenged the earlier neo-classical economicparadigm, which had held that provided it was unfettered by government interference, the market would naturally establish full employment equilibrium. In doing so Keynes was partly setting himself against his former teachers Marshall and Pigou. Keynes believed the classical theory was a "special case" that applied only to the particular conditions present in the 19th century, his own theory being the general one. Classical economists had believed in Say's law, which, simply put, states that "supply creates its own demand", and that in a free market workers would always be willing to lower their wages to a level where employers could profitably offer them jobs.

An innovation from Keynes was the concept of price stickiness – the recognition that in reality workers often refuse to lower their wage demands even in cases where a classical economist might argue it is rational for them to do so.

Due in part to price stickiness, it was established that the interaction of "aggregate demand" and "aggregate supply" may lead to stable unemployment equilibria – and in those cases, it is the state, and not the market, that economies must depend on for their salvation.

The *General Theory* argues that demand, not supply, is the key variable governing the overall level of economic activity. Aggregate demand, which equals total un-hoarded income in a society, is defined by the sum of consumption and investment.

In a state of unemployment and unused production capacity, one can *only* enhance employment and total income by *first* increasing expenditures for either consumption or investment. Without government intervention to increase expenditure, an economy can remain trapped in a low employment equilibrium – the demonstration of this possibility has been described as the revolutionary formal achievement of the work.

The book advocated activist economic policy by government to stimulate demand in times of high unemployment, for example by spending on public works. "Let us be up and doing, using our idle resources to increase our wealth," he wrote in 1928. "With men and plants unemployed, it is ridiculous to say that we cannot afford these new developments. It is precisely with these plants and these men that we shall afford them."

The *General Theory* is often viewed as the foundation of modern macroeconomics. Few senior American economists agreed with Keynes through most of the 1930s. Yet his ideas were soon to achieve widespread acceptance, with eminent American professors such as Alvin Hansen agreeing with the *General Theory* before the outbreak of World War II.

Keynes himself had only limited participation in the theoretical debates that followed the publication of the *General Theory* as he suffered a heart attack in 1937, requiring him to take long periods of rest.

Hyman Minsky and other post-Keynesian economists have argued that as result of this, Keynes's ideas were diluted by those keen to compromise with classical economists or to render his concepts with mathematical models like the IS/LM model (which, they argue, distort Keynes's ideas). Keynes began to recover in 1939, but for the rest of his life his professional energies were largely directed towards the practical side of economics – the problems of ensuring optimum allocation of resources for the War efforts, post-War negotiations with America, and the new international financial order that was presented at Bretton Woods, New Hampshire.

In The General Theory and later, Keynes responded to the socialists and left-wing liberals who argued, especially during the Depression of the 1930s, that capitalism caused war.

He argued that if capitalism were managed, domestically and internationally (with coordinated international Keynesian policies, an international monetary system that didn't pit the interests of countries against each other, and a high degree of freedom of trade), then this system of managed capitalism could promote peace rather than conflict between countries.

His plans during World War II for post-wear international economic institutions and policies (which contributed to the creation at Bretton Woods of theInternational Monetary Fund and the World Bank, and later to the creation of the General Agreement on Tariffs and Trade and eventually the World Trade Organization) were aimed to give effect to this vision.

World War II

During World War II, Keynes argued in *How to Pay for the War*, published in 1940, that the war effort should be largely financed by higher taxation and especially by compulsory saving (essentially workers lending money to the government), rather than deficit spending, in order to avoid inflation.

Compulsory saving would act to dampen domestic demand, assist in channelling additional output towards the war efforts, would be fairer than punitive taxation and would have the advantage of helping to avoid a post war slump by boosting demand once workers were allowed to withdraw their savings.

In September 1941 he was proposed to fill a vacancy in the Court of Directors of the Bank of England, and subsequently carried out a full term from the following April. In June 1942, Keynes was rewarded for his service with a hereditary peerage in the King's Birthday Honours.

On 7 July his title was gazetted as "BARON KEYNES, of Tilton, in the County of Sussex" and he took his seat in the House of Lords on the Liberal Party benches.

As the Allied victory began to look certain, Keynes was heavily involved, as leader of the British delegation and chairman of the World Bank commission, in the mid-1944 negotiations that established the Bretton Woods system. The Keynes-plan, concerning an international clearing-union argued for a radical system for the management of currencies.

He proposed the creation of a common world unit of currency, the bancor, and new global institutions – a world central bank and the International Clearing Union. Keynes envisaged these institutions managing an international trade and payments system with strong incentives for countries to avoid substantial trade deficits or surpluses.

The USA's greater negotiating strength, however, meant that the final outcomes accorded more closely to the more conservative plans of Harry Dexter White. According to US economist Brad Delong, on almost every point where he was overruled by the Americans, Keynes was later proved correct by events.

The two new institutions, later known as the World Bank and International Monetary Fund (IMF), were founded as a compromise that primarily reflected the American vision.

There would be no incentives for states to avoid a large trade surplus; instead, the burden for correcting a trade imbalance would continue to fall only on the deficit countries, which Keynes had argued were least able to address the problem without inflicting economic hardship on their populations. Yet, Keynes was still pleased when accepting the final agreement, saying that if the institutions stayed true to their founding principles, "the brotherhood of man will have become more than a phrase."

Postwar

After the war, Keynes continued to represent the United Kingdom in international negotiations despite his deteriorating health. He succeeded in obtaining preferential terms from the United States for new and outstanding debts to facilitate the rebuilding of the British economy.

Just before his death in 1946, Keynes told Henry Clay, a professor of Social Economics and Advisor to the Bank of England of his hopes that Adam Smith's 'invisible hand' can help Britain out of the economic hole it is in: "I find myself more and more relying for a solution of our problems on the invisible hand which I tried to eject from economic thinking twenty years ago."

LEGACY

The Keynesian Ascendancy 1939–1979

From the end of the Great Depression to the mid-1970s, Keynes provided the main inspiration for economic policy makers in Europe, America and much of the rest of the world.

While economists and policy makers had become increasingly won over to Keynes's way of thinking in the mid and late 1930s, it was only after the outbreak of World War II that governments started to borrow money for spending on a scale sufficient to eliminate unemployment.

According to economist John Kenneth Galbraith (then a US government official charged with controlling inflation), in the rebound of the economy from wartime spending, "one could not have had a better demonstration of the

Keynesian ideas." The Keynesian Revolution was associated with the rise of modern liberalism in the West during the post-war period.

Keynesian ideas became so popular that some scholars point to Keynes as representing the ideals of modern liberalism, as Adam Smith represented the ideals of classical liberalism.

After the war Winston Churchill attempted to check the rise of Keynesian policy-making in the United Kingdom, and used rhetoric critical of the mixed economy in his 1945 election campaign.

Despite his popularity as a war hero Churchill suffered a landslide defeat to Clement Attlee whose government's economic policy continued to be influenced by Keynes's ideas.

Neo-Keynesian Economics

In the late 1930s and 1940s, economists (notably John Hicks, Franco Modigliani, and Paul Samuelson) attempted to interpret and formalise Keynes's writings in terms of formal mathematical models.

In a process termed "theneo-classical synthesis", they combined Keynesian analysis with neo-classical economics to produce Neo-Keynesian economics, which came to dominate mainstream macroeconomic thought for the next 40 years.

By the 1950s, Keynesian policies were adopted by almost the entire developed world and similar measures for a mixed economy were used by many developing nations.

By then, Keynes's views on the economy had become mainstream in the world's universities. Throughout the 1950s and 1960s, the developed and emerging free capitalist economies enjoyed exceptionally high growth and low unemployment.

Professor Gordon Fletcher has written that the 1950s and 1960s, when Keynes's influence was at its peak, appear in retrospect as a Golden Age of Capitalism.

In late 1965 *Time* magazine ran a cover article with a title comment from Milton Friedman (later echoed by U.S. President Richard Nixon) that "We are all Keynesians now".

The article described the exceptionally favourable economic conditions then prevailing, and reported that "Washington's economic managers scaled these heights by their adherence to Keynes's central theme: the modern capitalist economy does not automatically work at top efficiency, but can be raised to that level by the intervention and influence of the government."

The article also states that Keynes was one of the three most important economists who ever lived, and that his *General Theory* was more influential than the *magna opera* of other famous economists, like Smith's *The Wealth of Nations*.

Economics Out of Favour 1979–2007

Keynesian economics were officially discarded by the British Government in 1979, but forces had begun to gather against Keynes's ideas over 30 years earlier. Friedrich Hayekhad formed the Mont Pelerin Society in 1947, with the explicit intention of nurturing intellectual currents to one day displace Keynesianism and other similar influences.

Its members included Austrian School economist Ludwig von Mises along with the then young Milton Friedman. Initially the society had little impact on the wider world – Hayek was to say it was as if Keynes had been raised to sainthood after his death and that people refused to allow his work to be questioned.

Friedman however began to emerge as a formidable critic of Keynesian economics from the mid-1950s, and especially after his 1963 publication of *A Monetary History of the United States*.

On the practical side of economic life, big government had appeared to be firmly entrenched in the 1950s but the balance began to shift towards private power in the 1960s.

Keynes had written against the folly of allowing "decadent and selfish" speculators and financiers the kind of influence they had enjoyed after World War I. For two decades after World War II public opinion was strongly against private speculators, the disparaging label Gnomes of Zürich being typical of how they were described during this period.

International speculation was severely restricted by the capital controls in place after Bretton Woods. Journalists Larry Elliott and Dan Atkinson say 1968 was a pivotal year when power shifted in the favour of private agents such as currency speculators.

They pick out a key 1968 event as being when America suspended the conversion of the dollar into gold except on request of foreign governments, which they identify as when the Bretton Woods system first began to break down.

Criticisms of Keynes's ideas had begun to gain significant acceptance by the early 1970s as they were able to make a credible case that Keynesian models no longer reflected economic reality.

Keynes himself had included few formulas and no explicit mathematical models in his General Theory. For commentators such as economist Hyman Minsky, Keynes's limited use of mathematics was partly the result of his scepticism about whether phenomena as inherently uncertain as economic activity could ever be adequately captured by mathematical models.

Nevertheless, many models were developed by Keynesian economists, with a famous example being the Phillips curve which predicted an inverse relationship between unemployment and inflation. It implied that unemployment could be reduced by government stimulus with a calculable cost to inflation. In

1968 Milton Friedman published a paper arguing that the fixed relationship implied by the Philips curve did not exist. Friedman suggested that sustained Keynesian policies could lead to both unemployment and inflation rising at once – a phenomenon that soon became known as stagflation. In the early 1970s stagflation appeared in both the US and Britain just as Friedman had predicted, with economic conditions deteriorating further after the 1973 oil crisis.

Aided by the prestige gained from his successful forecast, Friedman led increasingly successful criticisms against the Keynesian consensus, convincing not only academics and politicians but also much of the general public with his radio and television broadcasts.

The academic credibility of Keynesian economics was further undermined by additional criticism from other Monetarists trained in the Chicago school of economics, by the Lucas critique and by criticisms from Hayek's Austrian School. So successful were these criticisms that by 1980 Robert Lucas was saying economists would often take offence if described as Keynesians.

Keynesian principles fared increasingly poorly on the practical side of economics – by 1979 they had been displaced by Monetarism as the primary influence on Anglo-American economic policy.

However many officials on both sides of the Atlantic retained a preference for Keynes, and in 1984 the Federal Reserve officially discarded monetarism, after which Keynesian principles made a partial comeback as an influence on policy making.

Not all academics accepted the criticism against Keynes – Minsky has argued that Keynesian economics had been debased by excessive mixing with neo-classical ideas from the 1950s, and that it was unfortunate the branch of economics had even continued to be called "Keynesian".

Writing in *The American Prospect*, Robert Kuttner argued it was not so much excessive Keynesian activism that caused the economic problems of the 1970s but the breakdown of the Bretton Woods system of capital controls, which allowedcapital flight from regulated economies into unregulated economies in a fashion similar to Gresham's Law (where weak currencies undermine strong currencies). Historian Peter Pugh has stated a key cause of the economic problems afflicting America in the 1970s was the refusal to raise taxes to finance the Vietnam War, which was against Keynesian advice.

A more typical response was to accept some elements of the criticisms while refining Keynesian economic theories to defend them against arguments that would invalidate the whole Keynesian framework – the resulting body of work largely composing New Keynesian economics.

In 1992 Alan Blinder was writing about a "Keynesian Restoration" as work based on Keynes's ideas had to some extent become fashionable once again in academia, though in the mainstream it was highly synthesised with Monetarism and other neo-classical thinking. In the world of policy making, free-market influences broadly sympathetic to Monetarism remained very strong at government level – in powerful normative institutions like the World Bank, IMF and US Treasury, and in prominent opinion-forming media such as the *Financial Times* and *The Economist*.

The Keynesian Resurgence of 2008–2009

The global financial crisis of 2007–08 led to public skepticism about the free market consensus even from some on the economic right. In March 2008, Martin Wolf, chief economics commentator at the *Financial Times*, announced the death of the dream of global free-market capitalism.In the same month macroeconomist James K.

Galbraith used the 25th Annual Milton Friedman Distinguished Lecture to launch a sweeping attack against the consensus for monetarist economics and argued that Keynesian economics were far more relevant for tackling the emerging crises. Economist Robert Shiller had begun advocating robust government intervention to tackle the financial crises, specifically citing Keynes.

Nobel laureate Paul Krugman also actively argued the case for vigorous Keynesian intervention in the economy in his columns for the *New York Times*. Other prominent economic commentators arguing for Keynesian government intervention to mitigate the financial crisis include George Akerlof, Brad Delong, Robert Reich, and Joseph Stiglitz. Newspapers and other media have also cited work relating to Keynes by Hyman Minsky, Robert Skidelsky, Donald Markwell and Axel Leijonhufvud.

A series of major bail-outs were pursued during the financial crisis, starting on 7 September with the announcement that the U.S. government was to nationalise the two government-sponsored enterprises which oversaw most of the U.S. subprime mortgage market – Fannie Mae andFreddie Mac.

In October, the British Chancellor of the Exchequer referred to Keynes as he announced plans for substantial fiscal stimulus to head off the worst effects of recession, in accordance with Keynesian economic thought.

Similar policies have been adopted by other governments worldwide. This is in stark contrast to the action permitted to Indonesia during its financial crisis of 1997, when it was forced by the IMF to close 16 banks at the same time, prompting a bank run.

Much of the recent discussion reflected Keynes's advocacy of international coordination of fiscal or monetary stimulus, and of international economic institutions such as the IMF and the World Bank, which many had argued should be reformed as a "new Bretton Woods" even before the crises broke out. IMF and United Nations economists advocated a coordinated international approach to fiscal stimulus.

Donald Markwel argued that in the absence of such an international approach, there would be a risk of worsening international relations and possibly even world war arising from similar economic factors to those present during the depression of the 1930s.

By the end of December 2008, the *Financial Times* reported that "the sudden resurgence of Keynesian policy is a stunning reversal of the orthodoxy of the past several decades." In December 2008, Paul Krugman released his book, *The Return of Depression Economics and the Crisis of 2008*, arguing that economic conditions similar to what existed during the earlier part of the 20th century had returned, making Keynesian policy prescriptions more relevant than ever. In February 2009 Shiller and George Akerlof published *Animal Spirits*, a book where they argue the current US stimulus package is too small as it does not take into account Keynes's insight on the importance of confidence and expectations in determining the future behaviour of businessmen and other economic agents.

In a March 2009 speech entitled *Reform the International Monetary System*, Zhou Xiaochuan, the governor of the People's Bank of China came out in favour of Keynes's idea of a centrally managed global reserve currency. Zhou argued that it was unfortunate that part of the reason for the Bretton Woods system breaking down was the failure to adopt Keynes's bancor. Zhou proposed a gradual move towards increased use of IMF special drawing rights (SDRs). Although Zhou's ideas have not yet been broadly accepted, leaders meeting in April at the 2009 G-20 London summit agreed to allow $250 billion of special drawing rights to be created by the IMF, to be distributed globally. Stimulus plans have been credited for contributing to a better than expected economic outlook by both the OECD and the IMF, in reports published in June and July 2009. Both organisations warned global leaders that recovery is likely to be slow, so counter recessionary measures ought not be rolled back too early.

While the need for stimulus measures has been broadly accepted among policy makers, there has been much debate over how to fund the spending. Some leaders and institutions such as Angela Merkel and the European Central Bank have expressed concern over the potential impact on inflation, national debt and the risk that a too large stimulus will create an unsustainable recovery.

Among professional economists the revival of Keynesian economics has been even more divisive. Although many economists, such as George Akerlof, Paul Krugman, Robert Shiller, and Joseph Stiglitz, support Keynesian stimulus, others do not believe higher government spending will help the United States economy recover from the Great Recession. Some economists, such as Robert Lucas, questioned the theoretical basis for stimulus packages. Others, like Robert Barro and Gary Becker, say that theempirical evidence for beneficial effects from Keynesian stimulus does not exist. However, there is a growing academic literature that shows that fiscal expansion helps an economy grow in the near term, and that certain types of fiscal stimulus are particularly effective.

RECEPTION

Praise

Keynes's economic thinking only began to achieve close to universal acceptance in the last few years of his life. On a personal level, Keynes's charm was such that he was generally well received wherever he went – even those who found themselves on the wrong side of his occasionally sharp tongue rarely bore a grudge.

Keynes's speech at the closing of the Bretton Woods negotiations was received with a lasting standing ovation, rare in international relations, as delegates acknowledged the scale of his achievements made despite poor health.

Austrian School economist Friedrich Hayek was Keynes's most prominent contemporary critic, with sharply opposing views on the economy. Yet after Keynes's death he wrote:

He was the one really great man I ever knew, and for whom I had unbounded admiration. The world will be a very much poorer place without him.

For his part, Keynes praised Hayek's book *The Road to Serfdom*, writing to the Austrian economist that, "Morally and philosophically I find myself in agreement with virtually the whole of it."

Lionel Robbins, former head of the economics department at the London School of Economics, who had many heated debates with Keynes in the 1930s, had this to say after observing Keynes in early negotiations with the Americans while drawing up plans for Bretton Woods: This went very well indeed. Keynes was in his most lucid and persuasive mood: and the effect was irresistible.

At such moments, I often find myself thinking that Keynes must be one of the most remarkable men that have ever lived – the quick logic, the birdlike swoop of intuition, the vivid fancy, the wide vision, above all the incomparable sense of the fitness of words, all combine to make something several degrees beyond the limit of ordinary human achievement.

Douglas LePan, an official from the Canadian High Commission, wrote:

I am spellbound. This is the most beautiful creature I have ever listened to. Does he belong to our species? Or is he from some other order? There is something mythic and fabulous about him. I sense in him something massive and sphinx like, and yet also a hint of wings.

Bertrand Russell named Keynes one of the most intelligent people he had ever known, commenting: Keynes's intellect was the sharpest and clearest that I have ever known. When I argued with him, I felt that I took my life in my hands, and I seldom emerged without feeling something of a fool.

Keynes's obituary in *The Times* included the comment: There is the man himself – radiant, brilliant, effervescent, gay, full of impish jokes... He was a humane man genuinely devoted to the cause of the common good.

Critiques

As a man of the centre described by some as having the greatest impact of any 20th-century economist, Keynes attracted considerable criticism from both sides of the political spectrum. In the 1920s, Keynes was seen as anti-establishment and was mainly attacked from the right. In the "red 1930s", many young economists favoured Marxist views, even in Cambridge, and while Keynes was engaging principally with the right to try to persuade them of the merits of more progressive policy, the most vociferous criticism against him came from the left, who saw him as a supporter of capitalism. From the 1950s and onwards, most of the attacks against Keynes have again been from the right.

In 1931 Friedrich Hayek extensively critiqued Keynes's 1930 *Treatise on Money*. After reading Hayek's *The Road to Serfdom*, Keyneswrote to Hayek saying: "Morally and philosophically I find myself in agreement with virtually the whole of it" but concluded the same letter with the recommendation:

What we need therefore, in my opinion, is not a change in our economic programmes, which would only lead in practice to disillusion with the results of your philosophy; but perhaps even the contrary, namely, an enlargement of them. Your greatest danger is the probable practical failure of the application of your philosophy in the United States.

On the pressing issue of the time, whether deficit spending could lift a country from depression, Keynes replied to Hayek's criticism in the following way:

I should... conclude rather differently. I should say that what we want is not no planning, or even less planning, indeed I should say we almost certainly want more. But the planning should take place in a community in which as many people as possible, both leaders and followers wholly share your own moral position. Moderate planning will be safe enough if those carrying it out are rightly oriented in their own minds and hearts to the moral issue.

Hayek explained the letter by saying:

Because Keynes believed that he was fundamentally still a classical English liberal and wasn't quite aware of how far he had moved away from it. His basic ideas were still those of individual freedom. He did not think systematically enough to see the conflicts.

According to some observers, Hayek felt that the post-World War II "Keynesian orthodoxy" gave too much power to the state and led towards socialism. While Milton Friedman described *The General Theory* as "a great book", he argues that its implicit separation of nominal from real magnitudes is neither possible nor desirable. Macroeconomic policy, Friedman argues, can reliably influence only the nominal. He and other monetarists have consequently argued that Keynesian economics can result in stagflation, the combination of low growth and high inflation that developed economies suffered in the early 1970s. More to Friedman's taste was the *Tract on Monetary Reform* (1923), which he regarded as Keynes's best work because of its focus on maintaining domestic price stability.

Joseph Schumpeter was an economist of the same age as Keynes and one of his main rivals. He was among the first reviewers to argue that Keynes's *General Theory* was not a general theory, but was in fact a special case. He said the work expressed "the attitude of a decaying civilization". After Keynes's death Schumpeter wrote a brief biographical piece called *Keynes the Economist* – on a personal level he was very positive about Keynes as a man, praising his pleasant nature, courtesy and kindness. He assessed some of Keynes biographical and editorial work as among the best he'd ever seen. Yet Schumpeter remained critical about Keynes's economics, linking Keynes's childlessness to what Schumpeter saw as an essentially short term view. He considered Keynes to have a kind of unconscious patriotism that caused him to fail to understand the problems of other nations. For Schumpeter "Practical Keynesianism is a seedling which cannot be transplanted into foreign soil: it dies there and becomes poisonous as it dies."

Austrian School economic commentator and journalist Henry Hazlitt's *The Failure of the New Economics* is a paragraph-by-paragraph refutation of *The General Theory*. In 1960 he published the book *The Critics of Keynesian Economics* where he gathered together the major criticisms of Keynes made up to that year.

President Harry Truman was skeptical of Keynesian theorizing, "Nobody can ever convince me that Government can spend a dollar that it's not got," he told Leon Keyserling, a Keynesian economist who chaired Truman's Council of Economic Advisers.

Keynes used the word "niggers" to refer to black people in casual conversations. However, this term was often used neutrally in British circles at that time, and was not necessarily an expression of negative feelings, as when, for example, he wrote to Duncan Grant that "the only really sympathetic and original thing in America are the niggers, who are charming". Non-etheless fellow British observers recount being shocked by some statements he made, such as the following, apropos the Washington summer: "It's far too hot. Much too hot for white men. All right for niggers." He also wrote that there was "beastliness in the Russian nature" as well as "cruelty and stupidity", and other comments which may be construed as anti-Russian. Some critics, such as Rothbard, have sought to infer that Keynes had sympathy with Nazism, and a number of writers have described him as antisemitic. Keynes's private letters express portraits and descriptions some of which can be characterised as antisemitic, others as philosemitic.Scholars have suggested that these reflect clichés current at the time that he accepted uncritically, rather than any racism. Keynes had many Jewish friends, including Isaiah Berlin and Piero Sraffa. Keynes several times used his influence to help his Jewish friends, most notably when he successfully lobbied for Ludwig Wittgenstein to be allowed residency in the United Kingdom explicitly in order to rescue him from being deported to Nazi-occupied Austria. Keynes was, furthermore, a supporter of Zionism, serving on committees supporting the cause.

Allegations that he was racist or had totalitarian beliefs have been rejected by biographers such as Robert Skidelsky. Professor Gordon Fletcher writes that "the suggestion of a link between Keynes and any support of totalitarianism cannot be sustained". Once the aggressive tendencies of the Nazis towards Jews and other minorities became apparent, Keynes made clear his loathing of Nazism. As a lifelong pacifist he had initially favoured peaceful containment, yet he began to advocate a forceful resolution while many conservatives were still arguing for appeasement. After the war started he roundly criticised the Left for losing their nerve to confront Hitler:

The intelligentsia of the Left were the loudest in demanding that the Nazi aggression should be resisted at all costs. When it comes to a showdown, scarce four weeks have passed before they remember that they are pacifists and write defeatist letters to your columns, leaving the defence of freedom and civilization to Colonel Blimp and the Old School Tie, for whom Three Cheers.

Keynes has been characterised as being indifferent or even positive about mild inflation. Keynes had indeed expressed a preference for inflation over deflation, saying that if one has to choose between the two evils it is "better to disappoint the rentier" than to inflict pain on working-class families. However, Keynes was also aware of the dangers of inflation. In *The Economic Consequences of the Peace*, Keynes had written:

Lenin is said to have declared that the best way to destroy the Capitalist System was to debauch the currency. By a continuing process of inflation, governments can confiscate, secretly and unobserved, an important part of the wealth of their citizens. There is no subtler, no surer means of overturning the existing basis of society than to debauch the currency. The process engages all the hidden forces of economic law on the side of destruction, and does it in a manner which not one man in a million is able to diagnose.

PERSONAL LIFE

Relationships

Keynes's early romantic and sexual relationships were exclusively with men. Keynes had been in relationships while at Eton and Cambridge; significant among these early partners were Dilly Knox and Daniel Macmillan. Keynes was open about his affairs, and between 1901 to 1915, kept separate diaries in which he tabulated his many sexual encounters. Keynes's relationship and later close friendship with Macmillan was to be fortuitous, as Macmillan's company first published his tract, *Economic Consequences of the Peace*.

Attitudes in the Bloomsbury Group, in which Keynes was avidly involved, were relaxed about homosexuality. Keynes, together with writerLytton Strachey, had reshaped the Victorian attitudes of the Cambridge Apostles: "since [their] time, homosexual relations among the members were for a time common", wrote Bertrand Russell.

The artist Duncan Grant, whom he met in 1908, was one of Keynes's great loves. Keynes was also involved with Lytton Strachey, though they were for the most part love rivals, and not lovers. Keynes had won the affections of Arthur Hobhouse, as well as Grant, both times falling out with a jealous Strachey for it. Strachey had previously found himself put off by Keynes, not least because of his manner of "treat[ing] his love affairs statistically".

Political opponents have used Keynes' sexuality to attack his academic work. One line of attack held that he was uninterested in the long term ramifications of his theories because he had no children.

Keynes' friends in the Bloomsbury Group were initially surprised when, in his later years, he began dating and pursuing affairs with women, demonstrating himself to bebisexual.

Ray Costelloe (who would later marry Oliver Strachey) was an early heterosexual interest of Keynes. In 1906, Keynes had written of this infatuation that, "I seem to have fallen in love with Ray a little bit, but as she isn't male I haven't [been] able to think of any suitable steps to take."

Marriage

In 1921, Keynes wrote that he had fallen "very much in love" with Lydia Lopokova, a well-known Russian ballerina, and one of the stars ofSergei Diaghilev's *Ballets Russes*. In the early years of his courtship, he maintained an affair with a younger man, Sebastian Sprott, in tandem with Lopokova, but eventually chose Lopokova exclusively.

They married in 1925. The union was happy, with biographer Peter Clarke writing that the marriage gave Keynes "a new focus, a new emotional stability and a sheer delight of which he never wearied". Lydia became pregnant in 1927 but miscarried.

Among Keynes's Bloomsbury friends, Lopokova was, at least initially, subjected to criticism for her manners, mode of conversation and supposedly humble social origins – the latter of the ostensible causes being particularly noted in the letters of Vanessa and Clive Bell, and Virginia Woolf. In her novel *Mrs Dalloway* (1925), Woolf bases the character of Rezia Warren Smith on Lopokova. E. M. Forster would later write in contrition: "How we all used to underestimate her".

Support for the Arts

Keynes was interested in literature in general and drama in particular and supported the Cambridge Arts Theatre financially, which allowed the institution, at least for a while, to become a major British stage outside of London.

Keynes's personal interest in classical opera and dance led him to support the Royal Opera House at Covent Garden and the Ballet Company at Sadler's Wells. During the War as a member of CEMA (Council for the Encouragement of Music and the Arts) Keynes helped secure government funds to maintain both companies while their venues were shut.

Following the War Keynes was instrumental in establishing the Arts Council of Great Britain and was the founding Chairman in 1946. Unsurprisingly from the start the two organisations that received the largest grant from the new body were the Royal Opera House and Sadler's Wells.

Like several other notable British authors of his time, Keynes was a member of the Bloomsbury Group. Virginia Woolf's biographer tells an anecdote on how Virginia Woolf, Keynes and T. S. Eliot would discuss religion at a dinner party, in the context of their struggle againstVictorian era morality.

Keynes may have been confirmed, but by university he was clearly an agnostic, which he remained until his death. According to one biographer, "he was never able to take religion seriously, regarding it as a strange aberration of the human mind."

Investments

Keynes was ultimately a successful investor, building up a private fortune. His assets were nearly wiped out following the Wall Street Crash of 1929, which he did not foresee, but he soon recouped.

At Keynes's death, in 1946, his net worth stood just short of £500,000 – equivalent to about £11 million ($16.5 million) in 2009. The sum had been amassed despite lavish support for various good causes and his personal ethic which made him reluctant to sell on a falling market in cases where he saw such behaviour as likely to deepen a slump.

Keynes built up a substantial collection of fine art, including works, not all of them minor, by Paul Cézanne, Edgar Degas, Amedeo Modigliani, Georges Braque, Pablo Picasso, and Georges Seurat (some of which can now be seen at the Fitzwilliam Museum).

He enjoyed collecting books: for example, he collected and protected many of Isaac Newton's papers. It is in part on the basis of these papers that Keynes wrote of Newton as "the last of the magicians."

Keynes also successfully managed the endowment of King's College, Cambridge, with the active component of his portfolio outperforming a British equity index by an average of 8perc ent a year over a quarter century, earning him favourable mention by later investors such as Warren Buffett and George Soros.

Political Causes

Keynes was a lifelong member of the Liberal Party, which until the 1920s had been one of the two main political parties in the United Kingdom, and as late as 1916 had often been the dominant power in government.

Keynes had helped campaign for the Liberals at elections from as early as 1906, yet he always refused to run for office himself, despite being asked to do so on three separate occasions in 1920.

From 1926 when Lloyd George became leader of the Liberals, Keynes took a major role in defining the party's economics policy, but by then the Liberals had been displaced into third party status by the Labour party.

In 1939 Keynes had the option to enter Parliament as an independent MP with the University of Cambridge seat. A by-election for the seat was to be held due to the illness of an elderly Tory, and the master of Magdalene College had obtained agreement that none of the major parties would field a candidate if Keynes chose to stand.

Keynes declined the invitation as he felt he would wield greater influence on events if he remained a free agent.

Keynes was a proponent of eugenics. He served as Director of the British Eugenics Society from 1937 to 1944. As late as 1946, shortly before his death, Keynes declared eugenics to be "the most important, significant and, I would add, genuine branch of sociology which exists."

Keynes once remarked that "the yes had religion and wanted to save Communism with pens which was worse than yes." Marxism "was founded upon nothing better than a misunderstanding of Ricardo", and, given time, he, Keynes, "would deal thoroughly with the Marxists" and other economists to solve the economic problems their theories "threaten[ed] to cause".

In 1931 Keynes went on to write the following on Marxism: How can I accept the Communist doctrine, which sets up as its bible, above and beyond criticism, an obsolete textbook which I know not only to be scientifically erroneous but without interest or application to the modern world?

How can I adopt a creed which, preferring the mud to the fish, exalts the boorish proletariat above the bourgeoisie and the intelligentsia, who with all their faults, are the quality of life and surely carry the seeds of all human achievement? Even if we need a religion, how can we find it in the turbid rubbish of the red bookshop? It is hard for an educated, decent, intelligent son of Western Europe to find his ideals here, unless he has first suffered some strange and horrid process of conversion which has changed all his values.

Death

Throughout his life, Keynes worked energetically for the benefit both of the public and his friends; even when his health was poor, he laboured to sort out the finances of his old college, and at Bretton Woods he worked to institute an international monetary system that would be beneficial for the world economy.

Keynes suffered a series of heart attacks, which ultimately proved fatal, beginning during negotiations for an Anglo-American loan in Savannah, Georgia, where he was trying to secure favourable terms for the United Kingdom from the United States, a process he described as "absolute hell". A few weeks after returning from the United States, Keynes died of a heart attack at Tilton, his farmhouse home near Firle, East Sussex, England, on 21 April 1946 at the age of 62.

Both of Keynes's parents outlived him: his father John Neville Keynes (1852–1949) by three years, and his mother Florence Ada Keynes (1861–1958) by twelve. Keynes's brother Sir Geoffrey Keynes (1887–1982) was a distinguished surgeon, scholar, and bibliophile.

His nephews include Richard Keynes (1919–2010) (a physiologist) and Quentin Keynes (1921–2003) (an adventurer and bibliophile). His widow, Lydia Lopokova, died in 1981.

JOHN R HICKS

Sir John Richard Hicks (8 April 1904 – 20 May 1989) was a British economist and one of the most important and influential economists of the twentieth century. The most familiar of his many contributions in the field of economics were his statement ofconsumer demand theory in microeconomics, and the IS/LM model (1937), which summarised a Keynesian view ofmacroeconomics. His book *Value and Capital* (1939) significantly extended general-equilibrium and value theory.

The compensated demand function is named the Hicksian demand function in memory of him.

In 1972 he received the Nobel Memorial Prize in Economic Sciences (jointly) for his pioneering contributions to general equilibrium theory and welfare theory.

BIOGRAPHY

Early Life

Hicks was born in 1904 at Warwick, England. His father was a journalist at a local newspaper. He was educated at Clifton College (1917–22) and at Balliol College, Oxford (1922–26), financed by mathematical scholarships. During his school days, and in his first year at Oxford, he specialised in mathematics but also had interests in literature and history. In 1923, he moved to Philosophy, Politics and Economics, the "new school" just being started at Oxford, graduating with second-class honours and, so he states, "no adequate qualification in any of the subjects" that he had studied.

Career, Influences, and Honours

From 1926 to 1935 Hicks lectured at the London School of Economics and Political Science. He started as a labour economist and did descriptive work on industrial relations but gradually he moved over to the analytical side, where his mathematics background returned to the fore.

Hick's influences included Lionel Robbins and such associates asFriedrich von Hayek, R.G.D. Allen, Nicholas Kaldor, and Abba Lerner – and Ursula Webb, who, in 1935, became his wife. He said of his personal transformation: "I can date my own personal 'revolution' rather exactly to May or June 1933. It was like this. It began...with Hayek."

From 1935 to 1938, he lectured at Cambridge where he was also a fellow of Gonville & Caius College. He was mainly occupied in writing *Value and Capital*, which was based on the work he had done in London. From 1938 to 1946, he was Professor at the University of Manchester. It was there that he did his main work on welfare economics, with its application to social accounting.

In 1946 he returned to Oxford, first as a research fellow of Nuffield College (1946–52), then as Drummond Professor of Political Economy (1952–65), and finally as a research fellow of All Souls College (1965–71) where he continued writing after retirement. He was also an honourary fellow of Linacre College. He died in 1989.

Hicks was knighted in 1964 and was co-recipient of the Nobel Prize in Economic Sciences (with Kenneth J. Arrow) in 1972. He donated the Nobel Prize to the London School of Economics and Political Science's Library Appeal in 1973.

CONTRIBUTIONS TO ECONOMIC ANALYSIS

Hicks's early work as a labour economist culminated in *The Theory of Wages* (1932, 2nd ed. 1963), still considered standard in the field. He collaborated with R.G.D. Allen in two seminal papers on value theory published in 1934.

His magnum opus is *Value and Capital* published in 1939. The book *built* on ordinal utility and mainstreamed the now-standard distinction between the substitution effect and theincome effect for an individual in demand theory for the 2-good case. It generalised the analysis to the case of one good and a composite good, that is, all other goods. It aggregated individuals and businesses through demand and supply across the economy. It anticipated the aggregation problem, most acutely for the stock of capital goods.

It introduced general equilibrium theory to an English-speaking audience, refined the theory for dynamic analysis, and for the first time attempted a rigourous statement of stability conditions for general equilibrium. In the course of analysis Hicks formalised comparative statics.

In the same year, he also developed the famous "compensation" criterion called Kaldor-Hicks efficiency for welfare comparisons of alternative public policies or economic states.

Hicks's most familiar contribution in macroeconomics was the Hicks-Hansen IS-LM model, which formalised an interpretation of the theory of John Maynard Keynes.

The model describes the economy as a balance between three commodities: money, consumption and investment.

Hicks himself did not embrace the theory as he interpreted it; and, in a paper published in 1980, Hicks asserted that it had omitted some crucial components of Keynes's arguments, especially those related to uncertainty.

MAURICE ALLAIS

Maurice Félix Charles Allais (31 May 1911 – 9 October 2010) was a French economist, and was the 1988 winner of the Nobel Memorial Prize in Economics "for his pioneering contributions to the theory of markets and efficient utilization of resources."

THE ECONOMIST

Born in Paris, France, Allais attended the Lycée Lakanal, graduated from the École Polytechnique in Paris and studied at the École nationale supérieure des mines de Paris.

His academic and non-academic posts have included being Professor of Economics at the École Nationale Supérieure des Mines de Paris (since 1944) and Director of its Economic Analysis Centre (since 1946).

In 1949 he received a Doctor-Engineer title from the University of Paris, Faculty of Science.

He also held teaching positions at various institutions, including at the University of Paris X-Nanterre, and the Graduate Institute of International and Development Studies in Geneva.

As an economist he made contributions to decision theory, monetary policy and other areas.

He was reluctant to write in or translate his work into English, and many of his major contributions became known to the dominant anglophone community only when they were independently rediscovered or popularized by English-speaking economists.

For example, in one of his major works,*Économie et Intérêt* (1947), he introduced the first overlapping generations model (later popularized by Paul

Samuelson in 1958), introduced the golden rule of optimal growth (later popularized by Edmund Phelps) or described the transaction demand for money rule (later found in William Baumol's work).

He was also responsible for early work in Behavioural economics, which in the US is generally attributed to Daniel Kahneman and Amos Tversky.

Allais attended the inaugural meeting of the Mont Pelerin Society, but alone among the attendees, refused to sign the statement of aims due a disagreement over the extent of property rights.

His name is particularly associated with what is commonly known as the Allais paradox, a decision problem he first presented in 1953 which contradicts the expected utility hypothesis.

In 1992, Maurice Allais criticized the Maastricht Treaty for its excessive emphasis on free trade.

He also expressed reservations on the single European currency. In 2005, he expressed similar reservations concerning the European constitution.

WORK IN DECISION THEORY

During the 1940s, Allais became interested in the theory of choice under uncertainty and developed a theory of cardinal utility.

Because of wartime conditions and his commitment to publishing in French this work was undertaken in isolation from that of von Neumann and Morgenstern whose Theory of Games and Economic Behaviour included the development of expected utility theory.

HIS INTEREST IN PHYSICS

Besides his career in economics, Maurice Allais performed experiments between 1952 and 1960 in the fields of gravitation, special relativity and electromagnetism, in order to investigate possible links between these fields.

He reported three effects with respect to these experiments:

- An unexpected anomalous effect in the angular velocity of the plane of oscillation of a paraconical pendulum, detected during two partial solar eclipses in 1954 and 1959. This claimed effect is now called the Allais effect.
- Anomalous irregularities in the oscillation of the paraconical pendulum, with periodicity 24h50min, which corresponds to the tidal lunar day.
- Anomalous irregularities in optical theodolite measurements, with the same tidal periodicity.

Over the years, a number of pendulum experiments were performed by scientists around the world to test his findings. However, the results were mixed.

DEATH

Allais died on 9 October 2010 at his home near Paris at the age of 99.

MILTON FRIEDMAN

Milton Friedman (July 31, 1912 – November 16, 2006) was an American economist, statistician, and writer who taught at the University of Chicago for more than three decades. He was a recipient of the 1976 Nobel Prize in Economic Sciences, and is known for his research on consumption analysis, monetary history and theory, and the complexity of stabilization policy.

As a leader of the Chicago school of economics, he profoundly influenced the research agenda of the economics profession. A survey of economists ranked Friedman as the second most popular economist of the twentieth century afterJohn Maynard Keynes, and *The Economist* described him as "the most influential economist of the second half of the 20th century ... possibly of all of it."

Friedman's challenges to what he later called "naive Keynesian" (as opposed to New Keynesian) theory began with his 1950s reinterpretation of the consumption function, and he became the main advocate opposing Keynesian government policies.

In the late 1960s, he described his own approach (along with all of mainstream economics) as using "Keynesian language and apparatus" yet rejecting its "initial" conclusions.

During the 1960s, he promoted an alternative macroeconomic policy known as "monetarism". He theorized there existed a"natural" rate of unemployment and argued that governments could only increase employment above this rate, *e.g.*, by increasing aggregate demand, only for as long as inflation was accelerating.

He argued that the Phillips curve was, in the long run, vertical at the "natural rate" and predicted what would come to be known as stagflation. Though opposed to the existence of the Federal Reserve System, Friedman argued that, given that it does exist, a steady, small expansion of themoney supply was the only wise policy.

Friedman was an economic adviser to Republican U.S. President Ronald Reagan. His political philosophy extolled the virtues of a free market economic system with minimal intervention.

He once stated that his role in eliminating U.S. conscription was his proudest accomplishment, and his support for school choice led him to found the Friedman Foundation for Educational Choice.

In his 1962 book *Capitalism and Freedom*, Friedman advocated policies such as a volunteer military, freely floating exchange rates, abolition of medical licenses, a negative income tax, and school vouchers.

His ideas concerningmonetary policy, taxation, privatization and deregulation influenced government policies, especially during the 1980s. Hismonetary theory influenced the Federal Reserve's response to the global financial crisis of 2007–08. In the field ofstatistics, Friedman developed the sequential sampling method of analysis.

Milton Friedman's works include many monographs, books, scholarly articles, papers, magazine columns, television programmes, videos, and lectures, and cover a broad range of topics of microeconomics, macroeconomics, economic history, and public policy issues. His books and essays were widely read, and have had an international influence, including in formerCommunist states.

EARLY LIFE

Friedman was born in Brooklyn, New York, to recent Jewish immigrants Sára Ethel (née Landau) and Jenõ Saul Friedman, from Beregszász in Carpathian Ruthenia, Kingdom of Hungary (now Berehove in Ukraine), both of whom worked as dry goodsmerchants. Shortly after Milton's birth, the family relocated to Rahway, New Jersey. In his early teens, Friedman was injured in a car accident, which scarred his upper lip.

A talented student, Friedman graduated from Rahway High School in 1928, just before his 16th birthday.

In 1932 Friedman graduated from Rutgers University, where he specialized in Mathematics and Economics and initially intended to become an actuary. During his time at Rutgers, Friedman became influenced by two economics professors, Arthur F. Burns andHomer Jones, who convinced him that modern economics could help end the Great Depression.

After graduating from Rutgers, Friedman was offered two scholarships to do graduate work — one in mathematics at Brown University and the other in economics at the University of Chicago. Friedman chose the latter, thus earning a Master of Artsdegree in 1933. He was strongly influenced by Jacob Viner, Frank Knight, and Henry Simons. It was at Chicago that Friedman met his future wife, economist Rose Director. During the 1933–1934 academic year he had a fellowship at Columbia University, where he studied statistics with renowned statistician and economist Harold Hotelling.

He was back in Chicago for the 1934–1935 academic year, working as a research assistant for Henry Schultz, who was then working on *Theory and Measurement of Demand*. That year, Friedman formed what would prove to be lifelong friendships with George Stigler and W. Allen Wallis.

PUBLIC SERVICE

Friedman was initially unable to find academic employment, so in 1935 he followed his friend W. Allen Wallis to Washington, whereFranklin D.

Roosevelt's New Deal was "a lifesaver" for many young economists. At this stage, Friedman said that he and his wife "regarded the job-creation programmes such as the WPA, CCC, and PWA appropriate responses to the critical situation," but not "theprice- and wage-fixing measures of the National Recovery Administration and the Agricultural Adjustment Administration.

"Foreshadowing his later ideas, he believed price controls interfered with an essential signaling mechanism to help resources be used where they were most valued.

Indeed, Friedman later concluded that all government intervention associated with the New Deal was "the wrong cure for the wrong disease," arguing that the money supply should simply have been expanded, instead of contracted.

In the publication, *A Monetary History of the United States, 1867–1960* by Friedman and Anna J. Schwartz, they argue that theGreat Depression was caused by monetary contraction, which was the consequence of poor policymaking by the Federal Reserve System and the continuous crises of the banking system.

During 1935, he began work for the National Resources Committee, which was then working on a large consumer budget survey.

Ideas from this project later became a part of his *Theory of the Consumption Function*.

Friedman began employment with theNational Bureau of Economic Research during autumn 1937 to assist Simon Kuznets in his work on professional income.

This work resulted in their jointly authored publication *Incomes from Independent Professional Practice*, which introduced the concepts of permanent and transitory income, a major component of the Permanent Income Hypothesis that Friedman worked out in greater detail in the 1950s. The book hypothesizes that professional licensing artificially restricts the supply of services and raises prices.

During 1940, Friedman was appointed an assistant professor teaching Economics at the University of Wisconsin–Madison, but encountered antisemitism in the Economics department and decided to return to government service.

From 1941 to 1943 Friedman worked on wartime tax policy for the Federal Government, as an advisor to senior officials of the United States Department of the Treasury. As a Treasury spokesman during 1942 he advocated a Keynesian policy of taxation.

He helped to invent the payroll withholding tax system, since the federal government badly needed money in order to fight the war. He later said, "I have no apologies for it, but I really wish we hadn't found it necessary and I wish there were some way of abolishing withholding now."

ACADEMIC CAREER

Early Years

In 1940, Friedman accepted a position at the University of Wisconsin–Madison, but left because of differences with faculty regarding United States involvement in World War II.

Friedman believed the United States should enter the war. In 1943, Friedman joined the Division of War Research at Columbia University (headed by W.

Allen Wallis and Harold Hotelling), where he spent the rest ofWorld War II working as a mathematical statistician, focusing on problems of weapons design, military tactics, and metallurgical experiments.

In 1945, Friedman submitted *Incomes from Independent Professional Practice* (co-authored with Kuznets and completed during 1940) to Columbia as his doctoral dissertation.

The university awarded him a PhD in 1946. Friedman spent the 1945–1946 academic year teaching at the University of Minnesota (where his friend George Stigler was employed). On February 12, 1945, his son, David D. Friedman was born.

University of Chicago

In 1946, Friedman accepted an offer to teach economic theory at the University of Chicago (a position opened by departure of his former professor Jacob Viner to Princeton University).

Friedman would work for the University of Chicago for the next 30 years. There he contributed to the establishment of an intellectual community that produced a number of Nobel Prize winners, known collectively as theChicago school of economics.

At that time, Arthur F. Burns, who was then the head of the National Bureau of Economic Research, asked Friedman to rejoin the Bureau's staff. He accepted the invitation, and assumed responsibility for the Bureau's enquiry into the role of money in the business cycle.

As a result, he initiated the "Workshop in Money and Banking" (the "Chicago Workshop"), which promoted a revival of monetary studies. During the latter half of the 1940s, Friedman began a collaboration with Anna Schwartz, an economic historian at the Bureau, that would ultimately result in the 1963 publication of a book co-authored by Friedman and Schwartz, *A Monetary History of the United States, 1867–1960*.

Friedman spent the 1954–1955 academic year as a Fulbright Visiting Fellow at Gonville and Caius College, Cambridge. At the time, the Cambridge economics faculty was divided into a Keynesian majority (including Joan Robinson and Richard Kahn) and an anti-Keynesian minority (headed by Dennis Robertson). Friedman speculated that he was invited to the fellowship, because his views were unacceptable to both of the Cambridge factions. Later his weekly columns for *Newsweek* magazine (1966–84) were well read and increasingly influential among political and business people.

From 1968 to 1978, he and Paul Samuelson participated in the Economics Cassette Series, a biweekly subscription series where the economist would discuss the days' issues for about a half-hour at a time.

Friedman was an economic adviser to Republican presidential candidate Barry Goldwater during 1964.

Nobel Prize in Economic Sciences

Friedman won the Nobel Memorial Prize in Economic Sciences, the sole recipient for 1976, "for his achievements in the fields of consumption analysis, monetary history and theory and for his demonstration of the complexity of stabilization policy."

RETIREMENT

In 1977, at the age of 65, Friedman retired from the University of Chicago after teaching there for 30 years. He and his wife moved to San Francisco where he became a visiting scholar at the Federal Reserve Bank of San Francisco. From 1977 on, he was affiliated with the Hoover Institution at Stanford University.

During the same year, Friedman was approached by the Free To Choose Network and asked to create a television programme presenting his economic and social philosophy.

The Friedmans worked on this project for the next three years, and during 1980, the ten-part series, titled *Free to Choose*, was broadcast by the Public Broadcasting Service(PBS).

The companion book to the series (co-authored by Milton and his wife, Rose Friedman), also titled *Free To Choose*, was the bestselling non-fiction book of 1980 and has since been translated into 14 foreign languages.

Friedman served as an unofficial adviser to Ronald Reagan during his 1980 presidential campaign, and then served on the President's Economic Policy Advisory Board for the rest of the Reagan Administration.

In 1988 he received the National Medal of Science and Reagan honoured him with the Presidential Medal of Freedom. Milton Friedman is known now as one of the most influential economists of the 20th century.

Throughout the 1980s and 1990s, Friedman continued to write editorials and appear on television.

He made several visits to Eastern Europe and to China, where he also advised governments. He was also for many years a Trustee of the Philadelphia Society.

SCHOLARLY CONTRIBUTIONS

Economics

Friedman was best known for reviving interest in the money supply as a determinant of the nominal value of output, that is, the quantity theory of money. Monetarism is the set of views associated with modern quantity theory. Its origins can be traced back to the 16th-century School of Salamanca or even further; however, Friedman's contribution is largely responsible for its modern popularization.

He co-authored, with Anna Schwartz, *A Monetary History of the United States, 1867–1960* (1963), which was an examination of the role of the money supply and economic activity in the U.S. history.

A striking conclusion of their research regarded the way in which money supply fluctuations contribute to economic fluctuations. Several regression studies with David Meiselman during the 1960s suggested the primacy of the money supply over investment and government spending in determining consumption and output.

These challenged a prevailing, but largely untested, view on their relative importance. Friedman's empirical research and some theory supported the conclusion that the short-run effect of a change of the money supply was primarily on output but that the longer-run effect was primarily on the price level.

Friedman was the main proponent of the monetarist school of economics. He maintained that there is a close and stable association between inflation and the money supply, mainly that inflation could be avoided with proper regulation of the monetary base's growth rate.

He famously used the analogy of "dropping money out of a helicopter.", in order to avoid dealing with money injection mechanisms and other factors that would overcomplicate his models.

Friedman's arguments were designed to counter the popular concept of Cost-push inflation, that the increased General Price Level at the time was the result of increases in the price of oil, or increases in wages; as he wrote,

Inflation is always and everywhere a monetary phenomenon.

—Milton Friedman, 1963.

Friedman rejected the use of fiscal policy as a tool of demand management; and he held that the government's role in the guidance of the economy should be restricted severely.

Friedman wrote extensively on the Great Depression, which he termed the Great Contraction, arguing that it had been caused by an ordinary financial shock whose duration and seriousness were greatly increased by the subsequent contraction of the money supply caused by the misguided policies of the directors of the Federal Reserve.

The Fed was largely responsible for converting what might have been a garden-variety recession, although perhaps a fairly severe one, into a major catastrophe.

Instead of using its powers to offset the depression, it presided over a decline in the quantity of money by one-third from 1929 to 1933 ... Far from the depression being a failure of the free-enterprise system, it was a tragic failure of government. —Milton Friedman, *Two Lucky People, 233*

Friedman also argued for the cessation of government intervention in currency markets, thereby spawning an enormous literature on the subject, as well as promoting the practice of freely floating exchange rates.

His close friend George Stigler explained, "As is customary in science, he did not win a full victory, in part because research was directed along different lines by the theory of rational expectations, a newer approach developed by Robert Lucas, also at the University of Chicago."

Friedman was also known for his work on the consumption function, the permanent income hypothesis (1957), which Friedman himself referred to as his best scientific work.This work contended that rational consumers would spend a proportional amount of what they perceived to be their permanent income. Windfall gains would mostly be saved.

Tax reductions likewise, as rational consumers would predict that taxes would have to increase later to balance public finances. Other important contributions include his critique of the Phillips curve and the concept of the natural rate of unemployment (1968).

This critique associated his name, together with that of Edmund Phelps, with the insight that a government that brings about greater inflation cannot permanently reduce unemployment by doing so. Unemployment may be temporarily lower, if the inflation is a surprise, but in the long run unemployment will be determined by the frictions and imperfections of the labour market.

Friedman's essay "The Methodology of Positive Economics" (1953) provided the epistemological pattern for his own subsequent research and to a degree that of the Chicago School.

There he argued that economics as *science* should be free of value judgements for it to be objective. Moreover, a useful economic theory should be judged not by its descriptive realism but by its simplicity and fruitfulness as an engine of prediction. That is, students should measure the accuracy of its predictions, rather than the 'soundness of its assumptions'. His argument was part of an ongoing debate among such statisticians as Jerzy Neyman, Leonard Savage, and Ronald Fisher.

Statistics

One of his most famous contributions to statistics is sequential sampling. Friedman did statistical work at the Division of War Research at Columbia. He and his colleagues came up with a sampling technique, known as sequential sampling, which became, in the words of *The New Palgrave Dictionary of Economics*, "the standard analysis of quality control inspection".

The dictionary adds, "Like many of Friedman's contributions, in retrospect it seems remarkably simple and obvious to apply basic economic ideas to quality control; that however is a measure of his genius."

PUBLIC POLICY POSITIONS

Federal Reserve

Friedman believed that the Federal Reserve should be abolished but if the money supply was to be centrally controlled (as by the Federal Reserve System) that the preferable way to do it would be with a mechanical system that would keep the quantity of money increasing at a steady rate.

However, instead of government involvement at all, he was open to a real, non-government, gold standard where money is produced by the private market: "A real gold standard is thoroughly consistent with [classical] liberal principles and I, for one, am entirely in favour of measures promoting its development."

He did however add this caveat, "Let me emphasize that this note is not a plea for a return to a gold standard ... I regard a return to a gold standard as neither desirable nor feasible — with the one exception that it might become feasible if the doomsday predictions of hyperinflation under our present system should prove correct."

He said the reason that it was not feasible was because "there is essentially no government in the world that is willing to surrender control over its domestic monetary policy."

However, it could be done if "you could re-establish a world in which government's budget accounted for 10 percent of the national income, in which laissez-faire reigned, in which governments did not interfere with economic activities and in which full employment policies had been relegated to the dustbin ..." Friedman was considered sympathetic to free banking.

He was critical of the Federal Reserve's influence on the economics profession. In a 1993 letter to University of Texas economics professor and former House Banking Committee investigator Robert Auerbach, Friedman wrote:

I cannot disagree with you that having something like 500 economists is extremely unhealthy. As you say, it is not conducive to independent, objective research. You and I know there has been censorship of the material published.

Equally important, the location of the economists in the Federal Reserve has had a significant influence on the kind of research they do, biasing that research towards non-controversial technical papers on method as opposed to substantive papers on policy and results.

School Choice

In his 1955 article "The Role of Government in Education" Friedman proposed supplementing publicly operated schools with privately run but publicly funded schools through a system of school vouchers.

Reforms similar to those proposed in the article were implemented in, for example, Chile in 1981 and Sweden in 1992. In 1996, Friedman, together with his wife, founded The Foundation for Educational Choice to advocate school choice and vouchers.

Conscription

Milton Friedman was a major proponent of a volunteer military, stating that the draft was "inconsistent with a free society."

In *Capitalism and Freedom*, he argued that conscription is inequitable and arbitrary, preventing young men from shaping their lives as they see fit. During the Nixon administration he headed the committee to research a conversion to paid/volunteer armed force.

He would later state that his role in eliminating the conscription in the United States was his proudest accomplishment. Friedman did, however, believe a nation could compel military *training* as a reserve in case of war time.

Foreign Policy

Biographer Lanny Ebenstein noted a drift over time in Friedman's views from an interventionist to a more cautious foreign policy. He supported US involvement in the Second World War and initially supported a hard line against Communism, but moderated over time.

He opposed the Gulf War and the Iraq War. In a spring 2006 interview, Friedman said that the USA's stature in the world had been eroded by the Iraq War, but that it might be improved if Iraq were to become a peaceful independent country.

Libertarianism and the Republican Party

He served as a member of President Reagan's Economic Policy Advisory Board starting at 1981. In 1988, he received the Presidential Medal of Freedom and the National Medal of Science.

He said that he was a libertarian philosophically, but a member of the U.S. Republican Party for the sake of "expediency" ("I am a libertarian with a small 'l' and a Republican with a capital 'R.' And I am a Republican with a capital 'R' on grounds of expediency, not on principle.") But, he said, "I think the term classical liberal is also equally applicable. I don't really care very much what I'm called. I'm much more interested in having people thinking about the ideas, rather than the person."

Public Goods and Monopoly

Friedman was supportive of the state provision of some public goods that private businesses are not considered as being able to provide. However, he argued that many of the services performed by government could be performed better by the private sector.

Above all, if some public goods are provided by the state, he believed that they should not be a legal monopoly where private competition is prohibited; for example, he wrote:

There is no way to justify our present public monopoly of the post office. It may be argued that the carrying of mail is a technical monopoly and that a government monopoly is the least of evils. Along these lines, one could perhaps justify a government post office, but not the present law, which makes it illegal for anybody else to carry the mail.

If the delivery of mail is a technical monopoly, no one else will be able to succeed in competition with the government. If it is not, there is no reason why the government should be engaged in it. The only way to find out is to leave other people free to enter.

HONOURS, RECOGNITION, AND INFLUENCE

George H. Nash, a leading historian of American conservatism, says that by, "the end of the 1960s he was probably the most highly regarded and influential conservative scholar in the country, and one of the few with an international reputation."

Friedman allowed the libertarian Cato Institute to use his name for its biannual Milton Friedman Prize for Advancing Liberty beginning in 2001. A Friedman Prize was given to the late British economist Peter Bauer in 2002, Peruvian economist Hernando de Soto in 2004,Mart Laar, former Estonian Prime Minister in 2006 and a young Venezuelan student Yon Goicoechea in 2008.

His wife Rose, sister of Aaron Director, with whom he initiated the Friedman Foundation for Educational Choice, served on the international selection committee. Friedman was also a recipient of the Nobel Prize in Economics.

Upon the death of Friedman, Harvard President Lawrence Summers called Friedman "The Great Liberator" saying "... any honest Democrat will admit that we are now all Friedmanites." He said Friedman's great popular contribution was "in convincing people of the importance of allowing free markets to operate."

In 2013 Stephen Moore, a member of the editorial forward of the *Wall Street Journal* said, "Quoting the most-revered champion of free-market economics since Adam Smith has become a little like quoting the Bible." He adds, "There are sometimes multiple and conflicting interpretations."

Hong Kong

Friedman once said, "If you want to see capitalism in action, go to Hong Kong." He wrote in 1990 that the Hong Kong economy was perhaps the best example of a free market economy.

One month before his death, he wrote the article "Hong Kong Wrong – What would Cowperthwaite say?" in the *Wall Street Journal*, criticizing Donald Tsang, the Chief Executive of Hong Kong, for abandoning "positive non-interventionism."

Tsang later said he was merely changing the slogan to "big market, small government," where small government is defined as less than 20perc ent of GDP. In a debate between Tsang and his rival, Alan Leong, before the 2007 Chief Executive election, Leong introduced the topic and jokingly accused Tsang of angering Friedman to death.

Chile

During 1975, two years after the military coup that brought military dictator President Augusto Pinochet to power and ended the government of Salvador Allende, the economy ofChile experienced a severe crisis. Friedman and Arnold Harberger accepted an invitation of a private Chilean foundation to visit Chile and speak on principles of economic freedom.

He spent seven days in Chile giving a series of lectures at the Universidad Católica de Chile. and the (National) University of Chile.

One of the lectures was entitled "The Fragility of Freedom" and according to Friedman, "dealt with precisely the threat to freedom from a centralized military government."

During his visit Friedman met with Pinochet, who asked him for his "... opinions about Chile's economic situation and policies".

In an April 21, 1975, letter to Pinochet that Friedman wrote to comply with Pinochet's request, Friedman considered the "key economic problems of Chile are clearly ... inflation and the promotion of a healthy social market economy".

He stated that "There is only one way to end inflation: by drastically reducing the rate of increase of the quantity of money ..." and that "... cutting government spending is by far and away the most desirable way to reduce the fiscal deficit, because it ... strengthens the private sector thereby laying the foundations for *healthy* economic growth".

As to how rapidly inflation should be ended, Friedman felt that "for Chile where inflation is raging at 10-20perc ent a month ... gradualism is not feasible. It would involve so painful an *operation* over so long a period that the *patient* would not survive."

Choosing "a brief period of higher unemployment..." was the lesser evil.. and that "the experience of Germany, ... of Brazil ..., of the post-war adjustment in the U.S. ... all argue for *shock treatment*". In the letter Friedman recommended to deliver what the *shock approach* with "... a package to eliminate the surprise and to relieve acute distress" and "... for definiteness let me sketch the contents of a package proposal ... to be taken as illustrative" although his knowledge of Chile was "too limited to enable [him] to be precise or comprehensive".

He listed a "sample proposal" of 8 monetary and fiscal measures including "the removal of as many as obstacles as possible that now hinder the private market. For example, suspend ... the present law against discharging employees". He closed, stating "Such a *shock programme* could end inflation in months".

His letter suggested that cutting spending to reduce the fiscal deficit would result in less transitional unemployment than raising taxes.

Sergio de Castro, a Chilean Chicago School graduate, became the nation's Minister of Finance in 1975. During his six-year tenure, foreign investment increased, restrictions were placed on striking and labour unions, and GDP rose yearly.

A foreign exchange programme was created between the Catholic University of Chile and the University of Chicago. Many other Chicago School alumni were appointed government posts during and after the Pinochet years; others taught its economic doctrine at Chilean universities. They became known as the Chicago Boys.

Friedman did not criticize Pinochet's dictatorship at the time, nor the assassinations, illegal imprisonments, torture, or other atrocities that were well known by then.

In 1976 Friedman defended his unofficial adviser position with: "I do not consider it as evil for an economist to render technical economic advice to the Chilean Government, any more than I would regard it as evil for a physician to give technical medical advice to the Chilean Government to help end a medical plague."

Friedman defended his activity in Chile on the grounds that, in his opinion, the adoption of free market policies not only improved the economic situation of Chile but also contributed to the amelioration of Pinochet's rule and to the eventual transition to a democratic government during 1990.

That idea is included in *Capitalism and Freedom*, in which he declared that economic freedom is not only desirable in itself but is also a necessary condition for political freedom. In his 1980 documentary *Free to Choose*, he said the following: "Chile is not a politically free system, and I do not condone the system.

But the people there are freer than the people in Communist societies because government plays a smaller role.... The conditions of the people in the past few years has been getting better and not worse. They would be still better to get rid of the junta and to be able to have a free democratic system." In 1984, Friedman stated that he has "never refrained from criticizing the political system in Chile."

In 1991 he said: "I have nothing good to say about the political regime that Pinochet imposed. It was a terrible political regime. The real miracle of Chile is not how well it has done economically; the real miracle of Chile is that a military junta was willing to go against its principles and support a free market regime designed by principled believers in a free market.

In Chile, the drive for political freedom, that was generated by economic freedom and the resulting economic success, ultimately resulted in a referendum that introduced political democracy.

Now, at long last, Chile has all three things: political freedom, human freedom and economic freedom. Chile will continue to be an interesting experiment to watch to see whether it can keep all three or whether, now that it has political freedom,that political freedom will tend to be used to destroy or reduce economic freedom."

He stressed that the lectures he gave in Chile were the same lectures he later gave in China and other socialist states. During the 2000 PBS documentary *The Commanding Heights* (based on the book), Friedman continued to argue that "free markets would undermine [Pinochet's] political centralization and political control.", and that criticism over his role in Chile missed his main contention that freer markets resulted in freer people, and that Chile's unfree economy had caused the military government. Friedman suggested that the economic liberalization he advocated caused the end of military rule and a free Chile.

Iceland

Friedman visited Iceland during the autumn of 1984, met with important Icelanders and gave a lecture at the University of Iceland on the "tyranny of the *status quo*." He participated in a lively television debate on August 31, 1984 with socialist intellectuals, including Ólafur Ragnar Grímsson, who later became the president of Iceland.

When they complained that a fee was charged for attending his lecture at the University and that, hitherto, lectures by visiting scholars had been free-of-charge, Friedman replied that previous lectures had not been free-of-charge in a meaningful sense: lectures always have related costs. What mattered was whether attendees or non-attendees covered those costs. Friedman thought that it was fairer that only those who attended paid. In this discussion Friedman also stated that he did not receive any money for delivering that lecture.

PERSONAL LIFE

According to a 2007 article in *Commentary* magazine, his "parents were moderately observant [Jews], but Friedman, after an intense burst of childhood

, rejected religion altogether." He described himself as an agnostic. Friedman wrote extensively of his life and experiences, especially in 1998 in his memoirs with his wife Rose, titled *Two Lucky People*.

He died of heart failure at the age of 94 years in San Francisco on November 16, 2006. He was survived by his wife (who died on August 18, 2009) and their two children, David, who is an anarcho-capitalisteconomist, and Janet. David's son, Patri Friedman, was the executive director of the The Seasteading Institute from 2008–2011.

MUHAMMAD YUNUS

Muhammad Yunus (born 28 June 1940) is a Bangladeshi social entrepreneur, banker, economist and civil society leader who was awarded the Nobel Peace Prize for founding the Grameen Bank and pioneering the concepts ofmicrocredit and microfinance.

These loans are given to entrepreneurs too poor to qualify for traditional bank loans. In 2006, Yunus and the Grameen Bank were jointly awarded the Nobel Peace Prize "for their efforts through microcredit to create economic and social development from below".

The Norwegian Nobel Committee noted that "lasting peace cannot be achieved unless large population groups find ways in which to break out of poverty" and that "across cultures and civilizations, Yunus and Grameen Bank have shown that even the poorest of the poor can work to bring about their own development".

Yunus has received several other national and international honours. He received the United StatesPresidential Medal of Freedom in 2009 and the Congressional Gold Medal in 2010.

In 2008, he was rated #2 in *Foreign Policy* magazine's list of the "Top 100 Global Thinkers".

In February 2011, Yunus together with Saskia Bruysten, Sophie Eisenmann and Hans Reitz co-founded Yunus Social Business – Global Initiatives (YSB). YSB creates and empowers social businesses to address and solve social problems around the world.

As the international implementation arm for Yunus' vision of a new, humane capitalism, YSB manages Incubator Funds for social businesses in developing countries and providing advisory services to companies, governments, foundations and NGOs.

In 2012, he became Chancellor of Glasgow Caledonian University in Scotland. He is a member of the advisory board atShahjalal University of Science and Technology.

Previously, he was a professor of economics at Chittagong University in Bangladesh. He published several books related to his finance work. He is a founding board member of Grameen Americaand Grameen Foundation, which support microcredit. Yunus also serves on the board of directors of the United Nations Foundation, a public charity created in 1998 by American philanthropist Ted Turner's $1 billion gift to support UN causes.

In March 2011, the Bangladesh government fired Yunus from his position at Grameen Bank, citing legal violations and an age limit on his position. Bangladesh's High Court affirmed the removal on 8 March. Yunus and Grameen Bank are appealing the decision, claiming Yunus' removal was politically motivated.

EARLY LIFE AND EDUCATION

Early Years

The third of nine children, Yunus was born on 28 June 1940 to a Muslim family in the village of Bathua, by the Boxirhat Road inHathazari, Chittagong in the Bengal Presidency of the British Raj, which today forms modern Bangladesh. His father was Hazi Dula Mia Shoudagar, a jeweler, and his mother was Sufia Khatun.

His early childhood was spent in the village. In 1944, his family moved to the city of Chittagong, and he moved from his village school to Lamabazar Primary School. By 1949, his mother was afflicted with psychological illness.

Later, he passed the matriculation examination from Chittagong Collegiate School ranking 16th of 39,000 students in East Pakistan. During his school years, he was an active Boy Scout, and travelled to West Pakistan and India in 1952, and to Canada in 1955 to attend Jamborees.

Later while Yunus studied at Chittagong College, he became active in cultural activities and won awards for drama. In 1957, he enrolled in the Department of Economics at Dhaka University and completed his BA in 1960 andMA in 1961.

After Graduation

After his graduation, Yunus joined the Bureau of Economics as a research assistant to the economics researches of Professor Nurul Islam and Rehman Sobhan. Later, he was appointed lecturer in economics in Chittagong College in 1961.

During that time, he also set up a profitable packaging factory on the side. In 1965, he received aFulbright scholarship to study in the United States. He obtained his PhD in economics from the Vanderbilt University Graduate Programme in Economic Development (GPED) in 1971. From 1969 to 1972, Yunus was assistant professor of economics at Middle Tennessee State University in Murfreesboro.

During the Bangladesh Liberation War in 1971, Yunus founded a citizen's committee and ran the Bangladesh Information Centre, with other Bangladeshis in the United States, to raise support for liberation. He also published the *Bangladesh Newsletter* from his home in Nashville.

After the War, he returned to Bangladesh and was appointed to the government's Planning Commission headed by Nurul Islam. However, he found the job boring and resigned to join Chittagong University as head of the Economics department.

After observing the famine of 1974, he became involved in poverty reduction and established a rural economic programme as a research project. In 1975, he developed a Nabajug (New Era) Tebhaga Khamar (three share farm) which the government adopted as the Packaged Input Programme.

In order to make the project more effective, Yunus and his associates proposed the *Gram Sarkar* (the village government) programme. Introduced by president Ziaur Rahman in the late 1970s, the Government formed 40,392 village governments as a fourth layer of government in 2003.

On 2 August 2005, in response to a petition by Bangladesh Legal Aids and Services Trust (BLAST) the High Court had declared village governments illegal and unconstitutional.

His concept of microcredit for supporting innovators in multiple developing countries also inspired programmes such as the Infolady Social Entrepreneurship Programme.

EARLY CAREER

In 1976, during visits to the poorest households in the village of Jobra near Chittagong University, Yunus discovered that very small loans could make a disproportionate difference to a poor person.

Village women who made bamboo furniture had to take usurious loans to buy bamboo, and repay their profits to the lenders. Traditional banks did not want to make tiny loans at reasonable interest to the poor due to high risk of default.

But Yunus believed that, given the chance, the poor will repay the money and hence microcredit was a viablebusiness model. Yunus lent US$27 of his money to 42 women in the village, who made a profit of BDT 0.50 (US$0.02) each on the loan. Thus Yunus is credited with the idea of microcredit alongside Dr. Akhtar Hameed Khan, founder of the Pakistan Academy for Rural Development (now Bangladesh Academy for Rural Development), whom Yunus greatly admired.

In December 1976, Yunus finally secured a loan from the government Janata Bank to lend to the poor in Jobra. The institution continued to operate, securing loans from other banks for its projects. By 1982, it had 28,000 members. On 1 October 1983, the pilot project began operation as a full-fledged bank for poor Bangladeshis and was renamed Grameen Bank ("Village Bank"). Yunus and his colleagues encountered everything from violent radical leftists to conservative clergy who told women that they would be denied a Muslim burial if they borrowed money from Grameen. By July 2007, Grameen had issued US$6.38 billion to 7.4 million borrowers. To ensure repayment, the bank uses a system of "solidarity groups".

These small informal groups apply together for loans and its members act as co-guarantors of repayment and support one another's efforts at economic self-advancement.

In the late 1980s, Grameen started to diversify by attending to underutilized fishing ponds and irrigation pumps like deep tube wells. In 1989, these diversified interests started growing into separate organizations.

The fisheries project became Grameen Motsho ("Grameen Fisheries Foundation") and the irrigation project became Grameen Krishi ("Grameen Agriculture Foundation").

In time, the Grameen initiative grew into a multi-faceted group of profitable and non-profit ventures, including major projects like Grameen Trust and Grameen Fund, which runs equity projects like Grameen Software Limited, Grameen CyberNet Limited, and Grameen Knitwear Limited, as well as Grameen Telecom, which has a stake in Grameenphone (GP), the biggest private phone company in Bangladesh.

From its start in March 1997 to 2007, GP's Village Phone (*Polli Phone*) project had brought cell-phone ownership to 260,000 rural poor in over 50,000 villages.

The success of the Grameen microfinance model inspired similar efforts in about 100 developing countries and even in developed countries including the United States. Many microcredit projects retain Grameen's emphasis of lending to women.

More than 94perc ent of Grameen loans have gone to women, who suffer disproportionately from poverty and who are more likely than men to devote their earnings to their families.

For his work with Grameen, Yunus was named an Ashoka: Innovators for the Public Global Academy Member in 2001.

In the book Grameen Social Business Model, Rashidul Bari shows how Grameen's social business model (GSBM)- has gone from being theory to an inspiring practice adopted by leading universities (*e.g.*, Glasgow), entrepreneurs (*e.g.*, Franck Riboud) and corporations (*e.g.*, Danone) across the globe.

Through Grameen Bank, Rashidul Bari claims that Yunus demonstrated howGrameen Social Business Model can harness the entrepreneurial spirit to empower poor women and alleviate their poverty.

One conclusion from Yunus' concepts is that the poor are like a "bonsai tree", and they can do big things if they get access to the social business that holds potential to empower them to become self-sufficient.

RECOGNITION

Yunus was awarded the 2006 Nobel Peace Prize, along with Grameen Bank, for their efforts to create economic and social development. In the prize announcement TheNorwegian Nobel Committee mentioned:

Muhammad Yunus has shown himself to be a leader who has managed to translate visions into practical action for the benefit of millions of people, not only in Bangladesh, but also in many other countries.

Loans to poor people without any financial security had appeared to be an impossible idea. From modest beginnings three decades ago, Yunus has, first and foremost through Grameen Bank, developed micro-credit into an ever more important instrument in the struggle against poverty.

Yunus was the first Bangladeshi to ever get a Nobel Prize. After receiving the news of the important award, Yunus announced that he would use part of his share of the $1.4 million award money to create a company to make low-cost, high-nutrition food for the poor; while the rest would go towards setting up an eye hospital for the poor in Bangladesh.

Former U.S. president Bill Clinton was a vocal advocate for the awarding of the Nobel Prize to Yunus. He expressed this in *Rolling Stone*magazine as well as in his autobiography *My Life.*

In a speech given at University of California, Berkeley in 2002, President Clinton described Yunus as "a man who long ago should have won the Nobel Prize [and] I'll keep saying that until they finally give it to him." Conversely, The Economist stated explicitly that Yunus was a poor choice for the award, stating: "...the Nobel committee could have made a braver, more difficult, choice by declaring that there would be no recipient at all."

He is one of only seven persons to have won the Nobel Peace Prize, Presidential Medal of Freedom, and the Congressional Gold Medal. Other notable awards include the Ramon Magsaysay Award in 1984, the World Food Prize, the International Simon Bolivar Prize (1996), the Prince of Asturias Award for Concord and the Sydney Peace Prize in 1998, and the Seoul Peace Prizein 2006.

Additionally, Yunus has been awarded 50 honourary doctorate degrees from universities across 20 countries, and 113 international awards from 26 different countries including state honours from 10 countries. Bangladesh government brought out a commemorative stamp to honour his Nobel Award.

Yunus was named by Fortune Magazine in March 2012 as one of 12 greatest entrepreneurs of the current era. In its citation, Fortune Magazine said 3 Yunus' idea inspired countless numbers of young people to devote themselves to social causes all over the world.3

In January 2012, Yunus featured in "Transformative Entrepreneurs: How Walt Disney, Steve Jobs, Muhammad Yunus and Other Innovators Succeeded" a book by Jeffrey Harris.

Yunus was named "Nobel-Laureate-in-Residence" at Universiti Kebangsaan Malaysia (National University of Malaysia) on 15 July 2011.

Yunus delivered the Seventh Nelson Mandela Annual Lecture.

In January 2008, Houston, Texas declared 14 January as "Muhammad Yunus Day".

On 15 May 2010, Yunus gave the commencement speech at Rice University for the graduating class of 2010. On 16 May 2010, Yunus gave the commencement speech at Duke University for the graduating class of 2010. During this ceremony, he was also awarded an honourary degree, Doctor of Humane Letters.

Yunus was invited and gave the Wharton School of Business commencement address on 17 May 2009, the MIT commencement address on 6 June 2008, Adam Smith Lecture at Glasgow University on 1 December 2008 and Oxford's Romanes Lecture on 2 December 2008.

He received the Dwight D. Eisenhower Medal for Leadership and Service from the Eisenhower Fellowships at a ceremony in Philadelphia on 21 May 2009. He was also voted 2nd in *Prospect Magazine*'s 2008 global poll of the world's top 100 intellectuals.

Yunus was named among the most desired thinkers the world should listen to by the FP 100 (world's most influential elite) in the December 2009 issue of *Foreign Policy*magazine. On 1 March 2010, Yunus was awarded the prestigious Presidential Award from the University of Illinois at Urbana–Champaign. This is the highest honour available from the University.

A documentary on Yunus' work titled *To Catch a Dollar* was shown at the 2010 Sundance Film Festival and is due to be released in theatres in the US on September 2010.

In 2010, The British Magazine *New Statesman* listed Yunus at 40th in the list of "The World's 50 Most Influential Figures 2010".

In October 2010, He received the Social Entrepreneur of the Year Award at The Asian Awards.

On 22 September 2011 the documentary film, *Bonsai People – The Vision of Muhammad Yunus*, the first documentary film that looks his full body of work from microcredit to social business, premiered at the United Nations.

Yunus received 50 honourary doctorate degrees from universities from Argentina, Australia, Bangladesh, Belgium, Canada, Costa Rica, India, Italy, Japan, Korea, Lebanon, Malaysia, Russia, South Africa, Spain, Thailand, Turkey, UK, USA and Peru.

United Nations Secretary General, Ban Ki-Moon, invited Yunus to serve as an MDG Advocate. Yunus sits on the Board ofUnited Nations Foundation, Schwab Foundation, Prince Albert II of Monaco Foundation, Grameen Credit Agricole Microcredit Foundation. He has been a member of Fondation Chirac's honour committee, ever since the foundation was launched in 2008 by former French president Jacques Chirac in order to promote world peace.

Yunus has appeared on *The Daily Show with Jon Stewart* and *The Oprah Winfrey Show* in 2006, *The Colbert Report* in 2008, *Real Time with Bill Maher* in 2009 and *The Simpsons* in 2010. On Google+, Yunus is one of the most followed person worldwide, with over 1.7 million followers.

In 2012 Yunus was installed as Chancellor of Glasgow Caledonian University. U.S House and Senate leaders held a ceremony to present Yunus with the Congressional Gold Medal on April 17, 2013 in Washington, D.C for his contributions to the fight against global poverty.

The Congressional Gold Medal is the highest civilian honour bestowed by the United States Congress. At the ceremony, which you can watch on YouTube, Sen. Dick Durbin (D-IL) explained why Yunus is such a visionary: "It's been said that almost anyone can make something complicated. It takes a genius to make something simple. My friends, make no mistake; Muhammad Yunus is a genius." The gold medal was awarded to Yunus with the 111th Congress Public Law 253.

POLITICAL ACTIVITY

In early 2006 Yunus, along with other members of the civil society including Professor Rehman Sobhan, Justice Muhammad Habibur Rahman, Dr Kamal Hossain, Matiur Rahman, Mahfuz Anam and Debapriya Bhattchariya, participated in a campaign for honest and clean candidates in national elections. He considered entering politics in the later part of that year.

On 11 February 2007, Yunus wrote an open letter, published in the Bangladeshi newspaper *Daily Star*, where he asked citizens for views on his plan to float a political party to establish political goodwill, proper leadership and good governance.

In the letter, he called on everyone to briefly outline how he should go about the task and how they can contribute to it. Yunus finally announced that he is willing to launch a political party tentatively called Citizens' Power (*Nagorik Shakti*) on 18 February 2007.

There was speculation that the army supported a move by Yunus into politics. On 3 May, however, Yunus declared that he had decided to abandon his political plans following a meeting with the head of the interim government, Fakhruddin Ahmed.

In July 2007, in Johannesburg, South Africa, Nelson Mandela, Graça Machel, and Desmond Tutu convened a group of world leaders "to contribute their wisdom, independent leadership and integrity to tackle some of the world's toughest problems." Nelson Mandela announced the formation of this new group, The Elders, in a speech he delivered on the occasion of his 89th birthday. Yunus attended the launch of the group and was one of its founding members. He stepped down as an Elder in September 2009, stating that he was unable to do justice to his membership due to the demands of his work.

Yunus is a member of the Africa Progress Panel (APP), a group of ten distinguished individuals who advocate at the highest levels for equitable and sustainable development in Africa. Every year, the Panel releases a report, the Africa Progress Report, that outlines an issue of immediate importance to the continent and suggests a set of associated policies. In 2012, the Africa Progress Report highlighted issues of Jobs, Justice, and Equity. The 2013 report will outline issues relating to oil, gas, and mining in Africa.

In July 2009, Yunus became a member of the SNV Netherlands Development Organisation International Advisory Board to support the organisation's poverty reduction work.

Since 2010, Yunus has served as a Commissioner for the Broadband Commission for Digital Development, a UN initiative which seeks to use broadband internet services to accelerate social and economic development.

He also serves on the advisory board of the Holcim Foundation for Sustainable Construction, a foundation supporting initiatives that combine sustainable construction solutions with architectural excellence.

In 2011, Yunus was part of the Jury which chose the universal Logo for Human Rights. Its goal was to create an internationally recognised logo to support the global human rights movement.

CONTROVERSIES

Since late November 2010, several allegations have been made against Yunus. They started with a critique of microcredit and blame of Grameen Bank on several points in the documentary *Caught in Micro Debt* on Norwegian television on 30 November 2010. This developed at a time when larger questions were being raised about the benefits of microfinance and its effects on poverty alleviation, particularly in regards to several microfinance institutions (MFIs) in India and Mexico.

The allegations against Yunus became political when the government of Bangladesh – led by Sheikh Hasina Wajed turned against him and the concept of microfinance, accusing it of "sucking blood from the poor". Wajed reportedly viewed Yunus as a political rival since Yunus considered creating a political party in 2007. – In the book Grameen Social Business Model, Rashidul Bari explained the political vendetta in Bangladesh by Sheikh Hasina against Yunus as a replay of the conflict between Pope Urban VIII and Galileo Galilei.

Pope Urban VIII put 70-year-old Galileo in prison in 1632 for condemning and rejecting Ptolemy's geocentric model, which was adopted by the early Christian Church. In the same spirit, Sheikh Hasina who labeled Yunus as a "blood sucker of poor people"—unleashed her propaganda machine (*e.g.*, AMA Muhith) to remove Yunus from Grameen—and used the High Court and

Supreme Court to justify her decision. Why did Pope Urban VIII insult the Father of Astronomy? Because Galileo rejected the accepted Christian Church view, that the earth is the centre of the universe, and that all other celestial objects orbit around it. Why has Hasina insulted the Father of Microcredit? Because, in 2007, Yunus criticized Hasina, accusing her of corruption.

The Government announced a review of Grameen Bank activities on 11 January 2011, which is ongoing. In February, several international leaders, such as Mary Robinson, stepped up their defence of Yunus through a number of efforts, including the founding of a formal network of supporters known as "Friends of Grameen".

On 15 February 2011, the Finance Minister of Bangladesh, Abul Maal Abdul Muhith, declared that Yunus should "stay away" from Grameen Bank while it is being investigated. On 2 March 2011, Muzammel Huq – a former Bank employee, whom the government had appointed Chairman in January – announced that Yunus had been fired as Managing Director of the Bank. However, Bank General Manager Jannat-E Quanine issued a statement that Yunus was "continuing in his office" pending review of the legal issues surrounding the controversy.

In March 2011, Yunus petitioned the Bangladesh High Court challenging the legality of the decision by the Bangladeshi Central Bank to remove him as Managing Director of Grameen Bank.

The same day, nine elected directors of Grameen Bank filed a second petition. Following Hillary Clinton, John Kerry expressed his support to Yunus in a statement on 5 March 2011 and declared that he was "deeply concerned" by this affair. The same day in Bangladesh, thousands of people protested and formed human chains to support Yunus. The High Court hearing on the petitions, was planned for 6 March 2011 but postponed. On 8 March 2011, the Court confirmed Yunus's dismissal.

Political Motivations Behind the Allegations

Though Grameen Bank was quickly cleared by the Norwegian government of all allegations surrounding misused or misappropriated funds in December 2010, in March 2011 the Bangladeshi government launched a three-month investigation of all Grameen Bank's activities. This enquiry prevented Muhammad Yunus from participating in the World Economic Forum.

In January 2011, Yunus appeared in court in a defamation case filed by a local politician from a minor left-leaning party in 2007, complaining about a statement that Yunus made to the AFP news agency: "Politicians in Bangladesh only work for power. There is no ideology here". At the hearing, Yunus was granted bail and exempted from personal appearance at subsequent hearings.

These investigations fueled suspicion that many attacks might be politically motivated, due to difficult relations between Sheikh Hasina and Yunus since early 2007, when Yunus created his own political party, an effort he dropped in May 2007.

Transition to New Management

At 72 years old, he was 12 years beyond the legal retirement age for civil servants in Bangladesh in 2011. Government spokespersons called for Yunus to step down and declared: "We need to redefine the bank's role and bring it under closer regulation."

The government as chairman Muzammel Huq, himself a foundational figure of the Grameen Bank and one of senior managers together with Yunus of GB Research and Operations until the early 2000s. He has publicly criticised Yunus, saying: "I think he is a good man with a small heart... He cannot give credit to anyone but himself".

PERSONAL LIFE

In 1967, while Yunus attended Vanderbilt University, he met Vera Forostenko, a student of Russian literature at Vanderbilt University and daughter of Russian immigrants toTrenton, New Jersey, US. They were married in 1970.

Yunus's marriage with Vera ended within months of the birth of their baby girl, Monica Yunus (born 1979 Chittagong), as Vera returned to New Jersey claiming that Bangladesh was not a good place to raise a baby.

Yunus later married Afrozi Yunus, who was then a researcher in physics at Manchester University. She was later appointed as a professor of physics at Jahangirnagar University. Their daughter Deena Afroz Yunus was born in 1986.

Yunus's brothers are also active in academia. His brother Muhammad Ibrahim is a professor of physics at Dhaka University and the founder of The Centre for Mass Education in Science (CMES), which brings science education to adolescent girls in villages.

His younger brother Muhammad Jahangir is a popular television presenter and a well known social activist in Bangladesh. He is also the moderator of several Talk show programmes in Bangladesh. Monica Yunus, his elder daughter, is a Bangladeshi-Russian Americanoperatic soprano, working in New York City.

PAUL SAMUELSON

Paul Anthony Samuelson (May 15, 1915 – December 13, 2009) was an American economist, and the first American to win theNobel Memorial Prize in Economic Sciences. The Swedish Royal Academies stated, when awarding the prize, that he "has done more than any other contemporary economist to raise the level of scientific analysis in economic theory". Economic historian Randall E. Parker calls him the "Father of Modern Economics", and *The New York Times* considered him to be the "foremost academic economist of the 20th century".

He was author of the largest-selling economics textbook of all time: *Economics: An Introductory Analysis*, first published in 1948. It was the second American textbook to explain the principles of Keynesian economics and how to think about economics, and the first one to be successful, and is now in its 19th edition, having sold nearly 4 million copies in 40 languages.

James Poterba, former head of MIT's Department of Economics, noted that by his book, Samuelson "leaves an immense legacy, as a researcher and a teacher, as one of the giants on whose shoulders every contemporary economist stands".

In 1996, when he was awarded the National Medal of Science, considered America's top science honour, President Bill Clinton commended Samuelson for his "fundamental contributions to economic science" for over 60 years.

He entered the University of Chicago at age 16, during the depths of the Great Depression, and received his PhD in economics from Harvard. After graduating, he became an assistant professor of economics at Massachusetts Institute of Technology (MIT) when he was 25 years of age and a full professor at age 32.

In 1966, he was named Institute Professor, MIT's highest faculty honour. He spent his career at MIT where he was instrumental in turning its Department of Economics into a world-renowned institution by attracting other noted economists to join the faculty, including Robert M. Solow, Franco Modigliani, Robert C. Merton,Joseph E. Stiglitz, and Paul Krugman, all of whom went on to win Nobel Prizes.

He served as an advisor to Presidents John F. Kennedy and Lyndon B. Johnson, and was a consultant to the United States Treasury, the Bureau of the Budget and the President's Council of Economic Advisers. Samuelson wrote a weekly column for*Newsweek* magazine along with Chicago School economist Milton Friedman, where they represented opposing sides: Samuelson took the Keynesian perspective, and Friedman represented the Monetarist perspective. Samuelson died on December 13, 2009, at the age of 94.

BIOGRAPHY

Samuelson was born in Gary, Indiana, on May 15, 1915, to Frank Samuelson, a pharmacist, and the former Ella Lipton. His family, he said, was "made up of upwardly mobile Jewish immigrants from Poland who had prospered considerably in World War I, because Gary was a brand new steel town when my family went there". In 1923 Samuelson moved to Chicago; he graduated from Hyde Park High School (now Hyde Park Career Academy); he then studied at the University of Chicago and received his Bachelor of Arts degree there in 1935. He said he was born as an economist, at 8.00am on January 2, 1932, in the University of Chicago classroom.

He felt there was a dissonance between neo-classical economics and the way the system seemed to behave, and he said Henry Simons and Frank Knight were a big influence on him.

He then completed his Master of Arts degree in 1936, and his Doctor of Philosophy in 1941 at Harvard University. He won the David A. Wells prize in 1941 for writing the best doctoral dissertation at Harvard University in economics. As a graduate student at Harvard, Samuelson studied economics under Joseph Schumpeter, Wassily Leontief, Gottfried Haberler, and the "American Keynes" Alvin Hansen.

Samuelson moved to MIT as an Assistant Professor in 1940 and remained there until his death. Samuelson comes from a family of well-known economists, including brother Robert Summers, sister-in-law Anita Summers, brother-in-law Kenneth Arrow and nephew Larry Summers. During his seven decades as an economist, Samuelson's professional positions included:

- Assistant Professor of Economics at M.I.T, 1940, Associate Professor, 1944.
- Member of the Radiation Laboratory 1944–1945.
- Professor of International Economic Relations (part-time) at the Fletcher School of Law and Diplomacy in 1945.
- Guggenheim Fellowship from 1948 to 1949
- Professor of Economics at MIT beginning in 1947 and Institute Professor beginning in 1962.
- Vernon F. Taylor Visiting Distinguished Professor at Trinity University (Texas) in Spring 1989.

Death

Samuelson died after a brief illness on December 13, 2009, at the age of 94. His death was announced by the Massachusetts Institute of Technology. James M. Poterba, an economics professor at MIT and the president of the National Bureau of Economic Research, commented that Samuelson "leaves an immense legacy, as a researcher and a teacher, as one of the giants on whose shoulders every contemporary economist stands".

Susan Hockfield, the president of MIT, said that Samuelson "transformed everything he touched: the theoretical foundations of his field, the way economics was taught around the world, the ethos and stature of his department, the investment practices of MIT, and the lives of his colleagues and students".

IMPACT

Samuelson is considered to be one of the founders of neo-Keynesian economics and a seminal figure in the development of neo-classical economics.

In awarding him the Nobel Memorial Prize in Economic Sciences the committee stated:

More than any other contemporary economist, Samuelson has helped to raise the general analytical and methodological level in economic science. He has simply rewritten considerable parts of economic theory. He has also shown the fundamental unity of both the problems and analytical techniques in economics, partly by a systematic application of the methodology of maximization for a broad set of problems. This means that Samuelson's contributions range over a large number of different fields.

He was also essential in creating the Neo-classical synthesis, which incorporated Keynesian and neo-classical principles and still dominates current mainstream economics. In 2003, Samuelson was one of the ten Nobel Prize–winning economists signing the Economists' statement opposing the Bush tax cuts.

SIR RICHARD STONE

Sir John Richard Nicholas Stone (30 August 1913 – 6 December 1991) was an eminent British economist, educated atWestminster School, Cambridge University (Caius and King's), who in 1984 received the Nobel Memorial Prize in Economic Sciences for developing an accounting model that could be used to track economic activities on a national and, later, an international scale.

BIOGRAPHY

Youth and Studies

Richard Stone was born in London, UK on August 30, 1913. He received an English upper middle class education when he was a child as he attended Cliveden Place and Westminster School.

However, he had not taught mathematics and science until secondary school. When he was 17 years old, he followed his father to India as his father was appointed as a judge in Madras. From India, he visited many Asian countries: Malaya, Singapore, and Indonesia, and had enjoyable time.

Only one year in foreign country, he went back to London and studied in Gonville and Caius College, Cambridge University in 1931. However, his study in law only lasted for two years.

The young Stone then changed to reading economics. He was interested in economics as he taught that "if there were more economists, the world would be a better place". At that time, the level of unemployment was very high and it motivated him to know what caused it and how to overcome it.

He faced a challenge from his parents as they were disappointed to his choice. However, Stone was very enthusiastic to be an economist and then enjoyed his time studied economics. At his new major, he got supervision from Richard Kahn and Gerald Shove. However, Stone's quantitative mind had been greatly influenced by Colin Clark, Stone's teacher in statistics at Cambridge. Colin then introduced Stone to his project in measuring the national income.

This project then brought the greatest name for Stone as he received Nobel Prize because of this topic. After their meeting at Cambridge, Stone and Clark then became a best friend.

First Employment

After graduating from Cambridge in 1936 and until World War II he worked at Lloyd's of London. During the war, Stone worked with James Meade as a statistician and economist for the British Government.

They were requested by the government to analyze the UK's economy related to the current total resources of the nation on the war time. It was at this time that they developed the early versions of the system of national accounts. Their work resulted in the first UK's national accounts in 1941.

The collaboration between Stone and Meade was over after 1941 as their office was split into two different offices.

They then worked separately, Meade was responsible for Economic Section and Stone was responsible for the national income. In his new office, the Central Statistical Office, Stone became John Maynard Keynes' assistant. When the World War II ended in 1945, Stone discontinued working for the UK's government.

Academic Career

After the war, Stone worked at Cambridge as the director of the new Department of Applied Economics (1945–1955). As the director, Stone made the Department focus on research programmes about economic theory and statistical methodology.

This strategy attracted many top economists in that era to join the Department. Some remarkable works at the Department were, for example, Durbin and Watson on testing serial correlation in econometrics, and Alan Prest and Derek Rowe on demand analysis.

This condition made DAE become one of the leading quantitative economic research centres in the world in his era. Stone himself had many projects in DAE: national accountingwhere he had employed Agatha Chapman as a research associate, the analysis of consumer demand, and the system of socio-demographic account.

In 1955, Stone gave up his Directorship at the department as he was appointed as the P.D. Leake Chair of Finance and Accounting at Cambridge (emeritus from 1980). Together with Alan Brown he began the Cambridge Growth Project, which developed the Cambridge Multisectoral Dynamic Model of the British economy (MDM) . In building the Cambridge Growth Project, they used Social Accounting Matrices (SAM), which also formed computable equilibrium model which then developed at the World Bank.

He was succeeded as leader of the Cambridge Growth Project by Terry Barker. In 1970, Stone was appointed as the Chairman of the Faculty Board of Economics and Politics for the next two years.

A company founded by members of the Department and limited by guarantee, Cambridge Econometrics, was founded in 1978 with Stone as its first honourary president. The company continues to develop MDM and to use the model to make economic forecasts. Before retired from Cambridge in 1980, Stone served as the President of the Royal Economic Society for 1978–1980.

Family Life

In 1936, he married Winifred Mary Jenkins who was also from Cambridge. Both of them had a passion for Economics and started a monthly called Trends, which was a supplement to the periodical, Industry Illustrated. It contained articles about the British economic conditions. Soon after, in 1939, he was asked to join the Ministry of Economic Warfare.

In 1941, Stone married his second wife Feodora Leontinoff after his first marriage was dissolved in 1940.

His second wife Feodora died in 1956, and in 1960, he married Giovanna Saffi, great grandchild of Italian patriot Aurelio Saffi, who became his partner in many of his works.

Stone died on 6 December 1991. With his third wife, Stone collaborated for some projects in economics, for example in rewriting his famous book "National Income and Expenditure" in 1961. He is survived by his third wife Giovanna, and his daughter Caroline.

WORK

Stone in 1984 received the Nobel Memorial Prize in Economic Sciences for developing an accounting model that could be used to track economic activities on a national and, later, an international scale.

While he was not the first economist to work in this field, he was the first to do so with double entry accounting. Double entry accounting basically states that every income item on one side of the balance sheet must be met by an expenditure item on the opposite side of the accounting sheet therefore creating a system of balance.

This double entry system is the basis of nearly all modern accounting today. This allowed for a reliable way of tracking trade and wealth transfer on a global scale.

He is sometimes known as the 'father of national income accounting', and is the author of studies of consumer demand statistics and demand modeling, economic growth, andinput-output. During his acceptance speech Stone mentioned François Quesnay as well as the *Tableau économique*. Stone stated that it was one of the very first works in economics to examine various sectors on such a global level and how they are all interconnected.

WILLIAM VICKREY

William Spencer Vickrey (21 June 1914 – 11 October 1996) was a Canadian-born professor of economics and Nobel Laureate. Vickrey was awarded the 1996 Nobel Memorial Prize in Economic Sciences with James Mirrlees for their research into the economic theory of incentives under asymmetric information. The announcement of the prize was made just three days prior to his death; his Columbia University economics department colleague C. Lowell Harriss accepted the prize posthumously on his behalf.

BIOGRAPHY

Early Years

Vickrey was born in Victoria, British Columbia and attended high school at Phillips Academy in Andover, Massachusetts. After obtaining his B.S. in mathematics at Yale University in 1935, he went on to complete his masters in 1937 and doctoral studies in 1948 at Columbia University where he would remain for most of his career.

Career

Vickrey's paper, *Counterspeculation, auctions and competitive sealed tenders*, was the first of its kind using the tools of game theory to explain the dynamics of auctions. In his paper, Vickrey derives several auction equilibria, and provides an early revenue equivalence result. The revenue equivalence theorem remains the centrepiece of modern auction theory. The Vickrey auction is named after him.

He also did important work in congestion pricing, the idea that roads and other services should be priced so that users see the costs that arise from the service being fully used when there is still demand. Congestion pricing gives a signal to users to adjust their behaviour or to investors to expand the service in order to remove the constraint. His theory was later partially put into action inLondon.

In public economics, Vickrey extended the marginal cost pricing approach of Harold Hotelling.

Vickrey's economic philosophy was influenced by John Maynard Keynes and Henry George. He was sharply critical of the Chicago school of economics and the political focus on achieving balanced budgets and fighting inflation in times of high unemployment.

Vickrey had many graduate students and proteges at Columbia University, including the economists Jacques Drèze, Lynn Turgeon, and Harvey J. Levin.

Personal Life

Vickrey was married to Cecile Thompson in 1951. He died in Harrison, New York in 1996 from heart failure. He was a Quaker and a member of Scarsdale Friends Meeting.

WORKS

- "Counterspeculation, Auctions, and Competitive Sealed Tenders" is a fundamental paper on auctions written by the Nobel Prize–winning economist William Vickrey in 1961.It has originated auction theory, a subfield of game theory (Bayesian games).

3

Basics of Economic Thought

Economics is the science that concerns itself with economies, from how societies produce goods and services, to how they consume them. It has influenced world finance at many important junctions throughout history and is a vital part of our everyday lives.

The assumptions that guide the study of economics, have changed dramatically throughout history. In this article, we'll look at the history of how economic thought has changed over time, and the major participants in its development.

INTRODUCTION

Economics may appear to be the study of complicated tables and charts, statistics and numbers, but, more specifically, it is the study of what constitutes rational human behaviour in the endeavor to fulfill needs and wants.

As an individual, for example, you face the problem of having only limited resources with which to fulfill your wants and needs, as a result, you must make certain choices with your money.

You'll probably spend part of your money on rent, electricity and food. Then you might use the rest to go to the movies and/or buy a new pair of jeans. Economists are interested in the choices you make, and enquire into why, for instance, you might choose to spend your money on a new DVD player instead of replacing your old TV.

They would want to know whether you would still buy a carton of cigarettes if prices increased by $2 per pack. The underlying essence of economics is trying to understand how both individuals and nations behave in response to certain material constraints. ((To learn how economic factors are used in currency trading, read *Forex Walkthrough: Economics*.)

We can say, therefore, that economics, often referred to as the "dismal science", is a study of certain aspects of society. Adam Smith (1723 - 1790), the "father of modern economics" and author of the famous book "An Enquiry into the Nature and Causes of the Wealth of Nations", spawned the discipline of economics by trying to understand why some nations prospered while others lagged behind in poverty. Others after him also explored how a nation's allocation of resources affects its wealth.

To study these things, economics makes the assumption that human beings will aim to fulfill their self-interests. It also assumes that individuals are rational in their efforts to fulfill their unlimited wants and needs.

Economics, therefore, is a social science, which examines people behaving according to their self-interests. The definition set out at the turn of the twentieth century by Alfred Marshall, author of "The Principles Of Economics" (1890), reflects the complexity underlying economics: "Thus it is on one side the study of wealth; and on the other, and more important side, a part of the study of man."

WHAT IS ECONOMICS?

In order to begin our discussion of economics, we first need to understand (1) the concept of scarcity and (2) the two branches of study within economics:microeconomics and macroeconomics.

SCARCITY

Scarcity, a concept we already implicitly discussed in the introduction to this tutorial, refers to the tension between our limited resources and our unlimited wants and needs. For an individual, resources include time, money and skill. For a country, limited resources include natural resources, capital, labour force and technology.

Because all of our resources are limited in comparison to all of our wants and needs, individuals and nations have to make decisions regarding what goods and services they can buy and which ones they must forgo. For example, if you choose to buy one DVD as opposed to two video tapes, you must give up owning a second movie of inferior technology in exchange for the higher quality of the one DVD. Of course, each individual and nation will have different values, but by having different levels of (scarce) resources, people and nations each form some of these values as a result of the particular scarcities with which they are faced.

So, because of scarcity, people and economies must make decisions over how to allocate their resources. Economics, in turn, aims to study why we make these decisions and how we allocate our resources most efficiently.

MACRO AND MICROECONOMICS

Macro and microeconomics are the two vantage points from which the economy is observed. Macroeconomics looks at the total output of a nation and the way the nation allocates its limited resources of land, labour and capital in an attempt to maximize production levels and promote trade and growth for future generations. After observing the society as a whole, Adam Smith noted that there was an "invisible hand" turning the wheels of the economy: a market force that keeps the economy functioning.

Microeconomics looks into similar issues, but on the level of the individual people and firms within the economy. It tends to be more scientific in its approach, and studies the parts that make up the whole economy.

Analyzing certain aspects of human behaviour, microeconomics shows us how individuals and firms respond to changes in price and why they demand what they do at particular price levels.

Micro and macroeconomics are intertwined; as economists gain understanding of certain phenomena, they can help nations and individuals make more informed decisions when allocating resources. The systems by which nations allocate their resources can be placed on a spectrum where the command economy is on the one end and the market economy is on the other.

The market economy advocates forces within a competitive market, which constitute the "invisible hand", to determine how resources should be allocated. The command economic system relies on the government to decide how the country's resources would best be allocated. In both systems, however, scarcity and unlimited wants force governments and individuals to decide how best to manage resources and allocate them in the most efficient way possible. Nevertheless, there are always limits to what the economy and government can do.

THE FATHER OF ECONOMICS

Adam Smith is widely credited for creating the field of economics, however, he was inspired by French writers, who shared his hatred of mercantilism. In fact, the first methodical study of how economies work, was undertaken by these French physiocrats. Smith took many of their ideas and expanded them into a thesis about how economies should work, as opposed to how they do work.

Smith believed that competition was self-regulating and that governments should take no part in business through tariffs, taxes or any other means, unless it was to protect free-market competition. Many economic theories today are, at least in part, a reaction to Smith's pivotal work in the field.

THE DISMAL SCIENCE OF MARX AND MALTHUS

Karl Marx and Thomas Malthus had decidedly poor reactions to Smith's treatise. Malthus predicted that growing populations would outstrip the food supply. He was proven wrong, however, because he didn't foresee technological innovations that would allow production to keep pace with a growing population. Non-etheless, his work shifted the focus of economics to the scarcityof things, versus the demand for them. This increased focus on scarcity led Karl Marx to declare that the means of production were the most important components in any economy. Marx took his ideas further and became convinced that a class war was going to be initiated by the inherent instabilities he saw in capitalism. However, Marx underestimated the flexibility of capitalism. Instead of creating a clear owner and worker class, investing created a mixed class where owners and workers hold the interests of both classes, in balance.

Despite his overly rigid theory, Marx did accurately predicted one trend: businesses grew larger and more powerful, in accordance to the degree of free-market capitalism allowed.

SPEAKING IN NUMBERS

Leon Walras, a French economist, gave economics a new language in his book "Elements of Pure Economics." Walras went to the roots of economic theory and made models and theories that reflected what he found there. General equilibrium theory came from his work, as well as the tendency to express economic concepts statistically and mathematically, instead of just in prose.

Alfred Marshall took the mathematical modeling of economies to new heights, introducing many concepts that are still not fully understood, such as economies of scale, marginal utility and the real-cost paradigm.

It is nearly impossible to expose an economy to experimental rigour, therefore, economics is on the edge of science. Through mathematical modeling, however, some economic theory has been rendered testable.

KEYNESIAN ECONOMICS

John Maynard Keynes' mixed economy was a response to charges levied by Marx, long ago, that capitalist societies aren't self-correcting. Marx saw this as a fatal flaw, whereas Keynes saw this as a chance for government to justify its existence. Keynesian economics is the code of action that the Federal Reservefollows, to keep the economy running smoothly.

BACK TO THE BEGINNING: MILTON FRIEDMAN

The economic policies of the last two decades all bear the marks of Milton Friedman's work. As the U.S. economy matured, Friedman argued that the government had to begin removing the redundant controls it had imposed upon the market, such as antitrust legislation. Rather than growing bigger on the increasing gross domestic product (GDP), Friedman thought that governments should focus on consuming less of an economy's capital, so that more remained in the system. With more capital in the system, it would be possible for the economy to operate without any government interference.

THE BOTTOM LINE

Economic thought has diverged into two streams: theoretical and practical. Theoretical economics uses the language of mathematics, statistics and computational modeling to test pure concepts that, in turn, help economists understand the truths of practical economics and shape them into governmental policy. The business cycle, boom and bust cycles, and anti-inflation measures, are outgrowths of economics; understanding them helps the market and government adjust for these variables.

HISTORY OF ECONOMIC THOUGHT

The history of economic thought deals with different thinkers and theories in the subject that became political economy andeconomics from the ancient world to the present day. It encompasses many disparate schools of economic thought.

Ancient Greek writers such as the philosopher Aristotle examined ideas about the art of wealth acquisition, and questioned whether property is best left in private or public hands. In medieval times, Scholastic scholars such as Thomas Aquinas argued that it was a moralobligation of businesses to sell goods at a just price.

Since medieval times, economics was developed almost exclusively in the West until the 20th century.

Scottish philosopher Adam Smith is often cited as "the Father of Modern Economics" for his treatise *The Wealth of Nations*(1776). His ideas built upon a considerable body of work from predecessors in the eighteenth century, particularly thePhysiocrats.

His book appeared on the eve of the Industrial Revolution, with associated major changes in the economy.

Smith's successors included such classical economists as Thomas Malthus, Jean-Baptiste Say, David Ricardo, and John Stuart Mill. They examined ways the landed, capitalist, and laboring classes produced and distributed national output and modeled the effects of population and international trade. In London, Karl Marx castigated the capitalist system, which he described as exploitative and alienating. From about 1870, neo-classical economics attempted to erect a positive, mathematical, and scientifically grounded field above normative politics.

After the two world wars of the early twentieth century, John Maynard Keynes led a reaction against governmental abstention from economic affairs, advocating interventionist fiscal policy to stimulate economic demand and growth. With a world divided between the capitalist first world, the communist second world, and the poor of the Third World, the post-war consensus broke down.

Others like Milton Friedman and Friedrich Hayek warned of *The Road to Serfdom* and the unworkability of socialism, focusing their theories on what could be achieved through better monetary policy and deregulation.

As Keynesian policies seemed to falter in the 1970s, there emerged New Classical Macroeconomics, developed by prominent theorists including Robert Lucas, and Edward C. Prescott, who tried to provide neo-classical microeconomic mechanisms to help analyze macroeconomic issues.

New Keynesian economists including Paul Krugman, Edmund Phelps, John B. Taylor and Huw Dixon responded to their critiques, eventually leading to the New Neo-classical Synthesis in macroeconomics. Meanwhiledevelopment economists like Amartya Sen, and information economists like Joseph Stiglitz introduced new ideas to economic thought.

ANCIENT ECONOMIC THOUGHT

The earliest discussions of economics date back to ancient times, *e.g.* Xenophon's *Oeconomicus* (written c. 360 BCE) and Chanakya's (born c. 350 BCE) *Arthashastra*. Until the 18th–19th century Industrial Revolution in the West, economics was not a separate discipline but part of philosophy.

PLATO AND ARISTOTLE

Ancient Athens was a slave-based society, but also one developing an embryonic model of democracy.

Plato's dialogue *The Republic* (ca. 380–360 BCE) described the ideal city-state, run by philosopher-kings, and contained references to specialization of labour and production. Plato was the first to advocate the Credit Theory of Money, that money originated as a unit of account for debt.

Plato's student Aristotle's *Politics* (ca. 350 BCE) was mainly concerned to analyze different forms of a state (monarchy, aristocracy, constitutional government, tyranny, oligarchy, democracy) as a critique of Plato's advocacy of a ruling class of philosopher-kings. In particular for economists, Plato had drawn a blueprint of society on the basis of common ownership of resources. Aristotle viewed this model as an oligarchical anathema. In *Politics*, Book II, Part V, he argued that:

"Property should be in a certain sense common, but, as a general rule, private; for, when everyone has a distinct interest, men will not complain of one another, and they will make more progress, because every one will be attending to his own business... And further, there is the greatest pleasure in doing a kindness or service to friends or guests or companions, which can only be rendered when a man has private property. These advantages are lost by excessive unification of the state."

Though Aristotle certainly advocated there be many things held in common, he argued that not everything could be, simply because of the "wickedness of human nature". "It is clearly better that property should be private", wrote Aristotle, "but the use of it common; and the special business of the legislator is to create in men this benevolent disposition." In *Politics* Book I, Aristotle discusses the general nature of households and market exchanges.

For him there is a certain "art of acquisition" or "wealth-getting", but because it is the same many people are obsessed with its accumulation, and "wealth-getting" for one's household is "necessary and honourable", while exchange on the retail trade for simple accumulation is "justly censured, for it is dishonourable". Of the people he stated they as a whole thought acquisition of wealth (chrematistike) as being either the same as, or a principle of oikonomia (*household management* – oikonomos), with *oikos* as house and *nomos* in fact translated as custom or law. Aristotle himself was highly disapproving of usury and cast scorn on making money through means of a monopoly.

Aristotle discarded Plato's credit theory of money for Metallism, the theory that money derives its value from the purchasing power of the commodity upon which it is based, and is only an "instrument", its sole purpose being a medium of exchange, which means on its own "it is worthless... not useful as a means to any of the necessities of life".

ECONOMIC THOUGHT IN THE MIDDLE AGES

THOMAS AQUINAS

Thomas Aquinas (1225–1274) was an Italian theologian and writer on economic issues. He taught in both Cologne and Paris, and was part of a group of Catholic scholars known as the Schoolmen, who moved their enquiries beyond theology to philosophical and scientific debates. In the treatise *Summa Theologica* Aquinas dealt with the concept of a just price, which he considered necessary for the reproduction of the social order.

Bearing many similarities with the modern concept of long run equilibrium a just price was supposed to be one just sufficient to cover the costs of production, including the maintenance of a worker and his family. He argued it was immoral for sellers to raise their prices simply because buyers were in pressing need for a product. Aquinas discusses a number of topics in the format of questions and replies, substantial tracts dealing with Aristotle's theory. Questions 77 and 78 concern economic issues, mainly relate to what a just price is, and to the fairness of a seller dispensing faulty goods.

Aquinas argued against any form of cheating and recommended compensation always be paid in lieu of good service. Whilst human laws might not impose sanctions for unfair dealing, divine law did, in his opinion.

DUNS SCOTUS

One of Aquinas' main critics was Duns Scotus (1265–1308), originally from Duns Scotland, who taught in Oxford, Cologne, and Paris. In his work *Sententiae* (1295), he thought it possible to be more precise than Aquinas in calculating a just price, emphasizing the costs of labour and expenses, although he recognized that the latter might be inflated by exaggeration because buyer and seller usually have different ideas of what a just price comprises.

If people did not benefit from a transaction, in Scotus' view, they would not trade. Scotus defended merchants as performing a necessary and useful social role, transporting goods and making them available to the public.

IBN KHALDUN

Until Joseph J. Spengler's 1964 work "Economic Thought of Islam: Ibn Khaldun", Adam Smith (1723–1790) was believed to be the "Father of Economics". Now there is a second candidate, Arab Muslim scholar Ibn Khaldun (1332–1406) of Tunisia, although how the Muslim world fell behind the West, or what influence Khaldun had in the West is unclear.

NICOLE ORESME

French philosopher Nicole Oresme (1320–1382) wrote a work on the medieval conception of money.

MERCANTILISM, NATIONALISM, AND INTERNATIONAL TRADE

Despite the localism of the Middle Ages, the waning of Feudalism saw new national economic frameworks begin to be strengthened. After the voyages ofChristopher Columbus et al. opened up new opportunities for trade with the New World and Asia, newly-powerful monarchies wanted a more powerful military state to boost their status. Mercantilism was a political movement and an economic theory that advocated the use of the state's military power to ensure that local markets and supply sources were protected, spawning Protectionism.

Mercantile theorists thought that international trade could not benefit all countries at the same time. Because money and precious metals were the only source of riches, there was a limited quantity of resources to be shared between countries, therefore, tariffsshould be used to encourage exports (bringing more money into the country) and discourage imports (sending money abroad).

In other words a positive balance of trade ought to be maintained via a surplus of exports, often backed by military might. Despite its prevalence, the term mercantilism was not coined until 1763 by Victor de Riqueti, marquis de Mirabeau (1715–1789), and popularized by Adam Smith in 1776, who vigorously opposed its ideas.

SCHOOL OF SALAMANCA

In the 16th century the Jesuit School of Salamanca in Spain developed economic theory to a high level, only to have their contributions forgotten until the 20th century.

SIR THOMAS MORE

In 1516 English humanist Sir Thomas More (1478–1535) published *Utopia*, which describes an ideal society where land is owned in common and there is universal education and religious tolerance, inspiring the English Poor Laws (1587) and the communism-socialism movement.

NICOLAUS COPERNICUS

In 1517 Polish astronomer Nicolaus Copernicus (1473–1543) published the first known argument for the Quantity Theory of Money. In 1519 he published the first known form of Gresham's Law: "Bad money drives out good".

JEAN BODIN

In 1568 Jean Bodin (1530–1596) of France published *Reply to Malestroit*, containing the first known analysis of economic inflation, which he claimed was being caused by the importation of gold and silver from South America, backing the Quantity Theory of Money.

BARTHÉLEMY DE LAFFEMAS

In 1598 French mercantilist economist Barthélemy de Laffemas (1545–1612) published *Les Trésors et richesses pour mettre l'Estat en splendeur*, which blasted those who frowned on French silks because the industry created employment for the poor, the first known mention of Underconsumption Theory, which is later refined by John Maynard Keynes.

LEONARDUS LESSIUS

In 1605 Flemish Jesuit theologian Leonardus Lessius (1554–1623) published *On Justice and Law*, the deepest moral-theological study of economics since Aquinas, whose just price approach he claimed was no longer workable. After comparing money's growth via avarice to the propagation of hares, he made the first statement of the price of insurance as being based on risk.

EDWARD MISSELDEN AND GERARD MALYNES

In 1622 English merchants Edward Misselden and Gerard Malynes began a dispute over free trade and the desirability of government regulation of companies, with Malynes arguing against foreign exchange as under the control of bankers, and Misselden arguing that international money exchange and fluctuations in the exchange rate depend upon international trade and not bankers, and that the state should regulate trade to insure export surpluses.

THOMAS MUN

English economist Thomas Mun (1571–1641) describes early mercantilist policy in his book *England's Treasure by Foreign Trade*, which was not published until 1664, although it was widely circulated in manuscript form during his lifetime. Mun was a member of the East India Company, writing about his experiences in *A Discourse of Trade from England unto the East Indies* (1621).

According to Mun, trade was the only way to increase England's treasure (national wealth), and in pursuit of this end he suggested several courses of action.

Important were frugal consumption to increase the amount of goods available for export, increased utilization of land and other domestic natural resources to reduce import requirements, lowering of export duties on goods produced domestically from foreign materials, and the export of goods with inelastic demand because more money could be made from higher prices.

SIR WILLIAM PETTY

In 1662 English economist Sir William Petty (1623–1687) began publishing short works applying the rational scientific tradition of Francis Bacon to economics, requiring that it only use measurable phenomena and seek quantitative precision, coining the term "political arithmetic", introducing statistical mathematics, and becoming the first scientific economist.

PHILIPP VON HÖRNIGK

Philipp von Hörnigk (1640–1712, sometimes spelt *Hornick* or *Horneck*) was born in Frankfurt and became an Austrian civil servant writing in a time when his country was constantly threatened by Ottoman invasion. In *Österreich Über Alles, Wann es Nur Will* (1684, *Austria Over All, If She Only Will*) he laid out one of the clearest statements of mercantile policy, listing nine principal rules of national economy:

"To inspect the country's soil with the greatest care, and not to leave the agricultural possibilities of a single corner or clod of earth unconsidered... All commodities found in a country, which cannot be used in their natural state, should be worked up within the country.

Attention should be given to the population, that it may be as large as the country can support... gold and silver once in the country are under no circumstances to be taken out for any purpose... The inhabitants should make every effort to get along with their domestic products... [Foreign commodities] should be obtained not for gold or silver, but in exchange for other domestic wares... and should be imported in unfinished form, and worked up within the country... Opportunities should be sought night and day for selling the country's superfluous goods to these foreigners in manufactured form... No importation should be allowed under any circumstances of which there is a sufficient supply of suitable quality at home."

Nationalism, self-sufficiency and national power were the basic policies proposed.

JEAN-BAPTISTE COLBERT AND PIERRE LE PESANT, SIEUR DE BOISGUILBERT

In 1665–1683 Jean-Baptiste Colbert (1619–1683) was minister of finance under King Louis XIV of France, setting up national guildsto regulate major industries. Silk, linen, tapestry, furniture manufacture and wine were examples of the crafts in which France specialized, all of which came to require membership of a guild to operate in until the French Revolution. According to Colbert, "It is simply and solely the abundance of money within a state [which] makes the difference in its grandeur and power."

In 1695 French economist Pierre Le Pesant, sieur de Boisguilbert (1646–1714) wrote a plea to Louis XIV to end Colbert's mercantilist programme, containing the first notion of an economical market, becoming the first economist to question the economic policy of mercantilism and value the wealth of a country by its production and exchange of goods instead of the amount of money it has.

CHARLES DAVENANT

In 1696 British mercantilist Tory MP Charles Davenant (1656–1714) published *Essay on the East India Trade*, displaying the first understanding of consumer demand and perfect competition.

SIR JAMES STEUART

In 1767 Scottish mercantilist economist Sir James Steuart (1713–1780) published *An Enquiry into the Principles of Political Economy*, the first book in English with the term "political economy" in the title, and the first complete economics treatise.

THE BRITISH ENLIGHTENMENT

In the 17th century Britain went through some of its most troubling times, enduring not only the political and religious division of the English Civil War, KingCharles I's execution, and the Cromwellian dictatorship, but also the Great Plague of London and Great Fire of London.

The monarchy was restored underCharles II, who had Roman Catholic sympathies, leading to turmoil and strife, but his Catholic-leaning successor King James II was swiftly ousted. Invited in his place were Protestant William of Orange and Mary, who assented to the Bill of Rights 1689, ensuring that the Parliament was dominant in what became known as the Glorious Revolution.

The upheaval was accompanied by a number of major scientific advances, including Robert Boyle's discovery of the gas pressure constant (1660) and Sir Isaac Newton's publication of *Philosophiae Naturalis Principia*

Mathematica (1687), which described Newton's Laws of Motion and his Universal Law of Gravitation.

All these factors spurred the advancement of economic thought. For instance, Richard Cantillon (1680–1734) consciously imitated Newton's forces of inertia and gravity in the natural world with human reason and market competition in the economic world. In his *Essay on the Nature of Commerce in General*, he argued rational self-interest in a system of freely-adjusting markets would lead to order and mutually-compatible prices. Unlike the mercantilist thinkers however, wealth was found not in trade but in humanlabor. The first person to tie these ideas into a political framework was John Locke.

JOHN LOCKE

John Locke (1632–1704) was born near Bristol, and educated in London and Oxford. He is considered one of the most significant philosophers of his era mainly for his critique of Thomas Hobbes' defence of absolutism in *Leviathan* (1651) and the development of social contract theory. Locke believed that people contracted into society, which was bound to protect their property rights. He defined property broadly to include people's lives and liberties, as well as their wealth. When people combined their labour with their surroundings, that created property rights. In his words from his *Second Treatise on Civil Government* (1689):

"God hath given the world to men in common... Yet every man has a property in his own person. The labour of his body and the work of his hands we may say are properly his.

Whatsoever, then, he removes out of the state that nature hath provided and left it in, he hath mixed his labour with, and joined to it something that is his own, and thereby makes it his property."

Locke was arguing that not only should the government cease interference with people's property (or their "lives, liberties and estates"), but also that it should positively work to ensure their protection. His views on price and money were laid out in a letter to a Member of Parliament in 1691 entitled *Some Considerations on the Consequences of the Lowering of Interest and the Raising of the Value of Money* (1691), arguing that the "price of any commodity rises or falls, by the proportion of the number of buyers and sellers", a rule which "holds universally in all things that are to be bought and sold."

DUDLEY NORTH

Dudley North (1641–1691) was a wealthy merchant and landowner. He worked as an official for the Treasury and was opposed to most mercantile policy. In his *Discourses upon trade* (1691), which he published anonymously, he argued that the assumption of the necessity of a favourable trade balance was wrong. Trade, he argued, benefits both sides, it promotes specialization, the division of labour and produces an increase in wealth for everyone. Regulationof trade interfered with these benefits by reducing the flow of wealth.

DAVID HUME

David Hume (1711–1776) agreed with North's philosophy and denounced mercantilist assumptions. His contributions were set down in*Political Discourses* (1752), and later consolidated in his *Essays, Moral, Political, Literary* (1777).

Adding to the fact that it was undesirable to strive for a favourable balance of trade, Hume argued that it is, in any case, impossible.

Hume held that any surplus of exports that might be achieved would be paid for by imports of gold and silver. This would increase themoney supply, causing prices to rise. That in turn would cause a decline in exports until the balance with imports is restored.

FRANCIS HUTCHESON

Francis Hutcheson (1694–1746), the teacher of Adam Smith in 1737–1740 is considered to be at the end of a long tradition of thought on economics as "household or family management", stemming from Xenophon's work *Oeconomicus*.

THE PHYSIOCRATS AND THE CIRCULAR FLOW

Similarly disenchanted with regulation on trademarks inspired by mercantilism, a Frenchman named Vincent de Gournay (1712–1759) is reputed to have asked why it was so hard to *laissez faire ("let it be"), laissez passer* ("let it pass"), advocating free enterprise and free trade. He was one of the earlyPhysiocrats, a Greek word meaning "Government of nature", who held that agriculture was the source of wealth.

As historian David B. Danbom wrote, the Physiocrats "damned cities for their artificiality and praised more natural styles of living. They celebrated farmers."

Over the end of the seventeenth and beginning of the eighteenth century big advances in natural science and anatomy were being made, including the discovery of blood circulation through the human body. This concept was mirrored in the physiocrats' economic theory, with the notion of a circular flow of income throughout the economy.

François Quesnay (1694–1774) was the court physician to King Louis XV of France. He believed that trade and industry were not sources of wealth, and instead in his book *Tableau économique* (1758, Economic Table) argued that agricultural surpluses, by flowing through the economy in the form of rent, wages, and purchases were the real economic movers. Firstly, said Quesnay, regulation impedes the flow of income throughout all social classes and therefore economic development. Secondly, taxes on the productive classes, such as farmers, should be reduced in favour of rises for unproductive classes, such as landowners, since their luxurious way of life distorts the income flow. David Ricardo later showed that taxes on land are non-transferable to tenants in his Law of Rent.

In 1761 English Presbyterian minister Thomas Bayes (1701–1761) died, leaving an article describing Bayes' Theorem of conditional probabilities, which was generalized by statisticians and widely adopted by economists.

Jacques Turgot (1727–1781) was born in Paris and from an old Norman family. His best known work, *Réflexions sur la formation et la distribution des richesses* (*Reflections on the Formation and Distribution of Wealth*) (1766) developed Quesnay's theory that land is the only source of wealth. Turgot viewed society in terms of three classes: the productive agricultural class, the salaried artisan class (*classe stipendice*) and the landowning class (*classe disponible*). He argued that only the net product of land should be taxed and advocated the complete freedom of commerce andindustry.

In August 1774 Turgot was appointed to be minister of finance, and in the space of two years he introduced many anti-mercantile and anti-feudal measures supported by the king. A statement of his guiding principles, given to the king were "no bankruptcy, no tax increases, no borrowing." Turgot's ultimate wish was to have a single tax on land and abolish all other indirect taxes, but measures he introduced before that were met with overwhelming opposition from landed interests. Two edicts in particular, one suppressing corvées (charges from farmers to aristocrats) and another renouncing privileges given to guilds inflamed influential opinion. He was forced from office in 1776.

ADAM SMITH AND THE WEALTH OF NATIONS

Adam Smith (1723–1790) is popularly seen as the father of modern political economy. His 1776 publication *An Enquiry Into the Nature and Causes of the Wealth of Nations* happened to coincide not only with the American Revolution, shortly before the Europe-wide upheavals of the French Revolution, but also the dawn of a new industrial revolution that allowed more wealth to be created on a larger scale than ever before.

Smith was a Scottish moral philosopher, whose first book was *The Theory of Moral Sentiments* (1759). He argued in it that people's ethical systems develop through personal relations with other individuals, that right and wrong are sensed through others' reactions to one's behaviour. This gained Smith more popularity than his next work, *The Wealth of Nations*, which the general public initially ignored. Yet Smith's political economic magnum opus was successful in circles that mattered.

ADAM SMITH'S INVISIBLE HAND

Smith argued for a "system of natural liberty" where individual effort was the producer of social good. Smith believed even the selfish within society were kept under restraint and worked for the good of all when acting in a competitive market. Prices are often unrepresentative of the true value of goods and services. Following John Locke, Smith thought true value of things derived from the amount of labour invested in them.

Every man is rich or poor according to the degree in which he can afford to enjoy the necessaries, conveniencies, and amusements of human life. But after the division of labour has once thoroughly taken place, it is but a very small part of these with which a man's own labour can supply him.

The far greater part of them he must derive from the labour of other people, and he must be rich or poor according to the quantity of that labour which he can command, or which he can afford to purchase.

The value of any commodity, therefore, to the person who possesses it, and who means not to use or consume it himself, but to exchange it for other commodities, is equal to the quantity of labour which it enables him to purchase or command. Labour, therefore, is the real measure of the exchangeable value of all commodities. The real price of every thing, what every thing really costs to the man who wants to acquire it, is the toil and trouble of acquiring it.

When the butchers, the brewers and the bakers acted under the restraint of an open market economy, their pursuit of self-interest, thought Smith, paradoxically drives the process to correct real life prices to their just values. His classic statement on competition goes as follows. When the quantity of any commodity which is brought to market falls short of the effectual demand, all those who are willing to pay... cannot be supplied with the quantity which they want.

Some of them will be willing to give more. A competition will begin among them, and the market price will rise... When the quantity brought to market exceeds the effectual demand, it cannot be all sold to those who are willing to pay the whole value of the rent, wages and profit, which must be paid to bring it thither... The market price will sink...

Smith believed that a market produced what he dubbed the "progress of opulence". This involved a chain of concepts, that the division of labour is the driver of economic efficiency, yet it is limited to the widening process of markets. Both labour division and market widening requires more intensive accumulation of capital by the entrepreneurs and leaders of business and industry. The whole system is underpinned by maintaining the security of property rights.

LIMITATIONS [H

Smith's vision of a free market economy, based on secure property, capital accumulation, widening markets and a division of labour contrasted with the mercantilist tendency to attempt to "regulate all evil human actions." Smith believed there were precisely three legitimate functions of government.

The third function was... erecting and maintaining certain public works and certain public institutions, which it can never be for the interest of any individual or small number of individuals, to erect and maintain... Every system which endeavours... to draw towards a particular species of industry a greater share of the capital of the society than what would naturally go to it... retards, instead of accelerating, the progress of the society towards real wealth and greatness.

In addition to the necessity of public leadership in certain sectors Smith argued, secondly, that cartels were undesirable because of their potential to limit production and quality of goods and services.

Thirdly, Smith criticised government support of any kind of monopoly which always charges the highest price "which can be squeezed out of the buyers".

The existence of monopoly and the potential for cartels, which would later form the core ofcompetition law policy, could distort the benefits of free markets to the advantage of businesses at the expense of consumer sovereignty.

WILLIAM PITT THE YOUNGER

William Pitt the Younger (1759–1806), Tory Prime Minister in 1783–1801 based his tax proposals on Smith's ideas, and advocated free trade as a devout disciple of *The Wealth of Nations*. Smith was appointed a commissioner of customs and within twenty years Smith had a following of new generation writers who were intent on building the science of political economy.

EDMUND BURKE

Adam Smith expressed an affinity to the opinions of Irish MP Edmund Burke (1729–1797), known widely as a political philosopher: "Burke is the only man I ever knew who thinks on economic subjects exactly as I do without any previous communication having passed between us.

Burke was an established political economist himself, known for his book *Thoughts and Details on Scarcity*. He was widely critical of liberal politics, and condemned the French Revolution which began in 1789.

In *Reflections on the Revolution in France* (1790) he wrote that the "age of chivalry is dead, that of sophisters, economists and calculators has succeeded, and the glory of Europe is extinguished forever." Smith's contemporary influences included François Quesnay and Jacques Turgot whom he met on a visit to Paris, and David Hume, his Scottish compatriot.

The times produced a common need among thinkers to explain social upheavals of the Industrial revolution taking place, and in the seeming chaos without the feudal and monarchical structures of Europe, show there was order still.

CLASSICAL POLITICAL ECONOMY

The classical economists were referred to as a group for the first time by Karl Marx. One unifying part of their theories was the labour theory of value, contrasting to value deriving from a general equilibrium of supply and demand. These economists had seen the first economic and social transformation brought by the Industrial Revolution: rural depopulation, precariousness, poverty, apparition of a working class.

They wondered about the population growth, because the demographic transition had begun in Great Britain at that time. They also asked many fundamental questions, about the source of value, the causes of economic growth and the role of money in the economy. They supported a free-market economy, arguing it was a natural system based upon freedom and property. However, these economists were divided and did not make up a unified current of thought.

A notable current within classical economics was underconsumption theory, as advanced by the Birmingham School and Malthus in the early 19th century. These argued for government action to mitigate unemployment and economic downturns, and was an intellectual predecessor of what later became Keynesian economics in the 1930s. Another notable school was Manchester capitalism, which advocated free trade, against the previous policy of mercantilism.

JEREMY BENTHAM

Jeremy Bentham (1748–1832) was perhaps the most radical thinker of his time, and developed the concept of utilitarianism. Bentham was an atheist, aprison reformer, animal rights activist, believer in universal suffrage, free speech, free trade and health insurance at a time when few dared to argue for any. He was schooled rigourously from an early age, finishing university and being called to the bar at 18.

His first book, *A Fragment on Government* (1776) published anonymously was a trenchant critique of William Blackstone's *Commentaries of the laws of England*. This gained wide success until it was found that the young Bentham, and not a revered Professor had penned it. In *An Introduction to the Principles of Morals and Legislation* (1789) Bentham set out his theory of utility.

The aim of legal policy must be to decrease misery and suffering so far as possible while producing the greatest happiness for the greatest number.Bentham even designed a comprehensive methodology for the calculation of aggregate happiness in society that a particular law produced, a felicific calculus.

Society, argued Bentham, is nothing more than the total of individuals, so that if one aims to produce net social good then one need only to ensure that more pleasure is experienced across the board than pain, regardless of numbers. For example, a law is proposed to make every bus in the city wheel chair accessible, but slower moving as a result than its predecessors because of thenew design. Millions of bus users will therefore experience a small amount of displeasure (or "pain") in increased traffic and journey times, but a minority of people using wheel chairs will experience a huge amount of pleasure at being able to catch public transport, which outweighs the aggregate displeasure of other users.

Interpersonal comparisons of utility were allowed by Bentham, the idea that one person's vast pleasure can count more than many others' pain. Much criticism later showed how this could be twisted, for instance, would the felicific calculus allow a vastly happy dictator to outweigh the dredging misery of his exploited populace? Despite Bentham's methodology there were severe obstacles in measuring people's happiness.

HENRY THORNTON

In 1802 English banker-economist ("Father of the Modern Central Bank") Henry Thornton (1760–1815) published *An Enquiry into the Nature and Effects of the Paper Credit of Great Britain*, which disputed that the 1797 British banking credit crisis was caused by an increase in paper credit, opposing the Real Bills Doctrine of John Law, Adam Smith et al. that claims that a bank should issue notes only in the discount of "good bills" at not more than 60-day due dates to prevent collapse; the doctrine is "thoroughly discredited" in 1945.

JEAN-BAPTISTE SAY

Jean-Baptiste Say (1767–1832) was a Frenchman born in Lyon who helped popularize Adam Smith's work in France. His book *A Treatise on Political Economy* (1803) contained a brief passage, which later became orthodoxy in political economics until the Great Depression, now known as Say's Law of markets.

Say argued that there could never be a general deficiency of demand or a general glut of commodities in the whole economy. People produce things, to fulfill their own wants, rather than those of others, therefore production is not a question of supply, but an indication of producers demanding goods.

Say agreed that a part of the income is saved by the households, but in the long term, savings are invested. Investment and consumption are the two elements of demand, so that production *is* demand, so it is impossible for production to outrun demand, or for there to be a "general glut" of supply. Say also argued that money was neutral, because its sole role is to facilitate exchanges, therefore, people demand money only to buy commodities; "money is a veil".

To sum up these two ideas, Say said "products are exchanged for products". At most, there will be different economic sectors whose demands are not fulfilled. But over time supplies will shift, businesses will retool for different production and the market will correct itself. An example of a "general glut" could be unemployment, in other words, too great a supply of workers, and too few jobs. Say's Law advocates would suggest that this necessarily means there is an excess demand for other products that will correct itself.

This remained a foundation of economic theory until the 1930s. Say's Law was first put forward by James Mill (1773–1836) in English, and was advocated by David Ricardo, Henry Thornton, and James Mill's son John Stuart Mill. However two political economists, Thomas Malthus and Jean Charles Léonard de Sismondi, were unconvinced.

CHARLES HALL

In 1805 English physician Charles Hall (1740-1825) published *The Effects of Civilization on the People in European States*, which blasted capitalism for being unable to provide for the poor during the famines of 1795-1801, calling for a progressive tax and luxury tax, later drawing praise from Karl Marx.

THOMAS MALTHUS AND WILLIAM GODWIN

Thomas Malthus (1766–1834) was a Tory minister in the United Kingdom Parliament who, in contrast to Jeremy Bentham, believed in strict government abstention from social ills.

Malthus devoted the last chapter of his book *Principles of Political Economy* (1820) to rebutting Say's Law, arguing that the economy could stagnate with a lack of "effectual demand" caused by a "general glut" of goods.

In that case, wages that total less than the costs of production cannot purchase the total output of industry, causing deflation; price falls decrease incentives to invest, creating a downward spiral.

Malthus is more notorious however for his 1798 work *An Essay on the Principle of Population*, a reply to the popular 1793 work *An Enquiry Concerning Political Justice* by William Godwin (1756–1836), which describes an ideal society based on the assumed perfectibility of the human race. Malthus argued that all government intervention would ultimately prove futile because of two factors, population growth and limited resources.

"Food is necessary to the existence of man", wrote Malthus. "The passion between the sexes is necessary and will remain nearly in its present state", he added, meaning that the "power of the population is infinitely greater than the power in the Earth to produce subsistence for man. "Nevertheless growth in population is checked by "misery and vice".

Any increase in wages for the masses would cause only a temporary growth in population, which given the constraints in the supply of the Earth's produce would lead to misery, vice and a corresponding readjustment to the original population. However more labour could mean more economic growth, either one of which was able to be produced by an accumulation of capital.

JEAN CHARLES LÉONARD DE SISMONDI

In 1819 Swiss economist Jean Charles Léonard de Sismondi (1773–1842) published *New Principles of Economic Philosophy*, breaking ranks with Adam Smith by predicting that so-called general equilibrium would be marred by periodic economic crises, and calling for the state "to regulate the progress of wealth".

ROBERT OWEN

Robert Owen (1771–1858) was British industrialist who worked to improve the conditions of his workers. He bought textile mills in New Lanark, Scotland where he forbade children under ten to work, limited the workday to 6 a.m. to 7 p.m., and provided evening schools for children when they finished.

Such meagre measures were still substantial improvements, and his business remained solvent through higher productivity, though his pay rates were lower than the national average.

In 1816 he published his vision in *The New View of Society* during the passage of the Factory Acts, but his attempts from 1824 to begin a new utopian community in New Harmony, Indiana ended in failure.

DAVID RICARDO

David Ricardo (1772–1823) was born in London. By the age of 26, he had become a wealthy stock market trader, and bought himself a constituency seat in Ireland to gain a platform in the British parliament's House of Commons.

Ricardo's best known work is his *Principles of Political Economy and Taxation* (1817), which contains his critique of barriers to international trade and a description of the manner the income is distributed in the population. Ricardo made a distinction between the workers, who received a wage fixed to a level at which they can survive, the landowners, who earn a rent, and capitalists, who own capital and receive a profit, a residual part of the income.

If population grows, it becomes necessary to cultivate additional land, whose fertility is lower than that of already cultivated fields, because of the law of decreasing productivity.

Therefore, the cost of the production of the wheat increases, as well as the price of the wheat: The rents increase also, the wages, indexed to inflation (because they must allow workers to survive) too. Profits decrease, until the capitalists can no longer invest. The economy, Ricardo concluded, is bound to tend towards a steady state.

To postpone the steady state, Ricardo advocates to promote international trade to import wheat at a low price to fight landowners. The Corn Laws of the UK had been passed in 1815, setting a fluctuating system of tariffs to stabilise the price of wheat in the domestic market. Ricardo argued that raising tariffs, despite being intended to benefit the incomes of farmers, would merely produce a rise in the prices of rents that went into the pockets of landowners.

Furthermore, extra labour would be employed leading to an increase in the cost of wages across the board, and therefore reducing exports and profits coming from overseas business. Economics for Ricardo was all about the relationship between the three "factors of production": land, labour and capital. Ricardo demonstrated mathematically that thegains from trade could outweigh the perceived advantages of protectionist policy.

The idea of comparative advantage suggests that even if one country is inferior at producing all of its goods than another, it may still benefit from opening its borders since the inflow of goods produced more cheaply than at home, produces a gain for domestic consumers. According to Ricardo, this concept would lead to a shift in prices, so that eventually England would be producing goods in which its comparative advantages were the highest.

ALEXANDER HAMILTON, HENRY CLAY, AND THE AMERICAN SYSTEM

Basing his approach on the protectionist philosophy of U.S. Treasury secretary Alexander Hamilton (1755–1804), U.S. Senator Henry Clay (1777–1852) promoted the American System of developmental capitalism utilizing protective tariffs and government intervention to insure national self-sufficiency. In 1822 Irish-born American economist Mathew Carey (1760–1839) published *Essays on Political Economy; or, The Most Certain Means of Promoting the Wealth, Power, Resources, and Happiness of Nations, Applied Particularly to the United States*, one of the first treatises favouring Alexander Hamilton's protectionist economic policy.

In 1837–1840 his son Henry Charles Carey (1793–1879) published *Principles of Political Economy*, which soon became the standard representation of the American school of economic thought, dominating the U.S. economic system until after World War II. In 1851 Henry Charles Carey published *The Harmony of Interests: Agricultural, Manufacturing, and Commercial* (1851), which rejects the "British System" of*laissez faire* free trade capitalism in favour of the American System.

JOHANN HEINRICH VON THÜNEN

In 1826 German economist Johann Heinrich von Thünen (1783–1850) published *The Isolated State*, founding Economic Geography.

FRIEDRICH LIST AND THE NATIONAL SYSTEM

In 1841 after a stay in the U.S. convinced him of the value of Henry Clay's American System, German economist Friedrich List (1789-1846) published *The National System of Political Economy*, advocating protectionism and government involvement in the economy to catch up with rivals, along with an alliance between Germany and Britain against the U.S. and Russia, which became the biggest selling German economics book after Karl Marx's "Das Kapital", and influenced National Socialism and the European Economic Community.

WILHELM ROSCHER, CHARLES GIDE AND THE HISTORICAL SCHOOL OF ECONOMICS

In the mid-1840s German economist Wilhelm Roscher (1817–1894) founded the German Historical School of Economics, which promoted the cyclical theory of nations (whose economies allegedly pass through youth, manhood, and senility), and spread to academia in Britain and the U.S., dominating for the rest of the 19th century.

Charles Gide (1847–1932) continued the historical school tradition in France.

PIERRE-JOSEPH PROUDHON

One Karl Marx's influences was French mutualist anarchist Pierre-Joseph Proudhon (1809–1865). While deeply critical of capitalism and in favour of workers' associations to replace it, he also objected to those contemporary socialists who idolized centralized state-run associations.

In *System of Economic Contradictions* (1846) Proudhon made a wide-ranging critique of capitalism, analyzing the contradictory effects of machinery, competition, property, monopoly and other aspects of the economy.

Instead of capitalism, he argued for a mutualist system "based upon equality, – in other words, the organization of labour, which involves the negation of political economy and the end of property." In his book *What is Property?* (1840) he argue that property is theft, a different view than the classical Mill, who had written that "partial taxation is a mild form of robbery".

However, towards the end of his life, Proudhon modified some of his earlier views. In the posthumously published *Theory of Property*, he argued that "property is the only power that can act as a counterweight to the State."

JOHN STUART MILL

John Stuart Mill (1806–1873) was the dominant figure of political economic thought of his time, as well as being a Member of Parliament for the seat of Westminster, and a leading political philosopher.

Mill was a child prodigy, reading Ancient Greek from the age of 3, and being vigorously schooled by his father James Mill. Jeremy Bentham was a close mentor and family friend, and Mill was heavily influenced by David Ricardo. Mill's textbook, first published in 1848 and titled *Principles of Political*

Economy was essentially a summary of the economic wisdom of the mid nineteenth century.

Principles of Political Economy (1848) was used as the standard texts by most universities well into the beginning of the twentieth century. On the question of economic growth Mill tried to find a middle ground between Adam Smith's view of ever expanding opportunities for trade and technological innovation and Thomas Malthus' view of the inherent limits of population.

In his fourth book Mill set out a number of possible future outcomes, rather than predicting one in particular. The first followed the Malthusian line that population grew quicker than supplies, leading to falling wages and rising profits.

The second, per Smith, said if capital accumulated faster than population grew then real wages would rise.

Third, echoing David Ricardo, should capital accumulate and population increase at the same rate, yet technology stay stable, there would be no change in real wages because supply and demand for labour would be the same.

However growing populations would require more land use, increasing food production costs and therefore decreasing profits. The fourth alternative was that technology would advance faster than population and capital stock increased.

The result would be a prospering economy. Mill felt the third scenario most likely, and he assumed technological advances would have to end at some point. But on the prospect of continuing economic growth, Mill was more ambivalent.

"I confess I am not charmed with the ideal of life held out by those who think that the normal state of human beings is that of struggling to get on; that the trampling, crushing, elbowing, and treading on each other's heels, which form the existing type of social life, are the most desirable lot of human kind, or anything but the disagreeable symptoms of one of the phases of industrial progress."

Mill is also credited with being the first person to speak of supply and demand as a relationship rather than mere quantities of goods on markets, the concept of opportunity cost and the rejection of the wage fund doctrine.

FREDERIC BASTIAT

Frederic Bastiat (1801–1850) was a French political economist who in his short career produced many brilliant broadsides against statism, arguing that the only just purpose of government is to protect peoples' life, liberty, and property, not to engage in "legalized plunder".

His 1850 essay "That Which is Seen and That Which is Unseen" contains the famous Parable of the broken window. His works later inspired the Austrian School of Economics.

CAPITALISM, COMMUNISM, AND KARL MARX

Just as the term "Mercantilism" had been coined and popularized by its critics like Adam Smith, so was the term "Capitalism" or*Kapitalismus* used by its critics, primarily Karl Marx (1818–1883), who was, and in many ways still remains the pre-eminent Socialist economist.

The Socialist movement that Marx joined had emerged in response to the miserable conditions of the working class in the new industrial era, and the classical economics which it was based on. The combination of economic-political theory published in*The Communist Manifesto* (1848) and *Das Kapital* (1867) with the dialectic theory of history inspired by Friedrich Hegel (1770–1831) provided a revolutionary critique of nineteenth-century capitalism.

FRIEDRICH ENGELS

In 1845 German radical Friedrich Engels (1820–1895) published *The Condition of the Working Class in England in 1844*,describing workers in Manchester as "the most unconcealed pinnacle of social misery in our day." After Marx died, Engels completed the second volume of *Das Kapital* from his notes.

DAS KAPITAL

Marx wrote his magnum opus *Das Kapital* (1867) at the British Museum's library in London. Karl Marx begins it with the concept of commodities. Before capitalist societies, says Marx, the mode of production was based on slavery (*e.g.* in ancient Rome) before moving to feudal serfdom(*e.g.* in medieval Europe).

As society has advanced, economic bondage has become looser, but the current nexus of labour exchange has produced an equally erratic and unstable situation allowing the conditions for revolution. People buy and sell their labour in the same way as people buy and sell goods and services. People themselves are disposable commodities. As he wrote in *The Communist Manifesto*,

"The history of all hitherto existing society is the history of class struggles. Freeman and slave, patrician and plebeian, lord and serf, guildmaster and journeyman, in a word, oppressor and oppressed, stood in constant opposition to one another... The modern bourgeois society that has sprouted from the ruins of feudal society has not done away with class antagonisms. It has but established new classes, new conditions of oppression, new forms of struggle in place of the old ones. "From the first page of *Das Kapital*:

"The wealth of those societies in which the capitalist mode of production prevails, presents itself as an immense accumulation of commodities,its unit being a single commodity. Our investigation must therefore begin with the analysis of a commodity."

Marx's use of the word "commodity" is tied to an extensive metaphysical discussion of the nature of material wealth, how the objects of wealth are perceived and how they can be used. The concept of a commodity contrasts to objects of the natural world. When people mix their labour with an object it becomes a "commodity". In the natural world there are trees, diamonds, iron ore and people. In the economic world they become chairs, rings, factoriesand workers. However, says Marx, commodities have a dual nature, a dual value. He distinguishes the use value of a thing from its exchange value, which can be entirely different. The use value of a thing derives from the amount of labour used to produce it, says Marx, following the classical economists in the labour theory of value.

However, Marx did not believe labour only was the source of use value in things. He believed value can derive too from natural goods and refined his definition of use value to "socially necessary labour time" (the time people need to produce things when they are not lazy or inefficient). Furthermore, people subjectively inflate the value of things, for instance because there's a commodity fetish for glimmering diamonds, and oppressive power relations involved in commodity production.

These two factors mean exchange values differ greatly. An oppressive power relation, says Marx applying the use/exchange distinction to labour itself, in work-wage bargains derives from the fact that employers pay their workers less in "exchange value" than the workers produce in "use value". The difference makes up the capitalist's profit, or in Marx's terminology, "surplus value". Therefore, says Marx, capitalism is a system of exploitation.

Marx's work turned the labour theory of value, as the classicists called it, on its head. His dark irony goes deeper by asking what is the socially necessary labour time for the production of labour (*i.e.* working people) itself. Marx answers that this is the bare minimum for people to subsist and to reproduce with skills necessary in the economy.

People are therefore alienated from both the fruits of production and the means to realize their potential, psychologically, by their oppressed position in the labour market. But the tale told alongside exploitation and alienation is one of capital accumulation and economic growth.

Employers are constantly under pressure from market competition to drive their workers harder, and at the limits invest in labour displacing technology (*e.g.* an assembly line packer for a robot). This raises profits and expands growth, but for the sole benefit of those who have private property in these means of production.

The working classes meanwhile face progressive immiseration, having had the product of their labour exploited from them, having been alienated from the tools of production. And having been fired from their jobs for machines, they end unemployed. Marx believed that a reserve army of the unemployedwould grow and grow, fueling a downward pressure on wages as desperate people accept work for less. But this would produce a deficit of demand as the people's power to purchase products lagged. There would be a glut in unsold products, production would be cut back, profits decline until capital accumulation halts in an economic depression. When the glut clears, the economy again starts to boom before the next cyclical bust begins. With everyboom and bust, with every capitalist crisis, thought Marx, tension and conflict between the increasingly polarized classes of capitalists and workers heightens.

Moreover smaller firms are being gobbled by larger ones in every business cycle, as power is concentrated in the hands of the few and away from the many. Ultimately, led by the Communist party, Marx envisaged a revolution and the creation of a classless society. How this may work, Marx never suggested. His primary contribution was not in a blue print for how society would be, but a criticism of what he saw it was.

MARX'S DISCIPLES

The first volume of *Das Kapital* was the only one Marx alone published. The second and third volumes were produced with the help ofFriedrich Engels; Karl Kautsky, who had become a friend of Engels, saw through the publication of volume four.

Marx began a tradition of economists who became political activists, including Rosa Luxemburg (1871–1919), a member of the Social Democratic Party of Germany who later turned towards the Communist Party of Germany because of their stance against the First World War, and Beatrice Webb (1858–1943) of England, a socialist who helped found both the London School of Economics (LSE) and the Fabian Society.

ECONOMIC (BUSINESS) CYCLE THEORY

In the early 19th century German-born English astronomer Sir William Herschel (1738–1822) noted a connection between 11-yearsunspot cycles and wheat prices. In 1860 French economist Clément Juglar (1819–1905) proposed the existence of 7-11-yearBusiness (Economic) Cycles. In 1925 Russian (Soviet) economist Nikolai Kondratiev (1892–1938) proposed the existence of 50-60-yearKondratiev Waves in Western capitalist economies.

NEO-CLASSICAL ECONOMIC THOUGHT: THE MARGINALIST SCHOOL, THE CAMBRIDGE SCHOOL, AND THE AUSTRIAN SCHOOL

In the 1870s the Neo-classical economics revolution took place in economics. The new ideas were that of the Marginalist school. Writing simultaneously and independently, a Frenchman (Léon Walras), an Austrian (Carl Menger), and an Englishman (Stanley Jevons) launched the revolution.

Instead of the price of a good or service reflecting the labour that has produced it, it reflects the marginal usefulness (utility) of the last purchase. This meant that in equilibrium, people's preferences determined prices, including, indirectly, the price of labour.

This current of thought was not united, and there were three main independent schools. The Cambridge School was founded with the 1871 publication of Jevons' *Theory of Political Economy*, developing theories of partial equilibrium and focusing on market failures. The main representatives were Stanley Jevons, Alfred Marshall, and Arthur Pigou.

The Austrian School of Economics was made up of Austrian economists Carl Menger, Eugen von Böhm-Bawerk, and Friedrich von Wieser, who developed the theory of capital and tried to explain the presence of economic crises. It was founded with the 1871 publication of Menger's *Principles of Economics*.

The Lausanne School, led by Léon Walras and Vilfredo Pareto developed the theories of general equilibrium andPareto efficiency. It was founded with the 1874 publication of Walras' *Elements of Pure Economics*.

HERMANN HEINRICH GOSSEN, CARL MENGER, WILLIAM STANLEY JEVONS, LEON WALRAS, JOHN BATES CLARK, AND MARGINAL UTILITY

In 1854 German economist Hermann Heinrich Gossen (1810–1858) published *Entwickelung der Gesetze des menschlichen Verkehrs, und der daraus fließenden Regeln für menschliches Handeln* (The Development of the Laws of Human Intercourse and the Consequent Rules of Human Action), which proposed Gossen's Laws, the first statement of the principles of marginal utility. Unfortunately, the German Historical School gave it an icy reception, and it had little impact.

In 1871 Austrian School economist Carl Menger (1840–1921) restated the basic principles of marginal utility in *Grundsätze der Volkswirtschaftslehre* (*Principles of Economics*): Consumers act rationally by seeking to maximize satisfaction of all their preferences; people allocate their spending so that the last unit of a commodity bought creates no more satisfaction than a last unit bought of something else.

In 1871 Menger's English counterpart Stanley Jevons (1835–1882) independently published *Theory of Political Economy* (1871), stating that at the margin the satisfaction of goods and services decreases. An example of the Theory of Diminishing Marginal Utility is that for every orange one eats, the less pleasure one gets from the last orange until one stops eating oranges completely. In 1874 again working independently, French economist Léon Walras (1834–1910) generalized marginal theory across the economy in*Elements of Pure Economics*: Small changes in people's preferences, for instance shifting from beef to mushrooms, would lead to a mushroom price rise, and beef price fall; his stimulates producers to shift production, increasing mushrooming investment, which would increase market supply and a new price equilibrium between the products, *e.g.* lowering the price of mushrooms to a level between the two first levels.

For many products across the economy the same would happen if one assumes markets are competitive, people choose on the basis of self-interest, and there's no cost for shifting production.

Early attempts to explain away the periodic crises of which Marx had spoken were not initially as successful. After finding a statistical correlation of sunspots and business fluctuations and following the common belief at the time that sunspots had a direct effect on weather and hence agricultural output, Stanley Jevons wrote:

"When we know that there is a cause, the variation of the solar activity, which is just of the nature to affect the produce of agriculture, and which does vary in the same period, it becomes almost certain that the two series of phenomena – credit cycles and solar variations – are connected as effect and cause."

American economist John Bates Clark (1847–1938) promoted the marginalist revolution, publishing *The Distribution of Wealth* (1899), which proposed Clark's Law of Capitalism: "Given competition and homogeneous factors of production labour and capital, the repartition of the social product will be according to the productivity of the last physical input of units of labour and capital", also expressed as "What a social class gets is, under natural law, what it contributes to the general output of industry." In 1947 the John Bates Clark Medal was established in his honour.

ANTOINE AUGUSTIN COURNOT, JOSEPH LOUIS FRANCOIS BERTRAND, FRANCIS EDGEWORTH, VILFREDO PARETO, ALFRED MARSHALL, LOUIS BACHELIER, HAROLD HOTELLING, PAUL LÉVY (MATHEMATICIAN) AND MATHEMATICAL ECONOMICS

In 1838 French mathematician Antoine Augustin Cournot (1801–1877) published *Researches on the Mathematical Principles of the Theory of Wealth*, which introduced functions and probability into economics, deriving the first equation for supply and demand as a function of price and publishing the first supply-demand curves, founding modern economic analysis. In it he proposed the Cournot Duopoly Model of Competition, where firms decide the amount of output they will produce. In 1883 French mathematician Joseph Louis

Francois Bertrand (1822–1900) reworked it using prices instead of quantities, proposing the Bertrand Model of Competition.

In 1881 Irish economist Francis Ysidro Edgeworth (1845–1926) published *Mathematical Psychics: An Essay on the Application of Mathematics to the Moral Sciences*, which introduced indifference curves and the generalized utility function, along with Edgeworth's Limit Theorem, extending the Bertrand Model to handle capacity constraints, and proposing Edgeworth's Paradox for when there is no limit to what the firms can sell.

Italian economist Vilfredo Pareto (1848–1923) was best known for developing the concept of an economy that would permit maximizing the utility level of each individual given the feasible utility level of others from production and exchange. Such a result came to be calledPareto Efficiency. Pareto devised mathematical representations for such a resource allocation, notable in abstracting from institutional arrangements and monetary measures of wealth or income distribution.

Alfred Marshall (1842–1924) is also credited with an attempt to put economics on a more mathematical footing. The first professor of economics at the University of Cambridge, his 1890 work *Principles of Economics* abandoned the term "political economy" for his favourite "economics". He viewed math as a way to simplify economic reasoning, although he had reservations as revealed in a letter to his student Arthur Cecil Pigou:

"(1) Use mathematics as shorthand language, rather than as an engine of enquiry. (2) Keep to them till you have done. (3) Translate into English. (4) Then illustrate by examples that are important in real life. (5) Burn the mathematics. (6) If you can't succeed in 4, burn 3. This I do often."

Coming after the marginal revolution, Marshall concentrated on reconciling the classical labour theory of value which had concentrated on the supply side of the market with the new marginalist theory that concentrated on the consumer demand side.

Marshall's graphical representation is the famous Supply and Demand Graph, a.k.a. the Marshallian Cross, which treats the intersection of the supply and demand curves as the equilibrium of price in a competitive market. Over the long run, he argued, the costs of production and the price of goods and services tend towards the lowest point consistent with continued production.

In 1900 French mathematician Louis Bachelier (1870–1946) published his dissertation *The Theory of Speculation*, pioneering the study of Brownian Motion and stochastic processes and applying it to random walks of market prices, nearly coming up with the Black-Scholes Option Pricing Model.

American statistician Harold Hotelling (1895–1973) was a major figure in the application of statistics to economics. In 1929 he proposed Hotelling's Law, that in many markets it is rational for producers to make their products as similar as possible. In 1931 he proposed Hotelling's Rule, that the most socially and economically profitable extraction path of a non-renewable resource is one along which the price of the resource, determined by the marginal net revenue from the sale of the resource, increases at the rate of interest.

In 1932 he proposed Hotelling's Lemma, that a firm's net supply function is the partial derivative of the profit function with respect to the price. In 1938 he pioneered the study of non-convexity in economics.

In 1939 French mathematician Paul Pierre Lévy (1886–1971) introduced the concept of Martingales into probability theory, where the expectation of the next value in a sequence is the present observed value, modeling fair games, getting widely adopted by economists.

THE AUSTRIAN SCHOOL OF ECONOMICS

While economics at the end of the nineteenth century and the beginning of the twentieth was dominated increasingly by mathematical analysis, the followers of Carl Menger (1840–1921) and his disciples Eugen von Böhm-Bawerk (1851–1914) and Friedrich von Wieser(1851–1926) (coiner of the term "marginal utility") followed a different route, advocating the use of deductive logic instead.

This group became known as the Austrian School of Economics, reflecting the Austrian origin of many of the early adherents. Thorstein Veblen in*The Preconceptions of Economic Science* (1900) contrasted neo-classical marginalists in the tradition of Alfred Marshall with the philosophies of the Austrian School.

JOSEPH ALOIS SCHUMPETER

Joseph Alois Schumpeter (1883–1950) was an Austrian School economist and political scientist best known for his works on business cycles and innovation. He insisted on the role of the entrepreneurs in an economy.

In *Business Cycles: A theoretical, historical and statistical analysis of the Capitalist process* (1939), Schumpeter synthesized the theories about business cycles, suggesting that they could explain the economic situations. According to Schumpeter, capitalism necessarily goes through long-term cycles because it is entirely based upon scientific inventions and innovations.

A phase of expansion is made possible by innovations, because they bringproductivity gains and encourage entrepreneurs to invest.

However, when investors have no more opportunities to invest, the economy goes into recession, several firms collapse, closures and bankruptcy occur.

This phase lasts until new innovations bring a creative destruction process, *i.e.* they destroy old products, reduce the employment, but they allow the economy to start a new phase of growth, based upon new products and new factors of production.

LUDWIG VON MISES

Ludwig von Mises (1881–1973) was a central figure in the Austrian School. In his 1949 magnum opus on economics, *Human Action*, Mises introducedPraxeology, "the science of human action", as a more general conceptual foundation of the social sciences.

Praxeology views economics as a series of voluntary trades that increase the satisfaction of the involved parties. In 1920 Mises argued that socialism suffers from an unsolvable economic calculation problem, which according to him could only be solved through free market price mechanisms, launching the Economic calculation debate with socialist economists.

FRIEDRICH HAYEK

Mises' outspoken criticisms of socialism had a large influence on the economic thinking of Austrian School economist Friedrich Hayek(1899–1992), who, while initially sympathetic, became one of the leading academic critics of collectivism in the 20th century.

In echoes of Smith's "system of natural liberty", Hayek argued that the market is a "spontaneous order" and actively disparaged the concept of "social justice". Hayek believed that all forms of collectivism (even those theoretically based on voluntary cooperation) could only be maintained by a central authority.

In his book, *The Road to Serfdom* (1944) and in subsequent works, Hayek claimed that socialism required central economic planning and that such planning in turn would lead towards totalitarianism. Hayek attributed the birth of civilization to private property in his book *The Fatal Conceit* (1988).

According to him, price signals are the only means of enabling each economic decision maker to communicate tacit knowledge or dispersed knowledge to each other, to solve the economic calculation problem. Along with his Socialist Swedish contemporary and opponentGunnar Myrdal (1898–1987), Hayek was awarded the Nobel Prize in Economics in 1974.

MAFFEO PANTALEONI AND PUBLIC CHOICE THEORY

In 1882 Italian economist Maffeo Pantaleoni (1857–1924) published *Theory of Tax Shifting*, founding Public Choice Theory.

THE AMERICAN ECONOMIC ASSOCIATION,RICHARD T. ELY AND LAND ECONOMICS

In 1885 the American Economic Association (AEA) was founded by Richard T. Ely (1854–1943) et al., publishing the *American Economic Review* starting in 1911. In 1918 Ely published *Private Colonization of Land*, founding Lambda Alpha International in 1930 to promote Land Economics.

GEORG FRIEDRICH KNAPP AND CHARTALISM

In 1905 German economist Georg Friedrich Knapp (1842–1926) published *The State Theory of Money*, which founded the Chartalist school of monetary theory, which opposes metallism and argues that money has no intrinsic value but is only a "creature of law", *i.e.*, fiat money, with its value established by taxation.

THE LONDON SCHOOL OF ECONOMICS

In 1895 the London School of Economics (LSE) was founded by Fabian Society members Sidney Webb (1859–1947), Beatrice Webb(1858–1943), and George Bernard Shaw (1856–1950), joining the University of London in 1900. In the 1930s LSE member Sir Roy G.D. Allen (1906–1983) popularized the use of mathematics in economics.

THORSTEIN VEBLEN AND THE AMERICAN WAY

Thorstein Veblen (1857–1929), who came from rural midwestern America and worked at the University of Chicago is one of the best-known early critics of the "American Way".

In *The Theory of the Leisure Class* (1899) he scorned materialistic culture and wealthy people who conspicuously consumed their riches as a way of demonstrating success.

In *The Theory of Business Enterprise* (1904) Veblen distinguished production for people to use things and production for pure profit, arguing that the former is often hindered because businesses pursue the latter. Output and technological advance are restricted by business practices and the creation of monopolies.

Businesses protect their existing capital investments and employ excessive credit, leading to depressions and increasing military expenditure and war through business control of political power.

These two books, focusing on criticism of consumerism andprofiteering did not advocate change.

However, in 1918 he moved to New York to begin work as an editor of a magazine called *The Dial*, and then in 1919, along with Charles A. Beard, James Harvey Robinson, and John Dewey he helped found the New School for Social Research, known today as The New School) He was also part of the Technical Alliance, created in 1919 by Howard Scott.

From 1919 through 1926 Veblen continued to write and to be involved in various activities at The New School. During this period he wrote *The Engineers and the Price System (1921).*

EVOLUTIONARY ECONOMICS

In 1898 Thorstein Veblein (1857–1929) published *Why is Economics not an Evolutionary Science*, which coins the term Evolutionary economics, making use of anthropology to deny that there is a universal human nature, emphasizing the conflict between "industrial" or instrumental and "pecuniary" or ceremonial values, which became known as the Ceremonial/Instrumental Dichotomy.

GABRIEL TARDE AND ECONOMIC PSYCHOLOGY

In 1902–1903 French social psychologist Gabriel Tarde (1843–1904) published *La Psychologie economique*, founding Economic Psychology.

MAX WEBER AND THE PROTESTANT ETHIC

In 1905 German sociologist-economist Max Weber (1864–1920) published The Protestant Ethic and the Spirit of Capitalism, which claimed that it was the Protestant work ethic rather than atheistic dialectical materialism that drove the development of capitalism, causing a sea change in the debate and becoming one of the most important sociological works of the 20th century.

HENRY CHARLES TAYLOR AND AGRICULTURAL ECONOMICS

In 1909 American economist Henry Charles Taylor (1873–1969) founded Agricultural Economics with the first department devoted to its study at theUniversity of Wisconsin–Madison.

ALFRED MITCHELL-INNES AND THE CREDIT THEORY OF MONEY

In 1913 English economist-diplomat Alfred Mitchell-Innes (1864-1950) published *What is Money?*, which was reviewed favourably by John Maynard Keynes, followed in 1914 by*The Credit Theory of Money*, advocating the Credit Theory of Money, which economist L. Randall Wray called "The best pair of articles on the nature of money written in the twentieth century."

WORLD WAR I AND THE GREAT DEPRESSION: CONSEQUENCES TO ECONOMIC THOUGHT

At the outbreak of World War I (August 1, 1914 – November 11, 1918), Alfred Marshall was still working on his last revisions of his *Principles of Economics*. The 20th century's initial climate of optimism was soon violently dismembered in the trenches of the Western Front as the civilized world tore itself apart. For four years the production of Britain, Germany, and France were geared entirely towards the industry of death. In 1917 Russia crumbled into revolution led by Vladimir Lenin and the Bolshevik Party, who touted Marxist theory as the savior, and promised a broken country "peace, bread and land" by collectivizing the means of production.

Also in 1917 the United States of America entered the war on the side of the Allies (France and Britain), with President Woodrow Wilson claiming to be "making the world safe for democracy", devising a peace plan ofFourteen Points.

In 1918 Germany launched a spring offensive which failed, and as the allies counterattacked and more millions were slaughtered, Germany slid into theGerman Revolution, its interim government suing for peace on the basis of Wilson's Fourteen Points.

After the war, Europe lay in ruins, financially, physically, psychologically, and its future was dependent on the dictates of the Versailles Conference in 1919.

ECONOMIC THOUGHT BETWEEN THE WORLD WARS

After World War I, Europe and the Soviet Union lay in ruins, and the British Empire was nearing its end, leaving the United States as the pre-eminent global economic power.

Before World War II, American economists had played a minor role. During this time institutional economists had been largely critical of the "American Way" of life, especially theconspicuous consumption of the Roaring Twenties before the Wall Street Crash of 1929. After the crash a more orthodox body of thought took root, reacting against the lucid debating style of Keynes, and remathematizing the profession.

The orthodox centre was also challenged by a more radical group of scholars based at the University of Chicago, who advocated "liberty" and "freedom", looking back to 19th century-style non-interventionist governments.

ECOLOGY AND ENERGY

By the twentieth century, the industrial revolution had led to an exponential increase in the human consumption of resources. The increase in health, wealth and population was perceived as a simple path of progress.

However, in the 1930s economists began developing models of non-renewable resource management and the sustainability of welfare in an economy that uses non-renewable resources.

Concerns about the environmental and social impacts of industry had been expressed by some Enlightenment political economists and in the Romantic movement of the 1800s. Overpopulation had been discussed in an essay by Thomas Malthus, while John Stuart Mill foresaw the desirability of a "stationary state" economy, thus anticipating concerns of the modern discipline of ecological economics.

ECOLOGICAL ECONOMICS

Ecological economics was founded in the works of Kenneth E. Boulding, Nicholas Georgescu-Roegen, Herman Daly and others. The disciplinary field of ecological economics also bears some similarity to the topic of green economics.

According to ecological economist Malte Faber, ecological economics is defined by its focus on nature, justice, and time. Issues of intergenerational equity, irreversibility of environmental change, uncertainty of long-term outcomes, and sustainable development guide ecological economic analysis and valuation.

ENERGY ACCOUNTING

Energy accounting was proposed in the early 1930s as a scientific alternative to a price system, or money method of regulating society. Joseph Tainter suggests that a diminishing ratio of energy returned on energy invested is a chief cause of the collapse of complex societies. Falling EROEI due to depletion of non-renewable resources also poses a difficult challenge for industrial economies. Sustainability becomes an issue as survival is threatened due to climate change.

JOHN R. COMMONS AND INSTITUTIONAL ECONOMICS

In 1919 Yale economist Walton H. Hamilton coined the term "Institutional economics". In 1934 John R. Commons (1862–1945), another economist from midwestern America published *Institutional Economics* (1934), based on the concept that the economy is a web of relationships between people with diverging interests, including monopolies, large corporations, labour disputes, and fluctuating business cycles.

They do however have an interest in resolving these disputes. Government, thought Commons, ought to be the mediator between the conflicting groups. Commons himself devoted much of his time to advisory and mediation work on government boards and industrial commissions.

ARTHUR CECIL PIGOU

In 1920 Alfred Marshall's student Arthur Cecil Pigou (1877–1959) published *Wealth and Welfare*, which insisted on the possibility of market failures, claiming that markets are inefficient in the case of economic externalities, and the state must interfere to prevent them. However, Pigou retained free market beliefs, and in 1933, in the face of the economic crisis, he explained in *The Theory of Unemployment* that the excessive intervention of the state in the labour market was the real cause of massive unemployment because the governments had established a minimal wage, which prevented wages from adjusting automatically.

This was to be the focus of attack from Keynes. In 1943 Pigou published the paper *The Classical Stationary State*, which popularized thePigou (Real Balance) Effect, the stimulation of output and employment during deflation by increasing consumption due to a rise in wealth

JOHN MAYNARD KEYNES AND KEYNESIANISM

John Maynard Keynes (1883–1946) was born in Cambridge, educated at Eton, and supervised by both A. C. Pigou and Alfred Marshall at Cambridge University.

He began his career as a lecturer before working for the British government during the Great War, rising to be the British government's financial representative at the Versailles Conference, where he profoundly disagreed with the decisions made.

His observations were laid out in his book *The Economic Consequences of the Peace* (1919), where he documented his outrage at the collapse of American adherence to the Fourteen Points and the mood of vindictiveness that prevailed towards Germany., and he resigned from the conference, using extensive economic data provided by the conference records to argue that if the victors forced war reparations to be paid by the defeated Axis, then a world financial crisis would ensue, leading to a second world war.

Keynes finished his treatise by advocating, first, a reduction in reparation payments by Germany to a realistically manageable level, increased intra-governmental management of continental coal production and a free trade union through the League of Nations; second, an arrangement to set off debt repayments between the Allied countries; third, complete reform of international currency exchange and an international loan fund; and fourth, a reconciliation of trade relations with Russia and Eastern Europe.

The book was an enormous success, and though it was criticized for false predictions by a number of people, without the changes he advocated, Keynes's dark forecasts matched the world's experience through the Great Depression which began in 1929, and the descent into World War II in 1939.

World War I had been touted as the "war to end all wars", and the absolute failure of the peace settlement generated an even greater determination to not repeat the same mistakes.

With the defeat of Fascism, the Bretton Woods Conference was held in July 1944 to establish a new economic order, in which Keynes was again to play a leading role.

THE GENERAL THEORY

During the Great Depression, Keynes published his most important work, *The General Theory of Employment, Interest and Money* (1936). The Great Depression had been sparked by the Wall Street Crash of 1929, leading to massive rises in unemployment in the United States, leading to debts being recalled from European borrowers, and an economic domino effect across the world. Orthodox economics called for a tightening of spending, until business confidence and profit levels could be restored.

Keynes by contrast, had argued in *A Tract on Monetary Reform* (1923) (which argues for a stable currency) that a variety of factors determined economic activity, and that it was not enough to wait for the long run market equilibrium to restore itself. As Keynes famously remarked:

"...this long run is a misleading guide to current affairs. In the long run we are all dead. Economists set themselves too easy, too useless a task if in tempestuous seasons they can only tell us that when the storm is long past the ocean is flat again."

On top of the supply of money, Keynes identified the propensity to consume, inducement to invest, marginal efficiency of capital, liquidity preference, and multiplier effect as variables which determine the level of the economy's output, employment, and price levels.

Much of this esoteric terminology was invented by Keynes especially for his *General Theory*. Keynes argued that if savings were being withheld from investment in financial markets, total spending falls, leading to reduced incomes and unemployment, which reduces savings again.

This continues until the desire to save becomes equal to the desire to invest, which means a new "equilibrium" is reached and the spending decline halts. This new "equilibrium" is a depression, where people are investing less, have less to save and less to spend.

Keynes argued that employment depends on total spending, which is composed of consumer spending and business investment in the private sector. Consumers only spend "passively", or according to their income fluctuations.

Businesses, on the other hand, are induced to invest by the expected rate of return on new investments (the benefit) and the rate of interest paid (the cost). So, said Keynes, if business expectations remained the same, and government reduces interest rates (the costs of borrowing), investment would increase, and would have a multiplied effect on total spending. Interest rates, in turn, depend on the quantity of money and the desire to hold money in bank accounts (as opposed to investing).

If not enough money is available to match how much people want to hold, interest rates rise until enough people are put off. So if the quantity of money were increased, while the desire to hold money remained stable, interest rates would fall, leading to increased investment, output and employment. For both these reasons, Keynes therefore advocated low interest rates and easy credit, to combat unemployment.

But Keynes believed in the 1930s, conditions necessitated public sector action. Deficit spending, said Keynes, would kick-start economic activity. This he had advocated in an open letter to U.S. President Franklin D. Roosevelt in the *New York Times* (1933).

The New Deal programme in the U.S. had been well underway by the publication of the*General Theory*. It provided conceptual reinforcement for policies already pursued. Keynes also believed in a more egalitarian distribution of income, and taxation on unearned income arguing that high rates of savings (to which richer folk are prone) are not desirable in a developed economy. Keynes therefore advocated both monetary management and an active fiscal policy.

JOAN ROBINSON, RICHARD KAHN, PIERO SRAFFA, JOHN HICKS AND THE CAMBRIDGE CIRCUS

During World War II Keynes acted as adviser to HM Treasury again, negotiating major loans from the U.S., helping formulate the plans for the International Monetary Fund, theWorld Bank, and the International Trade Organisation at the 1944 Bretton Woods Conference, a package designed to stabilize world economy fluctuations that had occurred in the 1920s and create a level trading field across the globe.

Keynes passed away little more than a year later, but his ideas had already shaped a new global economic order, and all Western governments followed the Keynesian economics programme of deficit spending to avert crises and maintain full employment.

One of Keynes's pupils at Cambridge was Joan Robinson (1903–1983), a member of Keynes's Cambridge Circus, who contributed to the notion thatcompetition is seldom perfect in a market, an indictment of the theory of markets setting prices.

In *The Production Function and the Theory of Capital* (1953) Robinson tackled what she saw to be some of the circularity in orthodox economics. Neo-classicists assert that a competitive market forces producers to minimize the costs of production. Robinson said that costs of production are merely the prices of inputs, like capital.

Capital goods get their value from the final products. And if the price of the final products determines the price of capital, then it is, argued Robinson, utterly circular to say that the price of capital determines the price of the final products. Goods cannot be priced until the costs of inputs are determined.

This would not matter if everything in the economy happened instantaneously, but in the real world, price setting takes time – goods are priced before they are sold. Since capital cannot be adequately valued in independently measurable units, how can one show that capital earns a return equal to the contribution to production? Richard Kahn (1905–1989) was a member of the Cambridge Circus who in 1931 proposed the Multiplier.

Piero Sraffa (1898–1983) came to England from Fascist Italy in the 1920s, and became a member of the Cambridge Circus. In 1960 he published a small book called *Production of Commodities by Means of Commodities*, which explained how technological relationships are the basis for production of goods and services. Prices result from wage-profit tradeoffs, collective bargaining, labour and management conflict and the intervention of government planning. Like Robinson, Sraffa was showing how the major force for price setting in the economy was not necessarily market adjustments.

John Hicks (1904–1989) of England was a Keynesian who in 1937 proposed the Investment Saving – Liquidity Preference Money Supply Model, which treats the intersection of the IS and LM curves as the general equilibrium in both markets.

FRED M. TAYLOR, OSKAR R. LANGE, ABBA LERNER AND MARKET SOCIALISM

In response to the Economic Calculation Problem proposed by the Austrian School of Economics that disputes the efficiency of a state-run economy, the theory of Market Socialism was developed in the late 1920s and 1930s by economists Fred M. Taylor (1855–1932),Oskar R. Lange (1904–1965), Abba Lerner (1903–1982) et al., combining Marxian economics with neo-classical economics after dumping the labour theory of value. In 1938 Abram Bergson (1914–2003) defined the Social Welfare Function.

THE STOCKHOLM SCHOOL OF ECONOMICS

In the 1930s the Stockholm School of Economics was founded by Eli Heckscher (1879–1952), Bertil Ohlin (1899–1977), Gunnar Myrdal(1898–1987) et al. based on the works of John Maynard Keynes and Knut Wicksell (1851–1926), advising the founders of the Swedish Socialist welfare state.

In 1933 Olin and Heckscher proposed the Heckscher-Ohlin Model of International Trade, which claims that countries will export products that use their abundant and cheap factors of production and import products that use their scarce factors of production. In 1977 Ohlin was awarded a share of the Nobel Economics Prize.

In 1957 Myrdal published his theory of Circular Cumulative Causation, in which a change in one institution ripples through others. In 1974 he received a share of the Nobel Economics Prize.

ECONOMETRICS

In the 1930s Norwegian economist Ragnar Frisch (1895–1973) and Dutch economist Jan Tinbergen (1903–1994) pioneeredEconometrics, receiving the first-ever Nobel Prize in Economics in 1969.

In 1936 Russian-American economist Wassily Leontief (1905–1999) proposed the Input-Output Model of economics, which uses linear algebra and is ideally suited to computers, receiving the 1973 Nobel Economics Prize. After World War II, Lawrence Klein (1920–) pioneered the use of computers in econometric modeling, receiving the 1980 Nobel Economics Prize.

In 1963–1964 as John Tukey of Princeton University was developing the revolutionary Fast Fourier Transform, which greatly speeded up the calculation of Fourier Transforms, his British assistant Sir Clive Granger (1934–2009) pioneered the use of Fourier Transforms in economics, receiving the 2003 Nobel Economics Prize.

Ragnar Frisch's assistant Trygve Haavelmo (1911–1999) received the 1989 Nobel Economics Prize for clarifying the probability foundations of econometrics and for analysis of simultaneous economic structures.

ADOLF BERLE, GARDINER C. MEANS AND CORPORATE GOVERNANCE

The Great Depression was a time of significant upheaval in the world economy. One of the most original contributions to understanding what went wrong came from Harvard University lawyer Adolf Berle (1895–1971), who like John Maynard Keynes had resigned from his diplomatic job at the Paris Peace Conference, 1919 and was deeply disillusioned by the Versailles Treaty.

In his book with American economist Gardiner C. Means (1896–1988) *The Modern Corporation and Private Property* (1932) he detailed the evolution in the contemporary economy of big business, and argued that those who controlled big firms should be better held to account.

Directors of companies are held to account to the shareholders of companies, or not, by the rules found in company law statutes. This might include rights to elect and fire the management, require for regular general meetings, accounting standards, and so on.

In 1930s America the typical company laws (*e.g.* in Delaware) did not clearly mandate such rights. Berle argued that the unaccountable directors of companies were therefore apt to funnel the fruits of enterprise profits into their own pockets, as well as manage in their own interests.

The ability to do this was supported by the fact that the majority of shareholders in big public companies were single individuals, with scant means of communication, in short, divided and conquered. Berle served in President Franklin Delano Roosevelt's administration through the Great Depression as a key member of his Brain Trust, developing many New

Deal policies. In 1967 Berle and Means issued a revised edition of their work, in which the preface added a new dimension. It was not only the separation of controllers of companies from the owners as shareholders at stake. They posed the question of what the corporate structure was really meant to achieve:

"Stockholders toil not, neither do they spin, to earn [dividends and share price increases]. They are beneficiaries by position only. Justification for their inheritance... can be founded only upon social grounds... that justification turns on the distribution as well as the existence of wealth. Its force exists only in direct ratio to the number of individuals who hold such wealth. Justification for the stockholder's existence thus depends on increasing distribution within the American population. Ideally the stockholder's position will be impregnable only when every American family has its fragment of that position and of the wealth by which the opportunity to develop individuality becomes fully actualized."

EDWARD CHAMBERLIN AND INDUSTRIAL ORGANIZATION ECONOMICS

In 1933 American economist Edward Chamberlin (1899–1967) published *The Theory of Monopolistic Competition*. The same year British economist Joan Robinson (1903–1983) published *The Economics of Imperfect Competition*. Together they founded Industrial Organization Economics. Chamberlin also founded Experimental Economics.

BENJAMIN GRAHAM, DAVID DODD AND VALUE INVESTING

In 1934 after learning the lessons from the 1929 Stock Market Crash, Columbia University economists Benjamin Graham (1894–1976) and David Dodd(1895–1988) published *Security Analysis*, promoting Value Investing, which became the bible for investors. In 1949 Graham published *The Intelligent Investor*, which billionaire investor Warren Buffett later called "the best book about investing ever written".

LEONID KANTOROVICH AND LINEAR PROGRAMMING

In 1939 Russian economist Leonid Kantorovich (1912–1986) developed Linear Programming for the optimal allocation of resources, receiving the 1975 Nobel Economics Prize.

JOHN VON NEUMANN, OSKAR MORGENSTERN, JOHN FORBES NASH AND GAME THEORY

In 1944 Hungarian-American mathematician John von Neumann (1903–1957) and Austrian School economist Oskar Morgenstern(1902–1977) published *Theory of Games and Economic Behaviour*, founding Game Theory, which was widely adopted by economists.

In 1951 Princeton mathematician John Forbes Nash Jr. (1928-) published the article *Non-Cooperative Games*, becoming the first to define a Nash Equilibrium for non-zero-sum games, receiving a share of the 1994 Nobel Economics Prize.

POST-WORLD WAR II ECONOMIC THOUGHT: THE GLOBALIZATION ERA

The globalization era began with the end of World War II and the rise of the U.S. as the world's leading economic power, along with theUnited Nations.

To prevent another global depression, the victorious U.S. forgave Germany its war debts and used its surpluses to rebuild Europe and encourage reindustrialization of Germany and Japan. In the 1960s it changed its role to recycling global surpluses.

JOHN KENNETH GALBRAITH AND THE AFFLUENT SOCIETY

After World War II, Canadian-born John Kenneth Galbraith (1908–2006) became one of the standard bearers for pro-active government and liberal-democrat politics. In *The Affluent Society* (1958), Galbraith argued that voters reaching a certain material wealth begin to vote against the common good. He also argued that the "conventional wisdom" of the conservative consensus was not enough to solve the problems of social inequality.

In an age of big business, he argued, it is unrealistic to think of markets of the classical kind.

They set prices and use advertising to create artificial demand for their own products, distorting people's real preferences. Consumer preferences actually come to reflect those of corporations – a "dependence effect" – and the economy as a whole is geared to irrational goals.

In *The New Industrial State* Galbraith argued that economic decisions are planned by a private-bureaucracy, a technostructure of experts who manipulate marketing cand public relations channels.

This hierarchy is self-serving, profits are no longer the prime motivator, and even managers are not in control. Because they are the new planners, corporations detest risk, require steady economic and stable markets. They recruit governments to serve their interests with fiscal and monetary policy, for instance adhering to monetarist policies which enrich money-lenders in the City through increases in interest rates.

While the goals of an affluent society and complicit government serve the irrational technostructure, public space is simultaneously impoverished. Galbraith paints the picture of stepping from penthouse villas onto unpaved streets, from landscaped gardens to unkempt public parks. In *Economics and the Public Purpose* (1973) Galbraith advocates a "new socialism" as the solution, nationalising military production and public services such as health care, introducing disciplined salary and price controls to reduce inequality.

PAUL SAMUELSON

In contrast to Galbraith's linguistic style, the post-war economics profession began to synthesize much of Keynes' work with mathematical representations. Introductory university economics courses began to present economic theory as a unified whole in what is referred to as the neo-classical synthesis.

"Positive economics" became the term created to describe certain trends and "laws" of economics that could be objectively observed and described in a value-free way, separate from "normative economic" evaluations and judgements.

The best-selling textbook writer of this generation was Paul Samuelson (1915–2009), a student of Wassily Leontief.

His Ph.D. dissertation was an attempt to show that mathematical methods could represent a core of testable economic theory. It was published as *Foundations of Economic Analysis* in 1947.

Samuelson started with two assumptions. First, people and firms will act to maximize their self-interested goals. Second, markets tend towards anequilibrium of prices, where demand matches supply. He extended the mathematics to describe equilibrating behaviour of economic systems, including that of the then new macroeconomic theory of John Maynard Keynes.

Whilst Richard Cantillon had imitated Isaac Newton's mechanical physics of inertia and gravity in competition and the market, the physiocrats had copied the body's blood system into circular flow of income models, William Jevons had found growth cycles to match the periodicity of sunspots, Samuelson adapted thermodynamics formulae to economic theory.

Reasserting economics as a hard science was being done in the United Kingdom also, and one celebrated "discovery", of A. W. Phillips, was of a correlative relationship between inflation and unemployment.

The workable policy conclusion was that securing full employment could be traded-off against higher inflation. Samuelson incorporated the idea of the Phillips curve into his work. His introductory textbook *Economics* was influential and widely adopted.

It became the most successful economics text ever. Paul Samuelson was awarded the new Nobel Prize in Economics in 1970 for his merging of mathematics and political economy.

KENNETH ARROW

American economist Kenneth Arrow (1921–) is Paul Samuelson's brother-in-law. His first major work, forming his doctoral dissertation at Columbia

University was *Social Choice and Individual Values* (1951), which brought economics into contact with political theory. This gave rise to social choice theorywith the introduction of his "Possibility Theorem". In his words,

"If we exclude the possibility of interpersonal comparisons of utility, then the only methods of passing from individual tastes to social preferences which will be satisfactory and which will be defined for a wide range of sets of individual orderings are either imposed or dictatorial."

This sparked widespread discussion over how to interpret the different conditions of the theorem and what implications it had for democracy and voting. Most controversial of his four (1963) or five (1950/1951) conditions is the independence of irrelevant alternatives.

In the 1950s Kenneth Arrow and Gérard Debreu (1921–2004) developed the Arrow–Debreu model of general equilibria.

In 1963 Arrow published a paper which founded Health Economics. In 1971 Arrow and Frank Hahn published *General Competitive Analysis* (1971), which reasserted a theory of general equilibrium of prices through the economy. With John Hicks, Arrow won the Nobel Economics Prize in 1972, the youngest recipient to date. The year before, 1971, US President Richard Nixon's had declared that "We are all Keynesians now" The irony was that this was the beginning of a new revolution in economic thought. In 1983 Debreu won the Nobel Economics Prize.

THE CHICAGO SCHOOL OF ECONOMICS

The government-interventionist monetary and fiscal policies that the postwar Keynesian economists recommended came under attack by a group of theorists working at theUniversity of Chicago, which came in the 1950s to be known as the Chicago School of Economics.

Before World War II, the Old Chicago School of strong Keynesians was founded by Frank Knight (1885–1972), Jacob Viner (1892–1970), and Henry Calvert Simons (1899–1946).

The second generation was known for a more conservative line of thought, reasserting a libertarian view of market activity that people are best left to themselves to be free to choose how to conduct their own affairs.

RONALD COASE, RICHARD POSNER, AND THE ECONOMIC ANALYSIS OF LAW

Ronald Coase (1910–2013) of the Chicago School of Economics was the most prominent economic analyst of law, and the 1991 Nobel Prize in Economicswinner. His first major article *The Nature of the Firm* (1937) argued that the reason for the existence of firms (companies, partnerships, etc.) is the existence of transaction costs. Homo economicus trades through bilateral contracts on open markets until the costs of transactions make the use of corporations to produce things more cost-effective. His second major article *The Problem of Social Cost* (1960) argued that if we lived in a world without transaction costs, people would bargain with one another to create the same allocation of resources, regardless of the way a court might rule in property disputes.

Coase used the example of an old legal case about nuisance named *Sturges v Bridgman*, where a noisy sweets maker and a quiet doctor were neighbours and went to court to see who should have to move.

Coase said that regardless of whether the judge ruled that the sweets maker had to stop using his machinery, or that the doctor had to put up with it, they could strike a mutually beneficial bargain about who moves house that reaches the same outcome of resource distribution. Only the existence of transaction costs may prevent this.

So the law ought to preempt what *would* happen, and be guided by the mostefficient solution. The idea is that law and regulation are not as important or effective at helping people as lawyers and government planners believe.Coase and others like him wanted a change of approach, to put the burden of proof for positive effects on a government that was intervening in the market, by analyzing the costs of action.

In 1973 Coase disciple Richard Posner (1939–) published *Economic Analysis of Law*, which became a standard textbook, causing him to become the most cited legal scholar of the 20th century. In 1981 he published *The Economics of Justice*, which claimed that judges have been interpreting common law as it they were trying to maximize economic welfare.

GARY BECKER, JACOB MINCER AND NEW HOME ECONOMICS

In the 1960s Gary Becker (1930–2014) and Jacob Mincer (1922–2006) of the Chicago School of Economics founded New Home Economics, which spawned Family Economics.

MILTON FRIEDMAN AND CAPITALISM AND FREEDOM

Milton Friedman (1912–2006) of the Chicago School of Economics is one of the most influential economists of the late 20th, century, receiving the Nobel Prize in Economics in 1976. He is known for *A Monetary History of the United States* (1963), in which he argued that the Great Depression was caused by the policies of the Federal Reserve. Friedman argues that laissez-faire government policy is more desirable than government intervention in the economy. Governments should aim for a neutral monetary policy oriented towards long-run economic growth, by gradual expansion of the money supply. He advocates the quantity theory of money, that general prices are determined by money. Therefore active monetary (*e.g.* easy credit) or fiscal (*e.g.* tax and spend) policy can have unintended negative effects. In*Capitalism and Freedom* (1962), Friedman wrote:

"There is likely to be a lag between the need for action and government recognition of the need; a further lag between recognition of the need for action and the taking of action; and a still further lag between the action and its effects."

Friedman was also known for his work on the consumption function, the Permanent Income Hypothesis (1957), which Friedman referred to as his best scientific work. This work contended that rational consumers would spend a proportional amount of what they perceived to be their permanent income. Windfall gains would mostly be saved. Tax reductions likewise, as rational consumers would predict that taxes would have to rise later to balance public finances. Other important contributions include his critique of the Phillips Curve, and the concept of the natural rate of unemployment (1968). This critique associated his name with the insight that a government that brings about higher inflation cannot permanently reduce unemployment by doing so. Unemployment may be temporarily lower, if the inflation is a surprise, but in the long run unemployment will be determined by the frictions and imperfections in the labour market.

EUGENE FAMA AND THE EFFICIENT MARKET HYPOTHESIS

In 1965 Chicago School economist Eugene Fama (1939–) published *The Behaviour of Stock Market Prices*, which found that stock market prices follow a random walk, proposing the Efficient Market Hypothesis, that randomness is characteristic of a perfectly functioning financial market. The same year Paul Samuelson published a paper concluding the same thing with a mathematical proof, sharing the credit.

Earlier in 1948 Holbrook Working (1895–1985) published a paper saying the same thing, but not in a mathematical form. In 1970 Fama published *Efficient Capital Markets: A Review of Theory and Empirical Work*, proposing that efficient markets can be strong, semi-strong, or weak, and also proposing the Joint Hypothesis Problem, that the idea of market efficiency can't be rejected without also rejecting the market mechanism.

JAMES E. MEADE AND INTERNATIONAL ECONOMICS

In 1951 English economist James E. Meade (1907–1995) published *The Balance of Payments*, volume 1 of "The Theory of International Economic

Policy", which proposed the theory of domestic divergence (internal and external balance), and promoted policy tools for governments. In 1955 he published volume 2 *Trade and Welfare*, which proposed the theory of the "second-best", and promoted protectionism. He shared the 1977 Nobel Economic Prize with Bertil Ohlin.

SIR ARTHUR LEWIS, SIMON KUZNETS AND DEVELOPMENT ECONOMICS

In 1954 Saint Lucian economist Sir Arthur Lewis (1915–1991) proposed the Dual Sector Model of Development Economics, which claims that capitalism expands by making use of an unlimited supply of labour from the backward non-capitalist "subsistence sector" until it reaches the Lewisian breaking point where wages begin to rise, receiving the 1979 Nobel Economics Prize.

In 1955 Russian-born American economist Simon Kuznets (1901–1985), who introduced the concept of Gross domestic product (GDP) in 1934 published an article revealing an inverted U-shaped relation between income inequality and economic growth, meaning that economic growth increases income disparity between rich and poor in poor countries, but decreases it in wealthy countries. In 1971 he received the Nobel Economics Prize.

ROBERT SOLOW, TREVOR SWAN AND THE NEO-CLASSICAL GROWTH MODEL

In 1956 American economist Robert Solow (1924–) and Australian economist Trevor Swan (1918–89) proposed the Solow-Swan Neo-classical Growth Model, based on productivity, capital accumulation, population growth, and technological progress. In 1956 Swan also proposed the Swan Diagram of the internal-external balance. In 1987 Solow was awarded the Nobel Economics Prize.

NEW ECONOMIC HISTORY (CLIOMETRICS)

In 1958 American economists Alfred H. Conrad (1924–1970) and John R. Meyer (1927–2009) founded New Economic History, which in 1960 was called Cliometrics by American economist Stanley Reiter (1925–) after Clio, the muse of history. It uses neo-classical economic theory to reinterpret historical data, spreading throughout academia, causing economic historians untrained in economics to disappear from history departments. American cliometric economists Douglass Cecil North (1920–) and Robert William Fogel (1926–2013) were awarded the 1993 Nobel Economics Prize.

PAUL KRUGMAN AND NEW TRADE THEORY

In 1979 American economist Paul Krugman (1953–) published a paper founding New Trade Theory, which attempts to explain the role of increasing returns to scale and network effects in international trade. In 1991 he published a paper founding New Economic Geography. His textbook *International Economics* (2007) appears on many undergraduate reading lists. He was awarded the Nobel Prize in Economics in 2008.

NEW KEYNESIAN MACROECONOMICS

In 1977 Edmund Phelps (1933–) (who was awarded the 2006 Nobel Economics Prize) and John B. Taylor (1946–) published a paper proving that staggered setting of wages and prices gives monetary policy a role in stabilizing economic fluctuations if the wages/prices are sticky, even when all workers and firms have rational expectations, which caused Keynesian economics to make a comeback among mainstream economists with New Keynesian Macroeconomics.

Its central theme is the provision of a microeconomic foundation for Keynesian macroeconomics, obtained by identifying minimal deviations from the standard microeconomic assumptions which yield Keynesian macroeconomic conclusions, such as the possibility of significant welfare benefits from macroeconomic stabilization.

In 1985 George Akerlof (1940–) and his economist wife Janet Yellen (1946–) published menu costs arguments showing that, under imperfect competition, small deviations from rationality generate significant (in welfare terms) price stickiness.

In 1987 British economist Huw Dixon (1958–) published *A simple model of imperfect competition with Walrasian features*, the first work to demonstrate in a simple general equilibrium model that the fiscal multiplier could be increasing with the degree of imperfect competition in the output market, helping develop New Keynesian economics.

In 1997 American economist Michael Woodford (1955–) and Argentine economist Julio Rotemberg (1953–) published the first paper describing a microfounded DSGE New Keynesian macroeconomic model.

SIDNEY WEINTRAUB, PAUL DAVIDSON AND POST-KEYNESIAN ECONOMICS

In 1975 American economists Sidney Weintraub (1914–1983) and Henry Wallich (1914–1988) published *A Tax-Based Incomes Policy*, promoting Tax-Based Incomes Policy (TIP), using the income tax mechanism to implement an anti-inflationary incomes policy. In 1978 Weintraub and American economist Paul Davidson (1930–) founded the *Journal of Post Keynesian Economics*. This opened the door to many younger economists such as E. Ray Canterbery (1935-). Always Post Keynesian in his style and approach, Canterbery went on to make contributions outside traditional Post Keynesianism. His friend, John Kenneth Galbraith, was a long-time influence.

AMARTYA SEN AND DEVELOPMENT ECONOMICS

Indian economist Amartya Sen (1933–) is a leading development and welfare economist who expressed considerable skepticism about the validity of neo-classical assumptions, and was highly critical of rational expectations theory, devoting his work to Development Economics and human rights. He was awarded the Nobel Prize in Economics in 1998.

MUHAMMAD YUNUS AND MICROCREDIT

In the 1970s Bangladeshi economist Muhammad Yunus (1940–) developed the concepts of Microcredit and Microfinance, receiving the 2006 Nobel Peace Prize.

THE FELDSTEIN–HORIOKA PUZZLE

In 1980 American economists Martin Feldstein (1939–) and Charles Horioka (1956–) published an article revealing that in the long run capital tends to stay in the home country instead of flowing to the countries with the most productive investment opportunities, which was later called the Feldstein–Horioka puzzle.

ROBERT E. HALL AND THE FLAT TAX

In 1981 American economist Robert E. Hall (1943–) and American political scientist Alvin Rabushka proposed the Hall–Rabushka flat tax to simplify the U.S. federal income tax. The U.S. didn't accept it, but after the fall of the Soviet Union many former Soviet republics including Russia implemented it.

THE DOT-COM BUBBLE

In 2001 the Dot-Com Bubble of 1997–2000 caused American economists Ben Bernanke (1953–) and Mark Gertler (1951–) to publish *Should Central Banks Respond to Movements in Asset Prices?*, recommending that the Federal Reserve limit its policy to targeting inflation and price stability rather than the more aggressive approach of managing asset bubbles. In 2006 Bernanke became the Federal Reserve chairman.

THE 2008–2009 KEYNESIAN RESURGENCE AND THE GREAT RECESSION

The 2008–2009 Keynesian Resurgence emerged as a short-lived consensus among policy makers and economists for a Keynesian response to theFinancial Crisis of 2007–2008, contrasting sharply with the previous economic orthodoxy in its support for government intervention in the economy.

Key figures included Dominique Strauss-Kahn (1949–), Olivier Blanchard (1948–), Gordon Brown (1951–), Paul Krugman (1953–), andMartin Wolf (1946–). The crisis worsened into the global Great Recession, which still hasn't ended.

THE 2010 AUSTERITY WAVE

In October 2009 Italian economists Alberto Alesina (1957–) and Silvia Ardagna published *Large Changes in Fiscal Policy: Taxes Versus Spending,* a much-cited academic paper aimed at showing that fiscal austerity measures did not hurt economies, and actually helped their recovery, refuting the Keynesians. In 2010 the paper *Growth in a Time of Debt* by American economists Carmen Reinhart(1955–) and Kenneth Rogoff (1953–) was published, analyzing public debt and GDP growth among 20 advanced economies and claiming that high debt countries grew at "0.1perc ent since WWII, which was accepted, setting the stage for a wave of fiscal austerity that swept Europe. In April 2013 some analysts at the IMF and the Roosevelt Institute exposed flaws in the Reinhart-Rogoff paper, claiming +2.2perc ent. On June 6, 2013 Paul Krugman published *How the Case for Austerity Has Crumbled* in *The New York Review of Books*, arguing for an end to austerity measures.

THOMAS PIKETTY AND THE GLOBAL CAPITAL TAX

In February 2013 French economist Thomas Piketty published *Capital in the 21st Century* (released in English in April 2014), arguing that ever-increasing inequality is the inevitable outcome of free market capitalism, and calling for the global taxation of capital to prevent social upheaval.

OTHER CONTEMPORARY ECONOMISTS

In 1981 American economist Robert J. Shiller (1946–) published *Do stock prices move too much to be justified by subsequent changes in dividends?*, shocking the economics community by challenging the accepted Efficient Market Hypothesis, arguing that in a rational stock market, investors would base stock prices on the expected receipt of future dividends, discounted to a present value. In 2000 he published *Irrational Exuberance*, warning of a coming stock market collapse.

In 2003 he published *Is There a Bubble in the Housing Market?*, going on to predict the late 2008 U.S. housing market collapse a year in advance.

In 2001 Turkish economist Daron Acemoðlu (1967–) et al. published *The Colonial Origins of Comparative Development*, arguing that Europeans set up growth-inducing institutions in areas where the disease environment was favourable for their settlement, while in unfavourable environments such as central Africa they set up extractive institutions instead.

In 2001 American economist William Easterly (1957–) published *The Elusive Quest for Growth: Economists' Adventures and Misadventures in the Tropics*, criticizing foreign aid for failing to insure sustainable growth. In 2006 he published *The White Man's Burden: Why the West's Efforts to Aid the Rest Have Done So Much Ill and So Little Good*, a reply to Jeffrey Sachs' 2005 book *The End of Poverty*, dividing foreign aid providers into top-down Planners and bottom-up Searchers, claiming that the latter have the best chance for success.

In 2002 South Korean heterodox economist Ha-Joon Chang (1963–) published *Kicking Away the Ladder: Development Strategy in Historical Perspective*, which claims that developed countries climb to the top then try to keep developing countries down by kicking away the ladder. In 2008 he published *Bad Samaritans: The Myth of Free Trade and the Secret History of Capitalism*, which claims that the modern economic superpowers got that way by shameless protectionism and government intervention in industry, and are ramming a fairy tale about free trade down developing countries' throats.

In 2002 French economist Jean-Jacques Laffont (1947–2004) published *The Theory of Incentives: The Principal-Agent Model*, discussing the Principal-Agent Problem.

In 2002 Venezuelan economist Carlota Perez (1939–) published *Technological Revolutions and Financial Capital: The Dynamics of Bubbles and Golden Ages*, claiming techno-economic paradigm shifts in five past technological revolutions.

In 2005 American economist Jeffrey Sachs (1954–) published *The End of Poverty: Economic Possibilities for Our Time*, which argues that extreme poverty (defined by the World Bank as an income of less than $1 a day) can be eliminated globally by the year 2025 via carefully planned development aid.

In 2007 American economist Susan Athey (1970–) became the first female to win the John Bates Clark Medal for the top American economist under age 40. She went on to become chief economist at Microsoft.

In 2007 Argentine-American economist Graciela Chichilnisky (1944–) was the lead author of the Fourth Assessment Report of the Intergovernmental Panel on Climate Change (IPCC), which shared the 2007 Nobel Peace Prize with U.S. vice-president Al Gore. She was the originator of the Carbon Credit Emissions Trading Market proposal.

In 2009 American political economist Elinor Ostrom (1933–2012) became the first woman to be awarded the Nobel Economics Prize.

In 2009 Zambian economist Dambisa Moyo (1969–) published *Dead Aid: Why Aid is Not Working and How There is Another Way for Africa*, followed by *How the West Was Lost: Fifty Years of Economic Folly and the Stark Choices That Lie Ahead* (2011), and *Winner Take All: China's Race for Resources and What It Means for the World* (2012). They were all New York Times bestsellers.

In 2011 Indian economist Abhijit Banerjee (1961–) and French economist Esther Duflo (1972–) published *Poor Economics: A Radical Rethinking of the Way to Fight Global Poverty*, based on randomized control trials.

In 2011 Turkish economist Dani Rodrik (1957–) published *The Globalization Paradox*, arguing that only two of the triad of hyperglobalization, national sovereignty, and democratic politics can be sustained, and that globalization should be the first to be relaxed.

In 2011 after successfully predicting the Great Recession, Istanbul-born American economist Nouriel Roubini (1958–) published *A G-Zero World*, which claimed that "Old models of understanding global dynamics are struggling" to keep up with rapid changes:

"We are now living in a G-Zero world, one in which no single country or bloc of countries has the political and economic leverage—or the will—to drive a truly international agenda. The result will be intensified conflict on the international stage over vitally important issues, such as international macroeconomic coordination, financial regulatory reform, trade policy, and climate change. This new order has far-reaching implications for the global economy, as companies around the world sit on enormous stockpiles of cash, waiting for the current era of political and economic uncertainty to pass. Many of them can expect an extended wait."

In February 2012 after criticizing Pres. Barack Obama for being too pro-private sector, African-American economist Sandy Darity, Jr.(1952–) called for the creation of a National Investment Employment Corps that would guarantee all U.S. citizens over the age of 18 a job at a minimal salary of $20,000, as well as $10,000 in benefits, including medical coverage and retirement saving.

In May 2012 Indian economist Raghuram Rajan (1963–) (chief economist of the IMF in 2003–2007, known for predicting the Great Recession) got into a debate with Paul Krugman over the best way to end the Great Recession, with Rajan advocating supply-side solutions, and Krugman advocating Keynesian solutions.

On June 10, 2013 George Gilder (1939-) published *Knowledge and Power: The Information Theory of Capitalism and How it is Revolutionizing our World*, attempting to reformulate economics in terms of the information theory of Alan Turing and Claude Shannon.

4

Ancient Economic Thought

ANCIENT ECONOMIC THOUGHT

In the history of economic thought, ancient economic thought refers to the ideas from people before the Middle Ages.

Economics in the classical age is defined in the modern analysis as a factor of ethics and politics, only becoming an object of study as a separate discipline during the 18th century.

ANCIENT NEAR EAST

Economic organization in the earliest civilizations of the fertile crescent was driven by the need to efficiently grow crops in river basins. TheEuphrates and Nile valleys were homes to earliest examples of codified measurements written in base 60 and Egyptian fractions.

Egyptian keepers of royal granaries, and absentee Egyptian landowners reported in the Heqanakht papyri. Historians of this period note that the major tool of accounting for agrarian societies, the scales used to measure grain inventory, reflected dual religious and ethical symbolic meanings.

The Erlenmeyer tablets give a picture of Sumerian production in the Euphrates Valley around 2200-2100 BC, and show an understanding of the relationship between grain and labour inputs (valued in "female labour days") and outputs and an emphasis on efficiency. Egyptians measured work output in man-days.

The development of sophisticated economic administration continued in the Euphrates and Nile valleys during the Babylonian Empire and Egyptian Empires when trading units spread through the Near East within monetary systems.

Egyptian fraction and base 60 monetary units were extended in use and diversity to Greek, early Islamic culture, and medieval cultures. By 1202,Fibonacci's use of zero and Vedic-Islamic numerals, motivated Europeans to apply zero as an exponent, birthing modern decimals 350 years later.

The city-states of Sumer developed a trade and market economy based originally on the commodity money of the Shekel which was a certain weight measure of barley, while the Babylonians and their city-state neighbours later developed the earliest system of economicsusing a metric of various commodities, that was fixed in a legal code.

The early law codes from Sumer could be considered the first (written) economic formula, and had many attributes still in use in the current price system today: codified amounts of money for business deals (interest rates), fines in money for 'wrongdoing', inheritance rules, laws concerning how private property is to be taxed or divided, etc. For a summary of the laws, see Babylonian law.

Earlier collections of (written) laws, just prior to Hammurabi, that could also be considered rules and regulations as to economic law for their cities include the codex of Ur-Nammu, king of Ur (c. 2050 BC), the Codex of Eshnunna (c. 1930 BC) and the codex of Lipit-Ishtar of Isin (c. 1870 BC).

Õ=Ancient Greco-Roman World== Some scholars assert economic thought similar to the modern understanding occurred during the 18th century or the Enlightenment, as early economic thought was based on metaphysical principles which are incommensurate with contemporary dominant economic theories such as neo-classical economics.

Several ancient Greek and Roman thinkers made various economic observations, especially Aristotle and Xenophon. Many other Greek writings show understanding of sophisticated economic concepts.

For instance, a form of Gresham's Law is presented in Aristophanes' *Frogs*, and beyond Plato's application of sophisticated mathematical advances influenced by the Pythagoreans is his appreciation of fiat money in his *Laws* (742a–b) and in the pseudo-Platonic dialogue, *Eryxias*. Bryson of Heraclea was a neo-platonic who is cited as having heavily influenced early Muslim economic scholarship.

Within the pre-Classical and Classical culture, horses and cattle were considered to be a measure of wealth.

HESIOD

... Through work men grow rich in flocks and substance... — Hesiod

In the opinion of the Austrian School of economics the first economist is thought to be Hesiod, by the fact of his having written on the fundamental subject of the scarcity of resources, in *Works and Days*.

His contribution to economic thought is at least in his relevancy to the practice of economical activity in the depositing and lending of grain, as his writings are "... the chief resource for details as to Grecian agriculture..." and that according to Loudon (1825) he provided "... directions for the whole business of family economy in the country".

XENOPHON

The influence of Babylonian and Persian thought on Greek administrative economics is present in the work of Greek historian Xenophon. Discussion of economic principles are especially present in his *Oeconomicus*, *Cyropaedia*, *Hiero*, and *Ways and Means*. *Hiero* is a minor work which includes discussion of leaders stimulating private production and technology through various means including public recognition and prizes. *Ways and Means*is a short treatise on economic development, and showed an understanding of the importance of taking advantage of economies of scale and advocated laws promoting foreign merchants.

The *Oeconomicus* discusses the administration of agricultural land. In the work, subjective personal value of goods is analyzed and compared with exchange value. Xenophon uses the example of a horse, which may be of no use to a person who does not know how to handle it, but still has exchange value.

Although this broadens the idea of value based in individual use to a more general social concept of value that comes through exchange, scholars note that this is not a market theory of value. In *Cyropaedia* Xenophon presents what in hindsight can be seen as the foundation for a theory of fair exchange in the market. In one anecdote, the young Cyrus is to judge the fairness of an exchange made between a tall and a short boy.

The tall boy forces the pair to exchange tunics, because the tall boy's tunic is too short, shorter than the short boys, which is too tall for him. Cyrus rules the exchange fair because it results in a better fit for both boys. Cyrus' mentors were not pleased with Cyrus' basing his decision on the values involved, as a just exchange must be voluntary.

Later in the biography, Xenophon discusses the concept of division of labour, referencing specialized cooks and workers in a shoemaking shop.Scholars have noted that Adam Smith's early notes about this concept "read like a paraphrase of Xenophon's discussion of the role of the carpenter as a "jack of all trades" in small cities and as a specialist in large cities.

Marx attributes to *Cyropaedia* the idea that the division of labour correlates to the size of a market. Xenophon also presents an example of mutual advantage from exchange in a story about Cyrus coordinating an exchange of surplus farmland from Armenians, who were herders, and surplus grazing land from Chaldeans, who were farmers.

ARISTOTLE

Allocation of scarce resources was a moral issue to Aristotle, and in book I of his *Politics*, Aristotle expresses that consumption was the objective of production, and the surplus should be allocated to the rearing of children, and personal satiation ought to be the natural limit of consumption. (To Aristotle, the question was a moral one: in his era child mortality was high.) In transactions, Aristotle used the labels of "natural" and "unnatural". Natural transactions were related to the satisfaction of needs and yielded wealth that was limited in quantity by the purpose it served. Un-natural transactions aimed at monetary gain and the wealth they yielded was potentially without limits. He explained the un-natural wealth had no limits because it became an end in itself rather than a means to another end—satisfaction of needs. This distinction is the basis for Aristotle's moral rejection of usury.

Later, in book VII Chapter 1 of *Politics*, Aristotle asserts

external goods have a limit, like any other instrument, and all things useful are of such a nature that where there is too much of them they must either do harm, or at any rate be of no use, to their possessors

and some interpret this as capturing a concept of diminishing marginal utility, though there has been marked disagreement about the development and role of marginal utility considerations in Aristotle's value theory. Certainly this book formulates an ordinal hierarchy of values, which later appeared in Maslow's contribution to motivation theory.

Aristotle's *Nicomachean Ethics*, particularly book V.v, has been called the most economically provocative analytic writing in ancient Greece. Therein, Aristotle discusses justice in distribution and exchange. Still considering isolated exchanges rather than markets, Aristotle sought to discuss just exchange prices between individuals with different subjective values for their goods. Aristotle suggested three different proportions to analyze distributive, corrective, and reciprocal or exchange transactions: the arithmetic, the geometric, and the harmonic. The harmonic proportion implies a strong commitment to the subjective values of the traders.

Sixth century AD philosopher Boethius used the example of 16 as the harmonic mean of 10 and 40. 16 is the same percentage larger than 10 as it is smaller than 40 (60 percent of 10 is 6, while 60 percent of 40 is 24). Thus if two bargainers have subjective prices for a good of 10 and 40, Aristotle points out that in exchange, it is most fair to price the good at 16, due to the equality proportional differences from their price to the new price. Another nuance in this analysis of exchange is that Aristotle also saw a zone ofconsumer surplus or mutual advantage to both consumers that had to be divided.

PLATO

Of Plato's works those considered the most important to study of economics are *Nomoi*, *Politeia* and *Politikos* (Backhaus). In his work *Laws (dialogue)* Plato writes on the three things as important to a person of these mind he stated as the most important, then body and lastly estate (×ñÞìáôá). In *Phaedo*, Plato makes the first distinction between things which are thought necessary and those thought a luxury (Bonar).

Plato promoted the exercise of temperance in respect to the pursuit of material wealth such that by strengthening moderation a person there-by preserves the order of their psyche. In *The Republic* he gives an account of the manner by which a state is to be formed with the skills (techne) of individuals supporting economic sustainability. With respect to the identification of skill Plato's writing in *the Republic* also deals with the specialization of skills as the concept of division of labour (Wagner 2007).

ROMAN LAW

Early Greek and Judaic law follow a voluntaristic principle of just exchange; a party was only held to an agreement after the point of sale. Roman law developed the contractrecognizing that planning and commitments over time are necessary for efficient production and trade.

The large body of law was unified as the Corpus Juris Civilis in the 530s by Justinian who was Emperor of the Eastern Roman Empire from 526-565. In Institutiones, the principle of just trade is stated as "tantum bona valent, quantum vendi possunt" ("goods are worth as much as they can be sold for").

ANCIENT INDIA

Chulavamsa records that Parakramabahu I of Sri Lanka had debased the currency of Ancient Sri Lanka in order to produce monies to support his large scale infrastructure projects. Parakramabahu I also pioneered free trade during his reign; a war was fought with Burma to defend free trade.

CHANAKYA

Chanakya (c. 350 BC-275 BC) considered economic issues. He was a professor of political science at the Takshashila University of ancient India, and later the Prime Minister of the Mauryan emperor Chandragupta Maurya. He wrote the *Arthashastra* (*"Science of Material Gain*" or ""'*Science of political economy*" in Sanskrit).

Many of the topics discussed in the *Arthashastra* are still prevalent in modern economics, including its discussions on the management of an efficient and solid economy, and the ethics of economics. Chanakya also focuses on issues of welfare (for instance, redistribution of wealth during a famine) and the collective ethics that hold a society together.

The *Arthashastra* argues for an autocracy managing an efficient and solid economy. The qualities described is in effect that of a command economy. It discusses the ethics of economics and the duties and obligations of a king.

The scope of *Arthaúâstra* is, however, far wider than statecraft, and it offers an outline of an entire civil and criminal code andbureaucratic framework for administering a kingdom, with a wealth of descriptive cultural detail on topics such as mineralogy, mining and metals, agriculture, animal husbandry and medicine. The *Arthaúâstra* also focuses on issues of welfare (for instance, redistribution of wealth during a famine) and the collective ethics that hold a society together.

Chanakya says that *artha* (sound economies) is the most important quality and discipline required for a Rajarshi, and that dharma & kama are both dependent on it.

According to Chanakya, a conducive atmosphere is necessary for the state's economy to thrive. This requires that a state's law and order be maintained. Arthashastra specifies fines and punishments to support strict enforcement of laws (the *Dandaniti*).

MAHAVIRA

Economics in Jainism is influenced by the Mahavira and his principles and philosophies. His philosophies have been used to explain the economics behind it. He was the last of the 24 Tirthankars, who spread Jainism. In the Economics context he explains the importance of the concept of 'anekanta' (non-absolutism).

There are two core political-economic system of the society recognized by the Mahavira. One is Communism and the other, Capitalism. The former is meant to be more socialistic and the latter capitalistic. However the Mahavira found no difference in both these systems because both were driven by materialism.

ANCIENT CHINA

FAN LI

Fan Li (later *Tao Zhugong*) Chinese businessman, politician and strategist, wrote on economic issues. He discussed seasonal effects on markets, and business strategy among other things.

CONFUCIANISM AND LEGALISM

In ancient China, Chinese scholar-officials would often debate about the role government should have in the economy, such as setting monopolies in lucrative industries and instating price controls. Confucian factions tended to oppose extensive government controls, while "Reform" or legalist factions favoured intervention.

The Confucians' rationale for opposing government intervention was that the government should not "compete for profit with the people" as it would tend to exploit the population whenever it was involved in mercantile activity.

One such debate is recorded in the Discourses on Salt and Iron, a debate over Salt and iron monopolies imposed by Emperor Wu of Han to fund wars and expansionism against the Xiongnu. Although Confucian laissez faire was largely dominant throughout China's history, legalist policies often gained prominence in times of war or with the patronage of rulers, such as under Qin

Shi Huang, Sang Hongyang, Wang Mang and Wang Anshi, though they were abolished shortly thereafter.

WANG ANSHI

Chancellor Wang Anshi (1021–1086), one of China's most prominent reformers, lived during the medieval Song Dynasty (960-1279). Espousing heated reaction by conservative ministers at court, Wang Anshi's political faction of the New Policies Group enacted a series of reforms that centered around military reform, bureaucratic reform, and economic reform.

Economic reforms introduced included low-cost loans for farmers (whom he considered the backbone of the Chinese economy in terms of production of goods and greatest source of the land tax), replacing the corvee labour service with a tax instead, enacting government monopolies on crucial industries producing tea, salt, and wine, introduction of a local militia to ease the budget spending on the official standing army of 1 million troops, and the establishment of a Finance Planning Commission staffed largely by political loyals so that his reforms could pass quickly with less time for conservatives to oppose it in court.

Reformers and conservatives would oust each other from power once they had the support of the emperor.

MEDIEVAL ISLAMIC WORLD

To some degree, the early Muslims based their economic analyses on the Qur'an (such as opposition to *riba*, interest), and from sunnah, the sayings and doings of Muhammad.

EARLY MUSLIM THINKERS

Al-Ghazali (1058–1111) classified economics as one of the sciences connected with religion, along with metaphysics, ethics, and psychology. Authors have noted, however, that this connection has not caused early Muslim economic thought to remain static.

Persian philosopher Nasir al-Din al-Tusi (1201–1274) presents an early definition of economics (what he calls hekmat-e-madani, the science of city life) in discourse three of his *Ethics*:

"The study of universal laws governing the public interest (welfare?) in so far as they are directed, through cooperation, towards the optimal (perfection)."

Many scholars trace the history of economic thought through the Muslim world, which was in a Golden Age from the 8th to 13th century and whose philosophy continued the work of the Greek and Hellenistic thinkers and came to influence Aquinas when Europe "rediscovered" Greek philosophy through Arabic translation.

A common theme among these scholars was the praise of economic activity and even self-interested accumulation of wealth.Persian philosopher Ibn

Miskawayh (born 1030) notes: "The creditor desires the well-being of the debtor in order to get his money back rather than because of his love for him. The debtor, on the other hand, does not take great interest in the creditor."

This view is in conflict with an idea Joseph Schumpeter called the Great (Schumpeterian) Gap, which comes from his 1954 book *History of Economic Analysis*, claiming a break in economic thought during the 500-year period between the decline of the Greco-Roman civilization in the eighth century and the thirteenth century work of Thomas Aquinas (1225–1274). However in 1964 Joseph J.

Spengler's "Economic Thought of Islam: Ibn Khaldun" appeared in the journal *Comparative Studies in Society and History* and took a large step in bringing knowledge of medieval Muslim economic scholars to the contemporary West.

The influence of earlier Greek and Hellenistic thought on the Muslim world began largely with Abbasid caliph al-Ma'mun, who sponsored the translation of Greek texts into Arabicin the 9th century by Syrian Christians in Baghdad.

But already by that time numerous Muslim scholars had written on economic issues, and early Muslim leaders had shown sophisticated attempts to enforce fiscal and monetary financing, use deficit financing, use taxes to encourage production, the use of credit instruments for banking, including rudimentary savings and checking accounts, and contract law.

Among the earliest Muslim economic thinkers was Abu Yusuf (731-798), a student of the founder of the Hanafi Sunni School of Islamic thought, Abu Hanifah. Abu Yusuf was chief jurist for Abbasid Caliph Harun al-Rashid, for whom he wrote the *Book of Taxation* (*Kitab al-Kharaj*).

This book outlined Abu Yusuf's ideas on taxation, public finance, and agricultural production. He discussed proportional tax on produce instead of fixed taxes on property as being superior as an incentive to bring more land into cultivation. He also advocated forgiving tax policies which favour the producer and a centralized tax administration to reduce corruption. Abu Yusuf favoured the use of tax revenues for socioeconomic infrastructure, and included discussion of various types of taxes, including sales tax, death taxes, and import tariffs.

The power of supply and demand was understood to some extent by various early Muslim scholars as well. Ibn Taymiyyah illustrates:

"If desire for goods increases while its availability decreases, its price rises. On the other hand, if availability of the good increases and the desire for it decreases, the price comes down." Ghazali suggests an early version of price inelasticity of demand for certain goods, and he and Ibn Miskawayh discuss equilibrium prices." Other important Muslim scholars who wrote about economics include al-Mawardi (1075–1158) and Ibn Taimiyah (1263–1328).

IBN KHALDUN

Perhaps the most well known Islamic scholar who wrote about economics was Ibn Khaldun of Tunisia (1332–1406), considered a father of modern economics,Ibn Khaldun wrote on economic and political theory in the introduction, or*Muqaddimah* (*Prolegomena*), of his *History of the World* (*Kitab al-Ibar*). In the book, he discussed what he called *asabiyyah* (social cohesion), which he sourced as the cause of some civilizations becoming great and others not. Ibn Khaldun felt that many social forces are cyclic, although there can be sudden sharp turns that break the pattern.

His idea about the benefits of the division of labour also relate to *asabiyya*, the greater the social cohesion, the more complex the successful division may be, the greater the economic growth. He noted that growth and development positively stimulate both supply and demand, and that the forces of supply and demand are what determine the prices of goods.

He also noted macroeconomic forces of population growth, human capital development, and technological developments effects on development. In fact, Ibn Khaldun thought that population growth was directly a function of wealth.

Although he understood that money served as a standard of value, a medium of exchange, and a preserver of value, he did not realize that the value of gold and silver changed based on the forces of supply and demand. He also introduced the concept known as the Khaldun-Laffer Curve (the relationship between tax rates and tax revenue increases as tax rates increase for a while, but then the increases in tax rates begin to cause a decrease in tax revenues as the taxes impose too great a cost to producers in the economy).

CHANAKYA

Chanakya (c. 370 – c. 283 BCE) was an Indian teacher, philosopher, and royal advisor.

Originally a professor of economics and political science at the ancient Takshashila University, Chanakya managed the first Mauryaemperor Chandragupta's rise to power at a young age. He is widely credited for having played an important role in the establishment of the Maurya Empire, which was the first empire in archaeologically recorded history to rule most of the Indian subcontinent. Chanakya served as the chief advisor to both Chandragupta and his son Bindusara.

Chanakya is traditionally identified as Kautilya or Vishnu Gupta, who authored the ancient Indian political treatise called*Arthasastra* (*Economics*). As such, he is considered as the pioneer of the field of economics and political science in India, and his work is thought of as an important precursor to classical economics. His works were lost near the end of the Gupta dynastyand not rediscovered until 1915.

ORIGIN

Birth

Chanakya was born in a Brahmin house. Chanakya's birthplace is a matter of controversy, and there are multiple theories about his origin. According to the Buddhist text*Mahavamsa Tika*, his birthplace was Taxila. The Jain scriptures, such as *Adbidhana Chintamani*, mention him as a *Dramila*, implying that he was a native of South India.

According to the Jain writer Hemachandra's *Parishishtaparva*, Chanakya was born in the Canaka village of the Golla region, to a Brahmin named Canin and his wife Canesvari. Other sources mention his father's name as Chanak and state that Chanakya's name derives from his father's name. According to some sources, Chanakya was Brahmin from north India, scholar in Vedas, and a devotee of Lord Vishnu. According to Jain accounts he became Jain in old age like Chandragupta Maurya.

Sources of Information

There is little purely historical information about Chanakya: most of it comes from semi-legendary accounts. Thomas R. Trautmann identifies four distinct accounts of the ancient Chankya-Chandragupta *katha* (legend):

Version of the legend	Example texts
Buddhist version	*Mahavamsa* and its commentar *Vamsatthappakasini* (Pali language).
Jain version	*Parisistaparvan* by Hemachandra.
Kashmiri version *Manjari* by Ksemendra.	*Kathasaritsagara* by Somadeva, *Brihat-Katha-*
Vishakhadatta's version Vishakhadatta.	*Mudrarakshasa,* a Sanskrit play by

The following elements are common to these legends:

- The King Dhana Nanda insults Chanakya, prompting Chanakya to swear revenge and destroy the Nanda Empire
- Chanakya searches for one worthy successor to the Nanda and finds the young Chandragupta Maurya
- With the help of some allies, Chanakya and Chandragupta bring down the Nanda empire, often using manipulative and secretive means

Identification with Kautilya or Vishnugupta

The ancient treatise *Arthashastra* has been traditionally attributed to Chanakya by a number of scholars. The *Arthaúhâstra* identifies its author by the name Kautilya, except for one verse that refers to him by the name Vishnugupta. Kautilya is presumably the name of the author's gotra (clan).

One of the earliest Sanskrit literatures to identify Chanakya with Vishnugupta explicitly was Vishnu Sharma's *Panchatantra* in the 3rd century BCE.

K. C. Ojha puts forward the view that the traditional identification of Vishnugupta with Kautilya was caused by a confusion of the text's editor and its originator. He suggests that Vishnugupta was a redactor of the original work of Kautilya. Thomas Burrow goes even further and suggests that Chanakya and Kautilya may have been two different people.

EARLY LIFE

Chanakya was educated at Takshashila, an ancient centre of learning located in north-western ancient India (present-day Pakistan). He later became a teacher (*acharya*) at the same place. Chanakya's life was connected to two cities: Takshashila and Pataliputra (present-day Patna in Bihar, India). Pataliputra was the capital of the Magadhakingdom, which was connected to Takshashila by Uttarapatha, the northern high road of commerce..

ROLE IN THE FALL OF THE NANDA EMPIRE

Chankaya and Chandragupta have been credited with defeating the powerful Nanda Empire and establishing the new Maurya Empire.

Mudrarakshasa ("The Signet of the Minister"), a play dated variously from the late 4th century to the early 8th century, narrates the ascent of Chandragupta Maurya to power: Sakatala, an unhappy royal minister, introduced Chanakya to the Nanda king, knowing that Chanakya would not be treated well in the court.

Insulted at the court, Chanakya untied the sikha (lock of hair) and swore that he would not tie it back till he destroyed the Nanda kingdom. According to *Mudrarakshasa*, Chandragupta was the son of a royal concubine named Mura and spent his childhood in the Nanda palace. Chanakya and Chandragupta signed a pact with Parvataka (identified with King Porusby some scholars) of north-west India that ensured his victory over the Nanda empire. Kingdom of Nepal provided safe sanctuary to the followers of Chanakya during his operations.

Their combined army had Shaka, Yavana (Greek), Kirata, Kamboja and Vahlik soldiers. Following their victory, the territories of the Nanda empire were divided between Parvataka and Chanakya's associate Chandragupta. However, after Parvataka's death, his son Malayaketu sought control of all the former Nanda territories. He was supported by Rakshasaa, the former Nanda minister, several of whose attempts to kill Chandragupta were foiled by Chanakya.

As part of their game plan, Chanakya and Chandragupta faked a rift between themselves. As a sham, Chandragupta removed Chanakya from his ministerial post, while declaring that Rakshasa is better than him. Chanakya's agents in

Malayaketu's court then turned the king against Rakshasa by suggesting that Rakshasa was poised to replace Chanakya in Chandragupta's court. The activities by Chanakya's spies further widened the rift between Malayaketu and Rakshasa. His agents also fooled Malayaketu into believing that five of his allies were planning to join Chandragupta, prompting Malayaketu to order their killings.

In the end, Rakshasa ends up joining Chandragupta's side, and Malayaketu's coaliation is completely undone by Chanakya's strategy.

According to the Buddhist texts, Chandragupta was the son of the chief of the Moriya clan of Pippalivana. Chanakya once saw him leading a band of local youth and was highly impressed. He picked Chandragupta as the leader of the anti-Nanda revolt.

Several modern adaptions of the legend narrate the story of Chanakya in a semi-fictional form, extending these legends. In*Chandragupta* (1911), a play by Dwijendralal Ray, the Nanda king exiles his half-brother Chandragupta, who joins the army of Alexander the Great. Later, with help from Chanakya and Katyayan (the former Prime Minister of Magadha), Chandragupta defeats Nanda, who is put to death by Chanakya.

Twenty-first-century works such as *Chanakya* (2001) by B. K. Chaturvedi and *Chanakya's Chant* (2010) by Ashwin Sanghi also present semi-fictional narratives of Chanakya's life. According to these, Chanakya's father Chanak was a friend of Shaktar, the Prime Minister of the Magadha kingdom, and Chanakya loved Shaktar's daughter Suvashini.

Shaktar had lost much of his political clout to another courtier called Rakshasa, and one night, Shaktar was imprisoned by the King Dhana Nanda. The rivalry of the Chanakya's family with King Dhana Nanda started when Chanak openly criticised the misrule of the king.

After the execution of Chanak by the King, the former Magadha minister Katyayan sent Chanakya to Acharya Pundarikaksha of Takshashila. Chanakya completed his education at Takshashila and became a teacher there. After some years, he returned to Pataliputra to meet his mother, only to learn that she was dead.

He also learnt that the Nanda administration had further deteriorated under the growing influence of Rakshasa, who had made Suvashini his mistress. When Chanakya visited the royal court to advise him, he was insulted and imprisoned by the king.

Chanakya was rescued by the men of General Maurya, another person who despised with the king's rule. Chanakya took Chandragupta Maurya to Takshashila, where he trained the young man. King Ambhi, the ruler of Takshashila, had allied with the invader Alexander the Great to defeat Parvataka. Chanakya and Chandragupta gathered a band of people discontented with Ambhi's rule and formed an alliance with Parvataka to defeat the Nanda king. Their initial attempts at conquering Magadha were unsuccessful. Once, Chanakya came across a mother scolding her child for burning himself by eating from the middle of a bowl of porridge rather than the cooler edge. Chanakya realized his initial strategic error: he was attacking Magadha, the centre of the Nanda territory.

He then changed his strategy and focused on capturing the areas located at the peripharies of the Nanda empire. With help from Suvashini, he drove a wedge between the king and Rakshasa. Finally, he defeated the last Nanda king and established a new empire with Chandragupta Maurya as the emperor.

AFTER THE ESTABLISHMENT OF THE MAURYA EMPIRE

Chanakya continued to serve as an advisor to Chandragupta after the establishment of the Maurya Empire. According to a popular legend mentioned in the Jain texts, Chanakya used to add small doses of poison to the food eaten by Emperor Chandragupta Maurya (mithridatism) in order to make him immune to the poisoning attempts by the enemies.

Unaware, Chandragupta once fed some of his food to his queen, Durdhara, who was seven days away from delivery. The queen, not immune to the poison, collapsed and died within a few minutes. In order to save the heir to the throne, Chanakya cut the queen's belly open and extracted the foetus just as she died. The baby was named Bindusara, because he was touched by a drop (*bindu*) of blood having poison.

When Bindusara was in his youth, Chandragupta gave up the throne and followed the Jain saint Bhadrabahu to present dayKarnataka and settled in the place of Shravana Belagola. He lived as an ascetic for some years and died of voluntary starvation according to Jain tradition. Chanakya meanwhile stayed in the court as an advisor to Bindusara.

DEATH

According to one legend, Chanakya retired to the jungle and starved himself to death. According to another legend mentioned by the Jain writer Hemachandra, Chanakya died as a result of a conspiracy by Subandhu, one of Bindusara's ministers.

Subandhu, who did not like Chanakya, told Bindusara that Chanakya was responsible for the murder of his mother. Bindusara asked the nurses, who confirmed the story of his birth. Bindusara was horrified and enraged. When Chanakya, who was an old man by this time, learned that the King was angry with him, he decided to end his life.

In accordance with the Jain tradition, he decided to starve himself to death. By this time, the King had found out the full story: Chanakya was not directly responsible for his mother's death, which was an accident. He asked Subandhu to convince Chanakya to give up his plan to kill himself. However, Subandhu, pretending to conduct a ceremony for Chanakya, burned Chanakya alive.

LITERARY WORKS

The *Arthashastra* discusses monetary and fiscal policies, welfare, international relations, and war strategies in detail. The text also outlines the duties of a ruler. Some scholars believe that *Arthashastra* is actually a compilation of a number of earlier texts written by various authors, and Chanakya might have been *one* of these authors (seeabove).

Chanakya Niti is a collection of aphorisms, said to be selected by Chanakya from the various shastras.

LEGACY

Arthashastra is serious manual on statecraft, on how to run a state, informed by a higher purpose, clear and precise in its prescriptions, the result of practical experience of running a state. It is not just a normative text but a realist description of the art of running a state.

Shiv Shankar Menon, National Security Advisor

Chanakya is regarded as a great thinker and diplomat in India. Many Indian nationalists regard him as one of the earliest people who envisaged the united India spanning the entire subcontinent.

India's National Security Advisor Shiv Shankar Menonpraised Chanakya's Arthashastra for its clear and precise rules which apply even today. Furthermore, he recommended reading of the book for broadening the vision on strategic issues.

The diplomatic enclave in New Delhi is named Chanakyapuri in honour of Chanakya. Institutes named after him includeTraining Ship Chanakya, Chanakya National Law University and Chanakya Institute of Public Leadership. Chanakya circle inMysore has been named after him.

XENOPHON

Xenophon (*Xenophôn*; c. 430 – 354 BC), son of Gryllus, of the deme Erchia of Athens, also known as Xenophon of Athens, was a Greek historian, soldier, mercenary, and student of Socrates. While not referred to as a philosopher by his contemporaries, his status as such is now a topic of debate.

He is known for writing about the history of his own times, the late 5th and early 4th centuries BC, especially for his account of the final years of the Peloponnesian War.

His *Hellenica*, which recounts these times, is considered to be the continuation of Thucydides' *History of the Peloponnesian War*. His youthful participation in the failed campaign of Cyrus the Younger to claim the Persian throne inspired him to write his most famous work,*Anabasis*. Despite his birth-association with Athens, Xenophon affiliated himself with Sparta for most of his life.

His pro-oligarchic views, service under Spartan generals in the Persian campaign and beyond, as well as his friendship with King Agesilaus II endeared Xenophon to the Spartans, and them to him. A number of his writings display his pro-Spartan bias and admiration, especially*Agesilaus* and *Constitution of Sparta*.

Other than Plato, Xenophon is the foremost authority on Socrates, having learned under the great philosopher while a young man. He greatly admired his teacher, and well after Socrates' death in 399 Xenophon wrote severalSocratic dialogues, including an *Apology* concerning the events of his trial and death.

Xenophon's works cover a wide range of genres and are written in very uncomplicated Attic Greek. Xenophon's works are among the first that many students of Ancient Greek translate on account of the straightforward and succinct nature of his prose.

This sentiment was apparent even in ancient times, as Diogenes Laertius states in his *Lives of Eminent Philosophers* (2.6) that Xenophon was sometimes known as the "Attic Muse" for the sweetness of his diction.

LIFE

Early Years

Little is known about Xenophon other than what he wrote about himself. Xenophon was born around 430 BC near the city of Athens to an aristocratic family.

The years of his youth are not well attested before 401 BC. It was in this year that Xenophon was convinced by his Boeotian friend Proxenus to participate in the expedition led by Cyrus the Younger against his older brother, King Artaxerxes II of Persia.

Anabasis

Expedition with Cyrus

Written years after these events, Xenophon's book *Anabasis* (Greek: íÜâáóéò, literally "going up") is his record of the entire expedition of Cyrus against the Persians and the Greek mercenaries' journey home. Xenophon writes that he had asked the veteran Socrates for advice on whether to go with Cyrus, and that Socrates referred him to the divinely inspired Delphic oracle. Xenophon's query to the oracle, however, was not whether or not to accept Cyrus' invitation, but "to which of the gods he must pray and do sacrifice, so that he might best accomplish his intended journey and return in safety, with good fortune". The oracle answered his question and told him to which gods to pray and sacrifice. When Xenophon returned to Athens and told Socrates of the oracle's advice, Socrates chastised him for asking so disingenuous a question.

Under the pretext of fighting Tissaphernes, the Persian satrap of Ionia, Cyrus assembled a massive army composed of native Persian soldiers, but also a large number of Greeks. Prior to waging war against Artaxerxes, Cyrus proposed that the enemy was the Pisidians, and so the Greeks were unaware that they were to battle against the larger army of King Artaxerxes II. At Tarsus the soldiers became aware of Cyrus's plans to depose the king, and as a result, refused to continue. However, Clearchus, a Spartan general, convinced the Greeks to continue with the expedition. The army of Cyrus met the army of Artaxerxes II in the Battle of Cunaxa. Despite effective fighting by the Greeks, Cyrus was killed in the battle. Shortly thereafter, Clearchus was invited to a peace conference, where, alongside four other generals and many captains, he was betrayed and executed.

Return

The mercenaries, known as the Ten Thousand, found themselves without leadership far from the sea, deep in hostile territory near the heart of Mesopotamia. They elected new leaders, including Xenophon himself, and fought their way north along the Tigris through hostile Persians and Medes to Trapezus on the coast of the Black Sea . They then made their way westward back to Greece via Chrysopolis. Once there, they helped Seuthes II make himself king of Thrace, before being recruited into the army of the Spartan general Thibron. The Spartans were at war with Tissaphernes andPharnabazus, Persian satraps in Anatolia, probably on account of the aforementioned treacherous slaughter of their general Clearchus. Xenophon's military activity with these Spartans marks the final episodes of the*Anabasis* .

Exile and Death

Upon his return to Greece proper, Xenophon continued to associate with the Spartans, even so far as to fight under the Spartan king Agesilaus II against his native Athens at Coronea in 394 BC. On account of this he was exiled from Athens. However, there may have been contributory causes, such as his support for Socrates, as well as the fact that he had taken service with the Persians. The Spartans gave him property at Scillus, near Olympia in Elis, where he likely composed the Anabasis. However, because his son Gryllus fought and died for Athens at the Battle of Mantinea while Xenophon was still alive, Xenophon's banishment may have been revoked. Nevertheless, after the Battle of

Leuktra in 371 and the end of Spartan hegemony, Xenophon moved to Corinth or Athens where he died. He died around 355, but the exact date is uncertain; historians know only that he survived his patron Agesilaus II, for whom he wrote an encomium which shared the Spartan king's name.

XENOPHON'S POLITICS

Xenophon has long been associated with the opposition of democracy. Although Xenophon seems to prefer oligarchy, or at least the aristocracy, especially in light of his associations with Sparta, none of his works explicitly attack democracy. Some scholars go so far as to say his views aligned with those of the democracy in his time. However, certain works of Xenophon, in particular the Cyropaedia, appear to display his pro-oligarchic politics. This historical-fiction serves as a forum for Xenophon to subtly display his political inclinations.

Cyropaedia

Persians as Centaurs

The *Cyropaedia* as a whole lavishes a great deal of praise on the first Persian emperor Cyrus the Great on account of his virtue and leadership quality, and it was through his greatness that the Persian Empire held together. Thus this book is normally read as a positive treatise about Cyrus. However, following the lead of Leo Strauss, David Johnson suggests that there is a subtle but strong layer to the book in which Xenophon conveys criticism of not only the Persians but the Spartans and Athenians as well.

In section 4.3 of the *Cyropaedia* Cyrus makes clear his desire to institute cavalry. He even goes so far to say that he desires that no Persian *kalokagathos* ("noble and good man" literally, or simply "noble") ever be seen on foot but always on a horse, so much so that the Persians may actually seem to be centaurs (4.3.22-23).

Centaurs were often thought of as creatures of ill repute, which makes even Cyrus' own advisors wary of the label. His minister Chrysantas admires the centaurs for their dual nature, but also warns that the dual nature does not allow centaurs to fully enjoy or act as either one of their aspects in full (4.3.19-20). In labeling Persians as centaurs through the mouth of Cyrus, Xenophon plays upon the popular post-Persian-war propagandistic paradigm of using mythological imagery to represent the Greco-Persian conflict.

Examples of this include the wedding of theLapiths, giantomachy, Trojan War, and Amazonomachy on the Parthenon frieze. Johnson reads even more deeply into the centaur label.

He believes that the unstable dichotomy of man and horse found in a centaur is indicative of the unstable and unnatural alliance of Persian and Mede formulated by Cyrus. The Persian hardiness and austerity is combined with the luxuriousness of the Medes, two qualities that cannot coexist. He cites the regression of the Persians directly after the death of Cyrus as a result of this instability, a union made possible only through the impeccable character of Cyrus.

In a further analysis of the centaur model, Cyrus is likened to a centaur such as Chiron, a noble example from an ignoble race. Thus this entire paradigm seems to be a jab at the Persians and an indication of Xenophon's general distaste for the Persians.

Against Empire/Monarchy

The strength of Cyrus in holding the empire together is praiseworthy according to Xenophon. However, the empire began to decline upon the death of Cyrus. By this example Xenophon sought to show that empires lacked stability and could only be maintained by a person of remarkable prowess, such as Cyrus.

Cyrus is idealized greatly in the narrative. Xenophon displays Cyrus as a cold, passionless man. This is not to say that he was not a good ruler, but he is depicted as surreal and not subject to the foibles of other men. By showing that only someone who is almost beyond human could conduct such an enterprise as empire, Xenophon indirectly censures imperial design.

Thus he also reflects on the state of his own reality in an even more indirect fashion, using the example of the Persians to decry the attempts at empire made by Athens and Sparta.

Although partially graced with hindsight, having written the *Cyropaedia* after the downfall of Athens in the Peloponnesian War, this work criticizes the Greek attempts at empire and "monarchy," dooming them to failure.

Against democracy

Another passage that Johnson cites as criticism of monarchy and empire concerns the devaluation of the *homotimoi*. The manner in which this occurs seems also to be a subtle yet poignant jab at democracy. Homotimoi were highly and thoroughly educated and thus became the core of the soldiery as heavy infantry.

As the name *homotimoi* ("equal," or "same honours" *i.e.* "peers") suggests, their small band (1000 when Cyrus fought the Assyrians) shared equally in the spoils of war.

However, in the face of overwhelming numbers in a campaign against the Assyrians, Cyrus armed the commoners with similar arms instead of their normal light ranged armament (*Cyropaedia* 2.1.9). Argument ensued as to how the spoils would now be split, and Cyrus enforced a meritocracy.

Many *homotimoi* found this unfair because their military training was no better than the commoners, only their education, and hand-to-hand combat was less a matter of skill than strength and bravery.

As Johnson asserts, this passage decries imperial meritocracy and corruption, for the *homotimoi* now had to sychophantize to the emperor for positions and honours; from this point they were referred to as *entimoi*, no longer of the "same honours" but having to be "in" to get the honour.

On the other hand, the passage seems to be critical of democracy, or at least sympathetic to aristocrats within democracy, for the*homotimoi* (aristocracy/oligarchs) are devalued upon the empowerment of the commoners (*demos*).

Although empire emerges in this case, this is also a sequence of events associated with democracy. Through his dual critique of empire and democracy, Xenophon subtly relates his support of oligarchy.

Constitution of the Spartans

The Spartans wrote nothing about themselves, or if they did it is lost. Therefore what we know about them comes exclusively from outsiders, such as Xenophon. Xenophon's affinity for the Spartans is clear in the *Constitution of the Spartans*, as well as his penchant for oligarchy.

The opening line reads:

"It occurred to me one day that Sparta, though among the most thinly populated of states, was evidently the most powerful and most celebrated city in Greece; and I fell to wondering how this could have happened.

But when I considered the institutions of the Spartans, I wondered no longer." Xenophon goes on to describe in detail the main aspects of the Lacedaemonian state, handing to us the most comprehensive extant analysis of the institutions of Sparta.

Old Oligarch

A short treatise on the *Constitution of Athens* exists that was once thought to be by Xenophon, but which was probably written when Xenophon was about five years old.

The author, often called in English the "Old Oligarch" or Pseudo-Xenophon, detests the democracy of Athens and the poorer classes, but he argues that the Periclean institutions are well designed for their deplorable purposes. Although the real Xenophon seems to prefer oligarchy over democracy, none of his works so ardently decry democracy as does the Constitution of the Athenians.

However, this treatise makes evident that anti-democratic sentiments were extant in Athens in the late 5th century and were only increased after its shortcomings were exploited and made apparent during the Peloponnesian War.

SOCRATIC WORKS AND DIALOGUES

Xenophon's variegated corpus includes a significant selection of Socratic dialogues. His completely preserved Socratic writings, along with the dialogues of Plato, are the only surviving representatives of the genre of *Sokratikoi logoi* (Socratic dialogues).

These works include his *Apology, Memorabilia, Symposium,* and *Oeconomicus*. The *Symposium* outlines the character of Socrates as he and his companions discuss what attribute they take pride in. In *Oeconomicus* Socrates explains how to manage the household well. Both the *Apology* and *Memorabilia* serve to defend Socrates' character and teachings.

The former is set during the trial of Socrates, essentially defending Socrates' loss and death, while the latter as a general defence of Socrates, explaining his moral principles and that he was not a corrupter of the youth.

Relationship with Socrates

Xenophon was a student of Socrates, and their personal relationship is evident through a direct conversation between the two in Xenophon's *Anabasis*. His admiration for his teacher is clear in writings such as *Symposium*, *Apology*, and *Memorabilia*. Xenophon was off on his Persian campaign when Socrates died, so he was not present for the trial of his old master.

Nevertheless, much of his Socratic writing, especially *Apology*, concerns that very trial and the defence Socrates put forward. In his Lives of Eminent Philosophers, the Greek biographer Diogenes Laertius reports how Xenophon came to be associated with Socrates.

"They say that Socrates met him in a narrow lane, and put his stick across it and prevented him from passing by, asking him where all kinds of necessary things were sold. And when he had answered him, he asked him again where men were made good and virtuous. And as he did not know, he said, 'Follow me, then, and learn.' And from this time forth, Xenophon became a follower of Socrates."

Socrates: Xenophon vs. Plato

Both Plato and Xenophon wrote an *Apology* concerning the death of Socrates. The two writers seem more concerned about answering questions that arose after the trial than about the actual charges.

In particular, Xenophon and Plato are concerned with the failures of Socrates to defend himself, such as his incompetence in court, his arrogance, and his defeat and execution.

The Socrates that Xenophon portrayed was different from Plato's in multiple respects. Xenophon asserts that Socrates dealt with his prosecution in an exceedingly arrogant manner, or at least was perceived to have spoken arrogantly. Conversely, while not omitting it completely, Plato worked to temper that arrogance in his own *Apology*. Xenophon framed Socrates' defence, which both men admit was not prepared at all, not as failure to effectively argue his side, but as striving for death even in the light of unconvincing charges. As Danzig interprets it, convincing the jury to condemn him even on unconvincing charges would be a rhetorical challenge worthy of the great persuader.

Xenophon uses this interpretation as justification for Socrates' arrogant stance and conventional failure. By contrast, Plato does not go so far as to claim that Socrates actually desired death, but seems to argue that Socrates was attempting to demonstrate a higher moral standard and teach a lesson, although his defence failed by conventional standards.

This places Socrates in a higher moral position than his prosecutors, a typical Platonic example of absolving "Socrates from blame in every conceivable way."

Historical Reality

It is quite clear that Socrates never would have said most of the things that Xenophon relates in his dialogues. Although Xenophon claims to have been present at the *Symposium*, this is impossible as he was only a young boy at the date which he proposes it occurred.

And again, Xenophon was not present at the trial of Socrates, having been on campaign in Anatolia and Persia. Thus he puts into the latter's mouth what he would have thought him to say.

Like Plato, it seems that Xenophon wrote his *Apology* and*Memorabilia* as defences of his former teacher, not to explain Socrates' relationship to the actual charges incurred, but for the fact that the great persuader failed in his defence.

The fact that Plato and Xenophon portray Socrates in different lights is evident of the fact that they were writing in reaction to his condemnation and death, portraying his loss in their own terms and rationalization. This is also indicative that they were not reflecting the literal reality of the court proceedings in their *Apologies*.

Modern Reception

Xenophon's standing as a political philosopher has been defended in recent times by Leo Strauss, who devoted a considerable part of his philosophic analysis to the works of Xenophon, returning to the high judgement of Xenophon as a thinker expressed by Shaftesbury, Winckelmann, Machiavelli and John Adams.

Xenophon's lessons on leadership have been reconsidered for their modern-day value. Jennifer O'Flannery holds that 'discussions of leadership and civic virtue should include the work of Xenophon....on public education for public service.' The *Cyropaedia*, in outlining Cyrus as an ideal leader having mastered the qualities of "education, equality, consensus, justice and service to state," is the work that she suggests be used as a guide or example for those striving to be leaders. The linking of moral code and education is an especially pertinent quality subscribed to Cyrus that O'Flannery believes is in line with modern perceptions of leadership.

FAN LI

Fan Li was an ancient Chinese advisor in the state of Yue in the Spring and Autumn Period. He had been to the state of Wu as hostage together with King Goujian of Yue. Three years later they came back and he helped Goujian to carry on a reform.

At last Yue was able to defeat the state of Wu. After the victory he resigned and renamed himself Tao Zhu Gong . He became abusinessman in his later years and became legendary for his success.

In the legend, after the fall of Wu, Fan Li retired from his ministerial post and lived with Xi Shi on a fishing boat, roaming like immortals in the misty wilderness of Lake Tai He. Fan became one of the prototypes of the later Chinese money god Cai Shen.

Fan Li managed a pharmacy selling traditional Chinese medicine. The pharmacy originally included only two elderly employees, "Questioning Uncle" and "Uncle Propriety" . The business began to expand only when Fan hired He Bo's youngest son, "Little Writing" .

He was credited with various books on business including *The Fish-Breeding Classic* , the earliest known work on fish farming, and the *Golden Rules of Business Success* . The later book, probably of a later origin, remains popular today. It includes 12 principles and 12 pitfalls describing the art of successful business management.

Fan Li was unusual among tycoons for his view of money. He believed that one who understood money would be willing to abandon it if it became a burden.

It is only a means to an end and should not be taken too seriously. Non-etheless, it must be handled and acquired according to principles. Fan Li also urged a somewhat loose construction of these principles, encouraging broad and flexible utilization in various situations. The Twelve Golden Rules are as follows:

- Ability to know people's character. You must perceive evidence of characteristics from experience.
- Ability to handle people. Never prejudge a prospect.
- Ability to stay focused on the business. Have a definite focus in life and business and avoid jumping around.
- Ability to be organized. A disorganized presentation is unappealing.
- Ability to be adaptable. Make sure you are organized enough to respond quickly.
- Ability to control credit. Do not allow non-payment. Make sure you collect what is owed.

- Ability to use and deploy people. Use employees in ways which bring out their potential(s).
- Ability to articulate and market. You must be able to educate customers on the value of goods.
- Ability to excel in purchasing. Use your best judgement in acquiring stock.
- Ability to analyze market opportunities and threats. Know what is selling according to areas and trends.
- Ability to lead by example. Have definite rules and standards. Make sure they are followed to ensure good relations.
- Ability to have business foresight. Know market trends and cycles.

The Twelve Golden Safeguards are:

- Don't be stingy. Never confuse efficiency with inhumanity.
- Don't be wishy-washy. Be confident in pursuing opportunities. Time is of the essence.
- Don't be ostentatious. Do not overspend in order to make an impression.
- Don't be dishonest. Truth is the only basis for business. Without it someone will get hurt.
- Don't be slow in debt collection. Without collections, liquidity is affected.
- Don't slash prices arbitrarily. This will only trigger a price war in which everyone will lose.
- Don't give in to herd instinct. Make sure the opportunities are real and not part of a craze.
- Don't work against the business cycle. When things fall in price, they will then rise and vice versa.
- Don't be a stick-in-the-mud. Keep up with things and make progress. Examine new things objectively.
- Don't overbuy on credit. Credit is not license to spend wildly.
- Don't under-save (keep reserve funds strong). When business is slow, one with money can expand while others close.
- Don't blindly endorse a product. Make sure your vendors are still following standard operating procedure.

Cartoon versions of this book are widely available in Singapore, both in Mandarin Chinese and in English. The Mandarin version includes Hanyu Pinyin and an English translation for each of the original business principles.

QIN SHI HUANG

Qin Shi Huang (260–210 BC), personal name Zheng, was the King of the state of Qin (r. 246–221 BC) who conquered all other Warring States and united China in 221 BC. Rather than maintain the title of king borne by the Shang and Zhou rulers, he ruled as the First Emperor of the Qin dynasty from 220 to 210 BC. The title emperor (*huangdi*) would continue to be borne byChinese rulers for the next two millennia.

During his reign, his generals greatly expanded the size of the Chinese state: campaigns south of Chu permanently added the Yuelands of Hunan and Guangdong to the Chinese cultural orbit; campaigns in Central Asia conquered the Ordos Loop from the nomadXiongnu, although eventually causing their confederation under Modu Chanyu.

Qin Shi Huang also worked with his minister Li Si to enact major economic and politic reforms aimed at the standardization of the diverse practices of the earlier Chinese states.

This process also led to the banning and burning of many books and the execution of recalcitrant scholars. His public works projects included the unification of diverse state walls into a single Great Wall of China and a massive new national road system, as well as the city-sized mausoleum guarded by the life-sized Terracotta Army. He ruled until his death, which occurred in 210 BC despite an infamous search for an elixir of immortality.

Modern Chinese names have two components, a surname and a given name. The nobles of ancient China, however, had two distinct surnames: the ancestral name comprised a larger group descended from a prominent ancestor, usually said to have lived during the time of the Three Sovereigns and Five Emperors of Chinese legend, and the clan name comprised a smaller group that showed a branch's current fief or recent title.

The ancient practice was to list men's names separately—Sima Qian's "Basic Annals of the First Emperor of Qin" introduces him as "given the name Zheng and the surname Zhao"—or to combine the clan surname with the personal name: Sima's account ofChu describes the sixteenth year of the reign of King Kaolie as the time when Zhao Zheng was enthroned as King of Qin".However, since modern Chinese surnames (despite usually descending from clan names) use the same character as the old*ancestral* names, it is much more common in modern Chinese sources to see the emperor's personal name written as Ying Zheng, using the ancestral name of the family who ruled both Qin and Zhao.

The rulers of Qin had styled themselves kings from the time of King Huiwen in 325 BC. Upon his ascension, Zheng became known as the King of Qin or King Zheng of Qin. This title made him the nominal equal of the rulers of Shang and of Zhou, the last of whose kings had been deposed by King Zhaoxiang of Qin in 256 BC.

Following the surrender of Qi in 221 BC, King Zheng had reunited all of the lands of the former Kingdom of Zhou. Rather than maintain his rank as king, however, he proclaimed the new title of emperor (*huángdì*). This derived from the titles of the divineThree Sovereigns and the legendary Five

Emperors of Chinese prehistory. The title was intended to appropriate some of the prestige of the Yellow Emperor, whose cult was popular in the later Warring States periodand who was considered to be a founder of the Chinese people. King Zheng chose the new regnal name of First Emperor (*ShĐ Huángdì*, formerly transcribed as Shih Huang-ti) on the understanding that his successors would be successively titled the "Second Emperor", "Third Emperor", and so on through the generations. (In fact, the scheme lasted only as long as his immediate heir, the Second Emperor.)

The First Emperor intended that his realm would remain intact through the ages but, following its overthrow and replacement by Han after his death, it became customary to prefix his title with Qin. Thus:

- *Qín* or Ch'in, "of Qin"
- *Shi* or Shih, "first"
- *Huángdì* or Huang-ti, "emperor", a new term coined from
- *Huáng* or Huang, literally "shining" or "splendid" and formerly most usually applied "as an epithet of Heaven", the high god of the Zhou
- *Dì* or Ti, the high god of the Shang, possibly composed of their divine ancestors, and used by the Zhou as a title of the legendary Five Emperors, particularly the Yellow Emperor

As early as Sima Qian, it was common to shorten the resulting four-character title, variously transcribed as Qin Shihuang or Qin Shi Huang. The new title carried religious overtones. For that reason, Sinologists—starting with Peter Boodbergor Edward Schafer—sometimes translate it as "thearch" and the First Emperor as the First Thearch.

Following his elevation as emperor, both Zheng's personal name and possibly its homophone became taboo. The First Emperor also arrogated the first-personChinese pronoun for his exclusive use and in 212 BC began calling himself The Immortal.Others were to address him as "Your Majesty" in person and "Your Highness" in writing.

LIFE

Birth

A rich merchant in the State of Han, named Lü Buwei, met Master Yiren. Lü Buwei's manipulation helped Yiren become King Zhuangxiang of Qin. At the time, Yiren was a prince of Qin who resided at the court of Zhao as a hostage to guarantee the armistice between the two states.

According to the *Records of the Grand Historian*, the first emperor was born in 259 BC as Yiren's eldest son. Prince Yiren had fallen in love at first sight with a concubinebelonging to Lü Buwei and Lü had consented to provide her to his protegé. The Lady Zhao bore the child on 18 February, but he was named Zheng from his birth during the first month of the Chinese lunar calendar. His clan name of Zhao came from his father's lineage and was unrelated both to his mother's surname and the location of his birth.

According to the *Records of the Grand Historian*, written by Sima Qian during the next dynasty, the first emperor was not the actual son of Prince Yiren. By the time Lü Buweiintroduced the dancing girl Zhao Ji to the prince, she was allegedly Lü Buwei's concubine and had already become pregnant by him. According to translations of the Annals of Lü Buwei, the woman gave birth to the future emperor in the city of Handan in 259 BC, the first month of the 48th year of King Zhaoxiang of Qin.

The idea that the emperor was an illegitimate child was widely believed throughout Chinese history and contributed to the generally negative view of the First Emperor.However, modern analysis has concluded that the sentence in the *Records of the Grand Historian* describing Qin Shi Huang's unusual birth is probably a later interpolation added in order to slander him. John Knoblock and Jeffrey Riegel, in their translation of Lü Buwei's *Spring and Autumn Annals*, call the story "patently false, meant both to libel Lü and to cast aspersions on the First Emperor." Claiming Lü Buwei – a merchant – as the First Emperor's biological father was meant to be especially disparaging, since later Confucian society held merchants to be the lowest of all social classes.

King of Qin

Regency

In 246 BC, when King Zhuangxiang died after a short reign of just three years, he was succeeded on the throne by his 13-year-old son. At the time, Zhao Zheng was still young, so Lü Buwei acted as the regent prime minister of the State of Qin, which was still waging war against the other six states.

Chengjiao, the Lord Chang'an, was Zhao Zheng's legitimate half-brother, by the same father but from a different mother. After Zhao Zheng inherited the throne, Chengjiao rebelled at Tunliu and surrendered to the state of Zhao. Chengjiao's remaining retainers and families were executed by Zhao Zheng.

Lao Ai's Attempted Coup

As King Zheng grew older, Lü Buwei became fearful that the boy king would discover his liaison with his mother Lady Zhao. He decided to distance himself and look for a replacement for the queen dowager. He found a man named Lao Ai. According to *the Record of Grand Historian*, Lao Ai was disguised as a eunuch by plucking his beard. Later Lao Ai and queen Zhao Ji got along so well they secretly had two sons together. Lao Ai then became ennobled as Marquis Lào Íi, and was showered with riches. Lao Ai's plot was supposed to replace King Zheng with one of the hidden sons. But during a dinner party drunken Lào Íi was heard bragging about being the young king's step father. In 238 BC the king was traveling to the ancient capital of Yông . Lao Ai seized the queen mother's seal and mobilized an army in an attempt to start a coup and rebel. When King Zheng found out this fact, he ordered Lü Buwei to let Lord Changping and Lord Changwen attack Lao Ai and their army killed hundreds of the rebels at the capital, although Lao Ai succeeded in fleeing from this battle.

A price of 1 million copper coins was placed on Lao Ai's head if he was taken alive or half a million if dead. Lao Ai's supporters were captured and beheaded; then Lao Ai was tied up and torn to five pieces by horse carriages, while his entire family was executed to the third degree. The two hidden sons were also killed, while mother Zhao Ji was placed under house arrest until her death many years later. Lü Buwei drank a cup of poison wine and committed suicide in 235 BC. Ying Zheng then assumed full power as the King of the Qin state. Replacing Lü Buwei, Li Si became the new chancellor.

First Attempted Assassination

King Zheng and his troops continued to take over different states. The state of Yan was small, weak and frequently harassed by soldiers. It was no match for the Qin state. SoCrown Prince Dan of Yan plotted an assassination attempt to get rid of King Zheng, begging Jing Ke to go on the mission in 227 BC. Jing Ke was accompanied by Qin Wuyang in the plot. Each was supposed to present a gift to King Zheng, a map of Dukang and the decapitated head of Fan Wuji.

Qin Wuyang first tried to present the map case gift, but trembled in fear and moved no further towards the king. Jing Ke continued to advance towards the king, while explaining that his partner "has never set eyes on the Son of Heaven", which is why he is trembling. Jing Ke had to present both gifts by himself. While unrolling the map, a dagger was revealed. The king drew back, stood on his feet, but struggled to draw the sword to defend himself. At the time, other palace officials were not allowed to carry weapons. Jing Ke pursued the king, attempting to stab him, but missed. King Zheng drew out his sword and cut Jing Ke's thigh. Jing Ke then threw the dagger, but missed again. Suffering eight wounds from the king's sword, Jing Ke realized his attempt had failed and knew that both of them would be killed afterwards. The Yan state was conquered by the Qin state five years later.

Second Attempted Assassination

Gao Jianli was a close friend of Jing Ke, who wanted to avenge his death. As a famous lute player, one day he was summoned by King Zheng to play the instrument. Someone in the palace who had known him in the past exclaimed, "This is Gao Jianli". Unable to bring himself to kill such a skilled musician, the emperor ordered his eyes put out. But the king allowed Gao Jianli to play in his presence. He praised the playing and even allowed Gao Jianli to get closer.

As part of the plot, the lute was fastened with a heavy piece of lead. He raised the lute and struck at the king. He missed, and his assassination attempt failed. Gao Jianli was later executed.

Unification of China

In 230 BC, King Zheng unleashed the final campaigns of the Warring States period, setting out to conquer the remaining independent kingdoms, one by one.

The first state to fall was Hán , in 230 BC. Then Qin took advantage of natural disasters in 229 BC to invade and conquer Zhào, where Qin Shi Huang had been born. He now avenged his poor treatment as a child hostage there, seeking out and killing his enemies.

Qin armies conquered the state of Zhao in 228 BC, the northern country of Yan in 226 BC, the small state of Wei in 225 BC, and the largest state and greatest challenge, Chu, in 223 BC.

In 222 BC, the last remnants of Yan and the royal family were captured in Liaodong in the northeast. The only independent country left was now state of Qi, in the far east, what is now the Shandong peninsula. Terrified, the young king of Qi sent 200,000 people to defend his western borders. In 221 BC, the Qin armies invaded from the north, captured the king, and annexed Qi.

For the first time, all of China was unified under one powerful ruler. In that same year, King Zheng proclaimed himself the "First Emperor", no longer a king in the old sense and now far surpassing the achievements of the old Zhou Dynasty rulers. The emperor made the He Shi Bi into the Imperial Seal, known as the "Heirloom Seal of the Realm". The words, "Having received the Mandate from Heaven, may (the emperor) lead a long and prosperous life." were written by Prime Minister Li Si, and carved onto the seal by Sun Shou. The Seal was later passed from emperor to emperor for generations to come.

In the South, military expansion in the form of campaigns against the Yue tribes continued during his reign, with various regions being annexed to what is now Guangdongprovince and part of today's Vietnam.

Emperor of Qin

Administrative Reforms

In an attempt to avoid a recurrence of the political chaos of early imperial China, the conquered states were not allowed to be referred to as independent nations. The empire was then divided into 36 commanderies , later more than 40 commanderies. The whole of China was now divided into administrative units: first commanderies, thendistricts , counties and hundred-family units. This system was different from the previous dynasties, which had loose alliances and federations.People could no longer be identified by their native region or former feudal state, as when a person from Chu was called "Chu person". Appointments were now based on merit instead of hereditary rights.

Economic Reforms

Qin Shi Huang and Li Si unified China economically by standardizing the Chinese units of measurements such as weights and measures, the currency, the length of the axles of carts to facilitate transport on the road system. The emperor also developed an extensive network of roads and canals connecting the provinces to improve trade between them. The currency of the different states were also standardized to the Ban liang coin . Perhaps most importantly, the Chinese script was unified. Under Li Si, the seal script of the state of Qin was standardized through removal of variant forms within the Qin script itself. This newly standardized script was then made official throughout all the conquered regions, thus doing away with all the regional scripts to form one language, one communication system for all of China.

Philosophy

Qin Shi Huang also followed the school of the five elements, earth, wood, metal, fire and water. Zhao Zheng's birth element is water, which is connected with the colour black. It was also believed that the royal house of the previous dynasty Zhou had ruled by the power of fire, which was the colour red.

The new Qin dynasty must be ruled by the next element on the list, which is water, represented by the colour black. Black became the colour for garments, flags, pennants. Other associations include north as the cardinal direction, winter season and the number six. Tallies and official hats were six inches long, carriages six feet wide, one pace was 6 ft (1.8 m).

While the previous Warring States era was one of constant warfare, it was also considered the golden age of free thought. Qin Shi Huang eliminated the Hundred Schools of Thought which incorporated Confucianism and other philosophies.

After the unification of China, with all other schools of thought banned, legalism became the endorsed ideology of the Qin dynasty, which was basically a system that required the people to follow the laws or be punished accordingly.

Beginning in 213 BC, at the instigation of Li Si and to avoid scholars' comparisons of his reign with the past, Qin Shi Huang ordered most existingbooks to be burned with the exception of those on astrology, agriculture, medicine, divination, and the history of the State of Qin. This would also serve the purpose of furthering the ongoing reformation of the writing system by removing examples of obsolete scripts. Owning the *Book of Songs* or the *Classic of History* was to be punished especially severely. According to the later *Records of the Grand Historian*, the following year Qin

Shi Huang had some 460 scholars buried alive for owning the forbidden books. The emperor's oldest son Fusu criticised him for this act. The emperor's own library still had copies of the forbidden books but most of these were destroyed later when Xiang Yu burned the palaces of Xianyang in 206 BC.

Third Attempted Assassination

In 230 BC, the state of Qin had defeated the state of Han. A Han aristocrat named Zhang Liang swore revenge on the Qin emperor. He sold all his valuables and in 218 BC, he hired a strongman assassin and built him a heavy metal cone weighing 120 jin (roughly 160 lb or 97 kg).

The two men hid among the bushes along the emperor's route over a mountain. At a signal, the muscular assassin hurled the cone at the first carriage and shattered it. However, the emperor was actually in the second carriage, as he was traveling with two identical carriages for this very reason. Thus the attempt failed. Both men were able to escape in spite of a huge manhunt.

Public Works

Great Wall

The Qin fought nomadic tribes to the north and northwest. The Xiongnu tribes were not defeated and subdued, thus the campaign was tiring and unsuccessful, and to prevent the Xiongnu from encroaching on the northern frontier any longer, the emperor ordered the construction of an immense defensive wall.

This wall, for whose construction hundreds of thousands of men were mobilized, and an unknown number died, is a precursor to the current Great Wall of China. It connected numerous state walls which had been built during the previous four centuries, a network of small walls linking river defences to impassable cliffs. A great monument of China to this day, the Great Wall still stands, open to the public to challenge its million steps.

Lingqu Canal

A famous South China quotation was "In the North there is the Great wall, in the South there is the Lingqu canal". In 214 BC the Emperor began the project of a major canal to transport supplies to the army. The canal allows water transport between north and south China. The canal, 34 kilometers in length, links the Xiang River which flows into the Yangtze and the Li Jiang, which flows into the Pearl River. The canal connected two of China's major waterways and aided Qin's expansion into the southwest. The construction is considered one of the three great feats of Ancient Chinese engineering, the others being the Great Wall and the Sichuan Dujiangyan Irrigation System.

Elixir of Life

Later in his life, Qin Shi Huang feared death and desperately sought the fabled elixir of life, which would supposedly allow him to live forever. He was obsessed with acquiring immortality and fell prey to many who offered him supposed elixirs. He visited Zhifu Island three times in order to achieve immortality.

In one case he sent Xu Fu, a Zhifu islander, with ships carrying hundreds of young men and women in search of the mystical Penglai mountain. They were sent to find Anqi Sheng, a 1,000-year-old magician whom Qin Shi Huang had supposedly met in his travels and who had invited him to seek him there. These people never returned, perhaps because they knew that if they returned without the promised elixir, they would surely be executed. Legends claim that they reached Japan and colonized it. It is also possible that the book burning, a purge on what could be seen as wasteful and useless literature, was, in part, an attempt to focus the minds of the Emperor's best scholars on thealchemical quest. Some of the executed scholars were those who had been unable to offer any evidence of their supernatural schemes. This may have been the ultimate means of testing their abilities: if any of them had magic powers, then they would surely come back to life when they were let out again. Since the great emperor was afraid of death and "evil spirits", he had workers build a series of tunnels and passage ways to each of his palaces (he owned over 200), because traveling unseen would supposedly keep him safe from the evil spirits.

Death

In 211 BC a large meteor is said to have fallen in Dôngjùn in the lower reaches of the Yellow River. On it, an unknown person inscribed the words "The First Emperor will die and his land will be divided". When the emperor heard of this, he sent an imperial secretary to investigate this prophecy. No one would confess to the deed, so all the people living nearby were put to death. The stone was then burned and pulverized.

The Emperor died during one of his tours of Eastern China, on September 10, 210 BC (Julian Calendar) at the palace in Shaqiu prefecture , about two months away by road from the capital Xianyang. Reportedly, he died due to ingesting mercury pills, made by his alchemists and court physicians. Ironically, these pills were meant to make Qin Shi Huang immortal.

After the Emperor's death, Prime Minister Li Si, who accompanied him, became extremely worried that the news of his death could trigger a general uprising in the Empire. It would take two months for the government to reach the capital, and it would not be possible to stop the uprising. Li Si decided to hide the death of the Emperor, and return to Xianyang. Most of the Imperial entourage accompanying the Emperor was left ignorant of the Emperor's death;

only a younger son, Ying Huhai, who was traveling with his father, the eunuch Zhao Gao, Li Si, and five or six favourite eunuchs knew of the death. Li Si also ordered that two carts containing rotten fish be carried immediately before and after the wagon of the Emperor. The idea behind this was to prevent people from noticing the foul smell emanating from the wagon of the Emperor, where his body was starting to decompose severely as it was summertime. They also pulled down the shade so no one could see his face, changed his clothes daily, brought food and when he had to have important conversations, they would act as if he wanted to send them a message.

Family

The following are some family members of Qin Shi Huang:

- Parents
- King Zhuangxiang of Qin
- Queen Dowager Zhao
- Half siblings:
- Chengjiao, Lord of Chang'an
- Two half-brothers born to Queen Dowager Zhao and Lao Ai
- Children:
- Fusu, Crown Prince (17th son)
- Gao
- Jianglü
- Huhai, later Qin Er Shi (18th son)

Qin Shi Huang had about 50 children, sons about 30, daughters about 15, but most of their names are unknown. He had numerous concubines but never seemed to name an empress.

Second Emperor Conspiracy

Eventually, after about two months, Li Si and the imperial court reached Xianyang, where the news of the death of the emperor was announced. Qin Shi Huang did not like to talk about his own death and he had never written a will. After his death, the eldest son Fusu would normally become the next emperor.

Li Si and the chief eunuch Zhao Gao conspired to kill Fusu because Fusu's favourite general was Meng Tian, whom they disliked and feared; Meng Tian's brother, a senior minister, had once punished Zhao Gao. They believed that if Fusu was enthroned, they would lose their power. Li Si and Zhao Gao forged a letter from Qin Shi Huang saying that both Fusu and General Meng must commit suicide. The plan worked, and the younger son Huhai became the Second Emperor, later known as Qin Er Shi or "Second Generation Qin."

Qin Er Shi, however, was not as capable as his father. Revolts quickly erupted. His reign was a time of extreme civil unrest, and everything built by the First Emperor crumbled away within a short period. One of the immediate revolt attempts was the 209 BC Daze Village Uprising led by Chen Sheng and Wu Guang.

LEGACY

Mausoleum

The Chinese historian Sima Qian, writing a century after the First Emperor's death, wrote that it took 700,000 men to construct the emperor's mausoleum. The British historian John Man points out that this figure is larger than any city of the world at that time and calculates that the foundations could have been built by 16,000 men in two years.While Sima Qian never mentioned the terracotta army, the statues were discovered by a group of farmers digging wells on March 29, 1974. The soldiers were created with a series of mix-and-match clay molds and then further individualized by the artists' hand. Han Purple was also used on some of the warriors. There are around 6,000 Terracotta Warriors and their purpose was to protect the Emperor in the afterlife from evil spirits. Also among the army are chariots and 40,000 real bronze weapons.

Tomb

One of the first projects the young king accomplished while he was alive was the construction of his own tomb. In 215 BC Qin Shi Huang ordered General Meng Tian with 300,000 men to begin construction. Other sources suggested he ordered 720,000 unpaid laborers to build his tomb to specification. Again, given John Man's observation regarding populations of the time, these historical estimates are debatable. The main tomb (located at 34°222 52.753 N 109°152 13.063 E) containing the emperor has yet to be opened and there is evidence suggesting that it remains relatively intact. Sima Qian's description of the tomb includes replicas of palaces and scenic towers, "rare utensils and wonderful objects", 100 rivers made with mercury, representations of "the heavenly bodies", and crossbows rigged to shoot anyone who tried to break in. The tomb was built at the foot of Li Mountain, and is only 30 kilometers away from Xi'an. Modern archaeologists have located the tomb, and have inserted probes deep into it. The probes revealed abnormally high quantities of mercury, some 100 times the naturally occurring rate, suggesting that some parts of the legend are credible.Secrets were maintained, as most of the workmen who built the tomb were killed.

Historiography

In traditional Chinese historiography, the First Emperor of the Chinese unified states was almost always portrayed as a brutal tyrant who had obsessive fear of assassination. Ideological antipathy towards the Legalist State of Qin was established as early as 266 BC, when Confucian philosopher Xunzi disparaged it. Later Confucian historians condemned the emperor who had burned the classics and buried Confucian scholars alive. They eventually compiled a list of the *Ten Crimes of Qin* to highlight his tyrannical actions.

The famous Han poet and statesman Jia Yi concluded his essay *The Faults of Qin* with what was to become the standard Confucian judgement of the reasons for Qin's collapse. Jia Yi's essay, admired as a masterpiece of rhetoric and reasoning, was copied into two great Han histories and has had a far-reaching influence on Chinese political thought as a classic illustration of Confucian theory. He attributed Qin's disintegration to its internal failures. Jia Yi wrote that:

Qin, from a tiny base, had become a great power, ruling the land and receiving homage from all quarters for a hundred odd years. Yet after they unified the land and secured themselves within the pass, a single common rustic could nevertheless challenge this empire... Why? Because the ruler lacked humaneness and rightness; because preserving power differs fundamentally from seizing power.

In more modern times, historical assessment of the First Emperor different from traditional Chinese historiography began to emerge. The reassessment was spurred on by weakness of China in the latter half of 19th century and early 20th century, and Confucian traditions at that time began to be seen by some as an impediment to China's entry into the modern world, opening the way for changing perspectives.

At a time when Chinese territory was encroached upon by foreign nations, leading Kuomintang historian Xiao Yishan emphasized the role of Qin Shi Huang in repulsing the northern barbarians, particularly in the construction of the Great Wall.

Another historian, Ma Feibai , published in 1941 a full-length revisionist biography of the First Emperor entitled *Qín ShĐ Huángdì Zhuàn* , calling him "one of the great heroes of Chinese history". Ma compared him with the contemporary leader Chiang Kai-shek and saw many parallels in the careers and policies of the two men, both of whom he admired. Chiang's Northern Expedition of the late 1920s, which directly preceded the new Nationalist government at Nanjing was compared to the unification brought about by Qin Shi Huang.

With the coming of the Communist Revolution in 1949, new interpretations again surfaced. The establishment of the new, revolutionary regime prompted another re-evaluation of the First Emperor, this time in accordance with Maoist thought. The new interpretation given of Qin Shi Huang was generally a combination of traditional and modern views, but essentially critical. This is exemplified in the *Complete History of China*, which was compiled in September 1955 as an official survey of Chinese history. The work described the First Emperor's major steps towards unification and standardisation as corresponding to the interests of the ruling group and the merchant class, not the nation or the people, and the subsequent fall of his dynasty as a manifestation of the class struggle. The perennial debate about the fall of the Qin Dynasty was also explained in Marxist terms, the peasant rebellions being a revolt against oppression – a revolt which undermined the dynasty, but which was bound to fail because of a compromise with "landlord class elements".

Since 1972, however, a radically different official view of Qin Shi Huang has been given prominence throughout China. The re-evaluation was initiated by Hong Shidi's biography *Qin Shi Huang*. The work was published by the state press as a mass popular history, and it sold 1.85 million copies within two years. In the new era, Qin Shi Huang was seen as a farsighted ruler who destroyed the forces of division and established the first unified, centralized state in Chinese history by rejecting the past. Personal attributes, such as his quest for immortality, so emphasized in traditional historiography, were scarcely mentioned. The new evaluations described how, in his time (an era of great political and social change), he had no compunctions against using violent methods to crush counter-revolutionaries, such as the "industrial and commercial slave owner" chancellor Lü Buwei. However, he was criticized for not being as thorough as he should have been, and as a result, after his death, hidden subversives under the leadership of the chief eunuch Zhao Gao were able to seize power and use it to restore the old feudal order.

To round out this re-evaluation, a new interpretation of the precipitous collapse of the Qin Dynasty was put forward in an article entitled "On the Class Struggle During the Period Between Qin and Han" by Luo Siding, in a 1974 issue of *Red Flag*, to replace the old explanation. The new theory claimed that the cause of the fall of Qin lay in the lack of thoroughness of Qin Shi Huang's "dictatorship over the reactionaries, even to the extent of permitting them to worm their way into organs of political authority and usurp important posts."

Mao Zedong, chairman of the People's Republic of China, was reviled for his persecution of intellectuals. On being compared to the First Emperor, Mao responded: "He buried 460 scholars alive; we have buried forty-six thousand scholars alive... You [intellectuals] revile us for being Qin Shi Huangs. You are wrong. We have surpassed Qin Shi Huang a hundredfold."

WANG ANSHI

Wang Anshi (December 8, 1021 – May 21, 1086) was a Chinese economist, statesman, chancellor and poet of the Song Dynasty who attempted controversial, major socioeconomic reforms. These reforms constituted the core concepts and motives of the Reformists, while their nemesis, Chancellor Sima Guang, led the Conservative faction against them. In economics, his reforms expanded the use of money, broke up private monopolies and introduced some forms of government regulation and social welfare. In military affairs, he supported the use of local militias; and in education and government, he expanded the examination system and tried to suppress nepotism. Though successful for a while, he eventually fell out of favour of the emperor.

BACKGROUND

Under the Song Dynasty, the unprecedented development of large estates, whose owners managed to evade paying their share oftaxes, resulted in an increasingly heavy burden of taxation on the peasantry. The drop in state revenues, a succession of budgetdeficits, and widespread inflation prompted the Emperor Shenzong of Song to seek advice from Wang.

EARLY CAREER

Though Wang was from the southern China, he came from a family of imperial scholars and was placed fourth in the imperial exam of 1042. He spent the first twenty years of his career in the regional government of the lower Yangtze region. During this period, he gained practical experience in local governance. This experience guided his analysis in formulating solutions to revitalize the ailing Song society.

MAJOR REFORM

Wang believed that the state has the responsibility to provide for its people the essentials for a decent living standard: "The state should take the entire management of commerce, industry, and agriculture into its own hands, with a view to succoring the working classes and preventing them from being ground into the dust by the rich."

Wang came to power as 2nd privy councilor in 1069. It was there that he introduced and promulgated his reform policy. There were three main components to this policy: 1) state finance and trade, 2) defence and social order, and 3) education and improving of governance.

Some of the finance reforms included paying cash for labour in place of corvee labour, increase the supply of copper coins, improve management of trade, direct government loan to farmers during planting seasons and to be repaid at harvest. He believed that foundation of the state rests on the well being of the common people. To limit speculation and eliminate private monopolies, he initiated price control and regulated wages and set up pensions for the aged and unemployed. The state also began to institute public orphanages, hospitals, dispensaries, hospices, cemeteries, and reserve granaries.

The military reform centered on a new institution of the baojia system or organized households. This was done to ensure collective responsibility in society and was later used to strengthen local defence. He also proposed the creation of systems to breed military horses, the more efficient manufacture of weapons and training of the militia.

To improve education and government, he sought to break down the barrier between clerical and official careers as well as improving their supervision to prevent connections being used for personal gain. Tests in law, military affairs and medicine were added to the examination system, with mathematics added in 1104. The National Academy was transformed into a real school rather than simply a holding place for officials waiting for appointments. However, there was deep-seated resistance to the education reforms as it hurt bureaucrats coming in under the old system.

WANG'S DOWNFALL

Although Wang had the alliance of such prominent court figures as Shen Kuo, imperial scholar-officials such as Su Dongpo and Ouyang Xiu bitterly opposed these reforms on the grounds of tradition.

They believed Wang's reforms were against the moral fundamentals of theTwo Emperors and would therefore prevent the Song from experiencing the prosperity and peace of the ancients. The tide tilted in favour of the conservatives due to renewed foreign conflict. He was even temporarily removed from power and imprisoned in 1075.

Like many Chinese officials of the era, Wang's career experienced many ups and downs, but the beginning of the end came in 1074. A famine in northern China drove many farmers off their lands. Their circumstances were made worse by the debts they had incurred from the seasonal loans granted under Wang's reform initiatives. Local officials insisted on collecting on the loans as the farmers were leaving their land. This crisis was depicted as being Wang's fault. The empress dowager was also an opponent of Wang. Wang wanted to resign, but the emperor still supported him, giving him high honours and an appointment to Jiangning (present-day Nanjing.)

He was recalled by the emperor the following year, but now he was seen as vulnerable and was openly attacked from groups of conservatives. Wang returned to Nanjing, which he preferred to Kaifeng. He wrote and engaged in scholarship through to his death in 1086.

With Shenzong's death in 1085, Wang was ousted and the New Policies were rolled back - some temporarily, some permanently.

POET

In addition to his political achievements, Wang Anshi was a noted poet. He wrote poems in the *shi* form, modelled on those of Du Fu. He was traditionally classed as one of the*Eight Great Prose Masters of the Tang and Song* .

LEGACY

Chinese politicians and historians have continued to look back on the reforms of Wang Anshi as either principled and measured or misguided and disastrous.

The twentieth-century Chinese warlord Yan Xishan cited the reforms of Wang Anshi to justify his use of a limited form of local democracy in Shanxi. Yan believed that the focus and intent of Wang's reforms was to strengthen the Song dynasty by persuading ordinary Chinese to give the dynasty their active support, instead of merely serving it. The system of "democratic" government that Yan justified via the philosophy of Wang Anshi was mostly focused on improving Yan's own popularity without holding any real power, and never became an effective alternative to military dictatorship. On the other hand, the popular scholar Lin Yutang cast Wang as the equivalent of communist totalitarian government in his biography of Wang's adversary Su Dongpo.

MUQADDIMAH

The *Muqaddimah,* also known as the *Muqaddimah of Ibn Khaldun* (Ibn Khaldun's Introduction) or *Ibn Khaldun's Prolegomena,* is a book written by the Arab, North African Muslim historian Ibn Khaldun in 1377 which records an early view of universal history. Some modern thinkers view it as the first work dealing with the philosophy of history or the social sciences of sociology, demography, historiography, cultural history, andeconomics. The *Muqaddimah* also deals with Islamic theology, political theory and the natural sciences of biology and chemistry. Ibn Khaldun wrote the work in 1377 as the preface or first book of his planned world history, the *Kitab al-Ibar* (Lessons, Record of Beginnings and Events in the history of the Arabs and Berbers and their Powerful Contemporaries"), but already in his lifetime it became regarded as an independent work.

CONTENT

Ibn Khaldun starts the *Muqaddimah* with a thorough criticism of the mistakes regularly committed by his fellow historians and the difficulties which await the historian in his work. He notes seven critical issues:

"All records, by their very nature, are liable to error...

1. ...Partisanship towards a creed or opinion...
2. ...Over-confidence in one's sources...
3. ...The failure to understand what is intended...
4. ...A mistaken belief in the truth...
5. ...The inability to place an event in its real context

6. ...The common desire to gain favour of those of high ranks, by praising them, by spreading their fame...
7. ...The most important is the ignorance of the laws governing the transformation of human society."

Against the seventh point (the ignorance of social laws) Ibn Khaldun lays out his theory of human society in the *Muqaddimah*. Sati' al-Husri suggested that Ibn Khaldun's *Muqaddimah* is essentially a sociological work, sketching over its six books a general sociology; a sociology of politics; a sociology of urban life; a sociology of economics; and a sociology of knowledge.

Scientific Method

Ibn Khaldun often criticized "idle superstition and uncritical acceptance of historical data." As a result, he introduced the scientific method to the social sciences, which was considered something "new to his age", and he often referred to it as his "new science" and developed his own new terminology for it.

His historical method also laid the groundwork for the observation of the role of state, communication, propaganda and systematic bias in history, leading to his development ofhistoriography.

SOCIOLOGY

'Asabiyyah

The concept of "'asabiyyah" (Arabic: 'tribalism', 'clanism', 'communitarism' or in a modern context 'nationalism') is one of the most well-known aspects of the *Muqaddimah*. Ibn Khaldun uses the term *Asabiyyah* to describe the bond of cohesion among humans in a group forming community. The bond, Asabiyyah, exists at any level of civilization, from nomadic society to states and empires.

Asabiyyah is most strong in the nomadic phase, and decreases as civilization advances. As this Asabiyyah declines, another more compelling Asabiyyah may take its place; thus, civilizations rise and fall, and history describes these cycles of Asabiyyah as they play out. Ibn Khaldun argues that each dynasty has within itself the seeds of its own downfall.

He explains that ruling houses tend to emerge on the peripheries of great empires and use the unity presented by those areas to their advantage in order to bring about a change in leadership.

As the new rulers establish themselves at the centre of their empire, they become increasingly lax and more concerned with maintaining their lifestyles.

Thus, a new dynasty can emerge at the periphery of their control and effect a change in leadership, beginning the cycle anew. Ibn Khaldun's model is an instinctive one, not requiring a conceptual social contract present in classical republicanism.

Conflict Theory

Ibn Khaldun conceived both a central social conflict ("town" versus "desert") as well as a theory (using the concept of a "generation") of the necessary loss of power of city conquerors coming from the desert.

ECONOMICS

Ibn Khaldun wrote on economic and political theory in the *Muqaddimah*, relating his thoughts on *asabiyya* to the division of labour: the greater the social cohesion, the more complex the division may be, the greater the economic growth.

Ibn Khaldun noted that growth and development positively stimulate both supply and demand, and that the forces of supply and demand are what determine the prices of goods.

He also noted macroeconomic forces of population growth, human capital development, and technological developments effects on development. Ibn Khaldun held that population growth was a function of wealth.

Ibn Khaldun understood that money served as a standard of value, a medium of exchange, and a preserver of value, though he did not realize that the value of gold and silver changed based on the forces of supply and demand. Ibn Khaldun also introduced the labour theory of value.

He described labour as the source of value, necessary for all earnings and capital accumulation, obvious in the case of craft. He argued that even if earning "results from something other than a craft, the value of the resulting profit and acquired (capital) must (also) include the value of the labour by which it was obtained. Without labour, it would not have been acquired." His theory of *asabiyyah* has often been compared to modern Keynesian economics, with Ibn Khaldun's theory clearly containing the concept of the multiplier.

A crucial difference, however, is that whereas for John Maynard Keynes it is the middle class's greater propensity to save that is to blame for economic depression, for Ibn Khaldun it is the governmental propensity to save at times when investment opportunities do not take up the slack which leads to aggregate demand.

Another modern economic theory anticipated by Ibn Khaldun is supply-side economics. He "argued that high taxes were often a factor in causing empires to collapse, with the result that lower revenue was collected from high rates." He wrote: "It should be known that at the beginning of the dynasty, taxation yields a large revenue from small assessments. At the end of the dynasty, taxation yields a small revenue from large assessments."

Laffer Curve

Ibn Khaldun introduced the concept now popularly known as the Laffer Curve, that increases in tax rates initially increase tax revenues, but eventually the increases in tax rates cause a decrease in tax revenues. This occurs as too high a tax rate discourages producers in the economy.

Ibn Khaldun used a dialectic approach to describe the sociological implications of tax choice (which now forms a part of economics theory):In the early stages of the state, taxes are light in their incidence, but fetch in a large revenue. As time passes and kings succeed each other, they lose their tribal habits in favour of more civilized ones.

Their needs and exigencies grow...owing to the luxury in which they have been brought up. Hence they impose fresh taxes on their subjects...and sharply raise the rate of old taxes to increase their yield. But the effects on business of this rise in taxation make themselves felt. For business men are soon discouraged by the comparison of their profits with the burden of their taxes. Consequently production falls off, and with it the yield of taxation.

This analysis is very similar to the modern economic concept known as the Laffer Curve. Laffer does not claim to have invented the concept himself, noting that the idea was present in the work of Ibn Khaldun and, more recently, John Maynard Keynes.

The Khaldun-Laffer curve has also been used in Solid State Physics and Chemistry to interpret the dependence of certain macroscopic properties of solids on hydrostatic pressure (*e.g.* dynamical effective charge, polarizability).

HISTORIOGRAPHY

The *Muqaddimah* is also held to be a foundational work for the schools of historiography, cultural history, and the philosophy of history. The *Muqaddimah* also laid the groundwork for the observation of the role of state, communication, propaganda and systematic bias in history. Franz Rosenthal wrote in the *History of Muslim Historiography*:

Muslim historiography has at all times been united by the closest ties with the general development of scholarship in Islam, and the position of historical knowledge in Muslim education has exercised a decisive influence upon the intellectual level of historical writing.

The Muslims achieved a definite advance beyond previous historical writing in the sociological understanding of history and the systematisation of historiography. The development of modern historical writing seems to have gained considerably in speed and substance through the utilization of a Muslim Literature which enabled western historians, from the seventeenth century on, to see a large section of the world through foreign eyes. The Muslim historiography helped indirectly and modestly to shape present day historical thinking.

Historical Method

In the *Muqaddimah*, Ibn Khaldun warned of seven mistakes that he thought that historians regularly committed. In this criticism, he approached the past as strange and in need of interpretation. The originality of Ibn Khaldun was to claim that the cultural difference of another age must govern the evaluation of relevant historical material, to distinguish the principles according to which it might be possible to attempt the evaluation, and lastly, to feel the need for experience, in addition to rational principles, in order to assess a culture of the past.

Ibn Khaldun often criticized "idle superstition and uncritical acceptance of historical data." As a result, he introduced a scientific method to the study of history, which was considered something "new to his age", and he often referred to it as his "new science", now associated with historiography.

His historical method also laid the groundwork for the observation of the role of state, communication, propaganda and systematic bias in history, and he is thus considered to be the "father of historiography" or the "father of the philosophy of history".

Ibn Khaldun' makes the following comments on his scientific historical method in his *Muqaddimah*:

- "History is a science"
- "History has a content and the historian should account for it"
- "The historian should account for the elements that gather to make the human history"
- "He should also work according to the laws of history"
- "History is a philosophical science"
- "History is composed of news about the days, states and the previous centuries. It is a theory, an analysis and justification about the creatures and their principles, and a science of how the incidents happen and their reasons"
- "Myths have nothing to do with history and should be refuted"
- "To build strong historical records, the historian should rely on necessary rules for the truth comparison"

Philosophy of History

Ibn Khaldun is considered a pioneer of the philosophy of history. Franz Rosenthal writes on the *Muqaddimah*:

It can be regarded as the earliest attempt made by any historian to discover a pattern in the changes that occur in man's political and social organization. Rational in its approach, analytical in its method, encyclopaedic in detail, it represents an almost complete departure from traditional historiography, discarding conventional concepts and cliches and seeking, beyond the mere chronicle of events, an explanation—and hence a philosophy of history.

Systematic Bias

The *Muqaddimah* emphasized the role of systemic bias in affecting the standard of evidence. Khaldun was quite concerned with the effect of raising the standard of evidence when confronted with uncomfortable claims, and relaxing it when given claims that seemed reasonable or comfortable. He was a jurist, and sometimes participated reluctantly in rulings that he felt were coerced, based on arguments he didn't respect. Besides al-Maqrizi (1364–1442), Ibn Khaldun's focused attempt to systematically study and account biases in the creation of history wouldn't be seen again until Hegel, Marx, and Nietzsche in 19th-century Germany, and Arnold J. Toynbee, a 20th-century British historian.

Ibn Khaldun also examines why, throughout history, it has been common for historians to sensationalize historical events and, in particular, exaggerate numerical figures:

Whenever contemporaries speak about the dynastic armies of their own or recent times, and whenever they engage in discussions about Muslim or Christian soldiers, or when they get to figuring the tax revenues and the money spent by the government, the outlays of extravagant spenders, and the goods that rich and prosperous men have in stock, they are quite generally found to exaggerate, to go beyond the bounds of the ordinary, and to succumb to the temptation of sensationalism. When the officials in charge are questioned about their armies, when the goods and assets of wealthy people are assessed, and when the outlays of extravagant spenders are looked at in ordinary light, the figures will be found to amount to a tenth of what those people have said. The reason is simple. It is the common desire for sensationalism, the ease with which one may just mention a higher figure, and the disregard of reviewers and critics. This leads to failure to exercise self-criticism about one's errors and intentions, to demand from oneself moderation and fairness in reporting, to reapply oneself to study and research. Such historians let themselves go and made a feast of untrue statements. "They procure for themselves enter-taining stories in order to lead (others) astray from the path of God." (Qur'an 31.6)

Military History

The *Muqaddimah* is the earliest known work to critically examine military history. It criticizes certain accounts of historical battles that appear to be exaggerated, and takesmilitary logistics into account when questioning the sizes of historical armies reported in earlier sources. In the Introduction to the *Muqaddimah*, Ibn Khaldun directs this criticism towards to famous historians such as Al-Masudi, who is today regarded as the "Herodotus of the Arabs" and who Ibn Khaldun himself regarded as one of the most famous historians up until his time.

As an example, Ibn Khaldun notes that Al-Masudi and other historians reported that Moses counted the Israelite army as 600,000 or more soldiers. Ibn Khaldun criticizes Al-Masudi for failing to take into account certain logistics, questioning whether Egypt and Syria could have possibly held such a large number of soldiers, or whether an army of that size would be able to march or fight as a unit. He notes that the whole available territory would have been too small for such a large army, and argues that if "it were in battle formation, it would extend" several times "beyond the field of vision."

He questions how two such parties could "fight with each other, or one battle formation gain the upper hand when one flank does not know what the other flank is doing," and that a co-ordinated battle movement in such a large group "would hardly be possible."

He argues that the "situation in the present day testifies to the correctness of this statement" since the "past resembles the future more than one drop of water another." He then compares it to thePersian Sassanid Empire, noting that it was far more vast than the Israelite Kingdom and yet the size of the Sassanid army at the Battle of al-Qâdisiyyah amounted to 120,000 troops at most (citing the 8th-century historian Sayf ibn Umar).

The *Muqaddimah* states that if the Israelites really did have such a large army, the extent of their empire would have been far larger, as "the size of administrative units and provinces under a particular dynasty is in direct proportion to the size of its militia and the groups that support the dynasty."

The *Muqaddimah* further notes that Moses lived only a few generations after Jacob, the founder of the Israelite tribes, according to the Levite tribe genealogy, as described by Al-Masudi.

Ibn Khaldun argues that it "is improbable that the descendants of one man could branch out into such a number within four generations." The *Muqaddimah* also states that there was a general assumption that Soloman's army was similarly large, but Ibn Khaldun refutes this, noting that Soloman came only eleven generations after Jacob, and argues that the "descendants of one man in eleven generations would not branch out into such a number, as has been assumed."

He then agrees with another statement from the "Israelite Stories" suggesting that Soloman's army had 12,000 soldiers and 1,400 horses. He notes that this was when the Israelite state was at its strongest, making other claims giving larger numbers for the Israelite army unlikely.

Ibn Khaldun notes that Jews have claimed the unrealistically large increase in the Israelite population within several generations was possible because it was a miracle of God, a claim that Ibn Khaldun did not dismiss completely. He considers such a miracle highly unlikely, but appears to be open to the possibility.

ISLAMIC THEOLOGY

The *Muqaddimah* contains discussions on Islamic theology which show that Ibn Khaldun was a follower of the orthodox Ash'ari school of Sunni

Islamic thought and a supporter of al-Ghazali's religious views. He was also a critic of Neo-platonism, particularly its notion of a hierarchy of being. He argued that theosis requires the participation of revelation and is not possible through reason alone.

He based his argument on the "irreducibility of the empirical nature of our knowledge of facts, which cannot then be converted into abstract and pure concepts at a higher level of human consciousness."

The *Muqaddimah* covers the historical development of kalam and the different schools of Islamic thought, notably the Mu'tazili and Ash'ari schools. Ibn Khaldun, being a follower of the Ash'ari school, criticizes the views of the Mu'tazili school, and bases his criticisms on the views of Abu al-Hasan al-Ash'ari, whom he describes as "the mediator between different approaches in the kalam."

Ibn Khaldun also covers the historical development of Islamic logic in the context of theology, as he viewed logic as being distinct from early Islamic philosophy, and believed that philosophy should remain separate from theology. The book also contains commentaries on verses from the Qur'an.

Islamic Psychology

In Islamic psychology, Ibn Khaldun wrote the following on dream interpretation:

Often, we may deduce (the existence of) that high spiritual world and the essences it contains, from visions and things we had not been aware of while awake but which we find in our sleep and which are brought to our attention in it and which, if they are true (dreams), conform with actuality. We thus know that they are true and come from the world of truth. "Confused dreams," on the other hand, are pictures of the imagination that are stored inside by perception and to which the ability to think is applied, after (man) has retired from sense perception.

Science of Hadith

Ibn Khaldun discussed the science of hadith. He disagreed with the use of reason in the evaluation of a hadith, arguing that "there is no place for the intellect in them, save that the intellect may be used in connection with them to relate problems of detail with basic principles."

On the authority of the *Sahih al-Bukhari*, the *Muqaddimah* also argues that, despite the Islamic belief that the Torah was altered by the Jews, the Muslims should neither believe nor disbelieve historical claims concerning the Torah made by Jews and Christians, particularly in regards to miraculous events. He states that:

The statement concerning the alteration (of the Torah by the Jews) is unacceptable to thorough scholars and cannot be understood in its plain meaning, since custom prevents people who have a (revealed) religion from dealing with their divine scriptures in such a manner. This was mentioned by al-Bukhari in the *Sahih*.

Sharia Law and Fiqh Jurisprudence

Ibn Khaldun was an Islamic jurist and discussed the topics of Sharia (Islamic law) and Fiqh (Islamic jurisprudence) in his *Muqaddimah*. Ibn Khaldun wrote that "Jurisprudence is the knowledge of the classification of the laws of God." In regards to jurisprudence, he acknowledged the inevitability of change in all aspects of a community, and wrote:

The conditions, customs and beliefs of peoples and nations do not indefinitely follow the same pattern and adhere to a constant course. There is rather, change with days and epochs, as well as passing from one state to another... such is the law of God that has taken place with regard to His subjects.

Ibn Khaldun further described Fiqh jurisprudence as "knowledge of the rules of God which concern the actions of persons who own themselves bound to obey the law respecting what is required (*wajib*), forbidden (*haraam*), recommended (*mandûb*), disapproved (*makruh*) or merely permitted (*mubah*)."

NATURAL SCIENCES

Biology

Some of Ibn Khaldun's thoughts, according to some commentators, anticipate the biological theory of evolution. Ibn Khaldun asserted that humans developed from "the world of the monkeys", in a process by which "species become more numerous" in Chapter 1 of the *Muqaddimah*:

This world with all the created things in it has a certain order and solid construction. It shows nexuses between causes and things caused, combinations of some parts of creation with others, and transformations of some existent things into others, in a pattern that is both remarkable and endless.

One should then take a look at the world of creation. It started out from the minerals and progressed, in an ingenious, gradual manner, to plants and animals. The last stage of minerals is connected with the first stage of plants, such as herbs and seedless plants.

The last stage of plants, such as palms and vines, is connected with the first stage of animals, such as snails and shellfish which have only the power of touch. The word 'connection' with regard to these created things means that the last stage of each group is fully prepared to become the first stage of the newest group.

The animal world then widens, its species become numerous, and, in a gradual process of creation, it finally leads to man, who is able to think and reflect. The higher stage of man is reached from the world of monkeys, in which both sagacity and perception are found, but which has not reached the stage of actual reflection and thinking. At this point we come to the first stage of man. This is as far as our (physical) observation extends.

Ibn Khaldun believed that humans are the most evolved form of animals, in that they have the ability to reason. The *Muqaddimah* also states in Chapter 6:

We explained there that the whole of existence in (all) its simple and composite worlds is arranged in a natural order of ascent and descent, so that everything constitutes an uninterrupted continuum.

The essences at the end of each particular stage of the worlds are by nature prepared to be transformed into the essence adjacent to them, either above or below them.

This is the case with the simple material elements; it is the case with palms and vines, (which constitute) the last stage of plants, in their relation to snails and shellfish, (which constitute) the (lowest) stage of animals. It is also the case with monkeys, creatures combining in themselves cleverness and perception, in their relation to man, the being who has the ability to think and to reflect.

The preparedness (for transformation) that exists on either side, at each stage of the worlds, is meant when (we speak about) their connection.

Plants do not have the same fineness and power that animals have. Therefore, the sages rarely turned to them.

Animals are the last and final stage of the three permutations. Minerals turn into plants, and plants into animals, but animals cannot turn into anything finer than themselves.

His evolutionary ideas appear to be similar to those found in the *Encyclopaedia of the Brethren of Purity* Ibn Khaldun was also an adherent of environmental determinism. He explained that black skin was due to the hot climate of sub-Saharan Africa and not due to their lineage. He thus dispelled the Hamitic theory, where the sons of Ham were cursed by being black, as a myth.

Chemistry

Ibn Khaldun was a critic of the practice of alchemy in the Islamic world. In chapter 23 of his work, entitled *Fi 'ilm al-kimya*, he discussed the history of alchemy, the views of alchemists such as Geber, and the theories of the transmutation of metals and elixir of life.

In chapter 26, entitled *Fi inkar thamrat al-kimya wa istihalat wujudiha wa ma yansha min al-mafasid*, he wrote a systematic refutation of alchemy on social, scientific, philosophical and religious grounds.

He begins his refutation on social grounds, arguing that many alchemists are incapable of earning a living because of the thought of becoming rich through alchemy and end up "losing their credibility because of the futility of their attempts".

He also argues that some alchemists resort to fraud, either openly by applying a thin layer of gold/silver on top of silver/copper jewellery, or secretly using an artificial procedure of covering whitened copper with sublimated mercury, though only skilled experimenters can carry out the latter.

He admits, however, that most alchemists are honest and carry out their investigations in good faith with the belief that the transmutation of metals is possible, but on the basis that there has never been any successful attempt to date, he argues that transmutation is an implausible theory without any reliable scientific evidence to support it.

He reports the earlier opinions of al-Farabi, Avicenna and al-Tughrai on alchemy, and then proceeds to advance his own arguments against it. One such argument is that "human science is powerless even to attain what is inferior to it" and that alchemy "resembles someone who wants to produce a man, an animal or a plant."

Another sociological argument he uses is that, even if transmutation were possible, the disproportionate growth of gold and silver "would make transactions useless and would run counter to divine wisdom." He ends his arguments with a restatement of his position:

Alchemy can only be achieved through psychic influences (*bi-ta'thirat al-nufus*). Extraordinary things are either miracles or witchcraft... They are unbounded; nobody can claim to acquire them.

OTHER THEORIES

Climate Theory

The *Muqaddimah* anticipated the meteorological climate theory of environmental determinism, later proposed by Montesquieu in the 18th century. Like Montesquieu, Ibn Khaldun studied "the physical environment in which man lives in order to understand how it influences him in his non-physical characteristics."

He explained the differences between different peoples, whether nomadic or sedentary peoples, including their customs and institutions, in terms of their "physical environment-habitat, climate, soil, food, and the different ways in which they are forced to satisfy their needs and obtain a living."

This was a departure from the climatic theories expressed by authors from Hippocratesto Jean Bodin. It has been suggested that Ibn Khaldun may have had an influence upon Montesquieu's theory through the traveller Jean Chardin, who travelled to Persia and described a theory resembling Ibn Khaldun's climatic theory.

Political Theory

The *Muqaddimah* deals with various questions of political theory. In some ways, his political theories show the influence of Aristotle, while in other ways they anticipate the works of Niccolò Machiavelli and Thomas Hobbes. In the *Muqaddimah*'s Introductory Remarks, Ibn Khaldun agrees with the classical republicanism of Aristotelian proposition that man is political by nature, and that man's interdependence creates the need for the political community.

Yet Ibn Khaldun argues, like Hobbes later, that men and tribes need to defend themselves from potential attack by beast or even unjust men, and thus political communities are formed.

The glue which holds such tribes together and eventually forms "royal authority" or the state, according to Ibn Khaldun, is *'asabiyah* or *group feeling*. Ibn Khaldun argues that the best type of political community is the Caliphate or the Islamic state, and argues that the neo-Platonist political theories of al-Farabi and Ibn Sina and the "perfect state" (Madina al-Fadilah) are useless because God's Law, the sharia, has been revealed to take account of public interest and the afterlife. The second most perfect state, Ibn Khaldun argues, is one based on justice and consideration for public welfare in this life, but not based on religious law and so not beneficial to one's afterlife. Ibn Khaldun calls this state blameworthy. Yet the worst type of state, according to Ibn Khaldun, is a tyranny wherein government usurps property rights and rules with injustice against the rights of men.

Ibn Khaldun also anticipates Machiavelli by attempting to answer the question of whether it is better for the ruler to be feared or loved. Ibn Khaldun, like Machiavelli, answers that it is best to be both (though in The Prince, Machiavelli argues it's ultimately more effective for a ruler to retain power through fear).

However, unlike Machiavelli, Khaldun believes that if that is not possible then it is better to be loved than feared because fear creates many negative effects in the state's population.

Ibn Khaldun writes that civilizations have lifespans like individuals, and that every state will eventually fall because sedentary luxuries distract them, and eventually government begins to overtax citizens and begin injustice against property rights, and "injustice ruins civilization." Eventually after one dynasty or royal authority falls, it is replaced by another, in a continuous cycle. Machiavelli has a similar notion of sedentary lifestyles, *ozio*, that corrupts the state, and argues that periodic wars rejuvenate a republic.

The British philosopher-anthropologist Ernest Gellner considered Ibn Khaldun's definition of government, "an institution which prevents injustice other than such as it commits itself", the best in the history of political theory.

ASSESSMENT OF VARIOUS CIVILIZATIONS

While discussing his "new science", now associated with the social sciences, Ibn Khaldûn states that no other author before him, as far as he was aware, had written about it. However, he was aware that much knowledge of the past had been lost, and thus he was open to the possibility that someone might have anticipated him but that their work had not survived:

Perhaps they have written exhaustively on this topic, and their work did not reach us. There are many sciences. There have been numerous sages among the nations of mankind. The knowledge that has not come down to us is larger than the knowledge that has.

Where are the sciences of the Persians that 'Umar ordered to be wiped out at the time of the conquest? Where are the sciences of the Chaladaeans, the Syrians and the Babylonians, and the scholarly products and results that were theirs? Where are the sciences of the Copts, their predecessors?

The sciences of only one nation, the Greeks, have come down to us, because they were translated through Al-Ma'mun's efforts. He was successful in this direction because he had many translators at his disposal and spent much money in this connection.

Ibn Khaldûn characterized Aristotle as "the First Teacher", for his having "improved the methods of logic and systematized its problems and details."

Arab and Persian Civilizations

Ibn Khaldun makes a clear distinction between two types of Arab people; those who are Arab by descent, *i.e.* of ethnic Arab descent, and those who are Arab by language, *i.e.* ethnically non-Arab populations who speak Arabic as a first language. He never refers to that final group as being Arabs, rather he called them by their ethnicity or places of origin (*i.e.* 'Persians' or 'the inhabitants of Egypt'):

In that connection, "non-Arab" meant non-Arab by descent. Such non-Arabs had a long (history of) sedentary culture which, as we have established, causes cultivation of the crafts and habits, including the sciences. Being non-Arab in language is something quite different, and this is what is meant here.

About ethnic Arabs, he wrote:

The Arabs dominate only of the plains, because they are, by their savage nature, people of pillage and corruption. They pillage everything that they can take without fighting or taking risks, then flee to their refuge in the wilderness, and do not stand and do battle unless in self-defence. So when they encounter any difficulty or obstacle, they leave it alone and look for easier prey. And tribes well-fortified against them on the slopes of the hills escape their corruption and destruction, because they prefer not to climb hills, nor expend effort, nor take risks.

On the Arab conquests of the 7th century:

Religious propaganda gives a dynasty at its beginning another power in addition to that of the group feeling it possessed as the result of the number of its supporters... This happened to the Arabs at the beginning of Islam during the Muslim conquests. The armies of the Muslims at al-Qadisiyah and at the Yarmuk numbered some 30,000 in each case, while the Persian troops at al-Qadisiyah numbered 120,000, and the troops of Heraclius, according to al-Waqidi, 400,000. Neither of the two parties was able to withstand the Arabs, who routed them and seized what they possessed.

Some of the content in the book is also related to the "Hadith of Persians and belief":

Thus the founders of grammar were Sibawaih and after him, al-Farisi and Az-Zajjaj. All of them were of non-Arab (Persian) descent... They invented rules of(Arabic) grammar... great jurists were Persians... only the Persians engaged in the task of preserving knowledge and writing systematic scholarly works. Thus the truth of the statement of the prophet becomes apparent, "If learning were suspended in the highest parts of heaven the Persians would attain it"... The intellectual sciences were also the preserve of the Persians, left alone by the Arabs, who did not cultivate them... as was the case with all crafts... This situation continued in the cities as long as the Persians and Persian countries, Iraq, Khorasan and Transoxiana, retained their sedentary culture.

Here again he uses the term "Arab" to refer to the ethnic Arabs of the Arabian Peninsula and "Ajam" to refer to non-Arabs in general, though it often it referred more specifically to Iranian peoples from a sedentary Persian culture on the Iranian plateau. Ibn Khaldun made a distinction between being linguistically Arabized and being culturally Arabized.

Cultural Arabization to him meant adopting a tribal, bedouin and desert livestyle and was opposite to the sedentary, urban culture, which was inherently non-Arab.

Throughout his work he makes the point that Arabs during the early Muslim expansion, were indeed de-Arabized and to some degree adopted Persian and Greek sedentary culture. Also note that in medieval Islamic literature, there were two regions known as Iraq: the Iraq-e-Arab (Arab Iraq) and the Iraq-e-Ajam (Persian Iraq). The Persian Iraq mentioned by Ibn Khaldun is the historic Iraq-e-Ajam (Persian Iraq) which constitutes the triangle of Isfahan, Shiraz and Hamadan.

Ibn Khaldun, however, notes that by his time, the study of science in Persian culture had declined and was eventually surpassed by the culture of Egypt of the Mamluk Sultanate:

This situation continued in the cities as long as the Persians and the Persian countries, the 'Iraq, Khurasan, and Transoxania, retained their sedentary culture. But when those cities fell into ruins, sedentary culture, which God has devised for the attainment of sciences and crafts, disappeared from them. Along with it, scholarship altogether disappeared from among the non-Arabs (Persians), who were (now) engulfed by the desert attitude. Scholarship was restricted to cities with an abundant sedentary culture.

Today, no (city) has a more abundant sedentary culture than Cairo (Egypt). It is the mother of the world, the great centre (Iwan) of Islam, and the mainspring of the sciences and the crafts.

Some sedentary culture has also survived in Transoxania, because the dynasty there provides some sedentary culture. Therefore, they have there a certain number of the sciences and the crafts, which cannot be denied. Our attention was called to this fact by the contents of the writings of a (Transoxanian) scholar, which have reached us in this country. He is Sa'd-ad-din at-Taftazani. As far as the other non-Arabs (Persians) are concerned, we have not seen, since the imamIbn al-Khatib and Nasir-ad-din at-Tusi, any discussions that could be referred to as indicating their ultimate excellence.

Ibn Khaldun discussed the history of science, and wrote the following on the history of Islamic science:

The Muslims desired to learn the sciences of foreign nations. They made them their own through translations. They pressed them into the mould of their own views. They took them over into their own language from the non-Arab languages and surpassed the achievements of the non-Arabs in them.

Jewish Civilization

On the Jewish civilization:

The other religious groups did not have a universal mission, and the holy war was not a religious duty to them, save only for purposes of defence... They are merely required to establish their religion among their own people. This is why the Israelites after Moses and Joshua remained unconcerned with royal authority for about four hundred years.

Their only concern was to establish their religion... The Israelites dispossessed the Canaanites of the land that God had given them as their heritage in Jerusalem and the surrounding region, as it had been explained to them through Moses.

The nations of the Philistines, the Canaanites, theArmenians, the Edomites, the Ammonites, and the Moabites fought against them. During that time political leadership was entrusted to the elders among them. The Israelites remained in that condition for about four hundred years.

They did not have any royal power and were harassed by attacks from foreign nations. Therefore, they asked God through Samuel, one of their prophets, that he permit them to make someone king over them. Thus, Saul became their king.

He defeated the foreign nations and killed Goliath, the ruler of Philistines. After Saul, David became king, and then Solomon. His kingdom flourished and extended to the borders of the land of the Hijaz and further to the borders of Yemen and to the borders of the land of the Byzantines. After Solomon, the tribes split into two dynasties. One of the dynasties was that of the ten tribes in the region of Nablus, the capital of which is Samaria (Sabastiyah), and the other that of the children of Judah andBenjamin in Jerusalem. Their royal authority had had an uninterrupted duration of a thousand years.

Sub-Saharan Africa

Ibn Khaldûn's description of the various Sub-Saharan African states:

The Western Sahel:

Many translations of Ibn Khaldun were translated during the colonial era in order to fit the colonial propaganda machine. *The Negro land of the Arabs Examined and Explained* was written in 1841 and gives excerpts of older translations that were not part of colonial propaganda:

When the conquest of the West (by the Arabs) was completed, and merchants began to penetrate into the interior, they saw no nation of the Blacks so mighty as Ghanah, the dominions of which extended westward as far as the Ocean. The King's court was kept in the city of Ghanah, which, according to the author of the Book of Roger (El Idrisi), and the author of the Book of Roads and Realms (El Bekri), is divided into two parts, standing on both banks of the Nile, and ranks among the largest and most populous cities of the world.

The people of Ghanah had for neighbours, on the east, a nation, which, according to historians, was called Susu; after which came another named Mali; and after that another known by the name of Kaukau; although some people prefer a different orthography, and write this name Kagho. The last-named nation was followed by a people called Tekrur.

The people of Ghanah declined in course of time, being overwhelmed or absorbed by the Molaththemun (or muffled people; that is, the Morabites), who, adjoining them on the north towards the Berber country, attacked them, and, taking possession of their territory, compelled them to embrace the Mohammedan religion. The people of Ghanah, being invaded at a later period by the Susu, a nation of Blacks in their neighbourhood, were exterminated, or mixed with other Black nations.

Ibn Khaldun suggests a link between the decline of Ghana and rise of the Almoravids. However, there is little evidence of there actually being an Almoravid conquest of Ghana Of those further south of Ghana he writes (it should be noted that the English translation of the text used the word "Negro" as a translation for the Arabic world "Zanj"),

To the south of this...there is a Negro people called Lamlam. They are unbelievers. They brand themselves on the face and temples. The people of Ghanah andTakrur invade their country, capture them, and sell them to merchants who transport them to the Maghrib.

There, they constitute the ordinary mass of slaves. Beyond them to the south, there is no civilization in the proper sense. There are only humans who are closer to dumb animals than to rational beings. They live in thickets and caves and eat herbs and unprepared grain. They frequently eat each other. They cannot be considered human beings.

Nubia:

In the middle of the first zone along the Nile, lie the countries of the Nubah and the Abyssinians and some of the oases down to Assuan. A settled part of the Nubah country is the city of Dongola, west of the Nile.

Beyond it are 'Alwah 83 and Yulaq.84 Beyond them, a six days' journey north of Yulaq, is the mountain of the cataracts. This is a mountain which rises to a great height on the Egyptian side but is much less elevated on the side of the country of the Nubah, The Nile cuts through it and flows down precipitately in tremendous cascades for a long distance. Boats cannot get through.

Cargoes from the Sudanese boats are taken off and carried on pack animals to Assuan at the entrance to Upper Egypt. In the same way, the cargoes of the boats from Upper Egypt are carried over the cataracts.

The distance from the cataracts to Assuan is a twelve day's journey. The oases on the west bank of the Nile there are now in ruins. They show traces of ancient settlement.

Abyssinia (Ethiopia):

In the middle of the first zone, in its fifth section, is the country of the Abyssinians, through which a river flows, which comes from beyond the equator and 85 flows towards the land of the Nubah, where it flows into the Nile and so on down into Egypt. Many people have held fantastic opinions about it and thought that it was part of the Nile of the Qumr (Mountain of the Moon).

Ptolemy mentioned it in the Geography. He mentioned that it did not belong to the Nile.

PLATO

Plato (348/347 BCE) was a philosopher, as well asmathematician, in Classical Greece, and an influential figure in philosophy, central in Western philosophy. He was Socrates' student, and founded the Academy in Athens, the first institution of higher learning in the Western world.

Along with Socrates and his most famous student, Aristotle, Plato helped to lay the foundations of Western philosophy and science.

Alfred North Whitehead once noted: "the safest general characterization of the European philosophical tradition is that it consists of a series of footnotes to Plato."

Plato's dialogues have been used to teach a range of subjects, including philosophy, logic, ethics, rhetoric, religion andmathematics. His theory of Forms began a unique perspective on abstract objects, and led to a school of thought called Platonism.

Plato's writings have been published in several fashions; this has led to several conventions regarding the naming and referencing of Plato's texts.

BIOGRAPHY

Early Life

Little can be known about Plato's early life and education, due to very few accounts. The philosopher came from one of the wealthiest and most politically active families in Athens.

Ancient sources describe him as a bright though modest boy who excelled in his studies. His father contributed all which was necessary to give to his son a good education, and, therefore, Plato must have been instructed in grammar, music, gymnastics and philosophy by some of the most distinguished teachers of his era.

Birth and family

The exact time and place of Plato's birth are not known, but it is certain that he belonged to an aristocratic and influential family. Based on ancient sources, most modern scholars believe that he was born in Athens or Aegina between 429 and 423 BCE. His father was Ariston.

According to a disputed tradition, reported by Diogenes Laertius, Ariston traced his descent from the king of Athens, Codrus, and the king of Messenia, Melanthus.

Plato's mother was Perictione, whose family boasted of a relationship with the famous Athenian lawmaker and lyric poet Solon. Perictione was sister of Charmides and niece of Critias, both prominent figures of the Thirty Tyrants, the brief oligarchic regime, which followed on the collapse of Athens at the end of the Peloponnesian War (404–403 BCE). Besides Plato himself, Ariston and Perictione had three other children; these were two sons, Adeimantusand Glaucon, and a daughter Potone, the mother of Speusippus (the nephew and successor of Plato as head of his philosophical Academy).

The brothers Adeimantus and Glaucon are mentioned in the Republic as sons of Ariston, and presumably brothers of Plato, but some have argued they were uncles. But in a scenario in the Memorabilia, Xenophon confused the issue by presenting a Glaucon much younger than Plato.

The traditional date of Plato's birth (428/427) is based on a dubious interpretation of Diogenes Laertius, who says, "When [Socrates] was gone, [Plato] joined Cratylus the Heracleitean and Hermogenes, who philosophized in the manner of Parmenides.

Then, at twenty-eight, Hermodorus says, [Plato] went to Euclides in Megara." As Debra Nails argues, "The text itself gives no reason to infer that Plato left immediately for Megara and implies the very opposite." In his Seventh Letter, Plato notes that his coming of age coincided with the taking of power by the Thirty, remarking, "But a youth under the age of twenty made himself a laughingstock if he attempted to enter the political arena." Thus, Nails dates Plato's birth to 424/423.

According to some accounts, Ariston tried to force his attentions on Perictione, but failed in his purpose; then the god Apollo appeared to him in a vision, and as a result, Ariston left Perictione unmolested. Another legend related that, when Plato was an infant, bees settled on his lips while he was sleeping: an augury of the sweetness of style in which he would discourse about philosophy.

Ariston appears to have died in Plato's childhood, although the precise dating of his death is difficult. Perictione then married Pyrilampes, her mother's brother, who had served many times as an ambassador to the Persian court and was a friend of Pericles, the leader of the democratic faction in Athens. Pyrilampes had a son from a previous marriage, Demus, who was famous for his beauty. Perictione gave birth to Pyrilampes' second son, Antiphon, the half-brother of Plato, who appears in *Parmenides*.

In contrast to reticence about himself, Plato often introduced his distinguished relatives into his dialogues, or referred to them with some precision: Charmides has a dialogue named after him; Critias speaks in both *Charmides* and *Protagoras*; and Adeimantus and Glaucon take prominent parts in the *Republic*.

These and other references suggest a considerable amount of family pride and enable us to reconstruct Plato's family tree. According to Burnet, "the opening scene of the *Charmides* is a glorification of the whole [family] connection... Plato's dialogues are not only a memorial to Socrates, but also the happier days of his own family."

Name

According to Diogenes Laërtius, the philosopher was named *Aristocles* after his grandfather. It was common in Athenian society for boys to be named after grandfathers (or fathers). But there is only one inscriptional record of an Aristocles, an early Archon of Athens in 605/4 BCE. There no record of a line of Aristocles's from this one that culminate in one who was father of Plato's father Ariston. However, if Plato was not named after an ancestor named Plato (there is no record of one), then the origin of his renaming as *Plato* becomes a conundrum. Diogenes' sources account for this fact by claiming that his wrestling coach, Ariston of Argos, dubbed him *Platon*, meaning "broad," on account of his robust figure or that Plato derived his name from the breadth of his eloquence, or else because he was very wide across the forehead. Recently a scholar has argued that even the name Aristocles for Plato was a much later invention. Although *Plato* was a fairly common name, (31 instances are known from Athens alone), the name does not occur in Plato's known family line.

Education

Apuleius informs us that Speusippus praised Plato's quickness of mind and modesty as a boy, and the "first fruits of his youth infused with hard work and love of study".

Plato must have been instructed in grammar, music, and gymnastics by the most distinguished teachers of his time. Dicaearchus went so far as to say that Plato wrestled at theIsthmian games.

Plato had also attended courses of philosophy; before meeting Socrates, he first became acquainted with Cratylus (a disciple of Heraclitus, a prominent pre-Socratic Greek philosopher) and the Heraclitean doctrines. W. A. Borody argues that an Athenian openness towards a wider range of sexuality may have contributed to the Athenian philosophers' openness towards a wider range of thought, a cultural situation Borody describes as "polymorphously discursive."

Plato and Pythagoras

Although Socrates influenced Plato directly as related in the dialogues, the influence of Pythagoras upon Plato also appears to have significant discussion in the philosophical literature.

Pythagoras, or in a broader sense, the Pythagoreans, allegedly exercised an important influence on the work of Plato. According to R. M. Hare, this influence consists of three points: (1) The platonic Republic might be related to the idea of "a tightly organized community of like-minded thinkers", like the one established by Pythagoras in Croton. (2) There is evidence that Plato possibly took from Pythagoras the idea that mathematics and, generally speaking, abstract thinking is a secure basis for philosophical thinking as well as "for substantial theses in science and morals". (3) Plato and Pythagoras shared a "mystical approach to the soul and its place in the material world". It is probable that both were influenced by Orphism.

Aristotle claimed that the philosophy of Plato closely followed the teachings of the Pythagoreans, and Cicero repeats this claim:*Platonem ferunt didicisse Pythagorea omnia* ("They say Plato learned all things Pythagorean"). Bertrand Russell, in his *A History of Western Philosophy*, contended that the influence of Pythagoras on Plato and others was so great that he should be considered the most influential of all Western philosophers.

Plato and Socrates

The precise relationship between Plato and Socrates remains an area of contention among scholars. Plato makes it clear in his *Apology of Socrates*, that he was a devoted young follower of Socrates. In that dialogue, Socrates is presented as mentioning Plato by name as one of those youths close enough to him to have been corrupted, if he were in fact guilty of corrupting the youth, and questioning why their fathers and brothers did not step forward to testify against him if he was indeed guilty of such a crime (33d-34a). Later, Plato is mentioned along with Crito, Critobolus, and Apollodorus as offering to pay a fine of 30 minas on Socrates' behalf, in lieu of the death penalty proposed by Meletus (38b). In the *Phaedo*, the title character lists those who were in attendance at the prison on Socrates' last day, explaining Plato's absence by saying, "Plato was ill."

Plato never speaks in his own voice in his dialogues. In the *Second Letter*, it says, "no writing of Plato exists or ever will exist, but those now said to be his are those of a Socrates become beautiful and new" (341c); if the Letter is Plato's, the final qualification seems to call into question the dialogues' historical fidelity. In any case, Xenophon and Aristophanes seem to present a somewhat different portrait of Socrates from the one Plato paints. Some have called attention to the problem of taking Plato's Socrates to be his mouthpiece, given Socrates' reputation for irony and the dramatic nature of the dialogue form.

Aristotle attributes a different doctrine with respect to the Ideas to Plato and Socrates (*Metaphysics* 987b1–11). Putting it in a nutshell, Aristotle merely suggests that Socrates' idea of forms can be discovered through investigation of the natural world, unlike Plato's Forms that exist beyond and outside the ordinary range of human understanding.

Later Life

Plato may have traveled in Italy, Sicily, Egypt and Cyrene, Libya. Said to have returned to Athens at the age of forty, Plato founded one of the earliest known organized schools in Western Civilization on a plot of land in the Grove of Hecademus or Academus.

The Academy was a large enclosure of ground about six stadia outside of Athens proper. One story is that the name of the Academy comes from the ancient hero, Academus. Another story is that the name came from a supposed a former owner, a citizen of Athens also named Academus. Yet another account is that it was named after a member of the army of Castor and Pollux, an Arcadian named Echedemus.

The Academy operated until it was destroyed by Lucius Cornelius Sulla in 84 BCE. Neo-platonists revived the Academy in the early 5th century, and it operated until AD 529, when it was closed by Justinian I of Byzantium, who saw it as a threat to the propagation of Christianity. Many intellectuals were schooled in the Academy, the most prominent one being Aristotle.

Throughout his later life, Plato became entangled with the politics of the city of Syracuse. According to Diogenes Laertius, Plato initially visited Syracuse while it was under the rule of Dionysius. During this first trip Dionysius's brother-in-law, Dion of Syracuse, became one of Plato's disciples, but the tyrant himself turned against Plato. Plato almost faced death, but he was sold into slavery, then Anniceris bought Plato's freedom for twenty minas, and sent him home. After Dionysius's death, according to Plato's*Seventh Letter*, Dion requested Plato return to Syracuse to tutor Dionysius II and guide him to become a philosopher king. Dionysius II seemed to accept Plato's teachings, but he became suspicious of Dion, his uncle. Dionysius expelled Dion and kept Plato against his will. Eventually Plato left Syracuse. Dion would return to overthrow Dionysius and ruled Syracuse for a short time before being usurped by Calippus, a fellow disciple of Plato.

Death

A variety of sources have given accounts of Plato's death. One story, based on a mutilated manuscript, suggests Plato died in his bed, whilst a young Thracian girl played the flute to him. Another tradition suggests Plato died at a wedding feast. The account is based on Diogenes Laertius's reference to an account by Hermippus, a third-century Alexandrian. According to Tertullian, Plato simply died in his sleep.

PHILOSOPHY

Recurrent Themes

Plato often discusses the father-son relationship and the question of whether a father's interest in his sons has much to do with how well his sons turn out. In ancient Athens, a boy was socially located by his family identity, and Plato often refers to his characters in terms of their paternal and fraternal relationships. Socrates was not a family man, and saw himself as the son of his mother, who was apparently a midwife.

A divine fatalist, Socrates mocks men who spent exorbitant fees on tutors and trainers for their sons, and repeatedly ventures the idea that good character is a gift from the gods. Crito reminds Socrates that orphans are at the mercy of chance, but Socrates is unconcerned. In the *Theaetetus*, he is found recruiting as a disciple a young man whose inheritance has been squandered. Socrates twice compares the relationship of the older man and his boy lover to the father-son relationship (*Lysis* 213a, *Republic* 3.403b), and in the *Phaedo*, Socrates' disciples, towards whom he displays more concern than his biological sons, say they will feel "fatherless" when he is gone.

In several of Plato's dialogues, Socrates promulgates the idea that knowledge is a matter of recollection, and not of learning, observation, or study. He maintains this view somewhat at his own expense, because in many dialogues, Socrates complains of his forgetfulness. Socrates is often found arguing that knowledge is not empirical, and that it comes from divine insight. In many middle period dialogues, such as the *Phaedo*, *Republic* and *Phaedrus* Plato advocates a belief in the immortality of the soul, and several dialogues end with long speeches imagining theafterlife. More than one dialogue contrasts knowledge and opinion, perception and reality, nature and custom, and body and soul.

Several dialogues tackle questions about art: Socrates says that poetry is inspired by the muses, and is not rational. He speaks approvingly of this, and other forms of divine madness (drunkenness, eroticism, and dreaming) in the *Phaedrus* (265a–c), and yet in the *Republic* wants to outlaw Homer's great poetry, and laughter as well. In *Ion*, Socrates gives no hint of the disapproval of Homer that he expresses in the *Republic*. The dialogue *Ion* suggests that Homer's *Iliad* functioned in the ancient Greek world as the Bible does today in the modern Christian world: as divinely inspired literature that can provide moral guidance, if only it can be properly interpreted.

Socrates and his company of disputants had something to say on many subjects, including politics and art, religion and science, justice and medicine, virtue and vice, crime and punishment, pleasure and pain, rhetoric and rhapsody, human nature and sexuality, as well as love and wisdom.

Metaphysics

"Platonism" is a term coined by scholars to refer to the intellectual consequences of denying, as Plato's Socrates often does, the reality of the material world. In several dialogues, most notably the *Republic*, Socrates inverts the common man's intuition about what is knowable and what is real.

While most people take the objects of their senses to be real if anything is, Socrates is contemptuous of people who think that something has to be graspable in the hands to be real. In the *Theaetetus*, he says such people are*eu amousoi* , an expression that means literally, "happily without the muses" (*Theaetetus* 156a). In other words, such people live without the divine inspiration that gives him, and people like him, access to higher insights about reality.

Socrates's idea that reality is unavailable to those who use their senses is what puts him at odds with the common man, and with common sense. Socrates says that he who sees with his eyes is blind, and this idea is most famously captured in his allegory of the cave, and more explicitly in his description of the divided line. The allegory of the cave (begins *Republic* 7.514a) is a paradoxical analogy wherein Socrates argues that the invisible world is the most intelligible ("noeton") and that the visible world ("(h)oraton") is the least knowable, and the most obscure.

Socrates says in the *Republic* that people who take the sun-lit world of the senses to be good and real are living pitifully in a den of evil and ignorance. Socrates admits that few climb out of the den, or cave of ignorance, and those who do, not only have a terrible struggle to attain the heights, but when they go back down for a visit or to help other people up, they find themselves objects of scorn and ridicule. According to Socrates, physical objects and physical events are "shadows" of their ideal or perfect forms, and exist only to the extent that they instantiate the perfect versions of themselves.

Just as shadows are temporary, inconsequential epiphenomena produced by physical objects, physical objects are themselves fleeting phenomena caused by more substantial causes, the ideals of which they are mere instances. For example, Socrates thinks that perfect justice exists (although it is not clear where) and his own trial would be a cheap copy of it.

The allegory of the cave (often said by scholars to represent Plato's own epistemology and metaphysics) is intimately connected to his political ideology (often said to also be Plato's own), that only people who have climbed out of the cave and cast their eyes on a vision of goodness are fit to rule.

Socrates claims that the enlightened men of society must be forced from their divine contemplations and be compelled to run the city according to their lofty insights. Thus is born the idea of the "philosopher-king", the wise person who accepts the power thrust upon him by the people who are wise enough to choose a good master. This is the main thesis of Socrates in the *Republic*, that the most wisdom the masses can muster is the wise choice of a ruler.

Theory of Forms

The theory of Forms (or theory of Ideas) typically refers to the belief that the material world as it seems to us is not the real world, but only an "image" or "copy" of the real world. In some of Plato's dialogues, this is expressed by Socrates, who spoke of forms in formulating a solution to the problem of universals. The forms, according to Socrates, arearchetypes or abstract representations of the many types of things, and properties we feel and see around us, that can only be perceived by reason. (That is, they are universals.) In other words, Socrates was able to recognize two worlds: the apparent world, which constantly changes, and an unchanging and unseen world of forms, which may be the cause of what is apparent.

Epistemology

Many have interpreted Plato as stating—even having been the first to write—that knowledge is justified true belief, an influential view that informed future developments in epistemology. This interpretation is partly based on a reading of the *Theaetetus* wherein Plato argues that knowledge is distinguished from mere true belief by the knower having an "account" of the object of her or his true belief. And this theory may again be seen in the *Meno*, where it is suggested that true belief can be raised to the level of knowledge if it is bound with an account as to the question of "why" the object of the true belief is so. Many years later, Edmund Gettier famously demonstrated the problems of the justified true belief account of knowledge. That the modern theory of justified true belief as knowledge which Gettier addresses is equivalent to Plato's is accepted by some scholars but rejected by others. Plato himself also identified problems with the *justified true belief* definition in the *Theaetetus*, concluding that justification (or an "account") would require knowledge of *differentness*, meaning that the definition of knowledge is circular .

Later in the *Meno*, Socrates uses a geometrical example to expound Plato's view that knowledge in this latter sense is acquired by recollection. Socrates elicits a fact concerning a geometrical construction from a slave boy, who could not have otherwise known the fact (due to the slave boy's lack of education). The knowledge must be present, Socrates concludes, in an eternal, non-experiential form.

In other dialogues, the *Sophist*, *Statesman*, *Republic*, and the *Parmenides*, Plato himself associates knowledge with the apprehension of unchanging Forms and their relationships to one another (which he calls "expertise" in Dialectic), including through the processes of *collection* and *division*. More explicitly, Plato himself argues in the *Timaeus* that knowledge is always proportionate to the realm from which it is gained.

In other words, if one derives one's account of something experientially, because the world of sense is in flux, the views therein attained will be mere opinions. And opinions are characterized by a lack of necessity and stability. On the other hand, if one derives one's account of something by way of the non-sensible forms, because these forms are unchanging, so too is the account derived from them.

That apprehension of forms is required for knowledge may be taken to cohere with Plato's theory in the *Theaetetus* and *Meno*. Indeed, the apprehension of Forms may be at the base of the "account" required for justification, in that it offers foundational knowledge which itself needs no account, thereby avoiding an infinite regression.

The State

Plato's philosophical views had many societal implications, especially on the idea of an ideal state or government. There is some discrepancy between his early and later views. Some of the most famous doctrines are contained in the *Republic* during his middle period, as well as in the *Laws* and the *Statesman*. However, because Plato wrote dialogues, it is assumed that Socrates is often speaking for Plato. This assumption may not be true in all cases.

Plato, through the words of Socrates, asserts that societies have a tripartite class structure corresponding to the appetite/spirit/reason structure of the individual soul. The appetite/spirit/reason are analogous to the castes of society.

- *Productive* (Workers) — the labourers, carpenters, plumbers, masons, merchants, farmers, ranchers, etc. These correspond to the "appetite" part of the soul.

- *Protective* (Warriors or Guardians) — those who are adventurous, strong and brave; in the armed forces. These correspond to the "spirit" part of the soul.
- *Governing* (Rulers or Philosopher Kings) — those who are intelligent, rational, self-controlled, in love with wisdom, well suited to make decisions for the community. These correspond to the "reason" part of the soul and are very few.

In the Timaeus, Plato locates the parts of the soul within the human body: Reason is located in the head, spirit in the top third of thetorso, and the appetite in the middle third of the torso, down to the navel.

According to this model, the principles of Athenian democracy (as it existed in his day) are rejected as only a few are fit to rule. Instead of rhetoric and persuasion, Plato says reason and wisdom should govern. As Plato puts it:

"Until philosophers rule as kings or those who are now called kings and leading men genuinely and adequately philosophise, that is, until political power and philosophy entirely coincide, while the many natures who at present pursue either one exclusively are forcibly prevented from doing so, cities will have no rest from evils,... nor, I think, will the human race." (*Republic* 473c-d)

Plato describes these "philosopher kings" as "those who love the sight of truth" (*Republic* 475c) and supports the idea with the analogy of a captain and his ship or a doctor and his medicine. According to him, sailing and health are not things that everyone is qualified to practice by nature. A large part of the *Republic* then addresses how the educational system should be set up to produce these philosopher kings.

However, it must be taken into account that the ideal city outlined in the *Republic* is qualified by Socrates as the ideal *luxurious* city, examined to determine how it is that injustice and justice grow in a city (*Republic* 372e). According to Socrates, the "true" and "healthy" city is instead the one first outlined in book II of the *Republic*, 369c–372d, containing farmers, craftsmen, merchants, and wage-earners, but lacking the guardian class of philosopher-kings as well as delicacies such as "perfumed oils, incense, prostitutes, and pastries", in addition to paintings, gold, ivory, couches, a multitude of occupations such as poets and hunters, and war.

In addition, the ideal city is used as an image to illuminate the state of one's soul, or the will, reason, and desires combined in the human body. Socrates is attempting to make an image of a rightly ordered human, and then later goes on to describe the different kinds of humans that can be observed, from tyrants to lovers of money in various kinds of cities. The ideal city is not promoted, but only used to magnify the different kinds of individual humans and the state of their soul. However, the philosopher king image was used by many after Plato to justify their personal political beliefs. The philosophic soul according to Socrates has reason, will, and desires united in virtuous harmony.

A philosopher has the moderate love for wisdom and the courage to act according to wisdom. Wisdom is knowledge about the Good or the right relations between all that exists.

Wherein it concerns states and rulers, Plato has made interesting arguments. For instance he asks which is better—a bad democracy or a country reigned by a tyrant. He argues that it is better to be ruled by a bad tyrant, than be a bad democracy (since here all the people are now responsible for such actions, rather than one individual committing many bad deeds.) This is emphasised within the *Republic* as Plato describes the event of mutiny on board a ship. Plato suggests the ships crew to be in line with the democratic rule of many and the captain, although inhibited through ailments, the tyrant. Plato's description of this event is parallel to that of democracy within the state and the inherent problems that arise.

According to Plato, a state made up of different kinds of souls will, overall, decline from an aristocracy (rule by the best) to a timocracy (rule by the honourable), then to anoligarchy (rule by the few), then to a democracy (rule by the people), and finally to tyranny (rule by one person, rule by a tyrant). Aristocracy is the form of government (*politeia*) advocated in Plato's *Republic*. This regime is ruled by a philosopher king, and thus is grounded on wisdom and reason. The aristocratic state, and the man whose nature corresponds to it, are the objects of Plato's analyses throughout much of the *Republic*, as opposed to the other four types of states/men, who are discussed later in his work. In Book VIII, Plato states in order the other four imperfect societies with a description of the state's structure and individual character. In timocracy the ruling class is made up primarily of those with a warrior-like character. In his description, Plato has Sparta in mind. Oligarchy is made up of a society in which wealth is the criterion of merit and the wealthy are in control. In democracy, the state bears resemblance to ancient Athens with traits such as equality of political opportunity and freedom for the individual to do as he likes. Democracy then degenerates into tyranny from the conflict of rich and poor. It is characterized by an undisciplined society existing in chaos, where the tyrant rises as popular champion leading to the formation of his private army and the growth of oppression.

Unwritten Doctrines

For a long time, Plato's unwritten doctrine had been controversial. Many modern books on Plato seem to diminish its importance; nevertheless, the first important witness who mentions its existence is Aristotle, who in his *Physics* (209 b) writes: "It is true, indeed, that the account he gives there [*i.e.* in *Timaeus*] of the participant is different from what he says in his so-called *unwritten teachings* (ãñáöá äüãìáôá)." The term "ãñáöá äüãìáôá" literally means *unwritten doctrines* and it stands for the most fundamental metaphysical teaching of Plato, which he disclosed only orally, and some say only to his most trusted fellows, and which he may have kept secret from the public. The importance of the unwritten doctrines does not seem to have been seriously questioned before the 19th century.

A reason for not revealing it to everyone is partially discussed in *Phaedrus* (276 c) where Plato criticizes the written transmission of knowledge as faulty, favouring instead the spoken logos: "he who has knowledge of the just and the good and beautiful... will not, when in earnest, write them in ink, sowing them through a pen with words, which cannot defend themselves by argument and cannot teach the truth effectually." The same argument is repeated in Plato's *Seventh Letter* (344 c): "every serious man in dealing with really serious subjects carefully avoids writing." In the same letter he writes (341 c): "I can certainly declare concerning all these writers who claim to know the subjects that I seriously study... there does not exist, nor will there ever exist, any treatise of mine dealing therewith." Such secrecy is necessary in order not "to expose them to unseemly and degrading treatment" (344 d).

It is, however, said that Plato once disclosed this knowledge to the public in his lecture *On the Good*, in which the Good is identified with the One, the fundamental ontological principle. The content of this lecture has been transmitted by several witnesses. Aristoxenus describes the event in the following words: "Each came expecting to learn something about the things that are generally considered good for men, such as wealth, good health, physical strength, and altogether a kind of wonderful happiness. But when the mathematical demonstrations came, including numbers, geometrical figures and astronomy, and finally the statement Good is One seemed to them, I imagine, utterly unexpected and strange; hence some belittled the matter, while others rejected it." Simplicius quotes Alexander of Aphrodisias, who states that "according to Plato, the first principles of everything, including the Forms themselves are One and Indefinite Duality, which he called Large and Small ", and Simplicius reports as well that "one might also learn this from Speusippus and Xenocrates and the others who were present at Plato's lecture on the Good".

Their account is in full agreement with Aristotle's description of Plato's metaphysical doctrine. In *Metaphysics* he writes: "Now since the Forms are the causes of everything else, he [*i.e.* Plato] supposed that their elements are the elements of all things.

Accordingly the material principle is the Great and Small [*i.e.* the Dyad], and the essence is the One, since the numbers are derived from the Great and Small by participation in the One" (987 b).

"From this account it is clear that he only employed two causes: that of the essence, and the material cause; for the Forms are the cause of the essence in everything else, and the One is the cause of it in the Forms. He also tells us what the material substrate is of which the Forms are predicated in the case of sensible things, and the One in that of the Forms - that it is this the duality, the Great and Small. Further, he assigned to these two elements respectively the causation of good and of evil" (988 a).

The most important aspect of this interpretation of Plato's metaphysics is the continuity between his teaching and the neo-platonic interpretation of Plotinus or Ficino which has been considered erroneous by many but may in fact have been directly influenced by oral transmission of Plato's doctrine. A modern scholar who recognized the importance of the unwritten doctrine of Plato was Heinrich Gomperz who described it in his speech during the 7th International Congress of Philosophy in 1930. All the sources related to the ãñáöá äüãìáôá have been collected by Konrad Gaiser and published as *Testimonia Platonica*. These sources have subsequently been interpreted by scholars from the German *Tübingen School of interpretation* such as Hans Joachim Krämer or Thomas A. Szlezák.

Dialectic

The role of dialectic in Plato's thought is contested but there are two main interpretations: a type of reasoning and a method of intuition. Simon Blackburn adopts the first, saying that Plato's dialectic is "the process of eliciting the truth by means of questions aimed at opening out what is already implicitly known, or at exposing the contradictions and muddles of an opponent's position." A similar interpretation has been put forth by Louis Hartz, who suggests that elements of the dialectic are borrowed from Hegel.According to this view, opposing arguments improve upon each other, and prevailing opinion is shaped by the synthesis of many conflicting ideas over time. Each new idea exposes a flaw in the accepted model, and the epistemological substance of the debate continually approaches the truth. Hartz's is a teleological interpretation at the core, in which philosophers will ultimately exhaust the available body of knowledge and thus reach "the end of history." Karl Popper, on the other hand, claims that dialectic is the art of intuition for "visualising the divine originals, the Forms or Ideas, of unveiling the Great Mystery behind the common man's everyday world of appearances."

THE DIALOGUES

Thirty-five dialogues and thirteen letters (the *Epistles*) have traditionally been ascribed to Plato, though modern scholarship doubts the authenticity of at least some of these. Plato's writings have been published in several fashions; this has led to several conventions regarding the naming and referencing of Plato's texts.

The usual system for making unique references to sections of the text by Plato derives from a 16th-century edition of Plato's works by Henricus

Stephanus. An overview of Plato's writings according to this system can be found in the Stephanus pagination article.

One tradition regarding the arrangement of Plato's texts is according to tetralogies. This scheme is ascribed by Diogenes Laertius to an ancient scholar and court astrologer toTiberius named Thrasyllus.

In the list below, works by Plato are marked (1) if there is no consensus among scholars as to whether Plato is the author, and (2) if most scholars agree that Plato is *not* the author of the work. Unmarked works are assumed to have been written by Plato.

- I. *Euthyphro*, *Apology (of Socrates)*, *Crito*, *Phaedo.*
- II. *Cratylus*, *Theaetetus*, *Sophist*, *Statesman.*
- III. *Parmenides*, *Philebus*, *Symposium*, *Phaedrus.*
- IV. *First Alcibiades* (1), *Second Alcibiades* (2), *Hipparchus* (2), *(Rival) Lovers* (2).
- V. *Theages* (2), *Charmides*, *Laches*, *Lysis.*
- VI. *Euthydemus*, *Protagoras*, *Gorgias*, *Meno*
- VII. *(Greater) Hippias (major)* (1), *(Lesser) Hippias (minor)*, *Ion*, *Menexenus.*
- VIII. *Clitophon* (1), *Republic*, *Timaeus*, *Critias.*
- IX. *Minos* (2), *Laws*, *Epinomis* (2), *Epistles* (1).

The remaining works were transmitted under Plato's name, most of them already considered spurious in antiquity, and so were not included by Thrasyllus in his tetralogical arrangement. These works are labelled as *Notheuomenoi* ("spurious") or *Apocrypha*.

Composition of the Dialogues

No one knows the exact order Plato's dialogues were written in, nor the extent to which some might have been later revised and rewritten. A significant distinction of the early Plato and the later Plato has been offered by scholars such as E.R. Dodds and has been summarized by Harold Bloom in his book titled *Agon*: "E.R. Dodds is the classical scholar whose writings most illuminated the Hellenic descent (in) *The Greeks and the Irrational* [...] In his chapter on Plato and the Irrational Soul [...] Dodds traces Plato's spiritual evolution from the pure rationalist of the *Protagoras* to the transcendental psychologist, influenced by the Pythagoreans and Orphics, of the later works culminating in the *Laws*."

Lewis Campbell was the first to make exhaustive use of stylometry to prove objectively that the *Critias*, *Timaeus*, *Laws*, *Philebus*,*Sophist*, and *Statesman* were all clustered together as a group, while the *Parmenides*, *Phaedrus*, *Republic*, and *Theaetetus* belong to a separate group, which must be earlier (given Aristotle's statement in his *Politics* that the *Laws* was written after the *Republic*; cf. Diogenes Laertius *Lives* 3.37).

What is remarkable about Campbell's conclusions is that, in spite of all the stylometric studies that have been conducted since his time, perhaps the only chronological fact about Plato's works that can now be said to be *proven* by stylometry is the fact that *Critias, Timaeus, Laws, Philebus, Sophist,* and *Statesman* are the latest of Plato's dialogues, the others earlier.

Increasingly in the most recent Plato scholarship, writers are skeptical of the notion that the order of Plato's writings can be established with any precision, though Plato's works are still often characterized as falling at least roughly into three groups.The following represents one relatively common such division. It should, however, be kept in mind that many of the positions in the ordering are still highly disputed, and also that the very notion that Plato's dialogues can or should be "ordered" is by no means universally accepted.

Among those who classify the dialogues into periods of composition, Socrates figures in all of the "early dialogues" and they are considered the most faithful representations of the historical Socrates. They include *The Apology of Socrates, Charmides, Crito, Euthyphro, Ion, Laches, Lesser Hippias, Lysis, Menexenus,* and *Protagoras* (often considered one of the last of the "early dialogues"). Three dialogues are often considered "transitional" or "pre-middle": *Euthydemus, Gorgias,* and *Meno.*

Whereas those classified as "early dialogues" often conclude in aporia, the so-called "middle dialogues" provide more clearly stated positive teachings that are often ascribed to Plato such as the theory of Forms. These dialogues include *Cratylus, Phaedo, Phaedrus, Republic, Symposium, Parmenides,* and *Theaetetus*. Proponents of dividing the dialogues into periods often consider the *Parmenides* and *Theaetetus* to come late in this period and be transitional to the next, as they seem to treat the theory of Forms critically (*Parmenides*) or not at all (*Theaetetus*). The first book of the *Republic* is often thought to have been written significantly earlier than the rest of the work, although possibly having undergone revisions when the later books were attached to it.

The remaining dialogues are classified as "late" and are generally agreed to be difficult and challenging pieces of philosophy. This grouping is the only one proven by stylometric analysis. While looked to for Plato's "mature" answers to the questions posed by his earlier works, those answers are difficult to discern. Some scholars indicate that the theory of Forms is absent from the late dialogues, its having been refuted in the *Parmenides*, but there isn't total consensus that the *Parmenides* actually refutes the theory of Forms. The so-called "late dialogues" include *Critias, Laws, Philebus, Sophist, Statesman,* and *Timaeus*.

Narration of the Dialogues

Plato never presents himself as a participant in any of the dialogues, and with the exception of the *Apology*, there is no suggestion that he heard any of the dialogues firsthand. Some dialogues have no narrator but have a pure "dramatic" form (examples: *Meno*, *Gorgias*, *Phaedrus*, *Crito*, *Euthyphro*), some dialogues are narrated by Socrates, wherein he speaks in first person (examples: *Lysis*, *Charmides*, *Republic*). One dialogue, *Protagoras*, begins in dramatic form but quickly proceeds to Socrates' narration of a conversation he had previously with the sophist for whom the dialogue is named; this narration continues uninterrupted till the dialogue's end.

Two dialogues *Phaedo* and *Symposium* also begin in dramatic form but then proceed to virtually uninterrupted narration by followers of Socrates. *Phaedo*, an account of Socrates' final conversation and hemlock drinking, is narrated by Phaedo to Echecrates in a foreign city not long after the execution took place. The *Symposium* is narrated by Apollodorus, a Socratic disciple, apparently to Glaucon. Apollodorus assures his listener that he is recounting the story, which took place when he himself was an infant, not from his own memory, but as remembered by Aristodemus, who told him the story years ago.

The *Theaetetus* is a peculiar case: a dialogue in dramatic form imbedded within another dialogue in dramatic form. In the beginning of the *Theaetetus* (142c-143b), Euclides says that he compiled the conversation from notes he took based on what Socrates told him of his conversation with the title character. The rest of the *Theaetetus* is presented as a "book" written in dramatic form and read by one of Euclides' slaves (143c). Some scholars take this as an indication that Plato had by this date wearied of the narrated form. With the exception of the *Theaetetus*, Plato gives no explicit indication as to how these orally transmitted conversations came to be written down.

Trial of Socrates

The trial of Socrates is the central, unifying event of the great Platonic dialogues. Because of this, Plato's *Apology* is perhaps the most often read of the dialogues. In the*Apology*, Socrates tries to dismiss rumors that he is a sophist and defends himself against charges of disbelief in the gods and corruption of the young. Socrates insists that long-standing slander will be the real cause of his demise, and says the legal charges are essentially false. Socrates famously denies being wise, and explains how his life as a philosopher was launched by the Oracle at Delphi. He says that his quest to resolve the riddle of the oracle put him at odds with his fellow man, and that this is the reason he has been mistaken for a menace to the city-state of Athens.

If Plato's important dialogues do not refer to Socrates' execution explicitly, they allude to it, or use characters or themes that play a part in it. Five dialogues foreshadow the trial: In the *Theaetetus* (210d) and the *Euthyphro* (2a–b) Socrates tells people that he is about to face corruption charges. In the *Meno* (94e–95a), one of the men who brings legal charges against

Socrates, Anytus, warns him about the trouble he may get into if he does not stop criticizing important people. In the *Gorgias*, Socrates says that his trial will be like a doctor prosecuted by a cook who asks a jury of children to choose between the doctor's bitter medicine and the cook's tasty treats (521e–522a). In the *Republic* (7.517e), Socrates explains why an enlightened man (presumably himself) will stumble in a courtroom situation. The *Apology* is Socrates' defence speech, and the *Crito* and *Phaedo* take place in prison after the conviction. In the *Protagoras*, Socrates is a guest at the home of Callias, son of Hipponicus, a man whom Socrates disparages in the *Apology* as having wasted a great amount of money on sophists' fees.

Unity and Diversity of the Dialogues

Two other important dialogues, the *Symposium* and the *Phaedrus*, are linked to the main storyline by characters. In the *Apology* (19b, c), Socrates says Aristophanes slandered him in a comic play, and blames him for causing his bad reputation, and ultimately, his death. In the *Symposium*, the two of them are drinking together with other friends. The character Phaedrus is linked to the main story line by character (Phaedrus is also a participant in the *Symposium* and the *Protagoras*) and by theme (the philosopher as divine emissary, etc.) The *Protagoras* is also strongly linked to the *Symposium* by characters: all of the formal speakers at the *Symposium* (with the exception of Aristophanes) are present at the home of Callias in that dialogue. Charmides and his guardian Critias are present for the discussion in the *Protagoras*. Examples of characters crossing between dialogues can be further multiplied. The *Protagoras* contains the largest gathering of Socratic associates.

In the dialogues Plato is most celebrated and admired for, Socrates is concerned with human and political virtue, has a distinctive personality, and friends and enemies who "travel" with him from dialogue to dialogue. This is not to say that Socrates is consistent: a man who is his friend in one dialogue may be an adversary or subject of his mockery in another. For example, Socrates praises the wisdom of Euthyphro many times in the *Cratylus*, but makes him look like a fool in the *Euthyphro*.

He disparages sophists generally, and Prodicus specifically in the *Apology*, whom he also slyly jabs in the *Cratylus* for charging the hefty fee of fifty drachmas for a course on language and grammar. However, Socrates tells Theaetetus in his namesake dialogue that he admires Prodicus and has directed many pupils to him. Socrates' ideas are also not consistent within or between or among dialogues.

Platonic Scholarship

Although their popularity has fluctuated over the years, the works of Plato have never been without readers since the time they were written. Plato's thought is often compared with that of his most famous student, Aristotle, whose reputation during the Western Middle Ages so completely eclipsed that of Plato that the Scholastic philosophers referred to Aristotle as "the Philosopher". However, in theByzantine Empire, the study of Plato continued.

The Medieval scholastic philosophers did not have access to most of the works of Plato, nor the knowledge of Greek needed to read them. Plato's original writings were essentially lost to Western civilization until they were brought from Constantinople in the century of its fall, by George Gemistos Plethon. It is believed that Plethon passed a copy of the Dialogues to Cosimo de' Medici when in 1438 the Council of Ferrara, called to unify the Greek and Latin Churches, was adjourned to Florence, where Plethon then lectured on the relation and differences of Plato and Aristotle, and fired Cosimo with his enthusiasm. During the early Islamic era, Persian and Arab scholars translated much of Plato into Arabic and wrote commentaries and interpretations on Plato's, Aristotle's and other Platonist philosophers' works. Many of these comments on Plato were translated from Arabic into Latin and as such influenced Medieval scholastic philosophers.

Only in the Renaissance, with the general resurgence of interest in classical civilization, did knowledge of Plato's philosophy become widespread again in the West. Many of the greatest early modern scientists and artists who broke with Scholasticism and fostered the flowering of the Renaissance, with the support of the Plato-inspired Lorenzo de Medici, saw Plato's philosophy as the basis for progress in the arts and sciences. By the 19th century, Plato's reputation was restored, and at least on par with Aristotle's.

Notable Western philosophers have continued to draw upon Plato's work since that time. Plato's influence has been especially strong in mathematics and the sciences. He helped to distinguish between pure and applied mathematics by widening the gap between "arithmetic", now called number theory and "logistic", now called arithmetic.

He regarded "logistic" as appropriate for business men and men of war who "must learn the art of numbers or he will not know how to array his troops," while "arithmetic" was appropriate for philosophers "because he has to arise out of the sea of change and lay hold of true being."

Plato's resurgence further inspired some of the greatest advances in logic since Aristotle, primarily through Gottlob Frege and his followers Kurt Gödel, Alonzo Church, and Alfred Tarski. Albert Einstein suggested that the scientist who takes philosophy seriously would have to avoid systematization and take on many different roles, and possibly appear as a Platonist or Pythagorean, in that such a one would have "the viewpoint of logical simplicity as an indispensable and effective tool of his research."

Many recent philosophers have diverged from what some would describe as the ontological models and moral ideals characteristic of traditional

Platonism. A number of these postmodern philosophers have thus appeared to disparage Platonism from more or less informed perspectives. Friedrich Nietzsche notoriously attacked Plato's "idea of the good itself" along with many fundamentals of Christian morality, which he interpreted as "Platonism for the masses" in one of his most important works, *Beyond Good And Evil*(1886).

Martin Heidegger argued against Plato's alleged obfuscation of *Being* in his incomplete tome, *Being and Time* (1927), and the philosopher of science Karl Popper argued in *The Open Society and Its Enemies* (1945) that Plato's alleged proposal for a utopian political regime in the *Republic* was prototypically totalitarian.

The political philosopher and professor Leo Strauss is considered by some as the prime thinker involved in the recovery of Platonic thought in its more political, and less metaphysical, form. Strauss' political approach was in part inspired by the appropriation of Plato and Aristotle by medieval Jewish and Islamic politicalphilosophers, especially Maimonides and Al-Farabi, as opposed to the Christian metaphysical tradition that developed from Neo-platonism.

Deeply influenced by Nietzsche and Heidegger, Strauss non-ethelessrejects their condemnation of Plato and looks to the dialogues for a solution to what all three latter day thinkers acknowledge as 'the crisis of the West.'

Textual Sources and History

Some 250 known manuscripts of Plato survive. The texts of Plato as received today apparently represent the complete written philosophical work of Plato and are generally good by the standards of textual criticism.

No modern edition of Plato in the original Greek represents a single source, but rather it is reconstructed from multiple sources which are compared with each other. These sources are medieval manuscripts written on vellum (mainly from 9th-13th century AD Byzantium), papyri (mainly from late antiquity in Egypt), and from the independent *testimonia* of other authors who quote various segments of the works (which come from a variety of sources).

The text as presented is usually not much different from what appears in the Byzantine manuscripts, and papyri and testimonia just confirm the manuscript tradition.

In some editions however the readings in the papyri or testimonia are favoured in some places by the editing critic of the text. Reviewing editions of papyri for the *Republic* in 1987, Slings suggests that the use of papyri is hampered due to some poor editing practices.

In the first century AD, Thrasyllus of Mendes had compiled and published the works of Plato in the original Greek, both genuine and spurious. While it has not survived to the present day, all the extant medieval Greek manuscripts are based on his edition. The oldest surviving complete manuscript for many of the dialogues is the Clarke Plato (Codex Oxoniensis Clarkianus 39, or Codex

Boleianus MS E.D. Clarke 39), which was written in Constantinople in 895 and acquired by Oxford University in 1809. The Clarke is given the siglum *B* in modern editions. *B* contains the first six tetralogies and is described internally as being written by "John the Calligrapher" on behalf of Arethas of Caesarea. It appears to have undergone corrections by Arethas himself.

For the last two tetralogies and the apocrypha, the oldest surviving complete manuscript is Codex Parisinus graecus 1807, designated *A*, which was written nearly contemporaneously to *B*, circa 900 AD.

A probably had an initial volume containing the first 7 tetralogies which is now lost, but of which a copy was made, Codex Venetus append. class. 4, 1, which has the siglum *T*.

The oldest manuscript for the seventh tetralogy is Codex Vindobonensis 54. suppl. phil. Gr. 7, with siglum *W*, with a supposed date in the twelfth century. In total there are fifty-one such Byzantine manuscripts known, while others may yet be found.

To help establish the text, the older evidence of papyri and the independent evidence of the testimony of commentators and other authors (*i.e.*, those who quote and refer to an old text of Plato which is no longer extant) are also used. Many papyri which contain fragments of Plato's texts are among the Oxyrhynchus Papyri.

The 2003 Oxford Classical Texts edition by Slings even cites the Coptic translation of a fragment of the *Republic* in the Nag Hammadi library as evidence. Important authors for testimony includeOlympiodorus the Younger, Plutarch, Proclus, Iamblichus, Eusebius, and Stobaeus.

During the early Renaissance, the Greek language and, along with it, Plato's texts were reintroduced to Western Europe by Byzantine scholars. In 1484 there was published a Latin edition of Plato's complete works translated by Marsilio Ficino at the behest of Cosimo de' Medici.

Cosimo had been influenced towards studying Plato by the many Byzantine Platonists in Florence during his day, including George Gemistus Plethon. Henri Estienne's edition, including parallel Greek and Latin, was published in 1578. It was this edition which established Stephanus pagination, still in use today.

Modern Editions

The Oxford Classical Texts offers the current standard complete Greek text of Plato's complete works. In five volumes edited by John Burnet, its first edition was published 1900-1907, and it is still available from the publisher, having last been printed in 1993.

The second edition is still in progress with only the first volume, printed in 1995, and the*Republic*, printed in 2003, available. The *Cambridge Greek and Latin Texts* and *Cambridge Classical Texts and Commentaries* series includes

Greek editions of the *Protagoras*, *Symposium*, *Phaedrus*, *Alcibiades*, and *Clitophon*, with English philological, literary, and, to an extent, philosophical commentary. One distinguished edition of the Greek text is E. R. Dodds' of the *Gorgias*, which includes extensive English commentary.

The modern standard complete English edition is the 1997 Hackett *Plato, Complete Works*, edited by John M. Cooper. For many of these translations Hackett offers separate volumes which include more by way of commentary, notes, and introductory material.

There is also the *Clarendon Plato Series* by Oxford University Press which offers English translations and thorough philosophical commentary by leading scholars on a few of Plato's works, including John McDowell's version of the *Theaetetus*. Cornell University Press has also begun the *Agora* series of English translations of classical and medieval philosophical texts, including a few of Plato's.

Bibliography

B. K. Chaturvedi: *Chanakya*, Diamond Pocket Books, 2001.

Badarayana Murthy; Miles Davis: *Sri Chanakya Niti-shastra; the Political Ethics of Chanakya Pandit Hardcover*, V.. Ram Kumar Press, 1981.

Dillery, John: *Xenophon and the History of His Times*, London; New York: Routledge, 1995.

Franco Modigliani and Arun Muralidhar: "*Rethinking Pension Reform*", Cambridge University Press, , 2004.

Helmuth von Glasenapp: *Jainism*, Motilal Banarsidass Publ, 1999.

Higgins, William Edward: *The Problem of the Individual and the Society of the "Polis"*, Albany: State University of New York Press, 1977.

Hirsch, Steven W: *The Friendship of the Barbarians; Xenophon and the Persian Empire*, University Press of New England, 1985.

Hutchinson, Godfrey: *Xenophon and the Art of Command*, London: Greenhill Books, 2000.

J.K. Kindahl: *The Behaviour of Industrial Prices*, Columbia University Press, 1970.

Kierkegaard, Soren A: *The Concept of Irony with Continual Reference to Socrates*, Princeton: Princeton University Press, 1992.

M. Srinivasachariar: *History of classical Sanskrit literature*, Motilal BanarsidassPubl, 1989.

Manohar Laxman Varadpand: *History of Indian Theatre*, Abhinav Publications, 2005.

Modigliani, Franco; Andrew B Abel; Simon Johnson: *The Collected Papers of Franco Modigliani*, MIT Press, 1980.

Nadon, Christopher: *Xenophon's Prince: Republic and Empire in the "Cyropaedia"*, Berkeley; Los Angeles; London: University of California Press, 2001.

Natubhai Shah: *Janism*:The World of Conquerors, Motilal Banarsidass Publishe, 2004.

Nury Vittachi: *The Kama Sutra of Business*: *Management Principles From Indian Classics*, Wiley India Pvt. Limited, 2007.

P. E. Granoff: *The Clever Adulteress and Other Stories; A Treasury of Jaina Literature*, Motilal Banarsidass Publ, 2012.

Padhy, K. S. (2011), *Indian Political Thought*, PHI Learning Pvt. Ltd.,

Raj Kumar Sen & Ratan Lal Basu: *Economics in Arthasastra*, Deep & Deep Publications Pvt. Ltd., 2006.

Ratan Lal Basu & Rajkumar Sen: *Ancient Indian Economic Thought, Relevance for Today*, Rawat Publications, 2008

S. K. Agarwal: *Towards Improving Governance*, Academic Foundation, 2008.

Strauss, Leo: *Xenophon's Socrates, Ithaca*, New York; London: Cornell University Press, 1972.

Subodh Kapoor: *The Indian Encyclopaedia*, Cosmo Publications, 2002.

V. K. Subramanian (1980): *Maxims of Chanakya: Kautilya*, Abhinav Publications, 1980.

Walter Miller: *Cyropaedia*, Harvard University Press, 1914.

Waterfield, Robin: *Xenophon's Retreat: Greece, Persia and the End of the Golden Age*, Cambridge, Massachusetts: The Belknap Press of Harvard University Press, 2006.

Wilhelm Geiger: *The DîpavaCsa and MahâvaCsa and their historical development in Ceylon. H. C. Cottle*, Government Printer, 1908.

Index

G

H

I

J

L

M

P

R

S

T

W